The Law of the Near & Middle East

The Law of the
Near & Middle East
Readings, Cases, & Materials

Herbert J. Liebesny

State University of New York Press Albany 1975

Herbert J. Liebesny
is Professorial Lecturer in Law
at George Washington University

First published in 1975 by
State University of New York Press
99 Washington Avenue, Albany, New York 12210

Library of Congress Cataloging in Publication Data

Liebesny, Herbert J.   1911–
   The Law of the Near & Middle East.
   Bibliography: p.
   Includes index.
     1. Law–Near East.   2. Law–Near East–History
and criticism. I. Title
Law   340′.0956   75–22046
ISBN 0–87395–256–1
ISBN 0–87395–257–x microfiche

To my wife

Contents

Preface

This book grew out of a graduate seminar on Near and Middle Eastern law that I have taught for over ten years at the National Law Center of George Washington University in Washington, D. C. It has two major aims. One is to trace the historical development of Islamic law, the systematic reception of Western law beginning in the nineteenth century, and the drafting of modern statutes and codes in the period before and after World War II. The second is to give a brief systematic survey of important legal institutions in their classical Islamic form as well as in their present-day appearance.

In order to keep the manuscript manageable, it was necessary to impose restrictions both geographically and topically. On the geographic side the study covers the Islamic countries from North Africa to Pakistan. There have been interesting developments in the law of other Islamic countries, such as Malaysia and Indonesia, but to include these would have overly expanded the book's contents. Topically, somewhat less emphasis is given to details of classical Islamic law than to the reception of Western law and developments in the nineteenth and twentieth centuries. The reason is that comprehensive discussions of Islamic law are available, to cite only among recent concise presentations, Joseph Schacht, *An Introduction to Islamic Law* and Noel J. Coulson, *A History of Islamic Law*, while no such comprehensive presentations exist for legal developments since the early nineteenth century. Again because there are adequate studies already available, Shi'i Islam is treated rather briefly.

In composing this book I have had two principal needs in mind. There is an increasing interest among American law students in foreign legal systems other than those of Western Europe. The law of the Near and Middle East is, to my mind, a useful subject for a study of non-European foreign law, because rather close interconnections have existed between this region and the West since ancient times.

There is another need which this book may serve. Legal transactions and law suits involving foreign law, including the law of the Near and Middle Eastern countries, play an increasingly important role in American legal practice. I therefore hope that this book will also help the practitioner who must deal with problems arising in this area to form an overall impression at least of this region's legal systems.

I further hope that this study will be of some aid to students of

Islamic law who are not lawyers, but who wish to gain some insight into the development of Islamic and present-day Near and Middle Eastern law.

The suggestions for further readings which are given in Appendix 1 are not designed as a comprehensive bibliography, but rather as a guide to those readers who want to go further in their study of the law of this region as a whole or of particular aspects.

In order not to overburden the text, detailed citations of sources have not been included, but can be found in Appendix 4 together with references to all places in this book where the work or study in question has been quoted. All translations into English are by me except as otherwise indicated.

The transliteration of Arabic words is always a problem in a book of this kind. Since the book is designed to serve the needs of many non-Arabists, I decided not to burden the text with diacritical marks, other than indicating *hamza* and *'ain*. However, in the glossary diacritical marks have been used following generally the rules of the U. S. Board of Geographic Names. Throughout the text I have aimed at uniformity in spelling of Arabic words, but I am aware that complete uniformity has not been achieved, partly because I felt that I should not change the spelling of proper names, particularly in case reports. Also, the names of modern Arab authors who have published in English or French were given in the spelling which they themselves use when publishing in those languages.

In the excerpts which I have quoted footnotes have generally been omitted, because most of them were rather technical and, I believe, would be of interest to only a few readers.

Finally, it is my pleasant duty to thank all those who have helped me in the work which has produced this book. Foremost, I wish to thank Professor J. N. D. Anderson whose interest in this undertaking and whose advice and counsel have been of very great assistance to me. My thanks are also due to lawyers in several of the countries of the Near and Middle East who were kind enough to provide me with information and documentation on their legal systems. I also would like to thank the students who have taken my seminar and who over the years have contributed to this study in its formative stages through their questions and criticism. I likewise want to express my gratitude to the authors and publishers who have so graciously given me permission to quote from their publications. Last, but not least, my deepest gratitude is due my wife who through her steady support and active participation in the production of this manuscript has given me the type of help and encouragement without which no author could accomplish a major publishing venture.

Herbert J. Liebesny

Arlington, Va.
November 1974

Part One

The Historical Development of the Law in Muslim Countries of the Near and Middle East

Chapter 1 Basic Characteristics of Islamic Law

A. Islamic Law as Religious Law

J. N. D. ANDERSON, "Law as a Social Force in Islamic Culture and History," pp. 13–14.*

The Theoretical Ideal

For centuries the law has held a paramount place in the civilization and structure of the Muslim world, at least in the Islamic ideal. The prestige it has enjoyed may indeed be regarded as without parallel in history, for this civilization was uniquely based on religion, and the religion of Islam has always accorded a pre-eminent place to law.

Nor is the reason for this pre-eminence far to seek. In the religion of Islam everything rested on divine revelation, without which man remains in a state of almost unrelieved ignorance. But, in the orthodox view, God has not revealed Himself and His nature, but rather His law. It is true that He may be said partially to have withdrawn the veil that surrounds the mystery of His Person by the use of the "Beautiful Names" by which revelation describes Him; but the Islamic doctrine of *mukhalafa* (difference or otherness — which postulates that even such names as the Compassionate and Merciful must not be thought to epitomize the same qualities as compassion and mercy when used of men) effectively precludes any certainty of knowledge, except of His utter transcendence and limitless power. But if the Person of God is, to the orthodox Muslim, beyond human knowledge, this is certainly not true of the divine commands. It is partly for this reason that law has normally taken precedence over theology in the Muslim world, for it is far more profitable and seemly to concentrate on the study of what may be known or deduced of God's commands regarding how man should behave, than to speculate on the essentially inscrutable mystery of His nature and attributes. It is enough to be certain that God is the Sovereign Lord and man his *ʿabd* (slave), whose primary duty is *ʿibada* (service). Nor in this context, should such *ʿibada* be limited to those religious duties which are commonly so classified, and which constitute the first section in almost all legal texts; for there is, in fact, no essential distinction in Islam between the sacred and the

*Reprinted by permission of the author and the School of Oriental and African Studies, University of London.

secular, and it is man's duty to serve his Maker in every circumstance and relationship of life. Similarly, from this viewpoint it may be said that there is no distinction in Islam between the law on the one hand and religion and morals on the other.

This same principle may be clearly seen in the constitutional theory of the Islamic ideal. To the orthodox Muslim the fount of divine revelation dried up with the death of Muhammad, for it was only he who could authoritatively reveal the divine will. After his death the community needed, indeed, a ruler (a *Khalifa* or successor, an *Imam* or leader) to administer the state, enforce its law, and command its armies. As such he had executive and judicial powers, but was—in the classical theory—denied any true legislative authority; for it was for him to uphold rather than promulgate the sacred law, to which ruler and ruled were alike subject. Not only so, but in the Islamic theory it is primarily the law which creates and upholds the Caliph, and only secondarily the Caliph who upholds, but does not create, the law. The Caliph, it became established, should be elected by the community through its learned men, rather than represent a hereditary kingship; he could demand obedience within the limits of the sacred law, and such obedience was commanded by that law itself; but he should conduct himself, the affairs of state, and even the finances of state according to the detailed precepts of the *shari'a* (the sacred law).

The *shari'a*, then, covers every aspect of life and every field of law—international, constitutional, administrative, criminal, civil, family, personal, and religious. In addition, it covers an enormous field which would not be regarded as law at all in any modern classification. Every human act is regarded as characterized to some degree by *husn* or *qubh*, seemliness or unseemliness, conformity or deformity; and these qualities can only be known by divine revelation. Everything—from murder to social etiquette, and from incest to the rules of religious retreat—is thus evaluated, and may be classified (according to a widely-accepted classification) as coming under one of five categories of things commanded, recommended, left legally indifferent, reprobated, or forbidden by God Himself. In large part this system is, of course, such as no human court would attempt to enforce, and any sanction, in these cases, can only be exacted at the bar of eternity; but, enforced or unenforced, this whole system of duties forms part of the sacred law. And it is only—in theory at least—within the category of things left legally indifferent by the Almighty that there is any essential place for human regulations.

Comment: Islam is rather unique in its emphasis on the divine character of the law, its immutability—in theory at least, the lack of legislative authority of the ruler, and the absence of any basic distinction between legal and ethical rules. The approach of most other legal systems in the ancient world was different. In ancient Egypt law was divine law, but it emanated from a king who was himself a God. The resultant situation has been described as follows:

JOHN A. WILSON, "Authority and Law in Ancient Egypt," pp. 5–7.*

. . . Despite all the written documents which have come down to us from ancient Egypt, we possess neither a body of law which is comparable to the Asiatic codes, nor any textual references to such laws elsewhere, nor even a later tradition about a king or official who was a law-giver or law-codifier until one comes down to the late tradition about King Bochoris, who reigned about 700 B.C. . . . . Since Egypt was blessed with having on earth a god as king, law proceeded from his mouth, always vitally renewed, and no codification was necessary or even proper. Of course legal procedure was followed in Egypt, but the specific practice must have stemmed from the customary law of the land before it was a unified state. It is even possible that such customary law differed in different parts of Egypt; that could well be within the divine understanding of the king as to what was good for his people . . . .

. . . Further, each king was a newly born god, a new source of verbal law, and it would be unfitting if he were to be made the heir to a long-standing code which came from outside him.

Comment: In the kingdoms of Mesopotamia the ruler was not regarded as a god. The ultimate source of the basic legal principles was divine, not human. The king, however, had the duty to proclaim and enforce the law and see to it that law enforcement was equitable. He also could make amendments to bring the basic legal principles in line with the needs of the day. These characteristics of Mesopotamian law are well illustrated by the famous code of the Babylonian King Hammurabi, who ruled in the late eighteenth and early seventeenth century B.C. On the stela which contains the code, Hammurabi is pictured as receiving the commission to write the code from the Sun God. In the prologue to the code Hammurabi states that the gods called him "to establish justice in the land." The prologue ends with a phrase which clearly indicates that it was the king who drafted the code by command of the gods and similar phrasing is found in the epilogue.

JAMES B. PRITCHARD, ed., *Ancient Near Eastern Texts Relating to the Old Testament*, p. 165.†

When Marduk [the chief god] commissioned me to guide the people aright, to direct the land, I established law and justice in the language of the land, thereby promoting the welfare of the people. At that time (I decreed): . . . .

[In the epilogue (*Ibid.*, p. 177) Hammurabi says of his code:] "The laws of justice, which Hammurabi, the efficient king, set up . . . ." Later on in the epilogue he states: "may my statutes have no one to scorn them." On several occasions in the epilogue Hammurabi also refers to "his words" as inscribed on the stela.

*Reprinted by permission of the American Oriental Society.
†Reprinted by permission of the Princeton University Press, copyright 1969.

Comment: Mesopotamian law thus has a basis in religion, but it is not religious law in the strict sense. Its character has been described as follows:

E. A. SPEISER, "Authority and Law in Mesopotamia," p. 14*

The fact should be stressed that, although state and church interpenetrated throughout the ancient Near East, Mesopotamian law as we know it from many sources that span scores of centuries, was strictly secular. It concerns itself with private and public property, trade and commerce, agriculture and land tenure, professions and wages, and the general administration of justice. It is not a religious pronouncement . . . .

Comment: Greek and Roman law were wholly secular during the classical period. This is clearly expressed by a great Roman jurist, Gaius, in his *Institutes* of Roman law.

GAIUS *Institutiones* I. I.

All peoples who are ruled by laws and customs, utilize partly the common law of all men; what each people establishes for itself as law, is its own specific law and called civil law, as being the specific law of the state.

Comment: The Romans drew a definite distinction between *fas,* divine law, and *ius*, secular law. *Fas* regulated the relations of man with the gods, whereas *ius* regulated relationships within the human community. Christianity was born into the Hellenistic era when well-developed and elaborate secular legal systems existed around the Mediterranean. This circumstance was clearly recognized in the New Testament.

MATTHEW 22: 21 (Revised Standard Version).†

Then (Jesus) said to (the Pharisees): "Render therefore to Caesar the things that are Caesar's and to God the things that are God's."

Comment: This thought of a division between the sphere of the secular state and that of religion is further elaborated in the first epistle of Peter:

I PETER 2: 13–14.†

Be subject, for the Lord's sake to every human institution, whether it be to the emperor as supreme, or to the governors as sent by him to punish those who do wrong and to praise those who do right.

Comment: The Canon Law of the Roman Catholic Church retained

*Reprinted by permission of the American Oriental Society.
†Reprinted by permission of the Division of Education and Ministry,
National Council of the Churches of Christ in the U.S.A., copyright 1947.

this distinction between the religious and secular sphere in the
Corpus Juris Canonici.

Corpus Juris Canonici, Decretum Gratiani, I. I,I

All laws are either divine or human. The divine laws consist of
those of nature, the human laws consist of customs . . . . The
divine law is called *fas*, the human law is called *ius*.

Comment: The law of the ancient Hebrews was closer in concept to
the divine law of Islam.

ZE'EV W. FALK, "Jewish Law," pp. 28–33*

Jewish law is an all-embracing body of religious duties, regulating
all aspects of Jewish life. It comprises on an equal footing norms
of worship and ritual, rules of private and social behavior, and
laws which are nowadays enforced by the courts. The system
recognizes distinctions between these classes of "laws," but they
are all equally binding in conscience.

    .   .   .   .

In order to study Jewish law we mainly rely on literary sources,
for neither a state nor any other form of social structure has
played a decisive role in the formation of its rules. It is learning
rather than practice which has influenced legal creation, so that
works of scholarship have often fulfilled the functions of both
legislature and judiciary.

    .   .   .   .   .

    The earliest collection of Jewish laws is the Pentateuch, but to a
lesser extent legal data can also be traced in the books of the
Prophets and the Writings . . . . Post-exilic Jewish tradition, on
the other hand, interpreted Scripture in the light of the so-called
Oral Law, which was ascribed together with the Pentateuchic
laws themselves to the divine revelation at Mount Sinai, and thus
became part of God's "covenant" with his people.

    The Oral Law was indeed transmitted in the academies at least
as from the Babylonian Exile (586–537 B.C.), though in its present
form the greater part dates from the Hasmonean and later times.
The material originally remained an oral tradition so as to distinguish it from Scripture. The idea may also have existed that
oral traditions could be tested in the academy as in court, whereas
any written source did not lend itself to cross-examination. The
Oral Law was gradually committed to writing, this process taking
from A.D. 200 till the Middle Ages . . . .

    Jewish law . . . is partly understood as the literal word of God
and partly its divinely inspired interpretation . . . . While a distinction was made by the rabbis between the commandments
defining the duties toward God and those concerning one's

*Reprinted by permission of Professor Derrett and Praeger Publishers, Inc.,
copyright 1968.

fellow man, both were considered equally to be of divine origin. . . . . Nevertheless, the sages remained aware of the legislative role played by man. Although biblical law was thought to embrace all problems and to be complete, the need was admitted for human legislation to interfere from time to time.

B. Personality of the Law

Comment: This is another important principle of Islamic law. The law which is applicable to a person can be determined according to one of two basic principles; the personality of the law or the territoriality of the law. The principle of personality of the law means that the law which is applicable is not determined territorially, but on the basis of the origin, nationality, tribal affiliation, or religion of the individual involved. This principle was dominant throughout much of antiquity. Only relatively late in the Roman Empire did a broad territorial application of the law develop. This development was reversed again in the Middle Ages when the controlling principle of law became once more that of personality. The situation that obtained in the Middle Ages was described by Vinogradoff:

PAUL VINOGRADOFF, *Roman Law in Medieval Europe*, pp. 25–26.*

. . . [In the Germanic kingdoms which were established on the soil of the Western Roman Empire] the legal rights of the Roman would be at variance with those of his German neighbors. These, again would act differently, each according to his peculiar nationality, as Salian Franks or Ripuarians, Bavarians or Burgundians, etc. The position became very intricate when members of different nationalities, living under different laws, were brought together to transact business with each other. As Bishop Agobard of Lyons tells us about 850 A.D., it happened constantly that of five people meeting in one room, each followed a law of his own. We find, in fact, in these cross-relationships very striking examples of so-called conflicts of law. Before proceeding to examine the material question at issue, it was necessary for the judges to discover to what particular body or bodies of law a case belonged . . . .

Comment: This principle that a person has to be judged according to his own law was clearly set forth in statutes of the period. Thus the so-called *Lex Ribuaria*, the code of law of a Frankish tribe, whose provisions go back to the sixth and seventh centuries A.D. provides as follows:

Lex Ribuaria, 31. 3 and 4.

If a Frank, Burgundian, Alamannian or a member of any other

*Reprinted by permission of the Clarendon Press, copyright 1929.

nation resides within the area of the Riburians and is summoned into court, he shall make his defense according to the law of his birthplace. If he is found guilty, his fine shall be set according to his own law and not according to Ribuarian law.

Comment: It was a logical extension of the principle of the personality of the law that both in antiquity and in the Middle Ages foreign communities were permitted not only to live according to their own laws, but to establish their own tribunals.

In the tribal society of pre-Islamic Arabia, the principle of personality of the law also was applied, indeed among nomadic tribes the concept of territoriality of the law cannot be expected to exist. The Prophet Muhammad built upon the existing foundations of the tribal society, but replaced the old concept of the tribal group by a new concept, that of the community of believers. All believers are brothers and they form the *umma* or community of believers and this community is substituted for the tribal community. Thus the Muslim community had a religious basis and Islamic law applied to all believers. At the same time it was not applicable, at least in principle, to non-believers. Since religion was the criterion for membership in the community of believers, the same criterion was used by the Muslims to classify non-Muslims, whether they were foreigners or inhabitants of Muslim countries or of countries conquered by the Muslims. In the Muslim realm certain religious communities were tolerated and allowed to live according to their own religion and law, they were the so-called *dhimmis*.

MAJID KHADDURI, *War and Peace in the Law of Islam*, pp. 175–177.*

. . . Islam provided an interesting experiment in the treatment of subject races that had originally entered into compacts with the Muslim authorities, the provisions of which became later part of the law of Islam. This law provides that it is in the competence of any member of the protected communities, in contrast to other penalized groups, at any moment to join the dominant community by merely pronouncing the *shahada*, the Muslim formula of professing the faith. As long as they remained attached to their own religion, the *dhimmis* were allowed to enforce their own law (except when Muslim interests were involved), but if they wanted to avail themselves of Muslim justice, they were not denied access to Muslim courts . . . .

The tolerated communities within Islam included not only the so-called *ahl al-Kitab* (people of the Book) or Scriptuaries, but also idolaters and fire worshippers, provided they had accepted residence in any Muslim territory, except the Arabian Peninsula. The Scriptuaries include Christians, Jews, Magians (Zoroastrians), Samaritans, and Sabians. Polytheists were, as a rule, denied the

*Reprinted by permission of the Johns Hopkins Press, copyright 1955.

status of *dhimmis* (especially in Arabia), since they had to choose between Islam and the sword . . . .

The term *ahl al-Kitab* was applied to all non-Muslims who possessed a scripture whether they resided within or without the *dar al-Islam*. The *ahl al-Kitab* who resided in the *dar al-Islam* (the territory of Islam) and accepted Muslim rule were called *dhimmis*. Literally the word *dhimma* means a compact which the believer agrees to respect, the violation of which makes him liable to *dhamm* (blame). Legally, the term refers to a certain status, the acquisition of which entitles the person to certain rights which must be protected by the state. These rights include, in addition to security of life and property, an indefinite *aman* (pledge of security) but it does not confer full citizenship, since the Scriptuary, although believing in Allah, fails to believe in His Apostle; he is therefore not a true believer and is not entitled to the full membership in the Muslim brotherhood. Punishment for disbelief in the Qur'an and Allah's Apostle is implied in certain disabilities; at the same time the *dhimmi*, by paying the poll tax is entitled to full protection against any possible encroachment or molestation.

Comment: Islam was universalist and ideally all the world should become Muslim. This patently was not the case. Khadduri discusses the resultant legal situation.

Ibid., pp. 52–53

[Because the universalist Muslim state could not expand over all of the known world] the world accordingly was sharply divided in Muslim law into the *dar al-Islam* (abode or territory of Islam) and the *dar-al-harb* (abode or territory of war). These terms may be rendered in less poetic words as the "World of Islam" and the "World of War." The first corresponded to the territory under Muslim rule. Its inhabitants were Muslims, by birth or conversion, and the communities of the tolerated religions (the *dhimmis*) who preferred to hold fast to their own cult, at the price of paying the *jizya* (poll tax). The Muslims enjoyed full rights of citizenship; the subjects of the tolerated religions enjoyed only partial rights, and submitted to Muslim rule in accordance with special charters regulating their relations with the Muslims. The *dar-al-harb* consisted of all the states and communities outside the world of Islam. Its inhabitants were often called infidels, or better unbelievers.

Comment: Islamic law thus dealt with the *dhimmis* as members of a non-Muslim religious community. The law of the *dhimmis* regulated their relationships to each other, and each of the *dhimmi* communities was led by its religious functionaries. Out of this concept developed the so-called *millet* system of the Ottoman Empire under which the various *dhimmi* communities lived according to their own laws within and as subjects of the Ottoman Empire. Remnants of this system are found today in most Arab states and in other parts of the Muslim world where matters of family relationships and frequently also of inheritance are regulated by the law of the individual community and not by legal rules applicable to all citizens of the state. This constitutes a survival of the concept of the personality of the law in an age when legal relationships are generally regulated on the basis of the territoriality of the law.

Chapter 2 Historical Development & Sources of Islamic Law

A. The Classical Theory of Islamic Law

J. N. D. ANDERSON, "Law as a Social Force in Islamic Culture and History," p. 15.

It is to revelation . . . that the Muslim turns as the primary and, in one sense, the only source of law. It was thus that the classical theory of Islamic jurisprudence, which has dominated all the orthodox schools of law since the third century of the Muslim era, concentrated on four sources of the law: the Qur'an or inspired book, the *sunna* or practice of Muhammad, the *ijma'* or consensus of Muslims, and *qiyas* or analogical deductions from these three primary sources. [These four sources are known as "roots" of Islamic jurisprudence.]

1. *The Qur'an*

DAVID SANTILLANA, *Istituzioni di Diritto Musulmano Malichita*, vol. 1, pp. 32–33.*

The supreme source of the Islamic law is the Qur'an . . . . The Qur'an is not a code of law, but a not very well coordinated collection of moral precepts, exhortations, biblical stories, polemics, and threats against the adversaries of the new faith. In the middle of all this, various legal rules emerge here and there. These rules do not even constitute the main part of the book; of 6219 verses contained in the 114 chapters (or *suras*) about 600 . . . [maximum] deal with legislation in the strict sense. This legislation is found particularly in the chapters of a later date. When one looks at the Qur'an one sees quickly that it is composed of chapters of unequal length which are also quite different in form. The oldest ones, dating from Mecca, that is, the first period of Muhammad's preaching, are very short, nearly exclusively religious in content, and written in a poetical, often lyrical style. The later Medinese chapters are much longer and less strict in form. They contain most of the political and legal precepts. This difference between the two revelations, that of Mecca and that of

*Reprinted by permission of the Istituto per l'Oriente, Rome, copyright 1938.

Medina, corresponds to the two periods into which the career of
the Prophet and of the movement which he founded can be
divided. The movement began at Mecca as a purely religious and
moral reaction against pagan society, it ended in Medina with the
establishment of a new political-religious community. This is
precisely why the Medinese chapters contain the first outline of
the legal and administrative framework required by the needs of
the small community of believers which was the prelude to the
future Islamic Empire.

2. *The Sunna*

IGNAZ GOLDZIHER, *Muhammedanische Studien*, vol. 2, p. 13

In those Arab circles where since the advent of Islam a way of life
and social institutions had developed which was in conformity
with the spirit of Muslim religious law, the concept of the *sunna*
was regarded from the beginning as a determinant norm in the
conduct of the life of the individual and of society.

Actually, the Muslims did not have to invent this concept and
its practical importance. It was already well known to the ancient
pagans of the period before Islam. To them *sunna* meant those
rules which were in conformity with the traditions of the Arab
world and the ancestral manners and customs. The term *sunna* is
still used in the same sense in the Islamic period by those Arab
circles which had been little touched by the influence of Muslim
religion. Islam changed the concept and meaning of this ancient
term. Among the pious successors of Muhammad and in the
oldest Muslim community *sunna* came to mean anything that
could be proven to have been the practice of the Prophet and his
oldest disciples. Just as the pagan Arab adhered to the *sunna* of
his ancestors, so was the Muslim community enjoined to uphold
and follow the new *sunna*. Thus the Muslim concept of *sunna* is a
variant of an ancient Arab concept . . . .

Ibid., pp. 19–21

The power of the *sunna* as a normative principle in the life of a
Muslim is as old as Islam itself. As early as the end of the first
century [of the Hijra] the principle had been established that "the
sunna was the judge over the Qur'an, but not the Qur'an over the
sunna." However, by examining the data from different periods it
can be seen that the omnipotence of the *sunna*—having in mind
constantly the theoretical concepts of the pious circles—increased
steadily in the course of time. In the early period [of Islam] some
free discussion concerning the practical application of the *sunna*
was still permissible . . . . Generally, however, the desire to make
the *sunna* a source of the law equal to the Qur'an becomes ever
stronger. The rules established by the Prophet as *sunna* in religious
matters . . . were made by him by order of God; they were
revealed to him in the same manner as the Qur'an . . . . [In the
second and third centuries of the Hijra] *sunna* and Qur'an exist

side by side as co-equals. The disputed question whether rules of the *sunna* can abrogate rules of the Qur'an is answered in the affirmative by al-Shaybani in the middle of the second century. Al-Shafi'i does not find anything extraordinary in this concept. In the third century the Qadi al-Hassaf (died 261 A.H.) assumes as a generally accepted doctrine that the *sunna mutawatira* (that is, the *sunna* recognized by an uninterrupted sequence of generations) has equal rank with the Qur'an. His contemporary Ibn Qutayba defended and established the doctrine of the divine origin of the *sunna*.

Ibid., p. 11

The term *hadith* has to be distinguished from the term sunna . . . . The difference between them is as follows: *hadith* is an oral communication which is traced back to the Prophet. *Sunna* is the usage in effect in the old Muslim community with regard to a point of law or religion, regardless of whether there exists an oral communication concerning this point or not . . . .

Ibid., p. 6

Every *hadith* consists of two parts. First is the chain of authoritative informants who transmit the information in question from the initial author to the last informant. The creditability of the information rests on these authoritative informants. The chain as a whole is called the *sanad* or *isnad*, that is, the support of the *hadith*. This formal element is followed by the text of the saying, called *matn*, the subject matter of the *hadith* . . . .

Comment: A passage from a work by the great Muslim jurist al-Shafi'i illustrates the weight given to the *sunna* by the classical jurists of Islam.

AL-SHAFI'I, *Risala*, p. 119.*

For the Apostle has laid down a *sunna* on matters for which there is a text in the book of God as well as for others concerning which there is no specific text. But whatever he laid down in the *sunna* God has ordered us to obey, and he regards our obedience to him, as obedience to Him, and our refusal to obey him as disobedience to Him for which no man will be forgiven; nor is an excuse for failure to obey the Apostle's *sunna* possible owing to what I have already stated and to what the Apostle himself has said.

Comment: The Muslim jurists were aware of the fact that not all of the many traditions ascribed to the Prophet were necessarily genuine. As a consequence they developed certain criteria by which the reliability of a specific *hadith* was judged. Ibn Khaldun discussed the science of the traditions in considerable detail.

*Reprinted by permission of the Johns Hopkins Press, copyright 1961.

IBN KHALDUN, *The Muqaddimah, An Introduction to History*,
vol. 2, pp. 448–460.*

Another of the sciences of tradition is the knowledge of the
norms that leading *hadith* scholars have invented in order to know
the chains of transmitters, the (individual) transmitters, their
names, how the transmission took place, their conditions, their
classes, and their different technical terminologies. This is because
general consensus makes it obligatory to act in accordance with
information established on the authority of the Messenger of
God. This requires probability for the assumption that the information is true. Thus, the independent student must verify
all the means by which it is possible to make such an assumption.

He may do this by scrutinizing the chains of transmitters of
traditions. For that purpose, one may use such knowledge of the
probity, accuracy, thoroughness, and lack of carelessness or
negligence, as the most reliable Muslims describe a transmitter as
possessing.

Then there are differences in rank that exist among transmitters. Further there is the way the transmission took place. . . .

Then there is the difference with regard to the (degree of)
soundness or acceptability of the transmitted material. The
highest grade of transmitted material is called "sound" by (the
hadith scholars). Next comes "good." The lowest grade is "weak."
(The classification of traditions) includes also: "skipping the
first transmitter on Muhammad's authority," "omitting one
link," "omitting two links," "affected by some infirmity,"
"singular," "unusual," and "singular and suspect." In some
cases, there is a difference of opinion as to whether (traditions so
described) should be rejected. In other cases, there is general
agreement that (they should be rejected). The same is the case
with (traditions with) sound chains. In some cases there is general
agreement as to their acceptability and soundness, whereas, in
other cases, there are differences of opinion . . . . Then there
follows the discussion of terms applying to the text of the traditions. A text may be "unusual", "difficult" (ambiguous), "affected
by some) misspelling (or misreading)," or "(containing) homo-
nyms," or "(containing) homographs."

On all these points *hadith* scholars have laid down a canon
explaining the (various) grades and terms, and adequate to protect
the transmission from possible defects . . . .

. . . . .

The *hadith* experts concerned themselves with knowledge of
the recensions of traditions and of the different chains of transmitters, such as the Hijazi and the Iraqi transmissions and others.
A certain tradition may be known in one way only or in numerous
ways, and it may be repeated in (different) chapters (of works of
jurisprudence) because it deals with several subjects.

There was Muhammad bin Isma'il al-Bukhari, the leading

*Reprinted by permission of the Princeton University Press, Bollingen
Foundation, copyright 1958 and 1967.

hadith scholar of his time. In his *Musnad al-Sahih*, he widened the area of tradition and published the orthodox traditions arranged according to subject. He combined all the different ways of the Hijazis, Iraqis, and Syrians, accepting the material upon which they all agreed, but excluding the material concerning which there were differences of opinion. He repeated a (given) tradition in every chapter upon which the contents of that particular tradition had some bearing. Therefore, his traditions were repeated in several chapters, because a (single) tradition may deal with different subjects, as we have indicated. His work thus comprised 7,200 traditions of which 3,000 are repeated . . . .

Then came the imam Muslim bin al-Hajjaj al-Qushayri. He composed his *Musnad al-Sahih* in which he followed al-Bukhari, in that he transmitted the material that was generally agreed upon, but he omitted the repetitions . . . . He arranged his work according to juridical categories and the chapter headings of jurisprudence.

. . . .

Abu Dawud al-Sijistani, Abu 'Isa al-Tirmidhi, and Abu 'Abd al-Rahman al-Nasa'i wrote *sunan* works which included more than merely "sound" traditions. Their intention was to include all traditions that amply fulfilled the conditions making them actionable traditions. They were either traditions with few links in the chain of transmitters, which makes them sound (traditions), as is (generally) acknowledged, or they were lesser traditions, such as "good" traditions and others. It was to serve as a guide to orthodox practice.

These are the collections of traditions that are used as reference works in Islam. They are the chief orthodox works on traditions . . . .

. . . With very few exceptions no attention has been paid to more than the five main works. Al-Bukhari's *Sahih* occupies the highest rank among them . . . .

The *Sahih* of Muslim has been given much attention by Maghribi scholars. They applied themselves to it and agreed that it was superior to the work of al-Bukhari . . . .

The other three collections of traditions contain the most extensive source material for jurists. Most comment on them is found in the law books . . . .

3. *Ijma'*

C. SNOUK HURGRONJE, "Le Droit Musulman," pp. 225–227.*

Ijma', the infallible consensus of the community is the third foundation of the law. From the standpoint of the practice one can say that it stands above everything. Only *ijma'* ends doubt.

. . . .

*Reprinted by permission of E. J. Brill, Leiden, copyright 1957.

The dogma of *ijma* was created during the period when the authorized personages still placed in the mouth of Muhammad their personal opinions on points in dispute; it was therefore unnecessary to look in the tradition for arguments in favor of *ijma'*. One could create them freely. The most important one consists of these words of the Prophet: "My community (*umma*) will not agree on an error." In other words, whatever my community agrees on, is the truth.

IGNAZ GOLDZIHER, *Vorlesungen über den Islam*, pp. 52–53.

Thus, whatever is accepted by the consensus of the believers of Islam in their universality is correct and can claim to be acknowledged as binding. It is correct only in the form the consensus has given it. Only that interpretation and application of the Qur'an and the *sunna* are correct which have been taken over by the consensus. In this sense consensus constitutes authoritative interpretation . . . . Those forms of religious worship and of legal practice which are approved by the consensus are removed from all theoretical criticism. Only those men and writings are regarded as authoritative whom the consensus of the community has acknowledged as such, not in synods or councils, but through a nearly subconscious voice of the people which in its universality was regarded as not being subject to error. . . .

The extent of *ijma'* was first determined by general instinct rather than by a clear theological definition of this matter. It was tried in vain to limit consensus with regard to time and place and to define as *ijma'* what could be shown as consensus of the companions of Muhammad or of the old authorities of Medina. Such a limitation was too restrictive for later developments. On the other hand, theology could not be satisfied to leave *ijma'* completely to the instinctive feeling of the masses. A formula to define *ijma'* was finally arrived at. The term was defined as the agreed opinion and teachings of the acknowledged Islamic jurist-theologians of a given period. They are to be regarded as . . . the men who are called to interpret the law and the teachings and to judge the accuracy of the application of the rules in practice.

GUSTAVE VON GRUNEBAUM, *Medieval Islam*, pp. 149–151.*

The means by which Muslim law succeeded at once in preserving its foundations of Qur'an and *sunna* and attuning its provisions to the ever changing needs of different places and times was the recognition of *ijma'*, the consensus, as another source of law. It is the consensus which can accept an innovation, at first considered heretical, and, by accepting it, make it part and parcel of the *sunna*, overriding traditional views in its way . . . . The *ijma'* of the doctors functions like the Roman *consensus prudentium* . . . .

By asserting that "never will my community be united in an error," the Prophet eliminated the uneasiness that the consensus might, on occasion, be misguided and thence misguiding. In the

*Reprinted by permission of the University of Chicago Press copyright 1946 and 1954. Phoenix Books (paperback ed. used).

beginning the consensus of the Companions was considered authoritative. Malik thought the consensus of the holy places, Mecca and Medina, decisive. Gradually *ijma'* came to be interpreted as the agreement of those competent to judge in religious matters; it became the agreement of the learned. There being no organization of the learned, it is not possible to poll them and to obtain a decision on a moot question.

The *ijma'* then, cannot be determined by resolutions of any kind regarding future settlement of this or that problem. It rather is to be determined by retrospection. At any given moment one is in a position to realize that such and such opinions, such and such institutions, have become accepted through *ijma'*. Deviation from *ijma'* is unbelief, *kufr*.

The doctrinal area covered by decisions of *ijma'*—these decisions may be expressed in statements, actions, or silence—constantly widens as the scope of what is left to its decision as steadily narrows. The questions to be settled by future *ijma'* will tend to become ever more minute and insignificant. This natural development diminishes considerably the potentialities of *ijma'* in reforming Islam. It may, of course, develop that, at some future time, the agreement will lend *ijma'* wider scope so at to allow it to sanction far-reaching changes concerning validity and content of the *fiqh*.

4. *Qiyas and Ijtihad*

DAVID SANTILLANA, *Istituzioni di Diritto Musulmano Malichita*, vol. 1, p. 46.

We have already outlined the three canonical sources of the law which depend more or less directly upon infallible divine inspiration. The fourth and last source depends, by contrast, upon the fallible judgment of man. Thus in cases where the Qur'an, the *sunna*, and the consensus of the Muslim community (*ijma'*) are of no help, recourse must be had to the analogical method.

As the name itself implies (*qiyas* means analogy), what is meant here is not the purely personal judgment, the application of personal opinion, but an inductive process governed by the rules of logic. If a jurist does not find in the law (Qur'an and *sunna*) a rule applicable to the case he has to solve, he has to search whether a rule cannot be deducted . . . from what has been decided in other similar cases. If analogical reasoning based on a single legal provision is not possible, then the jurist must examine whether a solution can be derived from the totality of the law, considering it carefully as a whole and applying to the case in question the solution which corresponds best to the general spirit of the law.

Ibid., pp. 70–71.

If there is no special legal provision and also no foundation for analogical interpretation, the jurist is still not left without recourse. If he is capable to do so . . . , he may have recourse to

ijtihad (personal reasoning). By concentrating all his mental
facilities on the penetration of the spirit and precise meaning of
the law, and not merely upon this or that specific provision, but
upon the totality of the law, the jurist relies upon his conscience,
thus illuminated and supported, to find the solution for the case in
question. *Ijtihad* therefore is not the arbitrary subjective and
personal opinion of the jurist, but the careful opinion. It is based
upon his legal conscience refined and disciplined by the intense
and profound contemplation of the law in its entirety . . . .

The general principle which is the starting point for the whole
system [of Islamic law] is thus reconfirmed. God has instituted
the laws for the good of mankind and the individual; man was not
made for the law, but law for man. In instances where the meaning
of the law or, in case of silence of the law, the rules applicable
are in doubt, the principal criterion is thus utility (*maslaha*). When
utility is general and effective, it is always the decisive argument.
By the same token, if there is a choice between general and individual utility, the first must always prevail . . . .

B. The Development of the Classical Schools of Jurisprudence

1. *The Rise of the Four Orthodox Schools*

Comment: During the Umayyad period groups of pious persons
developed who surveyed existing practices in all fields, including
law. In the early part of the second century of the Hijra these
groups formed the so-called ancient schools of law. These schools
continued to be composed of private individuals. At first these
schools were geographically determined, such as the Iraqi school
and the Hijazi school. Later, when the schools reached their full
development, they became known by the name of an individual
master whom the members of the school followed. Four great
schools or rites of orthodox Islam were formed which still exist
today. They were described by Ibn Khaldun.

IBN KHALDUN, *The Muqaddimah*, vol. 3, pp. 4, 6–9.

The jurists developed two different approaches to jurisprudence.
One was the use of opinion (reasoning) [*ra'y*] and analogy [*qiyas*].
It was represented by the Iraqis. The other was the use of tradi-
tions [*hadith*]. It was represented by the Hijazis.

. . . Few traditions circulated among the Iraqis. Therefore they
made much use of analogy and became skilled in it. That gave
them the name of representatives of opinion (reasoning). Their
chief, around whom and whose followers their school centered,
was the imam Abu Hanifa. The leader of the Hijazis was Malik bin
Anas and after him al-Shafi'i.

.   .   .   .

The leading authority of the Iraqis around whom their school centered, was Abu Hanifa al Nu'man bin Thabit. His place in jurisprudence is unrivalled. This has been attested by persons of his own caliber, in particular, Malik and al-Shafi'i.

The leading authority of the Hijazis was Malik bin Anas al-Asbahi, who held the leading position in Medina. He is distinguished by the fact that he added another source of law to those known to other scholars, namely, the practice of the Medinese. He was of the opinion that by virtue of their religion and traditionalism, the Medinese always necessarily followed each immediately preceding generation of Medinese, in respect of what they cared to do or not to do. The (process would have gone back) to the generation that was in contact with the actions of the Prophet, and they would have learned from him (what to and not to do). In (Malik's) opinion, the practice of the Medinese, thus, is basic legal evidence.

Many scholars have thought that the (practice of the Medinese) is (rather) one of the problems of the general consensus. Therefore, they have disapproved of (Malik's use of) it, because use of the general consensus as a source is not restricted to the inhabitants of Medina to the exclusion of other (Muslims), but extends to all Muslims. However, it should be known that general consensus means agreement concerning a religious matter on the strength of independent judgment. Malik did not consider the practice of the Medines in this light. He considered it in the light of the continuity of personal observation over successive generations, (going) back to the time of the lawgiver (Muhammad) . . . .

.   .   .   .

Malik bin Anas was followed by Muhammad bin Idris al-Muttalibi al-Shafi'i. He traveled to Iraq after Malik's time. He met the followers of the imam Abu Hanifa and learned from them. He combined the approach of the Hijazis with that of the Iraqis. He founded his own school and opposed Malik on many points.

Malik and al-Shafi'i were followed by Ahmad bin Hanbal. He was one of the highest ranking *hadith* scholars. His followers studied with those of Abu Hanifa, notwithstanding the abundant knowledge of traditions they themselves possessed. They founded another school.

These four authorities are the ones recognized by tradition in the (Muslim) cities . . . .

The Muslims today follow the tradition of one of the four (authorities).

2. *Divergencies Among the Orthodox Schools*

Comment: The four orthodox schools generally do not differ from each other in fundamentals, but they do diverge in many details. In their relationship to each other they have practiced mutual toleration. The interpretations of the four orthodox schools are regarded as equally valid and they are considered equally orthodox. The disagreement among the schools (*ikhtilaf*) has been discussed by Ibn Khaldun.

IBN KHALDUN, *The Muqaddimah*, vol. 3, pp. 3, 30–32.

Jurisprudence is the knowledge of the classification of the laws of God, which concern the actions of all responsible Muslims, as obligatory, forbidden, recommendable, disliked, or permissible. These (laws) are derived from the Qur'an and the *Sunna* (traditions), and from the evidence the Lawgiver (Muhammad) has established for the knowledge of (the laws). The laws evolved from the (whole) of this evidence are called "jurisprudence" (*fiqh*).

The early Muslims evolved the laws from that evidence, though, unavoidably, they differed in (the interpretation of) it. The evidence is mainly derived from texts. The texts are in Arabic. In many instances, and especially with regard to legal concepts, there are celebrated differences among them as to the meaning implicit in the words. Furthermore, the traditions (*Sunna*) differ widely in respect of the reliability of the recensions. Their legal contents, as a rule, are contradictory. Therefore, a decision is needed. This makes for differences of opinion. Furthermore, evidence not derived from texts causes (still other) differences of opinion. Then, there are new cases which arise and are not covered by the texts. They are referred by analogy to things that are covered by the texts. All of this serves to stir up unavoidable differences of opinion, and this is why differences of opinion occurred among the early Muslims and the religious leaders after them.

.   .   .   .

It should be known that the jurisprudence described, which is based upon religious evidence, involves many differences of opinion among scholars of independent judgment. Differences of opinion result from the different sources they use and their different outlooks, and are unavoidable, as we have stated before.

(These differences) occupied a very large space in Islam. (Originally,) people could adhere to any (juridical authority) they wished. Later on, the matter was in the hands of the four leading authorities in the Muslim cities. They enjoyed a very high prestige. Adherence was restricted to them, and people were thus prevented from adhering to anyone else . . . . Thus they were set up as the basic schools of Islam.

Differences of opinion among the adherents and the followers of their laws received equal status with differences of opinion concerning religious texts and legal principles (in general). The adherents of the four schools held disputations, in order to prove the correctness of their respective founders. These disputations took place according to sound principles and fast rules. Everyone argued in favor of the correctness of the school to which he adhered and which he followed. The disputations concerned all the problems of religious law and every subject of jurisprudence. The difference of opinion was on occasion between al-Shafiʿi and Malik, with Abu Hanifa agreeing with one of them. Or it was between Malik and Abu Hanifa, with al-Shafiʿi agreeing with one of them. Or it was between al-Shafiʿi and Abu Hanifa, with Malik agreeing with one of them. The disputations clarified the sources of the authorities as well as the motives of their differences and the occasions when they exercised independent judgment.

This kind of scholarship was called "controversial questions." The persons who cultivate it must know the basic rules through which laws can be evolved, just as they are known to scholars of independent judgment . . . . It is indeed a very useful discipline. It affords acquaintance with the sources and evidence of the authorities, and gives students practice in arguing what they wish to prove. Works by Hanefites and Shafiʿites are more numerous on the subject than those by Malikites . . . .

Comment: The earlier works giving comparative accounts of the teachings of the various schools reflect the discussions which were going on, while the later ones are handbooks presenting the different views of the schools without necessarily expressing preferences or arguing for one specific solution. The differences between schools have had practical significance in several respects. The authors of legal formularies which contained models for contracts and other documents, were careful in phrasing their models in such a way that the document would be valid, no matter what opinion the *qadi* followed in whose court it might be used. Also, a Muslim may not only join any orthodox school he wishes or change from one school to another without formalities, he even may apply to a specific transaction the rules of a school other than the one to which he belongs. Lastly, Islamic countries have made frequent use of divergent opinions of other schools in modern legislation in personal status matters so as to achieve desired results.

3. *Present Distribution of the Four Schools*

Comment: Today the four Sunni schools or rites are distributed geographically as follows:

The Hanefite rite was the official rite of the Ottoman Empire. It is prevalent among Muslims in Turkey, Syria, Lebanon, Jordan, India, Pakistan, and Afghanistan. It also has official status in Iraq, Egypt, Israel, the Sudan, and Libya. The Malikite rite is the rite of North Africa and of the Muslims of West Africa. Kuwait also is Malikite. The Shafiʿite rite is prevalent in Lower Egypt, the Hijaz, Southern Arabia, East Africa, Indonesia and Malaya. The Hanbalite school is the official rite of Saudi Arabia. It prevails in Eastern Saudi Arabia (the Najd and the Eastern Province) and in a few adjacent areas, such as Qatar.

4. *The Organization of Treatises on Islamic Law*

Comment: The treatises on Islamic law written by the adherents of the various schools cover purely religious as well as legal matters. The organization of the subject matter differs from school to school. All treatises, however, start with the treatment of purely religious subjects, such as prayer, the alms tax, the pilgrimage, ritual purity, and fasting during the month of Ramadan. These five subjects are considered basic religious performances and are known as the five *'ibadat*. (The word means religious performance.) Among the subjects which follow the variation among the different schools is greater. As an example of the organization of a work on Islamic jurisprudence (*fiqh*), the table of contents of a small Malikite treatise is given here.

IBN ABI ZAYD AL-QAYRAWANI, *Risala*. (Some of the more involved chapter titles are not given in full or are paraphrased.)

1. Chapter dealing with the compulsory religious duties and consisting of principles which the mouth shall express and in which the heart shall believe.

2. Chapter on the causes which make compulsory ablution and washing.

3. Chapter on the purity of the water, the garments, the place reserved for prayer and clothing permissible when praying.

4. Chapter on ablution and what it involves of traditional and divine obligations. Cleansing by water or stones (after bodily functions).

5. Chapter on purification through washing.

6. Chapter on the subject of believers who do not find water and on the characteristics of *tayammum* (ablutions with gravel or soil).

7. Chapter on wetting shoes by passing the hands over them.

8. Chapter on the times and names of prayers.

9. Chapter on the call to prayer and the repeated call.

10. Chapter describing the acts to be accomplished in the prayers resting on divine obligations. Additional and recommended practices of the tradition (*sunna*) relating to these prayers.

11. Chapter on the leadership (*imama*) of the prayer and the rules concerning the *imam* and the faithful praying behind an *imam*.

12. Chapter on overall rules on prayer.

13. Chapter on prostration during the reading of the Qur'an.

14. Chapter on prayer during a journey.

15. Chapter on the Friday prayer.

16.
17.
18. } Chapters dealing with different kinds of prayers.
19.

20. Chapter on practices relating to the dying, the washing of the dead, his envelopment in a shroud, his embalmment, his transportation and interment.

21. Chapter on the prayer at the bier carrying the dead and the invocation for the dead.

22. Chapter on the invocation for the little child who died, the prayer over its body and the washing of the body.

23. and 24. Chapters on fasting and spiritual retreat.

25.
26. } Chapters on various taxes.
27.

28. Chapter on the pilgrimage and the minor pilgrimage.

29. Chapter on various sacrifices. Rules concerning the hunt, circumcision, and forbidden foods and beverages.

30. Chapter on the Holy War.

31. Chapter on oaths and vows.

32. Chapter on marriage, repudiation, and various types of divorce.

33. Chapter on the *'idda* (period during which a divorced or widowed woman may not marry), on support (of the divorced or widowed wife), and related matters.

34. Chapter on sale and similar contracts.

35. Chapter on wills, on manumission after death, contractual manumission, simple manumission, the position of the concubine-mother, and the position of the former master.

36. Chapter on the right of preemption when joint property is sold, on gifts, alms, pious foundations, security for debts, deposit, finding lost property, and usurpation of property through violence.

37. Chapter on rules concerning homicide and penalties prescribed in the Qur'an.

38. Chapter on legal decisions and evidence.

39. Chapter on intestate succession.

40. Chapter on various religious obligations.

41. Chapter on various pious and forbidden practices.

42. Chapter on food and drink.

43. Chapter on formal greetings and other practices (such as recitation of the Qur'an, invocation of Allah, etc.)

44. Chapter on medicines, charms, auguries, astrology, castration (of animals), marks made with hot iron, of dogs and of good treatment of slaves.

45. Chapter on dreams, etc.

C. The Actual Historical Development

J. N. D. ANDERSON, "Law as a Social Force in Islamic Culture and History," pp. 18–21.

. . . The classical theory of the sources and origins of the law has been shown by modern research to represent a rationalization of history which is largely belied by the facts.* The *shari'a*, as we

*The summary which follows is based, in the main, on the conclusions of Professor J. Schacht. See M. Khadduri and H. J. Liebesny (ed.), *Law in the Middle East*, pp. 28–84; J. Schacht, *Origins of Muhammadan Jurisprudence, passim*; and J. Schacht, *An Introduction to Islamic Law, passim.*

know it, seems to have developed only around the turn of the first century of the Muslim era, and to have been based, in the main, on the existing customary law and administrative practice, provided this was not in flagrant conflict with a few basic Islamic norms. The period of the Caliphate of Medina was too much occupied with the phenomenal expansion of Islam, and with the organization of the conquered lands, to conform to the idealized picture of the classical theory. The conquered peoples were left to their own law, and such as survived of their own courts; while criminal and civil justice among the Muslim armies and their camp followers was administered by the generals and provincial governors, who might depute a "judicial secretary" to relieve them of part of this burden. It was only after some decades that religious specialists seem to have begun, in an unprofessional capacity, to wrestle with the problems of a law which should be truly Islamic; and they then appear to have worked through the existing customary law and administrative practice in the light of Qur'anic texts and Islamic principles—accepting, rejecting, or modifying their material and thus at one and the same time Islamicizing and systematizing the law—rather than, as the classical theory postulates, deducing the law straight from the Qur'an and traditions.

Nor can it be shown that any body of legal traditions was, in fact, in existence at this early date: on the contrary, the evidence indicates that, as these religious specialists began to form loosely-defined local schools, it was the "living tradition" of their common doctrine which represented the dynamic principle of evolution. It was only with the advent of Shafi'i and his commanding influence that the basic postulate of the traditionalists—that any specific tradition of what the Prophet had said or done must, if accepted as authentic, be regarded as binding and authoritative—came to prevail in the ancient schools of law; and it is only from this time that the term *sunna* was virtually confined to the content of these Prophetic traditions. Shafi'i's attempt to restrict the doctrine of consensus to that of the whole Muslim community, on the other hand, was doomed to failure, for the classical theory re-interpreted this consensus as that of the scholars, and thus opened the door to an arbitrary principle by which allegedly Prophetic traditions could be accepted or rejected.

It was only with the establishment of the 'Abbasid dynasty, moreover, with its ostentatious championship of the *shari'a,* that the law schools crystallized, that the classical theory of jurisprudence won acceptance, and that the office of *qadi* became—officially at least—reserved for those learned in the sacred law which this office particularly, and in theory exclusively, came to serve . . . .

There existed, therefore, a considerable gulf between theory and practice. In theory the sacred law, based exclusively on divine revelation and deductions therefrom, reigned supreme, and customary law had no official *locus standi* either in jurisprudence or substantive law. In practice, on the other hand, a great deal of customary law was incorporated in the *shari'a*; so much so, that even Qur'anic precepts were sometimes not applied by the courts if contrary thereto, while alleged Prophetic traditions were accepted or rejected in reality—although not in theory—by reference to this criterion, or were forged to provide custom with the authority which theory denied it. Other customary practices continued alongside the *shari'a*, and were either brought into superficial conformity with it or ignored in theory but followed in fact. There was a time, early in the 'Abbasid dynasty, when it appeared possible that this gulf —which had existed from the earliest days, when the religious specialists sought to Islamicize the existing law—would be bridged. But more and more the *shari'a* became, with the passage of time, an ideal law, parts only of which were consistently applied in practice.

.   .   .   .

It is not surprising, then, that there was little uniformity in the Muslim world. Even the differences between the precepts of the orthodox schools of law may, in fact, largely be explained on the basis of local conditions and existing practices; for while many countries were Islamicized, pre-Islamic practices almost everywhere survived. It is impossible, then, to assert that the *shari'a* in fact shaped society and its institutions nearly as radically or as exclusively as in theory it should have done. Yet there can be no manner of doubt that the *shari'a*, in spite of the differences between its schools, always and everywhere represented a strongly cohesive force. It had unique moral authority, and all, including the most absolute of rulers, paid at least lip service to its sway. The *shari'a*, moreover, was the exclusive province of the *'ulama'*, or religious specialists, who represent the nearest approach to clergy in strictly orthodox Islam and have wielded, all down the ages, an exceedingly powerful influence. It is interesting to observe, moreover, that while the office of jurist was universally respected, that of *qadi* or judge was frequently deprecated; for the former was regarded as exclusively concerned with the ideal law, while the latter's integrity was too often compromised—not only by the temptation to corruption but, still more, by the intrusions of the executive and the perils of an erroneous interpretation of the law or a mistaken application of its provisions to individual litigants.* Always and everywhere, the law has constituted the basic science of Islam; but it has remained throughout a lawyer's law, finding its most authoritative expression in the compendia of jurists, rather than a judge's law, resting on a system of case law or the principle of *stare decisis*.†

*Cf. N. J. Coulson, "Doctrine and Practice in Islamic Law." *Bulletin of the School of Oriental and African Studies* 18 (1956): 211–226.
†On the contrary, the Caliph 'Umar when told that a decision he had just given was diametrically contradictory to a previous decision which he had given on the same facts, is reputed to have observed: "It is better to return to the right path than to persist in an error."

D. The Closing of the Gate of Personal Reasoning (insidad bab al-ijtihad)

J. N. D. ANDERSON, "Law as a Social Force in Islamic Culture and History," p. 16.

In the orthodox view the law became increasingly rigid and static. At first the individual jurist had always enjoyed the right, if sufficiently learned, to go back to the original sources of the law and interpret them for himself. But with the crystallization of the schools of law in the second and third centuries A.H. this right of independent deduction, or *ijtihad*, was regarded as having progressively fallen into abeyance, and in the classical view the "door of *ijtihad*" became "closed" by about the end of the third century. Thenceforth every jurist was in practice regarded as a mere *muqallid*, one who had to take the decisions of his predecessors as authoritative without the exercise of independent thought. True, it was never denied that another great *mujtahid* (i.e., one who could exercise the right of *ijtihad*) might conceivably arise, and from time to time some jurist, greatly daring, would in fact claim to have reached the almost impossibly exacting qualifications postulated for such a claimant; but in practice any open or accepted use of the right of *ijtihad* had been in abeyance for centuries. The orthodox schools mutually recognized each other's orthodoxy, even in regard to the many points on which they differed; and within each school the vagaries of individual jurists became progressively unified in the doctrine which established itself as dominant.

Comment: Ibn Khaldun describes this process as follows:

IBN KHALDUN, *The Muqaddimah*, vol. 3, pp. 8–9.

... The technical terminology of the sciences has become very diversified, and there are obstacles preventing people from attaining the level of independent judgment. It is also feared that (the existence of differences of opinion) might affect unqualified people whose opinion and religion could not be trusted. Thus, (scholars) came to profess their inability (to apply independent judgment) and had the people adopt the tradition of the authorities) mentioned and of the respective group of adherents of each .... All that remained after the basic textbooks had been produced in the correct manner, and the continuity of their transmission had been established, was to hand down the respective school traditions and, for each individual adherent, to act in accordance with the traditions of his school. Today, jurisprudence means this, and nothing else. The person who would claim independent judgment nowadays would be frustrated and have no adherents.

Ibid., p. 13.

The school doctrine of each authority became, among his adherents, a scholarly discipline in its own right. They were no longer in a position to apply independent judgment and analogy. Therefore, they had to make reference to established principles from the school doctrine of their authority, in order to be able to analyze problems in their context and disentangle them when they got confused. A firmly rooted habit was required to enable a person to undertake such analysis and disentanglement and to apply the school doctrine of his particular authority to those (processes) according to the best of his ability. This habit is (what is meant) at this time by the science of jurisprudence.

Y. LINANT DE BELLEFONDS, *Traité de Droit Musulman Comparé*, vol. 1, pp. 20–22.*

. . . The decisions of the *qadis*, which had played a considerable role during the formative period of the law, have not had a creative function since the establishment of the schools of law among whom all Muslims are distributed. The same is true of custom which historically was one of the sources of *fiqh*, but which, from the orthodox point of view no longer has legal value, except as local usage which is taken into account in certain matters of secondary importance.

.   .   .   .

One does not, however, refer most frequently to the work of the founder of the school or of his immediate disciples in order to find the law. Although this may seem surprising, there exist in each school one or more works, sometimes of a late period, which have established themselves as the expression of the official doctrine of the school. Only these works are consulted in practice. They serve in a way as codes and the basic works of the founder of the school or of his immediate disciples are consulted only in rare instances, either for purposes of scholarly, historical study or in order to confirm the orthodoxy of the text utilized.

Actually, such a comparison always turns out to be unnecessary. The later works, those to which the practice refers, confine themselves usually to an often literal reproduction of the work of the Master. There are no innovations, rarely even slight deviations from the ancient doctrine dictated by the need felt to adapt this doctrine, if possible, to the economic and social changes which had occurred since it was devised. It actually could not be otherwise because *taqlid*, legal conformism, that is the obligation put upon all faithful to follow the teachings of the founder of the school and his immediate disciples, guarantees perfect conformity to the ancient original of all judicial production which has appeared during ten centuries.

Under these circumstances one can rightly ask why the many generations of faithful who have accepted the teachings of a certain school have not been satisfied with the work of the founder.

It is impossible to explain this phenomenon in a way valid for all schools. The output of legal writings which followed the time when the law was fixed (end of the third century of the *Hijra*) extends over more than ten centuries and over varied regions often quite distant from each other (Iraq, Arabia, Egypt, Spain, etc.).

Generally, and with due regard to the many local variants which cannot be systematized, the following explanation can be given: the work of the founder or founders of a school (the plural is applicable particularly to the Hanefite School) is always too voluminous and generally conceived in a spirit to which the needs of the practice accommodate only with difficulty.

Thus the official doctrine of the Hanefite School is contained in the six works of Muhammad al-Shaybani who died in 183 A.H. The *Umm* of the Imam al-Shafi'i, the basic work of Shafi'ite law, fills in its Egyptian edition, seven large volumes in quarto. The teachings of the Imam Malik, founder of the Malikite School, as reported by Sahnun (240 A.H.) in the famous *Mudawwana*, fill eight volumes (Egyptian edition 1323 A.H.). Under these circumstances one can understand why the need was soon felt for brief summaries which would give the essence of these enormous works and follow a more rigorous legal scheme than the work of the master.

·　·　·　·

However, the abridgement was not sufficient for the jurisconsult (*mufti*), the professor, the judge, or the layman who wanted information on legal matters. The reason was that the authors, in order to be concise, condensed matters to a point where their work ended up by being discouragingly difficult. To give just one example: the *Mukhtasar* of Khalil is in many places incomprehensible, even if one knows the key to the conventional formulas which he utilizes, unless one is aided by one of the many commentaries which this abridgement has given rise to. We have said that such an abridgement can have the same utility as a modern code. However, in all honesty one must say that a lawyer of our day would also be in difficulties if he had for his work only a code without any references, explanations, and above all without cases.

·　·　·　·

We come now to the commentary and the glosses. The basic text is put in parentheses and surrounded by the commentary. The gloss is generally put in the margin. What is contained in the commentaries and the glosses? Grammatical explanations, the opinion of the jurists who founded the school, divergences which arose within the school, on any point, and the prevailing solutions. Likewise, comparisons with the doctrine of the other schools and above all many practical examples . . . .

HERBERT J. LIEBESNY, "Stability and Change in Islamic Law," p. 19.*

Thus, the closing of the gate of independent reasoning and the

*Reprinted by permission of *The Middle East Journal.*

character of the later activity of the jurists may have been responsible for the fact that Islamic law did not progress to the point
where it drew general abstract rules from a number of similar
situations. For example, Islamic law did not develop a general
theory of obligations or of negligence. The question may at
least be raised whether this factor has been contributory to the
often found tendency of Middle Eastern peoples to think in
concrete rather than abstract terms and in terms of personalities
rather than institutions.

Comment: On the failure of Islamic jurisprudence to develop
general theories see also

Y. LINANT DE BELLEFONDS, *Droit Musulman*, vol. 1,
pp. 54–55.

In that enormous output which constitutes Muslim legal writing,
one finds only very rarely an attempt to systematize, to deduce a
general rule from the specific rules for each legal act. It has been
said that because of the religious character of the law, the Muslim
jurist felt a certain reticence to lay down principles which would
be generally applicable and thereby might seem to rival the
revealed precepts.

It goes too far to state (as has too often been repeated) that the
idea of synthesis was completely absent among Muslim jurists.
Nevertheless, it is true that the jurists, in accordance with their
traditional spirit, were always more inclined toward detailed
analyses than toward generalizing ideas.

Some works, however, have to be set apart, where the authors
have made an effort, a very rare one, we must repeat, at abstraction. Although these authors have not succeeded in creating a
general theory of the legal act, they were able to deduce some
general principles from the mass of commentaries and glosses of
their predecessors or contemporaries.

In Hanefite law the most original work from this point of view
is the *Ashbah wa-l-nadha'ir* (*Similarities and Resemblances*) of Ibn
Nujaym, an Egyptian, (died 970 A.H./1562–63 A.D.). This is a
small volume whose first part sets forth nineteen sayings or
general principles, while the second part (called *fawa'id*, valuable
information) reviews the basic rules governing various legal
acts and institutions.

These sayings and principles actually established the fame of
this work because they are literally reproduced in the *Majalla*, the
Ottoman code. In that code they form the substance of the first
hundred articles. They are not, however, strictly speaking legal
rules since one cannot find in them a normative character. Rather
they are statements of principles supposed to transmit the spirit
of Hanefite law, but they are so vague and so broad that they
constitute truisms or affirmations of general principles not in
agreement with positive law. . . .

Comment: A similar disinclination to abstract is shown by classical
Roman law.

FRITZ SCHULZ, *Principles of Roman Law*, pp. 41–52.*

A cursory glance at the Roman sources of law is sufficient to show how extremely reserved the Romans were when it came to abstraction. True, the Roman attitude was not the same at all times; the last century of the republic inclined more to abstraction than the classical period, the post-classical Byzantine era again more than the classical. But, compared with the jurisprudence of the eighteenth century (law of Nature) or with German legal science in the nineteenth, Roman jurisprudence on the whole shows a disinclination to the process. This attitude is by no means a sign of primitive incapacity—classical jurisprudence was evolved in the great period of Hellenistic science—but is based on a clear recognition of the dangers inherent in excessive abstraction. In law all general rules and conceptions are liable to cause catastrophes, as it is impossible, when formulating a rule, to foresee all possible complications which life may bring about.

.   .   .   .

... In the last century of the republic ... a tendency may be noticed, probably owing to Greek influence, toward abstract formulation of legal doctrines. It originated with Q. Mucius .... Cicero also expressly mentions the efforts of Servius to formulate *regulae* (rules) ....

Most of the "school rules" too, those epigrammatic statements handed down by classical writers as *regulae veterum* (rules of the old jurists), arose in this period. Too much importance should, however, not be attached to the results of this "maxim jurisprudence," as it has been called. On the whole only very elementary rules were at that time rendered in abstract formulae, and in classical times these efforts were only carried on with great reserve.

In the elementary introductory works of classical times ... the abstract method was followed; but apart from these the traditional casuistic method was employed .... Of course there are exceptions, but the casuistic method, which consistently avoids abstract formulation, remains predominant in the classical period ....

Comment: The nature of these brief rules was stated by the Roman jurist Paulus.

Digest of Justinian, 50. 17. 1:

A rule is a statement which briefly sets forth a matter. Law is not derived from such a rule, but the rule is derived from the law.

Comment: Paulus's statement would also be applicable to the brief maxims as formulated in Islamic law by Ibn Nujaym.

The casuistic approach of classical Roman law and classical Islamic law can be illustrated by extracts from the writings of representative authors. In both cases the examples are taken from

*Reprinted by permission of the Clarendon Press, Oxford, copyright 1936, reprinted 1956.

the law of torts. In Rome the *lex Aquilia* of 287 B.C. regulated a number of torts and established damages. This law was the object of considerable discussion among Roman jurists and a rich casuistic literature was developed.

ULPIANUS in *Digest of Justinian*, 9. 2. 7. 2–8 ; 9. 2. 9. 4.

. . . If someone is carrying too heavy a burden and throws it off and kills a slave, he is liable under the *lex Aquilia,* for it was left to his judgement not to burden himself so heavily. According to Pegasus* the *lex Aquilia* is also applicable if a person falls and crushes someone else's slave with his burden, if he either has burdened himself too heavily or has walked carelessly in a slippery place.

Proculus writes that if a person is pushed by another and does damage, neither the one who has done the pushing nor the one who was pushed is held liable, for the one who has pushed has not killed and the one who was pushed has not inflicted unlawful damage . . . . Proculus states that if a surgeon who is wanting in skill operates on a slave, he will be liable either under the contract of hire or under the *lex Aquilia*.

If persons throw javelins for amusement and kill a slave, they will be liable under the *lex Aquilia*. However, if they throw javelins in a field and the slave crosses there and is killed the *lex Aquilia* is not applicable because he should not have crossed the field while they were throwing javelins. A person who throws a javelin at the slave intentionally is nevertheless liable under the *lex Aquilia*.

ABU YUSUF, *Kitab al-Kharaj*, pp. 96–97. (French translation by Fagnan, *Livre de l'impôt foncier*, pp. 248–249.)†

If a person employs a workman to dig a ditch in a public roadway without an order of the ruler on this matter, and someone falls in and kills himself, the workman would be responsible according to the rule of analogy (*qiyas*). In this case, however, we reject analogy because the workmen would be no longer known in case the ditch is old and the responsibility falls on the employer's relatives who are liable for the blood money (*'aqila*). If a person trips on a stone and falls into the ditch, the one who has placed the stone there is responsible as if he had pushed the victim, but if it is not known who has put the stone there, then the owner is responsible. If the person has been pushed by an overburdened animal neither the owner of the ditch nor the master of the animal is responsible, unless the animal has been led or pushed or had been mounted by someone, then the latter is held responsible . . . . If someone slips on water spilled by another person on the road or on the water left over from ablutions, or the water used to wet the road, and if because of this water he falls into the pit or dies before he falls, the responsibility rests with him who has spilled the water. If, how-

---

*This name and the others in this excerpt are those of Roman jurists cited as authorities by Ulpian.

†Reprinted by permission of Librairie Orientaliste Paul Geuthner.

ever, it is rainwater which fell from the sky or an earth slide that led to his falling into the pit and killing himself, then the owner of the pit shall be responsible . . . . If a man falls into the pit but remains safe and sound and then tries to climb out, reaches a certain height, and falls back and dies, the owner of the pit is not responsible, because he was not there to push the person down . . . .

E. The Problem of Foreign Influences on Early Islamic Law

Comment: The question of the influence of foreign, particularly Roman law upon Islamic law has been much debated, with some scholars assuming a profound influence of Roman law upon Islamic law, while others deny practically any influence. The truth probably lies somewhere in the middle. In any event, it can be said that there was no conscious and methodical reception of foreign legal institutions during the formative period of Islamic law. Schacht's is a middle of the road opinion of a Western scholar.

JOSEPH SCHACHT, *Droit Byzantin et Droit Musulman*, pp. 6–10.*

. . . We know now that Islamic law as we know it, did not exist during the first century of the Hijra, that the first specialists in religious Moslem law began to study questions of immediate religious interest toward the end of that century, that the technical legal problems, in the sense in which we understand this term, were not approached by them until the beginning of the second century, that the first center of this activity was not Medina but Iraq, and that the opinions attributed to the specialists of the first century are apocryphal. Thus, the whole first century of Islam represented, from the juristic point of view, a void which could be infiltrated by foreign influences, in this case Byzantine. Even more importantly, Islamic jurisprudence began to develop at a time when the gates of Islamic civilization were wide open to potential transmitters [of foreign culture], the educated converts.

During the first two centuries of the Hijra a large proportion of the new converts actually belonged to the high social classes. They were people who had enjoyed a liberal education, that is an education in Hellenistic rhetoric, which was the normal education in all the Hellenized countries of the Near East. It is well known that during the last centuries of the ancient world the preparation of the advocate-orators, a profession quite distinct from that of the jurists proper, included a course in rhetoric and the teaching of the elementary principles of law. A general knowledge of the law was considered useful in all professions. Justinian had prohibited the technical teaching of law outside the three imperial universities of Rome, Beirut, and Constantinople. However, he

*Reprinted by permission of the Academia Nazionale dei Lincei, Rome, copyright 1956.

obviously could not purge the teaching of rhetoric which was designed not only to bring forth advocates, but also to provide a general education of all the elements of law which it contained. The infiltration at the "popular" level of Greek and Hellenistic ideas into Islamic theology and even Arabic grammar, well before the period of the translators, is due to these persons who, of course, were not specialists. They also are responsible for the presence in Islamic law of legal concepts of Byzantine origin. This fact explains the "popular" character of these borrowings. The technical solutions by the two sides are hardly ever identical, but there is a resemblance between the broad lines, a borrowing of the principle and not of the detail. Above all, the ideas involved are always widely spread, known not only to the specialists but also to laymen . . . .

All this is confirmed by remarkable parallels in the Talmudic law. D. Daube has shown that the methods of interpretation applied by the rabbis use reasoning identical with that of the Roman classical jurists. However, these methods were not derived directly from the writings of these jurists, but were transmitted to the rabbis through the intermediary of Hellenistic rhetoric. This also happened in Iraq, the country where Islamic jurisprudence came into being. Goldziher has already pointed out that parallels between Roman law and Islamic law are often duplicated by parallels in Talmudic law. In view of the profound influence which Talmudic law exercised on Islamic law one may thus wonder whether a specific rule came to Islamic law directly from Roman law or whether it came through the intermediary of Talmudic law.

We therefore have the right to consider according to its merits every case of possible or probable influence of Byzantine law on Islamic law, provided we strictly apply two criteria. The first criterion is the presence in Islamic law of some irregularity, be it historical, systematic, or sociological, which demands the hypothesis of foreign influence for an explanation. Parallels pure and simple, even if they are striking, are not enough. The same conditions and the same needs can well lead to the same solutions, even bring about parallel developments in both laws. The second criterion is that legal rules must be involved which would be known not only to the specialists but to the educated public at large. This follows from what I have said about the potential transmitters of Byzantine legal ideas to the Muslims. It is wholly out of the question to believe that the early Muslim jurists had consciously adopted foreign legal principles. No Byzantine law book was accessible to them in translation during the whole period with which we are concerned here.

. . . . .

The problem is somewhat different but not necessarily less difficult for the administrative and fiscal law, to which should be added real estate law. It has long been known that the Arabs throughout the first century of the Hijra did not hesitate to adopt much of the administrative and fiscal institutions existing in the conquered territories. This was well understood even before the new understanding of Islamic law, although the new viewpoint is helpful to a full understanding of the process.

Comment: Whatever the extent of foreign influence, there was one great difference between the Arabs and others, particularly the Germanic tribes who had invaded and conquered parts of the Roman Empire. The Arabs and their institutions were not Romanized, rather the conquered territories were gradually Islamicized. Pirenne deals with this phenomenon which is important as much for legal developments as for cultural development generally.

HENRI PIRENNE, *Mohammed and Charlemagne*, pp. 150–152.*

. . . [T]he great problem is to determine why the Arabs, who were certainly not more numerous than the Germans, were not, like the latter, absorbed by the populations of the regions which they had conquered, whose civilization was superior to their own. There is only one reply and it is of the moral order. While the Germans had nothing with which to oppose the Christianity of the Empire, the Arabs were exalted by a new faith. It was this, and this alone, that prevented their assimilation. For in other respects they were not more prejudiced than the Germans against the civilization of those whom they had conquered. On the contrary, they assimilated themselves to this civilization with astonishing rapidity; they learnt science from the Greeks, and art from the Greeks and the Persians. In the beginning, at all events, they were not even fanatical, and they did not expect to make converts of their subjects. But they required them to be obedient to the one God, Allah, and His Prophet Muhammad, and since Muhammad was an Arab, to Arabia. Their universal religion was at the same time a national religion. They were the servants of God.

. . . After the conquest they asked nothing better than to appropriate the science and art of the infidels as part of their booty; they would cultivate them to the glory of Allah. They would even adopt the institutions of the unbelievers in so far as these were useful to them. For that matter they were forced to do so by their own conquest. In governing the Empire which they had founded they could no longer rely on their tribal institutions; just as the Germans were unable to impose theirs upon the Roman Empire. But they differed from the Germans in this: wherever they went, they ruled. The conquered were their subjects; they alone were taxed; they were excluded from the community of the faithful. The barrier was insuperable. No fusion was possible between the conquered populations and the Muslims. What a contrast between them and Theodoric, who placed himself at the service of those he had conquered, and sought to assimilate himself to them!

In the case of the Germans, the conqueror spontaneously

approached the conquered. With the Arabs it was the other way about; the conquered had to approach the conquerors, and they could do so only by serving Allah, as the conquerors served Him, and by reading the Qur'an, like the conquerors; and therefore by learning the language, the sacred and consummate language of the conquerors.

.   .   .   .

The German became Romanized as soon as he entered "Romania." The Roman, on the contrary, became Arabized as soon as he was conquered by Islam. It is true that well into the Middle Ages certain small communities of Copts, Nestorians, and, above all, Jews, survived in the midst of the Muslim world. Nevertheless, the whole environment was profoundly transformed. There was a clean cut: a complete break with the past. Wherever his power was effective, it was intolerable to the new master that any influence should escape the control of Allah. His law, derived from the Qur'an, was substituted for Roman law, and his language for Greek and Latin.

F. The Concept of Jurists' Law

Comment: The role of the jurist-theologian in the development of Islamic law and also that of the *mufti* (see below) have frequently been compared with that of the Roman jurist in the development of Roman law. This latter role has been the subject of much discussion. A concise treatment of the problem comes from Professor Schiller of Columbia University.

A. ARTHUR SCHILLER, "Jurists' Law," pp. 1226–1232.*

The nature of [Roman] jurists' law may perhaps best be explained by describing the activities of the group from which it takes its name, the secular Roman jurists of the classical era, the period of the late Republic and the Principate, a period roughly from 150 B.C. to 250 A.D. These activities were classified in ancient times as falling within three categories: *cavere, agere,* and *respondere*—to aid in drafting documents, to advise in procedural matters and to respond to questions of law.

.   .   .   .

The jurists of the Principate continued the activities pursued by their predecessors. To the practice of providing answers to party litigant, *praetor* [judicial magistrate], and *index* [judge-juror], we may add the giving of advice to the emperor and imperial magistrates, and the growing custom of perpetuating their legal opinions in writings, whether in collections of answers to actual

*Reprinted by permission of the *Columbia Law Review* and the author.

or hypothetical questions of law, or in commentaries on the *ius
civile* and the edict of the *praetor*.

The sources tell us in passages which have been tampered with
that Augustus granted to some jurists, but not to all, the right of
giving responses publicly on the authority of the emperor . . . .

Patented or not, Roman jurists continued to be the prime force
in the development of Roman law, until the time of Hadrian at
least . . . .

There is a perplexing passage in Gaius' *Institutes* which refers
to the position of the jurists at this time. The responses of the
jurists (*responsa prudentium*) are noted as one of the constituent
elements of the Roman law. These *responsa* are defined as follows:

> The responses of the learned in the law are the decisions and
> opinions of those to whom it is granted to lay down the law.
> If the opinions of all of these are in accord that which they so
> hold has the force of statute. If, however, they differ, the *iudex*
> is free to follow the opinion he pleases; and this is indicated in
> a rescript of the late emperor Hadrian.

Some scholars have taken the position that anomalies in the text
are attributable to the misconceptions of a post-classical editor, or
that the whole is a product of post-classical times. Others see in
the passage the culmination of the development which began with
the grant of the *ius respondendi* by Augustus. Hadrian gave official
sanction to the principle that the responses of patented jurists were
binding, and only in the case of contradictory opinions was the
iudex free to choose the rule he favored.

These explanations fail to explain the coordination of "decisions and opinions," . . . or the power of the jurist to lay down
the law . . . . [T]here was a growing tendency by the jurists to
deal with specific cases in their writings, in addition to oral
responses. This is particularly true in those works which have
been termed "problematic literature," *i.e.*, collections of *responsa*,
epistulae, *quaestiones*, and *disputationes*. The first two collect answers
of law provided for cases in litigation, while *quaestiones* and
disputationes incorporate opinions given in response to hypothetical cases with actual ones. All are framed in the succinct,
casuistic fashion characteristic of juristic responses to questions
of law, whether the queries be raised in connection with actual
litigation, offered in discussion, or broached in adversary session.
In addition to problematic works, opinions on law are contained
within the jurists' commentaries on the *ius civile* and on the edict of
the *praetor*. No distinction can be made with respect to the force
of these decisions and opinions, wherever they may be found.
The validity of all juristic utterances, oral or written, depended on
what was termed *auctoritas prudentium*. The meaning of the phrase
is the recognition afforded the views of a person whose knowledge of the law has gained the highest respect and whose prestige
is such that his opinions on the law are accepted without the
slightest question. In a well-known passage of the jurist Papinian
we read that the *ius civile*—in this connotation the Roman positive
law—derives from the statutes, plebiscites, resolutions of the

Senate, enactments of the emperors, and from *auctoritas prudentium.*

Applying this to the Gaius passage, then, the *communis opinio* of
the jurists—the decisions and opinions which present the accepted
view—is just as much a source of law as statutes. The contributions to this *communis opinio* are not limited to any one form, but
they must come from "authoritative jurists," *i.e.*, those jurists who
have achieved *auctoritas prudentium,* whether or not they had
received the patent of the emperor. If there was agreement, the
iudex had no reason or power to depart from the opinion. But if
contradictory, he could chose one or another opinion, regardless
of the number of jurists who supported either view. Thus if
Gaius had specified and defined *auctoritas prudentium* instead of
responsa prudentium there would have been little difficulty in explaining the text . . . .

Four factors seem to be fundamental to the existence of jurists'
law, as revealed in the Roman experience. First, there was a
continued existence of a group of individuals dedicated to the
law . . . .

Secondly, the jurists possessed a comprehensive and expert
knowledge of the private law. For the most part, they paid little
attention to other fields of law. But in private law no one else had
even a remotely comparable grasp of the subject . . . .

In the third place the jurists were intimately and continuously
connected with the day to day administration of the law. It was
their concern with civil process which gave the jurists their
greatest opportunity to develop the law. Even in their writings
they dealt with cases . . . .

Finally, freedom of discussion and disputation, with its inevitable expression of divergent, even contradictory opinions, was a
basic premise of jurists' law . . . .

G. Further Development of the Law

1. *The Mufti*

Comment: Although theoretically the development of Islamic law
might have been regarded as having come to a halt with the
"closing of the gate of independent reasoning," in practice the
law, like any law, developed further. One means of this further
development was the activity of the *mufti.*

EMILE TYAN, *Histoire de l'Organisation Judiciaire en Pays d'Islam,*
pp. 219–220.*

An institution which is intimately connected with the Islamic
judicial system and which is the practical consecration of the
principle of *mashura* (consulting with experts) is the institution of
futya or *ifta'* (giving a legal opinion). It consists of providing an

*Reprinted by permission of E. J. Brill, Leiden, copyright 1960.

answer (*fatwa*) to a legal or theological question. The person who gives this answer is called a *mufti*; the person who requests and receives this answer is called a *mustafti*. This institution of the Islamic law corresponds to the Roman institution of the *ius publice respondendi* and there are many analogies between the two institutions.

It is most interesting to show what role this institution played. We believe that in Islam where there is, in principle, no legislative power, the role of the jurists in the legislative development was extremely important. It was because of the opinions of the *muftis*, opinions which were not reasoned and therefore gave the *mufti* much leeway, that legal doctrine, theoretically immutable, adapted itself in the course of the centuries to the practice and that legal development proceeded quietly.

Also, in controversial questions, in all those cases where the old doctrines clashed with the new realities of society, the solution which was in line with practical necessities was found and adopted through the means of a *fatwa*. The rule according to which the right to give opinions could be exercised only with regard to cases that arose in practice, and not with regard to theoretical questions, established even more strongly the role and influence of the Muslim *ius respondendi* . . . . This function of elaboration of the law became so important that it was felt necessary to bring the *fatwas* of famous *muftis* together in large collections.

It would appear that the considerable influence exerted by the *muftis* upon the interpretation and development of the law was the major reason for the interference of the state in this profession and for the control which it ultimately assumed over it.

Ibid., p. 229.

In principle, the question and the answer [of the *mufti*] may be formulated either orally or in writing. In practice written questions and answers prevail . . . .

The *mufti* does not have to give an immediate reply. Rather he should take time to reflect . . . .

[In writing out his answer] the *mufti* may not leave blank spaces between words or on either margin of the page. Erroneous passages may be erased. In principle, the *fatwa* need not contain reasons, but reasons may be indicated. The *mufti* is not allowed to formulate his response as his personal advice, because the *fatwa* must have an absolutely objective character. Furthermore, the *fatwa* must not contain any digressions or an answer to a question which was not asked.

Comment: In the Ottoman Empire the position of the *muftis* became strictly regulated. A chief *mufti*, appointed by the sultan, resided in Constantinople. He was the highest religious dignitary and had the title of *Shaykh al-Islam*. The *muftis* originally did not receive salaries and in principle held office for life. The organization of the *muftis* in the later Ottoman Empire and their activity around the turn of the century was described in the following work.

A. HEIDBORN, *Droit Public et Administratif de l'Empire Ottoman*, vol. 2, pp. 267–269.

In places where there is a *shari'a* judge there is also a *mufti* as an official organ of consultative justice. The *muftis* are usually taken from among those inhabitants who have a reputation of knowing the *shari'a* well and are elected for life by the administrative council upon proposal of the Muslim notables of the place. This choice has to be ratified by the *Shaykh al-Islam* who issues a certificate to the *mufti*. The *muftis* are *ex officio* members of the administrative councils and supervise the religious schools in their districts. In the more important cities they are assisted by one or more clerks . . . .

Fatwas are requested from the *mufti* nearly exclusively by the common people, Muslims and non-Muslims alike, and particularly by the farmers on market days, while well-to-do persons prefer to consult a lawyer. Generally, those who consult the *mufti* present their question orally and receive an oral answer, which, however, is given in writing for a very small fee. The form of the *fatwa* is consecrated by immemorial usage. Written on a piece of paper of about four inches in width and six inches in length it repeats the case as briefly as possible in form of a question, in terms of the *shari'a* and using the names Zeid, Amr, Hind, etc., to designate the parties, just as the Roman jurists used Titus, Gaius, Seia, etc., then follows the answer without further explanation in a single word, such as *olur* "that is right," *olmas* "that is not right," *ja'iz* "that is permissible," and the signature of the *fatwa*. [This form of a very abbreviated answer had developed in the Ottoman Empire] . . . .

Some *muftis* or clerks are very learned and answer right away without consulting books. In difficult and unusual cases they look for a precedent in *fatwa* collections. These collections contain the various *fatwas* arranged in the order used in the *fiqh* treatises. If the *mufti* does not find a parallel case, he should consult the *fiqh* treatises themselves as well as the commentaries and glosses to them. He cannot, however, decide a case according to the result of his own personal contemplation.

The *fatwa* does not prejudice the judicial decision. The *fatwa* accepts the facts as the requestor presents them in his question, it does not examine the facts and merely deals with the question what rule of the *shari'a* should apply to the facts as presented. The requestor may submit the *fatwa* to the judge during the trial and the judge himself may consult the *mufti*. In contrast to the *fatwa* [given to one of the parties] the judge will, however, base his decision on the presentation of both parties and the results of the trial.

At Constantinople there exists a special consultative office, established by Sultan Suleiman the Magnificent which is called *fetvahane* or more rarely *dar al-istifta'* (*fatwa* office). It owes its establishment to the fact that with the rapid growth of the capital the *mufti* by himself could no longer issue all the *fatwas* requested from him, particularly since he had been placed at the top of the religious-legal hierarchy as *Shaykh al-Islam* and charged with administrative and ceremonial functions.

The organization of the *fetvahane* [at the beginning of the twentieth century] was regulated by the law of the 13 Muharram 1292.* Under the presidency of the *fetva emini* it comprised some twenty secretaries . . . and a certain number of supernumeraries and candidates. One group of secretaries constitutes the judgment division which is charged with the revision of judgments of the *shari'a* courts. Another division renders *fatwas* . . . .

Comment: One of the outstanding *muftis* of the Ottoman Empire was Ebüssuud who was *Shaykh al-Islam* under two sultans, Suleiman the Magnificent and Selim II, from A.D. 1545 to A.D. 1574. His *fatwas* are contained in several collections. A number are found in a collection recently edited, from which some examples have been drawn.

FRIEDRICH SELLE, *Prozessrecht des 16. Jahrhunderts im Osmanischen Reich*, p. 82 (these cases deal with the testimony of witnesses), pp. 99 and 101 (dealing with hearsay evidence).†

35th Question: The following case: Amr and Bekr testify as witnesses: "Hind has appointed Zeyd to be her authorized representative at her marriage." Neither witness, however, has seen her or has heard her voice. Can their testimony be admitted?

Answer: No. Ebüssuud.

37th Question: If Zeyd has a quarrel with the inhabitants of a village regarding a certain matter and these inhabitants testify for each other against Zeyd, will their testimony be admitted?

Answer: Not if they are involved in that matter. Ebüssuud.

. . . . .

3rd Question: Can hearsay evidence be admitted in matrimonial causes?

Answer: Not in our time. Ebüssuud.

. . . .

4th Question: At the age of eighty Zeyd said: "Amr is my son" and insisted that it is so. Then he died. A number of people also testified: "We have heard the same thing from our fathers." Does this prove the relationship?

Answer: If these people testify who Amr is and who was the father of his father and the father of his father's father, then it is not necessary for the witnesses to have seen these ancestors or to have known them. If they merely testify, however: "This is what we have heard." then there is no proof . . . .

Comment: In modern times some very extensive *fatwas* have been issued often upon request by the government. As an example a

*Corresponds to 19 February 1875.
†Reprinted by permission of Otto Harrassowitz, Wiesbaden, copyright 1962.

modern Egyptian *fatwa* is presented. The question before the *mufti* of Egypt was whether Muslims were permitted to drink Coca-cola and Pepsi-cola.

Al-Ahram, 11 September 1951.

According to the Muslim Hanefite, Shafi'ite, etc., *imams* the rule in Islamic law of forbidding or allowing foods and beverages is based on the presumption that such things are permitted unless it can be shown that they are forbidden on the basis of the Qur'an, the *sunna*, or because of a specific or general harm which makes their prohibition necessary.

This opinion is based upon the saying of the Most High God in the *sura* on Cattle (Qur'an *sura* VI, 146, translation Pickthall)*: "Say: I find not in that which is revealed unto me aught prohibited to an eater that he eat thereof, except it be carrion, or blood poured forth, or swineflesh—for that verily is foul—or the abomination which was immolated to the name of other than Allah. But whoso is compelled (thereto), neither craving nor transgressing, (for him) lo! your Lord is Forgiving, Merciful."

On the basis of this rule the Muslim jurists stated that it remains generally permissible to partake of foods and beverages unless a person knows their origin and nature and it is established that they are forbidden by a statement in the Qur'an or the *sunna* or unless they are specifically or generally harmful. The jurists further stated that in case a person does not know the condition or ingredients of the food or beverage, be it meat or vegetable, such food or beverage shall, according to the rule, remain permitted until its nature is determined, inasmuch as nothing is forbidden without proof.

In order to give on this basis an answer on the merits of the case of these two beverages, whose problem has lately agitated the people, has become of the greatest importance, and has raised doubts, the Department of *Fatwas* has found it necessary to address itself to the Ministry of Public Health for the determination by analysis of the composition of the two beverages. The ministry is indeed the official specialized entity on whose research the Department of *Fatwas* can base its ruling because of that ministry's responsibility and the large number of research tools and instruments of analysis which it possesses.

On 25 August 1951 the ministry replied as follows: "To His Excellency the Mufti of Egypt, the peace, mercy and blessing of God be upon you.

I have the honor to communicate to Your Excellency, the results of the analysis of the two beverages 'Pepsi-cola' and 'Coca-cola' performed in the laboratories of the Ministry of Health in accordance with Your Excellency's letter of 8 August 1951.

Findings: The analyses performed with regard to the two beverages 'Pepsi-cola' and 'Coca-cola' show clearly that they

*Reprinted by permission, George Allen and Unwin, London, copyright 1930.

do not contain narcotic or alcoholic substances, nor do these analyses show the presence of pepsin. From the bacteriological point of view the beverages are free of microbes harmful to health. Please accept, Your Excellency, my heartfelt thanks and greetings. (Signed) Muhammad Nasr, Undersecretary of the Ministry of Health for Medical Questions. Confirmed by the Ministry of Health: the Ministry of Health confirmed the correctness of these findings under the date of 9 September 1951."

These findings deny the presence of alcoholic substances or of substances harmful to the body or the mind as well as of pepsin (or at least declare that proof of its presence is lacking). The latter element has raised doubts more than the others since it is taken from the stomach of the pig, which is absolutely forbidden by the Islamic *shari'a*.

In view of these communications and on the basis of the rule under which, as has been stated, food and beverages are declared permissible or forbidden under Islamic law, we rule that there is no legal prohibition against the consumption of these two beverages, that they are permitted, and that there is no reason to maintain that they are forbidden in the light of the communications on the results of the analyses made by the Ministry of Health.

God guide you to what is good and on the path of righteousness.

2. *Hyal (sing. hila)*

Comment: Another means to achieve desired results which were not in accord with the provisions of the *shari'a* law, was the use of "legal devices," or fictions through which the letter of the law was observed while the actual intent of the *shari'a* was evaded. The *hyal* literature has been studied intensively by Joseph Schacht.

ABU HATIM MAHMUD IBN AL-HASAN AL-QAZWINI, *Kitab al-Hiyal fil-Fiqh* (Shafi'ite), p. 10.

. . . [T]here are three kinds of legal devices, forbidden ones, disapproved ones, and permitted ones; the jurist may not disclose the forbidden ones to the public, but he may communicate them to (other) jurists, so that they can incorporate them into the *fiqh*, and he must be able to evaluate them if they occur. With regard to those which are disapproved, it will be dissapproved if he points them out to somebody else. The devices which are permitted he has to communicate if asked about them and is bound to make public.

Ibid., p. 26.

If a co-owner gives his share as a valid gift to someone and the recipient returns the value as a gift, then [the transaction is valid] and the other co-owner has no right of preemption with regard to this share. (This is a permissible *hila*.)

3. *Qanun*

Comment: According to Islamic doctrine the ruler was not permitted to legislate; he could, however, enact regulations carrying
out the *shari'a* law and filling in gaps. This power of the ruler was
used particularly in fields where the *shari'a* was weak, such as
criminal law, police regulations, various aspects of taxation, etc.
The administrative power of the ruler which extended to the
executive as well as the judicial sphere, was called *siyasa shar'iyya*,
since it had to be exercised within the limits of the *shari'a*—at
least in legal theory. Under the Ottoman sultans the field of
administrative regulations was widened, although these regulations continued to be regarded as merely supplementing the
shari'a rules. Thus in the Ottoman period the regulations of the
sultans became important instruments in the further development of the law. These regulations were called *qanun*, from the
Greek κανών which means regulation, and were collected in so-
called *Qanun-name*. The early sultans issued relatively few *qanuns*,
but this changed as the Ottoman Empire expanded. Mehmet the
Conqueror, so called because of his conquest of Constantinople,
who ruled from A.D. 1451 to A.D. 1481 enacted many important
qanuns dealing with the organization of the empire, education,
judicial administration and many other matters. At least as important was the activity in this field of Suleiman the Magnificent,
who is called by the Turks the Lawgiver (*Suleiman Qanuni*).
Suleiman ruled from A.D. 1520 to A.D. 1566 and regulated many
areas of the law, among them real estate transactions, feudal
holdings, military matters, and various matters in the field of
criminal law. The exercise of various trades also was made the
subject of detailed regulation.*

H. Heterodox Schools of Law

Comment: The most important heterodox group in Islam is that of
the Shi'a. The split between the Shi'a and the Sunnis occurred on
a political and constitutional issue. 'Ali, the son-in-law of the
Prophet, the husband of the Prophet's daughter Fatima and the
fourth caliph, was deprived of the caliphate through an arbitration which ended the civil war between him and Mu'awiya, the
governor of Syria. Two years after the arbitration 'Ali was
murdered. Mu'awiya assumed the caliphate and became the
founder of the Umayyad dynasty. The Shi'ite (the name comes
from a word meaning "partisans of someone") followers of 'Ali
declined to recognize the new caliph and maintained that the
caliphate belonged to 'Ali and his descendants. The Shi'ites also
believed that the ruler, the *imam*, was divinely inspired and the
spiritual as well as secular leader of the community. The Shi'ites

*See further on this topic Uriel-Heyd, *Studies in Old Ottoman Criminal Law*,
Oxford: Clarendon Press, 1973, particularly pp. 167–207.

are split into several sects. The most important are the *Ithna 'Ashari* or Twelvers (the Arabic word means twelve) and the *Isma 'ilis* or Seveners. The difference between these two groups stems from their divergence as to the line of succession after the fourth *imam*. The *Ithna 'Ashari* are concentrated in Iran and southern Iraq. The *Isma 'ilis* are concentrated in India with some pockets elsewhere. Another Shi'ite group, the *Zaydis*, combines Sunni and Shi'ite beliefs. It is found in the Yemen. The *Ithna 'Ashari* believe that the last *imam* disappeared and is hidden and that he will appear again to announce the last judgment and establish the rule of justice on earth.

Since the *imam* is divinely inspired, the Shi'ites do not basically recognize *ijma* and *qiyas*. The Ithna 'Ashari doctrine, however, permits *ijma* as interpretation of the commands of the *imams* on a particular question by the jurists (*mujtahids*). By the same token, the Shi'ites cannot recognize the closing of the gate of independent reasoning and the doctrine of *taqlid*. In practical terms, however, the Shi'ites have not deviated greatly from the traditional teachings. Nevertheless, there are a number of differences in substantive law, particularly with regard to the law of inheritance, which will be discussed later as far as they are pertinent.

Chapter 3 Legal Reforms in the Nineteenth Century

A. The Beginning of Legal Reform in the Ottoman Empire

Comment: Nineteenth-century legal reforms in the Ottoman Empire and elsewhere, led to considerable reception of foreign, Western law. In contrast to the very limited and nonsystematic reception of foreign institutions in early Islamic law, the adoption of foreign institutions in the nineteenth century was systematic and extensive. It was caused by political as well as legal considerations and constituted a conscious attempt at modernization of the legal system. In the Ottoman Empire the desire to modernize the country's institutions according to the European pattern led to an era of reform, the so-called *Tanzimat*. Modernization encompassed the army (the famous Janizary corps was abolished in 1826) education, and law and administration. Legal reform was initiated with the proclamation, on 3 November 1839, of the *Hatti-Sherif of Gülhane* (Imperial Edict of the Rose Chamber). This decree was designed to establish equality before the law of all Ottoman subjects and do away with a number of abuses. The text of the decree follows.

The Hatti-Sherif of Gülhane

All the world knows that in the first days of the Ottoman monarchy, the glorious precepts of the Qur'an and the laws of the Empire were always honored.

The Empire in consequence increased in strength and greatness, and all its subjects, without exception, had acquired the highest degree of ease and prosperity. In the last one hundred and fifty years a succession of accidents and divers causes have brought about a disregard for the sacred code of laws and the regulations flowing therefrom, and the former strength and prosperity have changed into weakness and poverty; an empire in fact loses all its stability as soon as it ceases to observe its laws.

These considerations are ever present in our mind and, from the day of our advent to the throne the thought of the public weal, of the improvement of the state of the provinces, and of relief to the [subject] peoples has not ceased wholly to engage it. If, therefore, the geographical position of the Ottoman provinces, the fertility of the soil, the aptitude and intelligence of the inhabitants are considered, the conviction will remain that by striving to find efficacious means, the result, which with the help of God we hope to attain, can be obtained within a few years. Full of confidence, therefore, in the help of the Most High and supported by the intercession of our Prophet, we deem it right to seek through new institutions to provide the provinces composing the Ottoman Empire with the benefit of a good administration.

These institutions must be principally carried out under three heads which are:

1. Guarantees insuring to our subjects perfect security of life, honor, and fortune.

2. A regular system of assessing and levying taxes.

3. An equally regular system for the levying of troops and the duration of their service.

And in fact, are not life and honor the most precious gifts that exist? What man, however much his character may be against violence, can prevent himself from having recourse to it, and thereby injure the government and the country, if his life and honor are endangered? If, on the contrary, he enjoys in that respect perfect security, he will not depart from the ways of loyalty and all his actions will contribute to the good of the government and of his brothers.

If there is an absence of security as to one's fortune, everyone remains insensible to the voice of the Prince and the country; no one interests himself in the progress of the public good, absorbed as he is in his own troubles. If, on the contrary, the citizen keeps possession in all confidence of all his goods, then, full of ardor in his affairs, which he seeks to enlarge in order to increase his comforts, he feels daily growing and doubling in his heart not only his love for the Prince and country, but also his devotion to his native land.

These feelings become in him the source of the most praiseworthy actions.

As to the regular and fixed assessment of the taxes, it is very important that this matter be regulated; for the state which is forced to incur many expenses for the defense of its territory, cannot obtain the money necessary for its armies and other services except by means of contributions levied on its subjects. Although, thanks be to God, the inhabitants of our Empire have for some time past been delivered from the scourge of monopolies, falsely considered at other times as a source of revenue, a fatal custom still exists, although it can only have disastrous consequences; it is that of venal concessions, known under the name of "*Iltizam.*"

Under this system the civil and financial administration of a locality is delivered over to the arbitrary control of a single man; that is to say, sometimes to the iron grasp of most violent and avaricious passions, for if that contractor is not a good man, he will only look to his own advantage.

It is therefore necessary that henceforth each member of Ottoman society should be taxed for a quota determined accord-

ing to his fortune and means, and that it should be impossible
that anything more could be exacted from him. It is also necessary
that special laws should fix and limit the expenses of our land and
sea forces.

Although, as we have said, the defense of the country is an
important matter, and that it is the duty of all the inhabitants to
furnish soldiers for that object, it has become necessary to establish laws to regulate the contingents to be furnished by each
locality according to the necessities of the time and to reduce the
term of military service to four or five years. For it is at the same
time doing an injustice and giving a mortal blow to agriculture
and to industry to take, without consideration to the respective
population of the localities, in the one more, in the other fewer
men than they can furnish; it also reduces the soldiers to despair
and contributes to the depopulation of the country by keeping
them all their lives in the service.

In short, without several laws, the necessity for which has just
been described, there can be neither strength, nor riches, nor
happiness, nor tranquility for the Empire; it must, on the contrary, look for them in the existence of these new laws.

From henceforth, therefore, the cause of every accused person
shall be judged publicly, as our divine law requires, after inquiry
and examination, and so long as a regular judgment shall not
have been pronounced, no one can secretly or publicly put another
to death by poison or in any other manner.

No one shall be allowed to attack the honor of any person
whatever.

Each person shall possess his property of every kind and shall
dispose of it in all freedom, without let or hindrance from any
person whatever; thus, for example, the innocent heirs of a
criminal shall not be deprived of their legal rights, and the property of the criminal shall not be confiscated. These imperial grants
shall extend to all our subjects, of whatever religion or sect they
may be; they shall enjoy them without exception. Perfect security
is thus given to the inhabitants of our Empire in their lives, their
honor, and their fortunes, as they are secured to them by the
sacred text of our law.

As for the other points, as they must be settled with the assistance of enlightened opinions, our council of justice (increased by
new members as shall be found necessary), to whom shall be
joined, on certain days which we shall determine, our ministers
and the notables of the Empire, shall assemble in order to frame
laws regulating these matters concerning the security of life and
fortune and the assessment of taxes. Each one in these assemblies
shall freely express his ideas and give his advice.

The laws regulating the military service shall be discussed by a
military council holding its meetings at the palace of the minister
of war. As soon as a law shall be completed in order to be forever
valid and in effect, it shall be presented to us; we shall give it our
approval, which we will write at the beginning with our imperial
sign-manual.

As the object of these institutions is solely to revivify religion, government, the nation, and the Empire, we engage not to do anything which is contrary thereto.

In testimony of our promise we will, after having deposited these presents in the hall containing the glorious mantle of the Prophet, in the presence of all the *'ulama'* and the grandees of the Empire, make oath thereto in the name of God, and shall afterwards cause the oath to be taken by the *'ulama'* and grandees of the Empire.

After that, those from among the *'ulama'* or the grandees of the Empire, or any other person whatsover who shall infringe these institutions, shall undergo, without respect of rank, position, and influence, the punishment corresponding to his crime, after the latter has been fully established. A penal code shall be compiled for that purpose.

As all the public servants of the Empire receive a suitable salary, and as the salaries of those whose duties have not up to the present time been sufficiently remunerated are to be fixed, a rigorous law shall be enacted against the traffic in favoritism and offices, which the divine law disapproves and which is one of the principal causes of the decay of the Empire.

Comment: The edict of Gülhane was never fully implemented. At the end of the Crimean War (1853–1856), the Western powers pressured Turkey to undertake further reforms, mainly to deprive the Russians, with whom peace negotiations were then under way, of any further pretense for intervention in the internal affairs of the Ottoman Empire. The result of these pressures was the proclamation of the *Hatti Humayun* (Imperial Rescript) of 18 February 1856.

The Hatti Humayun

Let it be done as herein set forth.

Most noble and eminent Minister . . . our present Grand Vizier, our *alter ego*, Mehmed Emin 'Ali Pasha . . . may God grant you imperishable greatness!

.   .   .   .   .

. . . [W]e have resolved upon and now order the following:

1. The guarantees promised on our part by the *Hatti-Sheriff of Gülhane* and by the laws of the *Tanzimat* to all our subjects without distinction of classes or of religion, for the security of their persons and property, and the preservation of their honor, are recalled and once more confirmed; efficacious measures shall be taken in order that they may have their full and entire effect.

2. All the privileges and spiritual immunities granted by our illustrious ancestors, and at subsequent dates, to all Christian and other non-Muslim communities, established in our Empire under our protection, shall be confirmed and maintained. Every Christian or other non-Muslim community shall procceed within a fixed period with the examination and revision of its present immunities and privileges; for that purpose they shall discuss by

means of councils formed *ad hoc* in the patriarchates with our sovereign approval and under the supervision of the Sublime Porte, the reforms required by the times as well as by the progress of enlightenment and civilization. The council must submit these reforms to our Sublime Porte . . . .

[The following provisions deal with the appointment of clerics, the administration of the non-Muslim communities, freedom of worship, and nondiscrimination on religious grounds in the filling of government positions.]

16. All commercial and criminal suits between Muslims and Christian or other non-Muslim subjects, or between Christian or other non-Muslim subjects of different sects shall be brought before mixed courts. The proceedings of these courts shall be public; the parties shall be present; the witnesses whom they produce shall confirm their depositions with an oath which shall always be sworn according to the religion and cult of the witness concerned.

17. Suits concerned with civil matters shall be tried according to the religious law and the regulations in the mixed provincial and subprovincial councils in the presence of the governor-general and the *qadi*. The records of cases tried in these tribunals and councils shall be public.

18. Special proceedings such as those relating to succession, be they between two Christians or between two other non-Muslim subjects, may, at the request of the parties be transferred for judgment to the patriarchs, the chiefs of the communities, and the councils of the communities in question.

19. Penal and commercial laws and rules of procedure for the mixed courts shall be completed as quickly as possible. They shall be coordinated and codified, then published and distributed in translation in the different languages used in our Empire.

20. The reform of the penitentiary system as it relates to prisons and all other places designated for preventive or penal detention shall be initiated with the least possible delay, so as to reconcile human rights with the demands of justice.

21. All corporal punishment, even in the prisons, shall be definitely suppressed and abolished except for that which is in accordance with disciplinary regulations issued by the Sublime Porte. Likewise abolished is all treatment which resembles torture.

22. Acts of cruelty which are perpetrated in contravention of the above shall be severely repressed. In addition, the officials who shall order these acts and those who shall carry them out, shall be discharged and punished according to the Penal Code.

23. The organization of the police in the capital, the provincial towns, and the rural districts shall be revised in such a manner as to give to all peaceable subjects of our Empire the strongest guarantees of protection for their persons as well as their property.

24. The equality of taxes entails the equality of other burdens, just as equality of rights entails equality of duties. Therefore, the Christian and other non-Muslim subjects must, like the Muslims, be subject to the recently promulgated law on military service.

25. The principle of personal exemption from military service, either through purchase or provision of a substitute, shall be admitted.

26. The necessary regulations concerning the admittance of non-Muslim subjects into the ranks of the army shall be drawn up and published as soon as possible.

27. The reform shall be initiated of the regulations of the provincial and subprovincial councils, so as to insure fairness in the choice of Muslim, Christian, and other members and guarantee freedom of voting. The Sublime Porte shall advise regarding the most efficient means of being informed exactly of the result of the deliberations and of knowing and controlling the decisions taken.

28. Since the laws concerning the purchase, sale, and ownership of real property are common to all Ottoman subjects, foreigners shall also be permitted to own land and shall conform to the law of the land and local police regulations. They shall bear the same charges as Ottoman subjects after arrangements have been made between my government and the foreign powers.

29. Taxes are to be levied under the same title from all our subjects without distinction of class or religion. The promptest means shall be considered for remedying the abuses existing today in collecting taxes and particularly the tithes. The system of direct collection of taxes shall be substituted gradually and as soon as possible for the system of tax farming. As long as the present system remains in effect all agents of the Sublime Porte and of the local councils [of the non-Muslim communities] shall be forbidden under severe penalties to have awarded to them any tax-farming contracts which are subject to public auction or to take any part in carrying out such a contract.

[The next four articles deal with specific provisions concerning public finances.]

34. The heads of the communities assisted by a delegate from each of them designated by us, shall be summoned specifically by our Grand Vizier to take part in the deliberations of the Grand Council in circumstances which are of interest to all our subjects. The delegates shall be appointed for one year. They shall take the oath upon entrance on their duties.

35. All members of the Grand Council shall, during ordinary or extraordinary sessions, freely voice their opinions and cast their vote and they shall not be annoyed in any way on this account.

36. The provisions of the law against corruption, extortion, and embezzlement shall apply, according to the legal forms, to all our subjects whatever class they may belong to and whatever may be their functions.

37. Banks and similar institutions shall be created to provide credit for the finances of the country and to reform the monetary system. The necessary capital shall be provided for such purposes as promote the material wealth of our Empire. Steps shall also be taken for the opening of roads and canals to create the proper facilities needed for the transportation of the products of the soil. Anything that impedes the development of commerce and agriculture shall be discarded.

38. To accomplish these objectives, means shall constantly be sought to profit from the knowledge, sciences, and capital of Europe.

You will thus, noble Vizier, cause this August Firman to be published in the customary form in Constantinople as well as in the provinces of the Empire. You will see to it that its terms are implemented and will take the necessary measures to see that its provisions are carried out forever . . . .

B. Legal Reform and the Reception of Continental European Codes

Comment: As part of the legal reform movement in the Ottoman Empire, certain comprehensive foreign statutes were selected and taken over, usually only with minor changes. At the time the Ottoman Empire embarked on this process, comprehensive legal codification had already been in progress in Europe for some time. Codes were in existence, particularly in France, which dealt with major subject matters of the legal system and could easily be taken over. Since the reception of continental European codes has characterized Near Eastern legal development to the present time, it will be necessary to discuss briefly the general principles of reception and the nature of the European code system.

1. *General Principles of Reception*

Comment: The theoretical and practical aspects of reception have occupied continental European scholars considerably more than those of Great Britain and the United States. This appears to be due primarily to two basic circumstances. First, continental Europe, particularly Germany, was the scene of one of the most important receptions in history, that of Roman law. Second, modern European codes have in their turn been received not only in some other European states but widely also in non-European countries, particularly in the Near and Middle East and in Asia. The following discussion is taken from a recent Swiss work on comparative law.

ADOLF F. SCHNITZER, *Vergleichende Rechtslehre*, vol. 1, pp. 59–64.*

. . . [L]aw means the regulation of the existing state of affairs. History teaches us that the various peoples go through different steps in the social order. Whenever a people has reached a certain point in its development, similar legal needs develop. This is true

*Reprinted by permission of the Verlag für Recht und Gesellschaft A. G., Basel, copyright 1961.

of societies of hunters or herdsmen, of agricultural societies, seafaring or commercial societies, and of the modern industrial state. Although the basic cultural notions may be quite different, similar or identical legal concepts may therefore be found in peoples which have the same low or high level of development. Thus blood vengeance . . . is found among the early Indo-Europeans and among African tribes. Feudal regulations are found among the Langobards as well as the Japanese. Commercial societies have developed similar regulations as seen in the laws of Hammurabi in Mesopotamia, those of the Phoenicians, the Genoese, the Venetians, or the English.

Foreign law thus is not unacceptable if it comes from a people at a similar stage of development . . . . If a similar state of development has been achieved, the foreign law does not appear intrinsically alien. The French *Code Civil* was an expression of the era of enlightenment, of the end of the *ancien régime*, of liberalism which had cast off feudal ties, of individualism, and of the doctrine of equal rights for all citizens. This law therefore appeared as an appropriate law to other European peoples who adhered to the same ideals as the French, more appropriate indeed than their own law. Since it furthermore was based on a mixture of Roman legal thought and Germanic customary law, it was also not alien in its intellectual basis to other peoples of Europe, Central and South America, whose own laws rested on the same historical basis.

·   ·   ·   ·

The most famous reception of earlier times is that of Roman law in Germany. The most important more recent receptions are those of European law by Asian and African peoples . . . .

The reception of Roman law was not forced upon the Germans by a foreign conqueror. Rather, German clerics studied canon law in Italy and brought it back with them. Also, German lawyers were trained in Roman law in Italy. This was done because the German princes for political reasons wanted to introduce into the courts the law of the Roman-Byzantine emperors which favored absolute rule. The princes hoped thereby to overcome the opposing tendencies of the popular courts and local customs. The introduction of Roman law as a subsidiary law existing side by side with the provincial and urban laws was facilitated also by the doctrine that the Empire was the Holy Roman Empire of the German Nation and the Emperor the successor of the Roman emperors. In this sense then Roman law was not foreign but imperial law. Roman law had been worked on by the post-glossators in the Italian law schools and had been adapted to the needs of the times. By contrast, the indigenous German law was fragmented into local customs. The laymen who dispensed the law according to these [Germanic] customs did not form a unified profession which could defend successfully the customary law against the territorial courts of the princes.

When non-European independent countries voluntarily introduced European laws in more recent times, political motivation also played a role. The European states which forcefully

opened foreign countries to trade, as for example in Japan, or
gained influence on the internal administration of a country because of its chaotic financial conditions, as in the Ottoman Empire, pressed for a legal order more in keeping with their own
concepts. Thus the Ottoman Empire began to modernize and
codify its laws in the middle of the nineteenth century.

Another factor also favored the reception of European law.
The Europeans originally lived according to their own laws in
the non-Christian countries in which they resided . . . and were
under the jurisdiction of their consuls. This state of affairs was
easy to maintain because of overwhelming European power. It
had been made possible even without this power by the prevalence of the principle of personality of the law, according to
which the indigenous law only applied to citizens. Furthermore,
where religious law was used, it was applied not even to all
citizens but only to those who belonged to the same religious
community.

The abolition of the privileged European legal position which
by now has taken place everywhere, presupposed that legal conditions in the country conformed to certain principles which to
the European way of thinking were fundamental . . . .

A further important reason for the introduction of European
law was, however, the need of the country itself to modernize
and thereby facilitate the contacts with modern culture and
economics. Where the country did not have the resources to
create by itself a modern legal system, European lawyers prepared the laws . . . .

Whether such a massive reception is a good thing or not is a
question which cannot easily be answered yes or no.

The first question is whether it is merely a case of modernizing
the indigenous law by putting it into a European form and publishing it as a statute. This was done in Turkey with the *Majalla*
around the middle of the nineteenth century. Such a modernization is not a true reception, however. Matters were wholly different with regard to the Turkish Republic in the twentieth century. The new rulers deliberately wanted to break with the past and
replace the old religious law by a secular modern law for which
material was lacking within the country.

. . . [However] only as far as [a] common cultural basis exists
or can be established, is the reception of foreign law justified.
Even [without reception of foreign law] every change in the law
within a country poses the question whether the proposed change
is in keeping with existing conditions. In this respect two things
may be noted . . . . Conditions are not the same everywhere
within a country. Intellectual attitudes as well as needs are different in the cities and in the countryside, with the cities historically constituting the more progressive element. Besides, people
are different as individuals, some are more conservative and
traditionalist, others more receptive to innovations. Any legal
reform might therefore go too far for those parts of the country

which have not yet reached the stage of development assumed by the new law. At the same time new legislation may lag behind the desires of some [other] sections of the nation.

The same phenomenon can be observed in an intensified form when foreign law is received. It will be better fitted for the progressive individual and the more modernized sections of the country than for conservative elements and sections where an older economic and social order prevails. There may be the intent, however, to break with precisely these traditional concepts and methods. The question always arises whether the new concepts can succeed. Success will be most difficult where there is little inclination to give up the old customs and follow new rules . . . .

In receiving foreign law it has furthermore to be considered that specific areas of the legal system have different sensitivity to the reception of alien legal material. Resistant areas and areas where change is easy may be distinguished . . . . Generally, reception of foreign law is relatively easy in fields such as commercial law, negotiable instruments, communications, and in areas of the law which were only brought into being by modern economic and technological needs. It is much more difficult to introduce foreign law into fields where indigenous law has held sway for many centuries. This is the case particularly in the law of family relationships and of inheritance. It is true to a degree also of the law of real estate, since it is closely linked to the nature of the country and its social and political structure.

. . . . .

If one goes too far in disregarding established indigenous custom, the latter is likely to continue alongside with or in opposition to the new law . . . .

PAUL KOSCHAKER, *Europa und das römische Recht*, pp. 161–162.*

. . . Reception presupposes . . . the existence of a written codification of the law to be received. Codes of law are received not law as such, particularly not jurists' law which, being contained in countless decisions, is hard to comprehend for the foreigner. There would not have been a reception of Roman law without the *Corpus Iuris*. That is also why the Anglo-American law cannot be received, since nobody could seriously consider the introduction as a new law of thousands of volumes containing an even larger number of decisions in which this law is contained as case law . . . .

P. 162, note 1: . . . Nevertheless English law has spread over vast areas, but not through reception. It extended rather through conquest, although this word should not be understood in the sense of forceful introduction of English law in the conquered territories. The term *pénétration pacifique* would be more appropriate. In fact, in contrast to the modern continental European states which regarded introduction of their own private law into newly acquired territories nearly as self-understood, it has always been a principle of British policy not to force their own private law upon subject populations . . . .

Comment: To this discussion should be added that the reception of Anglo-American law appears to be greatly facilitated where that law is applied in the courts by judges trained in the common law. Thus, the common law has had very considerable influence in Palestine, India, Pakistan, and other areas where there were British courts. On the other hand, the influence of common law has been minor in Egypt, despite the long British occupation of the country, or in Iraq where Great Britain was the mandatory power after World War I.

As Schnitzer pointed out, various parts of a legal system are open or resistant to reception in different degrees. What one might call the penetrability of these parts by foreign influences can be graphically shown as follows:

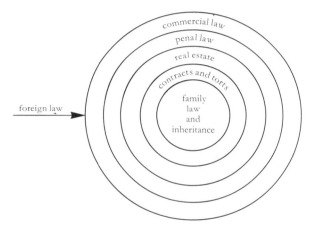

This figure is drawn to depict primarily the situation that obtained in the Ottoman Empire. The relatively easy penetrability of penal law is due to the fact that penal law was not treated exhaustively in classical Islamic law and was early subject to administrative regulation. Real estate law was based generally on indigenous rules, but on the formal side there were some foreign influences.

2. *General Nature of the European Code System*

a. *What is a Code?*

S. A. BAYITCH, "Codification in Modern Times," pp. 164–166.*

. . . [I]t may be stated safely that the notion of codification has

*Reprinted by permission of the Louisiana State University Press, copyright 1965.

some basic features in common throughout the world. First it
signifies enacted law, i.e., legal rules consciously formulated and
reduced to writing to be adopted as well as promulgated and
enforced in this form; this is a vital distinction from customary
law. Second, these rules emanate from the legislative branch,
sometimes from the executive, but never from the judicial
branch; as a consequence, the notion of codified law excludes not
only regulations, though they are comprehensive and general in
nature and enacted under the authority of the judicial law-making
power (e.g., rules of procedure), but also case law in whatever
form. Third, a codification contains abstract, general rules; this
excludes enactments dealing with individual situations (e.g.,
so-called private laws). Finally, a codification is concerned with
large areas of life in society, for example, private, commercial,
criminal, and aviation law; it is therefore comprehensive in scope
and systematically arranged . . . .

   In civil-law jurisdictions the terms codification and codes have
a precise meaning. This will be understood better by keeping in
mind that in these jurisdictions law emanates primarily from
statutory enactments while collateral sources (e.g., customs,
principles of justice, natural law) are considered subordinate.
These collateral sources become operative only insofar as they are
expressly referred to by statute or accepted, in various degrees, by
common usage (e.g., judicial opinions, doctrinal writings). This
well-established primacy of statutory law leaves lawmakers with
the choice limited to legislation by way of simple statutes or by
way of codes. This choice of alternatives, however, is not a mere
question of terminology. On the contrary, the adoption of one
alternative or the other carries significant substantive consequences. In determining these consequences, it must be remembered
that in civil-law jurisdictions an elaborate hierarchy of sources
prevails, with codes ranking higher than non-codified statutes.
This delicate structure requires further refinement in regard to
relations not only between simple statutory and codified law, but
also between various codes or groups of codes, (e.g., civil and
commercial) on the one hand and the special codes (e.g., labor,
aviation) on the other. It is therefore understandable that the
question whether to legislate by statute or by code is always
carefully considered. The final decision depends on whether the
branch of law to be codified is an autonomous branch of law, i.e.,
endowed with general legal principles of its own and at the same
time, on whether the area of life in society to be regulated is both
so important and so clearly individualized that it can be treated
properly only by an enactment of the status of a code. The prolonged discussions regarding the autonomy *vel non* of labor and
aviation law offer good examples. Finally, in civil-law jurisdictions
the drafting of codes as distinguished from simple statutes is, as a
rule, entrusted not to politically controlled bodies but to experts,
i.e., legal scholars . . . .

F. H. LAWSON, *A Common Lawyer Looks at the Civil Law*,
pp. 76–77.*

One effect of codification, which is really due to the work of the
institutional writers and therefore can also inure to the benefit of
uncodified laws of the same type, is that since a code must be
systematic and complete, every part of the Civil Law is subjected
to scientific study and formulation. In this the Civil Law differs
greatly from the Common Law, which may have little or nothing
to say about some obscure corner of life simply because there has
been no case on it. Moreover, the tendency in all countries is for
only the parts of the law which are taught to be properly discussed
and so to acquire consistency and form. The untaught portions,
unless by chance they fall into the hands of a judge with a scientific
or theoretical turn of mind, tend to remain disorderly, strung out
on threads of precedent and with no visible connection between
the rules. Perhaps this is an advantage: there have been many
instances of premature formulation. Perhaps it is right that some
parts only of the law should be systematic. At any rate, here is
a difference between the Civil Law and the Common Law. The
latter has many loose ends, the existence of which does not seem
to disturb the common lawyers. Even the American Restatement
is by no means complete. The Civil Law may at any moment and
place have a few loose ends, but civilians are not satisfied and
try to remedy what they consider a defect.

This implies, what is also true, that even though certain parts of
Civil Law are often left outside the Civil Code, yet attempts are
made to formulate them completely and systematically in separate
acts, which become, as it were, appendices to the Civil Code . . . .

b. *Codifications and Case Law*

PAUL KOSCHAKER, *Europa und das römische Recht*, pp. 183–187.

. . . Codifications try to prevent or at least limit the interpretation
by the lawyers of the law established by them. This is due to the
understandable endeavor to preserve the law established by
them with the least possible modification, since this law is meant
to represent an exhaustive new regulation [of the legal subject
matter]. Examples are the Emperor Justinian with his provisions
designed to limit the interpretation of the *Corpus Iuris*, the Prussian
Landrecht, and Italian codifications of the eighteenth and nineteenth centuries, which prohibit interpretation by the lawyers
or reference to such interpretations. We know today that such
endeavors by the legislator are based on illusions. It is wrong
to believe that a codification can regulate without lacunae the
legal subject matter encompassed by it. It is also fallacious to
believe that everything contained in a codification is living law.
Aside from the fact that no codification can avoid provisions
which are not enforced in practice and thus are stillborn, a codi-

fication presents at best only a snapshot of the law as it existed when the codification came into effect. Life does not stand still and presents the lawyer continuously with new problems which can be solved only through creative interpretation of the codification. No legislator can prevent that the provisions of a law, a codification, become encrusted with jurists' law [case law] soon after coming into effect.

These are no new insights . . . for the present-day lawyer, but it is noteworthy that these matters were already clear 150 years ago to the drafters of the French Civil Code, at a time when they were not yet universally accepted by the lawyers. This is shown by various passages from the *discours préliminaires* [Introductory Statements] by Portalis to the first draft of the *Code Civil* which I want to quote: "A code, no matter how complete it may appear to be, is no sooner finished than a thousand questions which have not been dealt with will present themselves to the judge. For the laws, once laid down, remain as they had been written. Men, by contrast, never rest, they always move and this movement, which does not stop and whose effects are modified in various ways by circumstances, produces at every moment some new arrangement, some new fact, some new result." Portalis also stated: "It is up to the judge and the lawyer, filled with the general spirit of the laws, to direct their application." Practice [to Portalis] is nothing but a supplement to legislation . . . . [The drafters of the *Code Civil*] . . . were pupils of the great practical jurists of the eighteenth century from whom an unbroken tradition leads back to their predecessors of the sixteenth century who had started to develop the *droit commun français*, in conjunction with Roman law, on the basis of the experiences of legal practice. The result of these teachings is the remarkable Article 4 of the *Code Civil*: "The judge who refuses to judge [a case] claiming that the law is silent, obscure, or insufficient, shall be prosecuted as being guilty of denial of justice." This article calls upon the judge to develop the law further . . . .

Thus, neither a single statute nor a codification can eliminate jurists' law. Rather, they need it for further development . . . .

RENÉ DAVID, *French Law, Its Structure, Sources and Methodology*, pp. 77–82.*

The French concept of *règle juridique* is not the exact equivalent of what the English understand by a legal rule: the concept of *règle juridique* has a greater generality than that of the legal rule . . . .

In the common law, the legal rule is ordinarily formulated by the judge. He faces a very precise, concrete question and responds to that question by applying a particular legal rule. He naturally has in mind the particular question posed as he formulates the rule and does not elaborate a rule that goes beyond the terms of this question. This is so true that if a slightly different question comes

before another judge later, he will consider himself justified in
distinguishing this question from the preceding . . . .

The situation in France is completely different. The law is not
essentially judges' law, but rather a law of jurists and the universities. French law has an aversion to case studies and seeks clarity
by looking beyond the decisions in particular cases to the principles proclaimed by the legislator and legal writers. What the
English call a legal rule the French regard as the disposition of a
dispute. Rules only exist at a higher level of abstraction. The very
concept of rule implies generality—abstraction . . . .

For a Frenchman, the English jurist's legal rule is nothing but
an isolated judicial decision; it is not a *règle juridique*. For an
Englishman, the French jurist's *règle juridique* is not a legal rule.
It does not have the precision that is the essence of such a rule.
Rather it is a legal principle. Contrary to what one might suppose,
this difference has more than theoretical interest. Its practical
importance is considerable.

Because of this difference in the conception of the legal rule,
legislative techniques in France and England are dissimilar.
Legislatures in both countries try to formulate legal rules, but the
realization of this intention is very different precisely because the
French *règle juridique* is not equivalent to the English legal rule. An
English statute will necessarily deal explicitly with particular
problems. A French statute will go into less detail, will give the
judge more discretion, will not try to foresee all problems, and
may include general formulae that to a common lawyer seem to
negate its effects as law and make it more a general principle than
a command.

.   .   .   .

Another difference between the two systems that results from
the contrast between the French and English conceptions of the
legal rule relates to the role of scholarly writing and judicial
opinions. Both have greater latitude in the French system than in
the common law precisely because only the former distinguishes
between the legal rule on the one hand and its application and
interpretation on the other. In common law countries, a sudden
change in case law is a serious thing. If a previously accepted rule
can be repudiated, what will become of the security of legal
relations? Why should other rules not be repudiated as well? In
France, even the question is not the same. Since a dissenting
writer or a change in the courts' position on a question affects
only the interpretation of a legal rule in its previous application,
it is not so dangerous. A certain flexibility in the courts' position is
acceptable, since the danger thereby created to the security of
legal relations is limited. There is no danger of its undermining
the law as a whole. The legal rules conceived of as entities superior
to judicial decisions, form a solid framework that limits the effect
of changes in the courts' position or that of dissenting writers. A
different attitude toward scholarly writing and judicial decisions
is the consequence of the different conceptions in France and
England concerning the very notions of *règle juridique* and legal rule.

An English lawyer looking at French law should not expect to find legal rules that are the full equivalent of legal rules in the common law. He should remember that French law is more doctrinal and academic than English law and that the legal rule is more abstract, more like a legal principle than a legal rule as those terms are used with reference to English law. He should remember that judicial decisions do not pose legal rules, but only apply preexisting rules which have significance beyond a particular case. If he understands these things, he can understand the technique of codification, as well as the lesser authority that judicial decisions have in French law as compared to the common law.

French judicial decisions always cite statutory provisions in their support. This is only possible because of the generality of the code and statute articles. These are often principles rather than commands. It is important to know how they have been applied, because judges will give considerable weight to this factor and will usually interpret a statute in the future as they have in the past. But one must keep in mind that in France the legal rule is found in the legislative provisions themselves, no matter how general they may be, and not in their application by the courts. It is because of this that French law is a "written law." It is essential to bear this in mind in order to understand not only how changes in courts' positions are possible in France, but also the limits of these changes.

. . . . .

Like all legislators, French legislators are sometimes tempted to try to foresee everything and make of the courts quasi-mechanical instruments of their will. French writers have criticized this poor legislative technique and decried the resulting defective legislation. The draftsmen of the Napoleonic codes, products of a sound tradition, were able to resist this temptation and did not surrender to the illusion that they could foresee everything. This is the source of these codes', and particularly the Civil Code's, exceptional value, long life, and influence on other countries. The drafters of the French codes were able to find a happy medium in the articles they drafted, between the detailed formulation that was adopted in the 1794 Prussian *Allgemeines Landrecht* and the overly general expressions that are often found in constitutions and declarations of rights . . . .

Ibid., pp. 180–186.

The role of court decisions in France can be examined from two points of view. The first question is whether, as a matter of law, courts can and do create new legal rules. The second is what authority court decisions have as a matter of empirical fact.

The first question must, in all areas of French law, including administrative law, be answered in the negative. The position of French law can be expressed by saying that a judicial decision can never be justified simply by stating that the rule of law applied has been applied previously by other judges.

The decision of a regular court will be reversed for "absence of legal basis" if the only justification it gives for its decision is an earlier decision of the Court of Cassation. There is nothing to prevent reference in the opinion to earlier court decisions, and the practice of citing precedents is in fact becoming more frequent. But reference to one or more prior cases does not constitute a self-sufficient legal argument and is not a valid basis for decision. The Court of Cassation in its opinions refrains rigorously from citation of earlier decisions it has made or the existence of an established line of precedents. Judges fear that this might give the impression that they consider themselves bound by doctrines adopted in their decisions. In addition it would be an unacceptable violation of Civil Code article 5, which prohibits judges from making general or regulatory decisions in connection with the disputes submitted to them. The role of the courts is to solve disputes that are brought before them, not to make laws or regulations. The principle of separation of powers, as it is understood in France, prevents the formal creation of legal rules by the courts.

.   .   .   .

No French court can create legal rules, since the principle of separation of powers prohibits it. But there is the additional question of what authority a court's interpretation of a statute has in fact: If the same legal question that has been decided, or an analogous question, comes up in the future, will the court considering the question be inclined to follow the doctrine previously applied, or will it regard this as of little importance and reject any arguments based on the fact that courts have previously interpreted the statute in a particular way?

.   .   .   .

The French judge is never required, legally, to follow a precedent. But to what extent will he in fact consider it? It is of course difficult to answer this question precisely, since many factors that are hard to evaluate will have their effect, such as the personality of the individual judge and the equities of the particular case . . . .

With respect to the Court of Cassation, two different situations must be considered: that where its own earlier decisions are cited to it and that where one or more decisions given by lower courts are invoked.

In the first case, it is understood that the Court of Cassation can always change its mind and reverse itself, but it is equally certain that it will not do so readily. The general rule here is that the Court of Cassation will follow the precedent that it has laid down, even if it is but a single decision rendered on the question. The Court of Cassation considers its principal role today as enforcement of the uniform application of the law. This function cannot be fulfilled if the Court of Cassation itself does not have a stable case law. There is no example of the Court of Cassation reversing a decision taken by it with all chambers sitting together. In the case where the precedents consist of one or several decisions of a single chamber of the Court of Cassation, reversals in the case law are well known. But still they are rare when compared to the number of cases where the court has remained faithful to its previous position in spite of active opposition to this position by scholarly writers.

. . . .

Or the Court of Cassation may never have had occasion to decide the question brought before it. The decisions cited before it may all come from lower courts. The authority of these decisions will be relatively slight before the Court of Cassation. They will become important only in certain very special circumstances. One possibility is that there may be many concordant decisions indicating an established case law. Or the lower court decision may have concerned a particular category of persons, who as a result have changed their practices in reliance on the decision (practice of notaries, form contracts in the area of insurance or maritime commerce).

Let us now consider the lower regular courts. It is easy to understand the authority in fact that court decisions have for them. If the decision cited is from the Court of Cassation, the civil and commercial courts of first instance and the courts of appeal will very probably follow the position taken, even if it has been stated in a single decision . . . .

The lower courts, of course, give less weight to decisions of other courts than to those of the Court of Cassation. In such a case, they are particularly sensitive to the existence of an established case law . . . .

Comment: There is no single "Napoleonic Code." Rather, the important legal subject matter was dealt with in five codes as follows:

Civil Code (1804)
Code of Civil Procedure (1806, now in the process of extensive revision)
Commercial Code (1807)
Penal Code (1810)
Penal Procedure Code (1811), replaced by a new code in 1958.

Thus an elaborate code system existed in France at the time modernization of the law began in the Ottoman Empire and the reception of French law in that country and many others, Egypt among them, was due to the generally high quality of the French code system as well as the position of cultural and political leadership which France at that time occupied in the world.

C. The Specific Reforms in the Ottoman Empire

Comment: The code system which was established in the Ottoman Empire was based in part on Western European principles, in part on principles of Islamic law. In form, however, all the

Ottoman codes followed the European prototypes of comprehensive codifications. A commercial code based on the French one was enacted in 1850. With regard to penal law several attempts were made to draft codes based generally on local and Muslim principles. In 1858, however, a penal code was enacted which was largely based on the French Penal Code. The relationship of the code to the *shari'a* is set forth in Article 1.

Ottoman Penal Code.

Article 1. It is the duty of the State to punish offenses directed against individuals because of the difficulties they cause to public tranquility as well as those directed against the State itself. This is why the present code determines the different degrees of punishment the application of which is delegated to the highest authority by the *shari'a*. These provisions cannot, however, in any case injure the rights of the individual consecrated by the *shari'a*.

Comment: This principle was quite clearly reflected in the code's retention of the right to blood money (*diya*) in the case of homicide.

A code of penal procedure was enacted in 1879 and a code of civil procedure a year later. Both are based on the respective French codes.

The three important codes that were not based upon Western legal principles or where Western legal principles played only a small role were the *Majalla* or Ottoman Civil Code, the Ottoman Land Law of 1858, and the Family Law of 1917.

HERBERT J. LIEBESNY, "Stability and Change in Islamic Law," pp. 22–23.

The Land Law reflected to a considerable degree the developments regarding land tenure which had taken place in the Ottoman Empire. The Code divided all land into five categories: *mulk* land, or land held in freehold ownership; *miri* land, or state-owned land which was leased to individuals; *waqf* land, or land established as a pious foundation; *matruka* land, or land reserved for public purposes; and *mawat* or dead land (Art. 1). The rulers of the Ottoman Empire had endeavored to make most land *miri* or *waqf*. The *miri* land was for the most part divided into fiefs and the peasants who worked this land had *tasarruf* (usufruct). This right of *tasarruf* could be transmitted by inheritance, but it could not be divided. In this way the rules of the Islamic law of inheritance were circumvented under which the property of the decedent had to be divided among his legal heirs. Since under the *shari'a* a person was allowed to dispose by will of only one-third of his estate, excessive fragmentation of property was inevitable. By making practically all agricultural land either *miri* or *waqf*, the Ottoman sultans tried to counteract the trend toward fragmentation. *Mulk* land was essentially the site of the houses in the villages and one half *dunum* surrounding them. The trees and vines in vineyards and orchards were also private property. Some provisions were made, however, to prevent also the fragmentation of property which was *mulk*.

Under the Ottoman Land Law the feudal relationship no longer existed. *Miri* land was granted directly to the cultivator. Doreen Warriner has pointed out that the object of this grant of the right to usufruct of *miri* land directly to the cultivators was an attempt on the part of the Ottoman Government to centralize power and restrict the power of large landowners and the tribal sheikhs.* The difference between *mulk* and *miri* land thus became minimal in practice. *Miri* land could be sold and the necessary agreement of the administrative authorities amounted to a mere formality. *Miri* land also could now be freely inherited. *Mulk* land was not regulated by the Land Law, but remained submitted to the *shari'a* law (Art. 2). This indicates that the Land Law was not regarded as a codification of *shari'a* rules. There were later amendments to the Land Law which introduced some European principles.

Ibid., pp. 21–22 (with slight changes).

The most interesting and important codification of this period was the *Majalla* or Ottoman Civil Code, called with its full name *Majallat-i Ahkami Adliye* and enacted in 1876. This work codified the rules of contracts and some procedural regulations on the basis of the Hanefite rite. Thus the *Majalla* was Islamic in content, but it was European in form. Like a European code it was subdivided into books, chapters and articles, but differed from the typical European codification in one basic respect. The European codes were regarded as exclusive as of the time of enactment, that is, unless the code itself contained statements to the contrary, the rules it contained superseded all earlier rules on the same subject. The *Majalla*, by contrast, was a compilation of the religious law of Islam and by its very nature could hardly have an exclusive character. In practical application, however, the *Majalla* achieved a position as an authoritative codification very much like that of a continental European code. This development was largely due to the factors which had led to the compilation of the *Majalla* in the first place, the difficulty of ascertaining the *shari'a* rules for a specific case from the masses of legal materials and the lack of jurists well-trained enough to utilize *shari'a* sources. The latter was true particularly after the establishment of a secular court system in the Ottoman Empire.

Substantively the *Majalla* covered both less and more than a continental European civil code. It dealt with contracts and some torts, but not with non-contractual obligations and did not regulate other areas of private law, such as marriage, divorce, inheritance, and various aspects of real property. On the other hand it contained some procedural rules. The approach of the *Majalla* was largely casuistic. Few broad principles were set forth, the code rather concentrated on defining and regulating specific

*Doreen Warriner, *Land and Poverty in the Middle East*, London and New York, 1948, p. 17.

subject matters. The *Majalla's* efforts to systematize the subject matters it dealt with were not wholly successful; some of the subjects were treated in different parts of the Code. The procedural provisions of the *Majalla* were replaced in 1880 by those of a Code of Civil Procedure based on French law. The *Majalla* has been criticized for its rigidity and the lack of attention to the economic realities of the day. Nevertheless, it constituted a very significant advance, since it was the first attempt to codify in modern form rules of Islamic law. Amendments to the *Majalla* were worked out by a committee in 1920–21. This committee, while still limited to Islamic law, went beyond the Hanefite rite and took various principles from other schools. The amendments were, however, never enacted into law, since Turkey soon embarked upon a new and much more radical legal reform.

J. N. D. ANDERSON, "Codification in the Muslim World," p. 245.*

... [The *Majalla's*] supreme importance ... lies not in its subject matter so much as the fact that it represents the first example in history of two highly significant developments; an official codification and promulgation of parts of the *shari'a* by the authority of the State, on the one hand, and the fact that this codification was not based exclusively on the dominant opinion in the school of law favored by that State (the Hanafi school), but on an eclectic choice between all those opinions which had enjoyed any Hanafi support whatever, even though some of them had in fact originated elsewhere. This law, moreover, was to be applied, like the other codes, by the new, secular *nizamiya* courts which the Tanzimat reforms had established.

Comment: Of interest for the genesis of the *Majalla* is the Report of the Commission appointed to draft the *Majalla*.

Majalla (French translation by G. Aristarchi Bey, *Législation Ottomane*, vol. 6, pp. 3–18).

Report to His Highness the Grand Vizir from the Drafting Committee for the Civil Code.

As Your Highness knows, that part of the *shari'a* which deals with temporal matters is divided into three categories: that which deals with questions concerning marriage, that which concerns transactions in general, and that which deals with penal law. The law of all civilized nations has reestablished this division into three sections, of which the one which regulates transactions is called civil law.

Since in recent times commercial relations have extended very considerably, it has been necessary to regulate in a special fashion many of the relevant matters such as bankruptcy and negotiable instruments. Therefore a separate code was enacted under the title of Commercial Code.

*Reprinted by permission of the author and Professor Konrad Zweigert, editor of *Rabel's Zeitschrift*.

If, however, in a commercial litigation which is being judged by a commercial court a secondary problem arises which concerns purely civil law, such as pledge, suretyship, agency, etc., the solution has to be found in the common law. The same is true when civil claims arise out of a penal offense.

At the present time the place of a civil code is taken in the Ottoman Empire by a series of laws and regulations promulgated at different times. Since these legislative provisions are not sufficient to cover all of the civil law, that part of the sacred law which deals with transactions generally and which is wholly sufficient to answer all needs, must be used to complement them.

It is sometimes difficult to decide whether the *shari'a* courts or the courts charged with the application of the new laws have jurisdiction. This difficulty has been remedied, however, by placing the newly instituted tribunals under the presidency of judges charged with the interpretation of the sacred law. Thereby these courts are competent to rule on questions arising from the *shari'a* as well as those arising from the special laws of the Empire applied by the *nizamiya* courts. All Ottoman legislation, however, is inspired by the precepts of the sacred law and in civil causes these precepts have to be referred to to resolve a host of incidental questions. Except for the president, the members of the *nizamiya* courts are not versed in the sacred law. As a result the presidents have been exposed to all sorts of suspicions and malicious rumors. They even have been accused of infringing upon the laws and regulations in force and of giving law suits whatever direction they wished.

The commercial courts which apply the Commercial Code have experienced great difficulties every time incidental questions arose in a commercial case which were outside the subject matter regulated by our commercial law. They could not have recourse to European laws to resolve these questions because these laws have not been sanctioned by the Sovereign, do not have force and effect in the Empire, and cannot therefore form the basis of a judgment. If the commercial courts referred such questions to the *shari'a* courts, the latter would have to examine the basic issue in controversy in order to rule on an incidental question. Since the procedure followed by the *shari'a* judges is totally different from that followed by the commercial courts, innumerable complications would arise which make such a solution impractical. If finally it were suggested that the judges of the commercial courts should themselves apply *shari'a* law, the answer is that the members of the commercial courts would find themselves in the same position as the judges of the *nizamiya* courts with regard to their knowledge of the sacred law.

In fact, Islamic jurisprudence resembles an immense ocean on whose bottom one has to search, at the price of very great efforts, for the pearls which are hidden there. A person has to possess great experience as well as great learning in order to find in the sacred law the proper solutions for all the questions which present themselves.

This is particularly true of the Hanefite rite. In this rite there are

many commentators whose opinions differ markedly from one
another. The doctrines are not as fixed and precise as those of the
Shafi'ite rite and the many subdivisions have made the knowledge
and application of Hanefite doctrine difficult. One can thus
understand how difficult it is to ascertain in all this diversity of
opinions the best one and to apply it to a given case.

. . . . .

. . . In our time the number of those competent in *shari'a* law
has become smaller and smaller and a point has been reached
where it is difficult not only to find members of the *nizamiya*
courts who can, when necessary, refer to the treatises of Islamic
jurisprudence to dispel their doubts, but also to find enough
qadis for the *shari'a* courts of the Empire.

The need has thus been felt for a long time for a work which
dealt with transactions in general on the basis of the sacred law
containing only the least contested and least controversial
opinions and composed in a manner which would be sufficiently
clear so that anyone could study it easily and act in conformity
with it. Such a work obviously would be immensely useful not
only for the judges of the *shari'a* courts, but also for those of the
nizamiya courts and for administrative officials who could by
consulting it inform themselves about the principles of *shari'a*
law and make them under all circumstances the rule of their
conduct. Such a work finally, being applicable in the *shari'a*
courts, would make it possible to dispense with the enactment of
new laws for civil matters dealt with by the *nizamiya* courts . . . .

Desirous to add this work to all those which have seen the
light of day under His Imperial Guidance, our August Sovereign
has ordered the drafting of a code based upon the sacred law,
which would fill the needs of the present age and would be sufficient to resolve the questions which arise daily in connection
with transactions. In fulfillment of this Imperial Command we
have assembled in the Supreme Judicial Council, have consulted
the most authoritative works of the Hanefite jurists dealing with
that part of the law which relates to civil transactions, and have
extracted the rules relating to the most important and most widely
used transactions of our time. We have brought together these
rules under the name of civil code in a work consisting of several
books. After having completed the first book, which was preceded
by a chapter containing a series of fundamental principles, we
submitted it for examination to His Highness the *Shaykh al-Islam*
and to other persons known for their legal expertise. We revised
this book according to the observations of these persons and have
today the honor to submit it to Your Highness. At this point the
work on the other books continues apace, while the first book is
being translated into Arabic.

In examining this book will Your Highness kindly note that
the second part of the preliminary section is composed of general
principles of law collected by Ibn Nujaym and other jurists of
his school. Although these principles alone are not sufficient to
enable a judge to render his decision unless they are amplified by

more explicit legal texts, they are nevertheless very useful for the study and understanding of the law since they make it possible to arrive more easily at the solution of a specific question. In them the administrative officials will find a sure guide for all cases which come up and through them each one of them will be able to conform his actions as far as possible to the precepts of the sacred law. This is why we have not composed a special title or chapter but rather a general introduction. Ordinarily in treatises of the sacred law, general principles are mixed in with specific questions. In the present code we have preferred to place at the beginning of each book an introduction containing definitions of all legal terms pertaining to the subject matter of the chapter . . . . Finally, in order to give more clarity to the basic provisions we have included after each of them various examples taken from *fatwa* collections.

.   .   .   .

. . . In drafting the present code we have never stepped outside the limits of the Hanefite rite and the rules which we have laid down are for the most part actually applied by the *fetvahane*. A discussion of these rules is therefore unnecessary. However, among the opinions of the most authoritative jurists of the Hanefite rite there are some which are less rigorous and more suitable for the needs of our times, and we have adopted these opinions . . . .

Comment: In order to provide an idea of the subject matter covered by the *Majalla* the main headings are given here.

Introductory Chapter
Section I.   Definition and Division of Islamic Law.
Section II.   Fundamental Principles of Islamic Law.
Book I.   The Contract of Sale.
Book II.   The Contract of Hire.
Book III.   The Contract of Guarantee.
Book IV.   The Transfer of a Debt.
Book V.   Pledge.
Book VI.   Deposit.
Book VII.   Gift.
Book VIII.   Usurpation and Damage to Another's Property.
Book IX.   Guardianship, Duress, and Right of Preemption.
Book X.   Joint Ownership and Partnerships.
Book XI.   Agency.
Book XII.   Compromise and Release.
Book XIII.   Admissions.
Book XIV.   Actions.
Book XV.   Evidence and Decisive Oath.
Book XVI.   Court Organization, Judgments, and
               Arbitration.

J. N. D. ANDERSON, "Codification in the Muslim World," pp. 245–246.

But none of [these reforms] extended to the family law, which was still applied by the *qadis* in the *shari'a* courts as it had always been. As a consequence there emerged a complete dichotomy in the courts, as between the new *nizamiya* courts, on the one hand, and the ancient *shari'a* courts, on the other, together with an extensive, but not wholly complete, dichotomy in the law these courts administered. In one sense, as we have seen, this was not altogether new. But the fundamental difference was that the new courts, and the new codes, now enjoyed the fullest possible recognition and became the basic courts of residual jurisdiction; henceforth it was the *shari'a* courts which were to enjoy only a very restricted competence, and the *shari'a* law which alone was to remain uncodified. Indeed, the *shari'a* courts continued for many years to administer this law in a way which was almost entirely unchanged, for personnel trained by the old, traditional methods still sought and applied the dominant Hanafi opinion as enshrined in the medieval compendia.

But the tide of social change could not, for long, be resisted, and by 1915 reforms had, perforce, to be effected even in the sacred sphere of family law. It was in fact the miserable position of the Muslim wives, under the dominant opinion in the Hanafi school, which forced the authorities to take action; for it was not uncommon for a Muslim to visit Istanbul from some distant land, marry one of the local women, and then sail away home without even troubling to divorce her, and she might remain for decades bound in marriage to a man who gave her neither his company nor support—while other women found themselves married without their knowledge or consent to men afflicted with leprosy or insanity. Both these defects in the Hanafi law were remedied by Imperial Edicts promulgated in 1915, based, in the first case, on the dominant Hanbali (and also Maliki,) opinion and, in the second, on a "weaker" Hanafi doctrine. But the dyke once breached, the pressure became almost irresistible, and in 1917, the "Ottoman Law of Family Rights"—a comparatively complete codification of the law of marriage, divorce, etc.—was enacted, based on an eclectic choice between opinions of all orthodox schools. This was repealed in Istanbul only two years later; but it was applied in Lebanon, Syria, Palestine and Jordan, and is still in force, even today, in Lebanon and Israel (although modified, to some extent, in the latter.)

OTTO OPET, "Die Neuregelung des türkischen Eherechts," pp. 341–343.

The new law . . . submits the whole population of the Turkish Empire, Muslims and non-Muslims, to its rule. In actual fact the group of non-Muslims comprises only Jews and Christians. The secular law of the Turkish state thus has become the source of the marriage law instead of *shari'a* and the rules of the Jewish and Christian communities . . . .

The creation of a unified formal source of marriage law has, however, not been accompanied by the creation of a substantively uniform marriage law for all groups of Turkey's population.

Substantively, the law of marriage has retained its religious
divisions. The legislation preserves a separate Muslim, Jewish,
and Christian marriage law . . . [T]he individual chapters and
sections contain the different rules which Muslim, Jewish, and
Christian law provide for the subject matter in question.

D. The Reforms in Egypt before World War I

HERBERT J. LIEBESNY, "Stability and Change in Islamic
Law," pp. 24–25.

Although Egypt was still nominally a part of the Ottoman
Empire, it did not follow the latter's pattern of legal reform, but
developed its own system which in several respects went further
in Westernization and secularization of the law than that of the
Empire. This was due, at least in part, to the influence of foreign
powers. Several attempts at judicial reform, following more or less
the Ottoman example, had failed in Egypt, largely because of
opposition from the representatives of the foreign powers. The
moving spirit for the badly needed reform of the legal system was
Nubar Pasha, the Foreign Minister of Khedive Isma'il. His tireless
efforts were largely responsible for the end of judicial chaos in
Egypt and for the creation of the Mixed Courts. The new judicial
system based upon agreement between Egypt and the great
powers, was inaugurated by the Khedive on June 28, 1875. It
necessitated not only a new court structure, but also new procedural and substantive laws. The new codes were taken largely
from French law and were, in fact, prepared by a French lawyer,
M. Manoury. Unlike the Ottoman Empire where, as we have
seen, contracts and torts remained largely regulated by Islamic
law, Egypt introduced considerable portions of the French
Civil Code. Those parts of the Civil Code which dealt with domestic relations were omitted, but the books regulating property
rights and obligations were largely adopted. Certain rules of
traditional Egyptian law, particularly those concerning certain
property rights, were incorporated into the new Egyptian Code.
The Commercial Code, the procedural codes and the Penal Code
also followed the French prototypes. The Penal Code and the
Code of Penal Procedure remained, however, largely inoperative
in the Mixed Courts, since these courts did not have full criminal
jurisdiction. The codes enacted for the Mixed Courts were extended eight years later with slight modifications to the newly
organized native courts, so that in effect these codes were the
general law of Egypt for the areas which they covered.

Comment: The Mixed Courts of Egypt which were established by
this reform and continued until 1949, had a considerable impact
on the development of law in Egypt. The basic document setting
up the mixed courts was their charter which was agreed to by the

foreign powers and was regarded by the courts as having the character of a treaty.

Charter of the Mixed Courts of 1875

Title I
Jurisdiction in Civil and Commercial Matters
Chapter I
Courts of First Instance and the Court of Appeal
I. *Institution and Composition*

Article 1. There shall be established three District Courts of first instance, at Alexandria, Cairo, and Mansura.

Article 2. Each of these Courts shall be composed of seven judges, four foreigners and three natives. Judgments shall be given by three judges of whom two shall be foreigners and one a native.

One of the foreign judges shall preside, with the title of Vice President. He shall be selected by a majority vote of the foreign and native members of the Court of Appeal from an alphabetical list, presented by the General Assembly of each District Court, which shall include five candidates in the case each of Alexandria and Cairo and three candidates in the case of Mansura.

In commercial affairs the District Court shall add to its number two merchants, one a native and one a foreigner, who shall enjoy the right to vote and who shall be chosen by election.

Article 3. There shall be at Alexandria a Court of Appeal composed of eleven justices, four natives and seven foreigners.

One of the foreign justices shall preside, with the title of Vice President. [In actual fact he was called President.] He shall be designated by an absolute majority of both foreign and native members of the Court.

The opinions of the Court of Appeal shall be rendered by five justices, three of whom shall be foreigners and two natives.

.   .   .   .   .

Article 5. The choice and appointment of the judges shall be made by the Egyptian Government; but in order to be assured of the qualifications possessed by the persons whom it may select, it shall address itself unofficially to the Ministers of Justice abroad and shall only engage persons who have received the approval and authorization of their Government.

.   .   .   .   .

II. *Jurisdiction*

Article 9. These courts shall have exclusive jurisdiction in all litigation involving civil and commercial matters arising between natives and foreigners and between foreigners of different nationalities, with the exception of personal status matters.

They shall also have exclusive jurisdiction in all suits concerning real estate between natives and foreigners and between foreigners of the same nationality or different nationalities . . . .

Article 10. The Egyptian Government, the administrative

offices, and the estates of the Khedive and of members of his family shall be subject to the jurisdiction of these courts in litigation with foreigners.

Article 11. The courts may not render decisions concerning the ownership of the public domain.

They likewise do not have jurisdiction over acts of sovereignty or over measures taken by the Government in execution of and conformity with the laws and regulations of public administration.

Notwithstanding their not being permitted to interpret an administrative act or to halt its execution, these courts shall have jurisdiction over cases involving infringements arising from such an act of the vested rights of a foreigner as recognized by treaty, law or contract.

.   .   .   .

Article 16. The judicial languages employed in the courts in pleadings, the preparation of documents and decisions are: Arabic, English, French, and Italian.

.   .   .   .

IV. *Execution of Judgments*

Article 18. The execution of judgments shall take place independently of any administrative, consular, or other action, upon order of the court. . . .

V. *Non-Removability of the Judges.*

Article 19. The judges who compose the Court of Appeal and the District Courts shall not be removable . . . .

Comment: In practice the jurisdiction of the Mixed Courts was very broad. It has been described as follows by Judge Brinton, an American, who was the last President of the Mixed Court of Appeal.

J. Y. BRINTON, *The Mixed Courts of Egypt,* pp. 64–66.*

According to the text of their Charter the jurisdiction of the Mixed Courts was founded primarily on a difference of nationality between parties to the litigation. In practice the courts went considerably beyond the letter of this definition.

In spite of this perfectly unambiguous language [complains the Judicial Adviser in 1899], the Mixed Tribunals have gradually established a principle (which is nowhere to be found in the law itself) under which they affirm their jurisdiction in all suits where a "mixed interest" is discoverable, although the actual parties to the suit may both be natives. It is easy to understand that with so vague and arbitrary a criterion of jurisdiction the powers of these tribunals have been extended in an ever widening circle.

Despite much similar criticism and of vigorous but unsuccessful efforts to induce the powers to repudiate this broad interpretation

*Reprinted by permission of the Yale University Press, copyright 1968.

of their mission, the Mixed Courts held firm to this principle of mixed interest, and its consistent application was a large factor in extending their influence in Egypt. They regarded themselves as the protector of foreign interest whether it became involved directly or indirectly in litigation before them, and never hesitated to look behind the parties on the record to discover its existence. Several important categories of cases illustrate the application of this principle.

A fertile field for its application was that of corporate law. Throughout the period of the regime of the Mixed Courts, private corporations doing business in Egypt were of two classes: foreign corporations organized under the law of a foreign country and having only business offices in Egypt, and corporations of Egyptian nationality, formed under Egyptian law, holding charters authorized by the government and issued under royal seal. Both classes of corporations were largely employed by foreign capital in Egypt . . . .

As far as the jurisdiction of the courts was concerned, the case of the foreign corporations raised no difficulty. Like all foreigners, the foreign company enjoyed the privilege of the jurisdiction of the Mixed Courts. By the application of the theory of the "mixed interest" a similar result was reached in the case of "Egyptian" companies. Acting on the possibility that the stock of every company was, partly at least, in the ownership of foreigners, the courts saw here a mixed interest sufficient to enable them to assume exclusive jurisdiction even in the case of suits between such companies and purely native litigants. An exception, however, was made in the case of the Bank Misr, the ownership of whose stock was restricted to Egyptians. The theory also brought within the jurisdiction of the Mixed Courts all the largest enterprises of the country, including the Suez Canal Company, the various municipal water, traction, and other public service companies, and practically the entire banking system. It was applied to purely governmental administrations, in which foreign interests were officially or otherwise represented . . . .

In bankruptcy, likewise, the application of the principle of mixed interest found wide scope. The existence of a single creditor of a nationality different from that of the alleged bankrupt was held sufficient to support the jurisdiction. The result was that the entire bankruptcy system of Egypt was in the hands of the Mixed Courts . . . .

Comment: This theory of the "mixed interest" has been very important in the development of Egyptian law. It meant that practically all suits involving important questions of commercial law, corporate organization, stocks and bonds, etc. were adjudicated by the Mixed Courts. Thus, until the abolition of these courts the experience of the native or, as they were later called, national courts in these matters was very limited. It was broadened somewhat after the establishment in the 1920s of the Bank Misr and the industries which depended upon this bank financially.

The Mixed Civil Code generally followed in its organization

the French Civil Code. Its provisions were confined, however, to property, contracts, and torts.

Organization of the Mixed Civil Code

(in force until 1949)

Preliminary regulations

First Title.	Property
Chapter 1.	Different Kinds of Property
Chapter 2.	Ownership
Chapter 3.	Usufruct
Chapter 4.	Servitudes
Chapter 5.	The Ways in Which Ownership and Real Rights are acquired
Chapter 6.	Loss of Ownership and of Real Rights
Second Title.	Obligations
Chapter 1.	Obligations in General
Chapter 2.	Contractual Obligations
Chapter 3.	Obligations Resulting from Fact
Chapter 4.	Obligations Resulting from Law
Chapter 5.	Extinction of the Obligations
Chapter 6.	Proof of Obligations and Discharge of Debts
Third Title.	Various Specific Contracts
Chapter 1.	Sale
Chapter 2.	Contracts of Hire
Chapter 3.	Partnership
Chapter 4.	Loan
Chapter 5.	Deposit
Chapter 6.	Suretyship
Chapter 7.	Agency
Chapter 8.	Settlement
Chapter 9.	Pledge
Fourth Title.	Rights of the Creditor
Chapter 1.	The Different Types of Creditors
Chapter 2.	Proof of Real Rights
Chapter 3.	Registration of Mortgages

Comment: The native courts were organized by a decree of the Khedive in 1883.

Decree of 14 June 1883 on the Reorganization of the Native Courts [as amended].

Article 5. A court of first instance is established in each of the following cities: Cairo, Tanta, Zagazig, Mansura, Alexandria, Beni-Souef, Assiut, and Keneh.

Article 6. Each of these courts shall be composed of at least five judges, of whom one shall be the President and one the Vice President. Judgment shall be given by three judges.

Article 8. Within the district of each court of first instance tribunals of summary justice shall be established. Their number, seat and venue shall be determined by regulation of the Ministry of Justice . . . .

Article 9. A court of appeal shall be established in Cairo.

Article 10. The decisions of the court of appeal shall be given by three justices.

Article 11. As the need arises, further courts of appeal may be established by decree and the number of the courts of first instance may also be increased . . . .

Article 12b. A Court of Cassation with its seat in Cairo is established. [Amendment of 1931].

The Court of Cassation shall consist of two chambers, one for civil causes and one for penal matters . . . .

The decisions of the Court of Cassation shall be given by five justices . . . .

Article 15. These courts shall have jurisdiction in all civil and commercial suits. In penal matters the jurisdiction shall extend to minor and major misdemeanors and to felonies . . . .

The civil and criminal jurisdiction of the native courts shall be excercised with regard to Egyptians and those foreigners who are not exempt from the jurisdiction of the native courts in certain or all matters by virtue of treaties, agreements or usage. In criminal cases involving the death penalty according to *shariʿa* law, the prior advice of the *mufti* shall be sought . . . .

Article 16. . . . [These courts] do not have jurisdiction in actions concerning the establishment of *waqfs*, marriage and other questions relating to marriage such as dowry, support [of wife and children] etc., as well as gifts, bequests, inheritance and all other questions concerning personal status.

They may not interpret the decisions rendered in these matters by the judge who has jurisdiction.

Comment: The Egyptian law reforms of the late nineteenth century thus established three separate court systems: the mixed courts, the native courts, and the religious courts (*shariʿa* courts and the courts of the Jewish and Christian communities). In addition there were consular courts which retained jurisdiction in some matters with regard to citizens of their country.

Chapter 4   Legal Reforms since the End of World War I

Comment: The most important result of World War I in the Near East was the dissolution of the Ottoman Empire. In its stead a number of successor states came into being. In Turkey itself Mustapha Kemal Atatürk created a strong secular nation state centered on Anatolia. The Near Eastern Arab provinces of the Empire became mandates under the League of Nations and were administered by Great Britain and France as mandatories. Iraq, Trans-Jordan, and Palestine became British mandates, while Syria and Lebanon were assigned to France. Iraq and Trans-Jordan were governed by Arab rulers under British control, Palestine was under direct British administration. In Syria and Lebanon France introduced republican constitutions, but the territory was subdivided in different ways on several occasions and the states of Syria and Lebanon as they exist today emerged only gradually. Iraq became independent in 1932. Syria and Lebanon achieved independence during World War II. In Trans-Jordan and Palestine the British mandate ended shortly thereafter. In 1949 the state of Israel, which included much of the territory of Palestine, was formed. Most of the remainder of Palestine became part of the kingdom of Jordan which also included the former Trans-Jordan. A narrow section along the Mediterranean, the so-called Gaza strip, came under Egyptian control. Egypt, which Great Britain had declared a protectorate at the outbreak of World War I, achieved independence in 1936. In the Arabian peninsula King 'Abd al-'Aziz Ibn Saud conquered the Nejd and the Hijaz and formed the independent kingdom of Saudi Arabia. The Yemen became completely independent from Ottoman suzerainty, while the rim areas of the pensinsula for the time being remained under British control. The British colony of Aden and its hinterland, the Aden protectorate, received independence in November 1967; it is now the People's Democratic Republic of Yemen. Kuwait at the head of the Persian Gulf, achieved complete independence in 1961 and the rest of the Arab sheikhdoms on the gulf in 1971.

Extensive legal reforms were initiated in the Near Eastern states after World War I with Turkey taking the lead. Iran followed with a thoroughgoing reform of its legal system under the rule of Reza Shah in the late 1920s and 1930s. In the Arab states the legal reform movement was somewhat slower during the interwar period and was influenced in many respects by the French and British as imperial powers. After World War II, legal reforms in the Arab countries, in some cases initiated before the outbreak of the war, received a tremendous impetus and new comprehensive legislation was enacted in most fields of the law. Turkey still remains the only country in the area, however, which has completely secularized its law.

A. Legal Reform in Turkey

HERBERT J. LIEBESNY, "Stability and Change in Islamic Law," pp. 25–26.

After some initial hesitation the government of Kemal Atatürk decided in 1924 to abolish *shari'a* law even in personal status matters and to put Turkish law on a completely secularized and Westernized basis. However, Atatürk broke new ground not only by this complete secularization, but by the abandonment of principal reliance upon French prototypes. This was due, no doubt, in part to the existence of greater choice. Germany, Italy and Switzerland had enacted new code systems which in many respects were more modern than those of France and the Turkish jurists endeavored to base the new legal system on the most modern codes available. For the civil law the choice fell upon the Swiss Civil Code and Code of Obligations . . . .

The Swiss codes were received verbatim for the largest part. Provisions necessitated by the federal system of Switzerland were, of course, omitted. Otherwise few changes were made. Of interest, however, is a small change in Article 1 which was due to the endeavour of the Turkish drafters to close all loopholes through which traditional practice could enter again. Article 1 of the Swiss Civil Code provided that in cases where the Code did not contain applicable provisions the judge should decide according to customary law, or if there were no applicable customary law, according to the rule which he himself would formulate were he the lawgiver. In the latter case the judge should follow "established doctrine and tradition." The Turkish code reproduced these rules, except that it did not refer to "tradition." Instead it directed the judge to follow doctrine and the practice established by judicial decisions.

The adoption of the Swiss Civil Code and Code of Obligations in 1926 was followed swiftly by the adoption of other European codes. The Criminal Code enacted in the same year was patterned after the Italian Penal Code of 1889; the Code of Criminal Procedure of 1929 followed the respective German code, and the Code of Civil Procedure of 1927 was based upon the corresponding code of the Swiss canton of Neuchâtel. Since the revision of the Swiss Code of Obligations which dealt with commercial matters had not been completed in 1926, a Commercial Code whose elements had been taken from various European prototypes was adopted in 1926. A Code of Maritime Commerce which followed the German Code became law in 1929. A new

Commercial Code replacing the old Commercial Code and the
Code of Maritime Commerce was enacted in 1956.

Turkey thus was the first and has so far remained the only
country in the Middle East where the *shari'a* law was eliminated
completely from the legal system. This radical step was due to
Atatürk's desire for a thorough secularization of Turkey's law
and administration. The law was to be and has been an important
element in the modernization and Westernization of Turkey and
thus became a conscious instrument in the promotion of cultural
change. Given the difficulties arising from the abolition of long-
established institutions and from the introduction of a new legal
system derived from a number of unrelated foreign codes and
lacking the homogeneity usually found in systems where the
various major codes were developed in close correlation to each
other, the Turkish legal system can be said to have worked well.
There have been difficulties, however. As was to be expected
these difficulties occurred primarily in the fields of family law and
land law.

Comment: The spirit of the Turkish reform of the Civil Code is
clearly apparent in the explanatory note attached to the Code by
the Minister of Justice, Mahmut Esat.

Explanatory Note to the Turkish Civil Code of 1926

The Turkish Republic does not at the present time possess a
civil code in the proper sense of that term. It has only the *Majalla*
which touches merely upon a small number of legal acts and
transactions. The drafting of that code, which contains 1851
articles, began on the 8 Muharram 1286 [20 April 1869] and was
completed on the 26 Sha'ban 1293 [22 February 1876], the date
when it went into effect. It can be said that barely 300 articles of
this code satisfy modern needs. The rest is nothing but a mass of
legal rules which are so primitive that they have no relationship
to the needs of our country and are inapplicable. The principles of
the *Majalla* are based on religion whereas human life undergoes
fundamental changes every day, even every minute . . . . The states
whose law is based on religion become incapable after a short time
to satisfy the needs of the country and the nation, because religions
express immutable rules. Life, however, marches on and requires
rapid changes. As life changes constantly, the religious laws
become nothing but empty words without meaning and formalities without value. Immutability is a dogmatic necessity for
religion . . . .

The laws inspired by religion fetter the nations in which they
are applied to the primitive periods when these laws first were
born and they constitute insuperable barriers to progress. There
is no doubt that our laws, based on religious principles and linked
permanently to the deity, have been the most powerful and most
effective factor which in modern times has tied the destiny of the
Turkish nation to medieval institutions and mentality.

The Turkish Republic would not have been responsive to the

needs of modern civilization or to the ideals and objectives inherent in the Turkish revolution if it had remained without a complete civil code inspired by the social life of the nation and establishing rules for it.

The modern state is distinguished from primitive societies by the fact that there are codified rules applicable to the relationships within the community. During the period of semi-civilization, in a nomadic society, the laws are not codified. The judge bases his judgment upon custom and tradition. Except for the three hundred articles of the *Majalla* mentioned above, the judges of the Turkish Republic have relied in their civil jurisdiction upon the works of the *fiqh* and religious principles. In his judgments the Turkish judge is not bound by any fixed and established interpretation, rule, or principle. Thus, two judgments rendered in two different sections of the country on an identical cause arising from identical circumstances, are very often dissimilar and even contradictory. Consequently, the Turkish people are constantly exposed to uncertainty and confusion in the dispensation of justice.

The fate of the individual is not determined by a precise and stable legal practice, but is subject to risks and chances because of the medieval and contradictory rules of the *fiqh*.

It was important therefore that justice in the Turkish Republic emerged from this chaos, this confusion, and the primitive state and adapted itself to the needs of the revolution and of modern civilization through the urgent adoption of a new civil code. This is why the Turkish Civil Code has borrowed the Swiss Civil Code, which is the most recent, the most perfect, and the most democratic. The work of adaptation was accomplished by a special commission of eminent jurists of our country.

There are no essential differences among the needs of the nations which belong to the family of modern civilized societies. The constant economic and social relations have actually made one family out of civilized humanity. It is unnecessary, therefore, to deal with the allegation that the application of the Turkish Civil Code, whose principles were borrowed from a foreign country, will not serve the needs of our country. Switzerland is composed of French, German, and Italian elements who have a different history and different traditions. A law which could be applied successfully in surroundings comprising so many heterogeneous elements of different cultural background should certainly be applicable even more successfully in Turkey where 80 per cent of the population is homogeneous . . . .

·   ·   ·   ·

The goal of legislation is not to maintain old customs or beliefs having their origin in religion, but to assure the economic and social unity of the nation. Also, modern legislation must establish a separation between law and religion. Otherwise the laws will support an intolerable tyranny over citizens who profess a religion other than that adopted by the state. The modern state excludes religion from its field of action and respects all religious beliefs which stay within their spiritual confines. When religion wanted to govern human society, it became the arbitrary instrument of sovereigns, despots, and strongmen. By separating the temporal and spiritual spheres, modern civilization has saved the world from many calamities and has given religion an imperishable place in the conscience of the believers.

For countries whose citizens belong to different religions, it is even more necessary to break with religion. Otherwise it would not be possible to issue laws applicable to all citizens. On the other hand, if laws are enacted for each religious minority, the political and social unity of the nation will be broken.

It should also be remembered that the state is in contact not only with its own citizens, but also with foreigners. In a theocratic system, the foreigners have the right to claim a special regime, that is, capitulations. In the course of the negotiations at Lausanne which led to the treaty of peace, the resistance of the western nations to the abolition of the capitulations was based on such considerations. Evidently the special regime established for foreigners since the time of Mehmed the Conqueror was made necessary by the religious character of our laws. Now, however, the ethnic and religious minorities of our country have declared that they would renounce the rights given them by the Treaty of Lausanne . . . .

Comment: The optimism expressed in the explanatory note, which did not foresee any particular problems in applying the Swiss codes to Turkey, was not fully borne out. Although the codes generally were applied with comparatively little difficulties, problems did develop in several fields. The Turkish lawyers have been fully aware of these problems and in September 1955 a symposium was held at the University of Istanbul at which the reception of Swiss law in Turkey was discussed by Turkish and foreign legal experts. A number of the papers read at that symposium were published in UNESCO's *International Social Science Bulletin,* vol. 9, no. 1 (1957). Others were published in *Les Annales de la Faculté de Droit d'Istanboul,* no. 6 (1956).

The general problem of the reception of the Swiss codes in Turkey was discussed by several speakers at the Istanbul symposium. Some excerpts from this interesting critical discussion of the results of the reception of a European code in a non-European country follow.

H. V. VELIDEDEOĞLU, "The Reception of the Swiss Civil Code in Turkey," pp. 61–63.*

. . . Until 1926, Turkish private law, with the exception of commercial law, was based principally upon religious principles. This means that while Turkey was a European country, its legal system was Islamic. In 1926 Turkish law ceased to belong to the group of legal systems classed as Muhammadan and became romano-germanic. At the same time, it ceased to be a system of religious law and became secular.

*Reprinted by permission of UNESCO.

The reception of alien civil codes in Europe during the nineteenth century was not in the nature of a legal revolution, for the new legislation was not transplanted to unfamiliar ground. In the first place, the background was uniformly furnished by Roman law. In the second place, the receiving states as much as the countries from which the codes emanated, were based on Christian culture and tradition. While Roman law had brought the European nations together in the field of law, the Renaissance and the Reformation had exercised the same effect in the cultural and spiritual sphere. Furthermore, no great climatic differences existed between these countries which could affect the biological conditions of their population. For all these reasons the new codes established themselves quickly in their new surroundings.

In Turkey the reception of foreign law occurred in entirely different circumstances. For centuries, Turkey had formed part of the Islamic world both culturally and in matters of religion. Religion moulded Turkish society and its outlook on problems of conscience, morals and law. Having been a theocratic state until 1839 and a semi-theocratic state until 1924, secularization was only achieved as a result of the abolition of the Caliphate and of the religious tribunals in 1924 and of the adoption of the Swiss Civil Code in 1926. To hope that the new Civil Code, based on romano-germanic and Christian traditions would operate without difficulties was to hope for a miracle. Naturally, the social structure of Turkey was opposed to it.

Technical difficulties arose from mistakes in the translation of the Code and from the failure to observe a strict uniformity in terminology. Moreover the Code was translated into the Turkish language from the French text, which was in turn a translation from the German original. Since the French version of the Swiss Civil Code is by no means perfect, the Turkish text suffers from corresponding imperfections.

Writers and the courts are attempting to eliminate the effects of these defects by a systematic treatment. Mistakes of translation are countered by the techniques of interpretation.

In addition, the Swiss Civil Code has been modified in other respects in the course of its reception in Turkey. These modifications may be classified as voluntary or involuntary.

As regards the former, some were necessary in view of the particular features of the administrative and judicial organization in Turkey. Others involved questions of principle, such as the rejection of the Swiss matrimonial property regime and the deliberate change in the quotas reserved as *légitime*. Religious, social and economic reasons caused changes in the effect of judicial separation, the period of desertion as grounds for divorce and in the time limits for bastardizing a child. Biological differences led to the reduction of the age of marriage and of majority. Geographical considerations influenced an extension of certain time limits.

On the other hand involuntary modifications include failure to include marginal notes, the merger of subsections of an article of the Code, the omission of certain articles and subsections, mistakes of translation, inaccurate terminology and unnecessary additions.

The legislature and the courts have made a strong effort to fill gaps in the Code and to adapt it to the structure of Turkish society . . . . Naturally the greatest difficulties arose in the field of family law. The new Code introduced the obligatory civil marriage in place of the religious marriage, while preserving the freedom to go through a religious ceremony following the civil marriage. Formerly, marriage was a simple contractual relationship entered into with the consent of the parties or of their parents in the presence of two witnesses. Although the conditions of marriage are laid down in the *Qur'an*, marriage in Turkey, as distinct from marriage in occidental law of former times, was never dependent upon a religious ceremony. The prayers of the *imam* were never a condition for a valid marriage, but assistance of an *imam* had become a tradition in social life and had invested the marriage ceremony with a religious character. A part of the population has continued to contract marriages in the presence of an *imam*, or even by consent only, without troubling to comply with the formalities required by law for the conclusion of a civil marriage. Since such marriages are void according to the Civil Code, considerable difficulties have arisen in connexion with the status of children born of such a union, and regarding the right to succeed to an inheritance.

Formerly polygamy was permitted in Turkey. The new Code has introduced monogamy. However, certain groups of the population have continued to practice polygamy. Since these marriages are void, according to the civil law, the legal position of the children born of such unions, and that of the wives has raised grave problems.

Faced with the conviction of the rural population that such marriages are still valid, legislation in 1933, 1945 and 1950 has legitimized the children of such unions and has recognized the unions themselves, if they were monogamous . . . . Until the cultural level of the rural population has been raised and until women in rural society obtain their proper place in social life, it will remain impossible to restrain certain sections of the population from marrying in the old form, and therefore, for some time to come, it will be necessary to pass legislation every five or ten years which legitimizes the issue of such unions . . .*

According to the old law, the husband had the unfettered right to repudiate his wife . . . . The new Code excludes unilateral repudiation and divorce by consent. Divorce is pronounced by a judicial decree on grounds laid down by law. It seems that the difficulty in obtaining a divorce is one of the reasons why the old form of marriage has survived. Men are accustomed to repudiate their wives unilaterally and do not wish to renounce this freedom of action by going through a civil marriage ceremony. It has been suggested that divorce should be made easier, but the Turkish legislature has been unwilling to follow this trend. Some Turkish

*Since this article was written, civil marriages among the rural population have increased significantly, see below p. 169.

courts, however, have relied on the provisions of the Code, which permits divorce on the ground of mutual incompatibility, in order to render the law of divorce more flexible, provided that marital life has really broken down. The practice of the Court of Cassation shows a more restrictive tendency.

According to the old law, successions were divided in unequal parts between male and female heirs; the parents of a deceased person shared the estate with his descendants. The new Code introduced equality of shares between sexes and excluded parents when there are descendants.

The principle of equality of shares between men and women has been accepted without opposition, and even with approval. On the other hand, the exclusion of the parents when competing with descendants has caused much discontent. It has been suggested that social needs could be met by granting the parents a life interest (usufruct) of part of the estate . . . .

In the sphere of property the greatest difficulties were encountered in the application of the rules of the new Code relating to land. Registration in the Land Register is required both for the creation and the transfer of rights in land. Nevertheless, arable land has continued to be transferred without registration, especially in the villages, even after the new Code came into force, and this has given rise to immense difficulties . . . .

The continuation of sales and purchases of land without registration in the Land Register is a social and legal fact which has compelled the legislature and the courts in Turkey to develop new rules in order to remedy this situation, and sometimes even to discard rules and principles laid down by the Civil Code.

The first measure was to effect the registration of all land. But the financial and technical means available have not permitted the simultaneous execution of this vast undertaking. The second measure attempts to educate the peasants to make conveyances of land in the presence of the Officer of the Land Register. This will take time and presents a social and cultural rather than a legal problem. The third measure was to develop a legal principle which makes it possible to sell and to transfer by simple delivery land which has not yet been registered, in the absence of a Land Register. After much hesitation and vacillation during a period of twenty years, the Turkish Court of Cassation found a solution in 1946. The lawful possession of unregistered land is now held to constitute a right of a proprietary nature which is *sui generis*. This practice is in keeping with the present social and economic situation in Turkey. A new rule has been created outside the Civil Code which recognizes ownership of non-registered land.

In the sphere of contracts, the introduction of the Swiss Code of Obligations has not caused any great difficulties. The reason is that contracts such as sale, hire and loan are known throughout the world and that a divergence in their regulation and effects does not impinge strongly upon the social structure, in contradistinction to family law and the law of succession.

Comment: While the codes are of primary importance in Turkey, court decisions have played a part in adapting the new legislation to Turkish needs. Basically, the courts have to make their decisions in conformity with the law as laid down in statutes and codes. The function of the judiciary is to interpret and apply the statutory law not to make new law. There will, of course, be cases where the judge cannot find a rule in the statutory law which can be applied to the problem before him. In such instances the Civil Code authorizes him to use certain other established principles and, in the last resort, to act himself as a lawgiver. The pertinent portions of Article 1 of the Turkish Civil Code read:

The law must be applied in all cases which come within the letter or spirit of any of its provisions. Where there are no applicable provisions, the judge should decide according to existing common usage and custom and in default thereof, according to the rules which he would lay down if he had himself to act as legislator. In this he must be guided by established legal doctrine and court decisions.

As in other civil law countries, the Turkish judge is generally not bound by precedent. However, again following the practice of some other civil law countries, certain decisions of the Court of Cassation are binding upon the lower courts and upon the Court of Cassation itself. These are the decisions made by the General Assembly of all Chambers of the Court of Cassation in cases where there is a contradiction between decisions made by the same chamber of the Court or between decisions made by two chambers, or where the Court decides that an established precedent should be changed. A decision by this Assembly is binding as soon as it has been published in the Official Gazette.

Not all of the other decisions of the Court of Cassation are published, none of them in the Official Gazette. Those that are published appear in a journal put out by the Ministry of Justice (*Adalet Dergisi*) or in private publications. While all decisions are reasoned, the reasoning is often brief and therefore not very enlightening.

While decisions other than those of the General Assembly are not binding upon the lower courts, the lower courts customarily follow the decisions of the highest court. Unless they feel very strongly about a matter, judges do not like to hand down decisions which they know will be reversed. This would not only be a futile gesture, but could also interfere with their advancement.

B. Developments in the Arab Countries

1. The Abolition of the Mixed Courts in Egypt

Comment: As Egyptian nationalism increased, particularly after World War I, the existence of special jurisdictions for foreigners came to be considered intolerable. After Egypt had achieved full independence in 1936, it pressed strongly for the abolition of the Mixed Courts and what remained of the consular jurisdictions. In 1937 the so-called Montreux Convention was concluded between Egypt and the powers whose subjects were justiciable by the Mixed Courts. This Convention provided for the abolition of the Mixed Courts after a transitional period of twelve years.

The Montreux Convention, 1937, US Treaty Series 939.

Article 1. The High Contracting Parties declare that they agree, each as far as he is concerned, to the complete abolition in all respects of the Capitulations in Egypt from all points of view.

Article 2. Subject to the application of the principles of international law, foreigners shall be subject to Egyptian legislation in criminal, civil, commercial, administrative, fiscal and other matters.

It is understood that the legislation to which foreigners will be subject, will not be inconsistent with the principles generally adopted in modern legislation and will not, with particular relation to legislation of a fiscal nature, entail any discrimination against foreigners or against companies incorporated in accordance with Egyptian law and wherein foreigners are substantially interested.

The immediately preceding paragraph, insofar as it does not constitute a recognized rule of international law, shall apply only during the transition period.

Article 3. The Mixed Court of Appeal and the Mixed Tribunals now existing shall be maintained until 14 October 1949. As from 15 October 1937, they shall be governed by an Egyptian law, establishing the *Réglement d'organisation judiciaire* [Rules of Judicial Organisation] the text of which is annexed to the present Convention.

At the date mentioned in paragraph 1 above all cases pending before the Mixed Tribunals shall be remitted, at the stage which they have then reached and without involving the parties in the payment of any fees, to the National Tribunals to be continued there until they are finally disposed of.

The period from 15 October 1937 to 14 October 1949 shall be known as the "transitional period.". . . .

Rules of Judicial Organization of the Mixed Courts of 1937.

Article 1. The Mixed Court of Appeal at Alexandria and the three Mixed Tribunals of First Instance at Cairo, Alexandria, and Mansurah shall be maintained within their existing territorial areas of jurisdiction . . . .

Article 2. The Court of Appeal shall be composed of 18 judges, 11 of whom shall be foreigners . . . . Vacancies occurring among the foreign judges of the Court of Appeal shall be filled through promotion of foreign judges from the Tribunals of First Instance.

Article 3. The Tribunals at Cairo, Alexandria, and Mansurah shall be composed on 15 October 1937 of sixty-one judges, forty of whom shall be foreigners.

As vacancies occur through retirement, death, resignation or

promotion among the foreign judges, they shall be replaced by
Egyptian judges.

Nevertheless, the number of foreign judges of the Tribunals of
First Instance shall not be smaller than one third of the total
number of judges composing these Tribunals.

.   .   .   .

Article 26. The Mixed Tribunals shall take cognizance of all
civil and commercial suits between foreigners and parties subject
to the jurisdiction of the National Courts.

However, the National Courts shall have jurisdiction in such
cases with regard to any foreigner who agrees to submit himself
to their jurisdiction . . . .

Article 34. In suits with parties subject to the jurisdiction of the
National Courts, companies of Egyptian nationality already
incorporated and in which there is a substantial foreign interest
are subject to the jurisdiction of the Mixed Tribunals, unless their
terms of incorporation contain a clause submitting them to the
jurisdiction of the National Courts or unless they have accepted
the jurisdiction of these Courts in accordance with Article 26.

Article 44. The Mixed Courts have jurisdiction in all penal cases
against a foreigner . . . .

Comment: Before 1937 the Mixed Courts in practice had had only
very limited penal jurisdiction over foreigners. Although the
Mixed Courts should have excercised a broad jurisdiction in penal
matters from the outset, consular jurisdiction over most offenses
was retained by the foreign powers, limiting the Mixed Courts to
jurisdiction over minor misdemeanors and such matters as bankruptcy and contempt of court. Very few felonies were adjudicated
by the Mixed Courts before 1937. Thus the Montreux Convention
considerably broadened the penal jurisdiction of these courts.

In personal status matters, fifteen powers availed themselves of
the option the Convention granted and retained consular jurisdiction in these cases. Where no such reservation was made,
personal status matters of foreigners were adjudicated by the
Mixed Courts, rather few cases in practice.

The Mixed Courts were abolished as of 15 October 1949, and
since that time Egypt has had a unified system of courts for
foreigners and Egyptians alike. There still remained a duality of
the court system, however, since the *shari'a* courts and the courts
of the other religious communities retained jurisdiction in personal status matters. These courts were abolished in 1955 and
their jurisdiction was transferred to the ordinary civil courts (see
p. 100).

*Law No. 115 of 1948 Abolishing the Mixed Courts and Consular
Courts.*

Article 1. The Mixed Courts and consular jurisdictions are
abolished as of 15 October 1949.

Article 2. Cases pending in the Mixed Courts on 14 October
1949 shall be transferred in the stage they are in and without costs

to the National Courts to continue their consideration in accordance with the codes of civil and criminal procedure in force in the National Courts and in accordance with Articles 4, 5, and 6. [These articles regulate the details of transfer.]

Article 3. Cases pending in the Mixed Court of Appeal sitting as Court of Cassation shall be transferred to the National Court of Cassation.

.   .   .   .   .

Article 7. Cases pending in consular courts on 14 October 1949 shall be transferred in the stage they are in and without costs to the National Courts to continue their consideration in accordance with the provisions of the Code of Procedure in Personal Status Matters . . . .

Comment: The Montreux Convention gave a strong impetus to legal drafting activities in Egypt, since the government wanted to have new unified codes ready for enactment when the Mixed Court jurisdiction came to an end. The first unified code to be enacted was the Penal Code of 1937.

Explanatory Note to the Penal Code of 1937.

After the abolition of the capitulations it has become necessary to give the country a Penal Code whose provisions are applicable to foreigners and Egyptians alike. The Egyptian Penal Code promulgated in 1904 is, of course, more recent than the Mixed Penal Code, and, since its promulgation, has been brought up to date through various amendments. It is, therefore, better suited to serve as the basis of the new code than the Mixed Penal Code. Changes and new provisions have only been introduced as far as they were dictated by the necessity to apply its provisions generally to all inhabitants of the country, and by urgent present-day needs . . . . [Because of the very restricted jurisdiction of the Mixed Courts in penal matters before 1937, the Mixed Penal Code had been little used. The consular courts decided on the basis of their own domestic law.]

Comment: The unified Egyptian Penal Code was still largely inspired by the French prototype. Work on other codes, particularly a unified civil code, was begun, but was not completed until after World War II. A general phenomenon in connection with legal reform in Egypt should be noted. In spite of the long occupation of Egypt by Great Britain, British legal thought has had relatively little influence in the country. This has been due not only to the firm establishment of French law in Egypt before the British occupation, but also to the fact that British courts never existed in Egypt and that the Egyptian bench and bar remained largely French-oriented in legal training and outlook. An important requirement for the reception of the noncodified law of the conqueror, namely its application in the courts, was thus absent.

2. *Developments in other Arab Countries in the Inter-War Period*

Comment: In contrast to Egypt where legal reform in the nineteenth century went its own independent way, the reform legislation of the *Tanzimat* was applied in the Arab provinces under full Ottoman control. Thus, Syria, Lebanon, Trans-Jordan, Palestine, and Iraq were governed by Ottoman laws when they came under British and French mandatory control. The state of judicial affairs at that time in one of these countries, Iraq, (then still called Mesopotamia) was described by a British official.

SIR EDGAR BONHAM-CARTER, in *Review of the Civil Administration of Mesopotamia*, pp. 93–95.

[*Civil and Commercial Law and Procedure*]

The procedure of the *Nizamiyah* Courts in civil matters is governed by the Code of Civil Procedure published in the year 1880, which follows in general the French Code of Civil Procedure of 1807. Considerable amendments of the Code, which were much needed, have been recently effected. The criminal procedure of the courts is regulated by the Criminal Code of Procedure, which was published in the year 1879, and which differs but little from the French Criminal Code of Procedure.

Commercial suits between Ottoman subjects were heard in accordance with the Code of Civil Procedure, but, if one of the parties was a foreigner, the Code of Commercial Procedure, which had received the assent of the Powers, was followed.

The substantive law administered by the courts consists of (1) the *Majalla*, (2) the Commercial Code, (3) the Marine Commercial Code, (4) the body of Ottoman Legislation.

The *Majalla* or Ottoman Civil Code is a Code published in the year 1869 of Hanafi Muhammadan Law . . . . A code of law which had remained unchanged for a thousand years cannot be a satisfactory instrument for determining legal rights at the present time. The best that can be said of it is that it is surprising how often its provisions are in agreement with modern law. So far as commercial transactions are concerned, it has been superseded by the Code of Commerce, and its provisions as regards actions have been replaced by the Code of Civil Procedure and later amendment. Unfortunately its provisions as regards evidence are still in force.

The Code of Commerce is a translation with some omissions of the sections of the French Code of Commerce relating to partnerships and companies (societies), bills of exchange, and bankruptcies.

The Marine Commercial Code is based principally on French law. The Baghdad Courts have little concern with it.

The general body of Ottoman legislation down to the year 1906, can be consulted in Mr. George Young's admirable *Corps de Droit Ottoman*, a work which has greatly facilitated the task of British lawyers and administrators in this country. Legislation subsequent to that work exists at Baghdad only in the Turkish originals.

It will be gathered from the foregoing summary that the organization of the *Nizamiyah* Courts was logical and complete and more than adequate for the needs of the country. It erred indeed in being over-complicated for the state of society in this *Wilayat** and for the personnel who administered it. The procedure of the courts, with the exception of the provisions of *Majalla* as regards evidence, is not unsatisfactory, though, being based on old models, it requires amendment to bring it up to date, and is also over-complicated for local conditions. And, subject to some reservations, the codes and the Turkish laws provide a body of law sufficiently modern and complete to enable cases which come before the court to be decided in a reasonable and just manner.

Nevertheless, it is generally agreed that the administration of justice was extremely unsatisfactory. Like so many other Turkish administrations, the courts presented a fair appearance on paper, but failed seriously in working. The principal causes of this failure are obvious.

In the first place, the salaries paid the judges were quite inadequate. A judge of a Court of First Instance received the wretched pay of from £T. 7½ to £T. 10 monthly. An ordinary judge of a Court of Appeal received £T. 15 monthly. The President of the Court of Appeal received £T. 35 monthly. The clerical staff was paid on a still more inadequate scale. The salaries were neither adequate to attract men of sufficient ability for the duties of a judge nor to maintain a standard of efficiency or honesty amongst judges or subordinate staff. Few of the judges were men of any general education or had had any sort of legal training beyond such as they acquired in subordinate positions as clerks of the court.

Secondly, the procedure of the courts is over-technical. And, as usually happens when a technical business is administered by persons of narrow education or of inadequate professional knowledge, this fault of the procedure was accentuated in practice.

Thirdly, all the proceedings of the court were conducted in Turkish, a language unknown to the mass of the population . . . .

[*Criminal Law and Procedure*]

. . . Ottoman law requires a multitude of courts, enquiring magistrates and prosecutors . . . the Ottoman Penal Code is ill-arranged, incomplete and difficult to interpret, while the Ottoman Criminal Procedure Code . . . is over-complicated and ill-adapted for application amongst the . . . rural and nomad population of Mesopotamia . . . .

Comment: During the mandatory period a new penal code and a new penal procedure code were enacted in Iraq which constituted an amalgam of provisions taken from Ottoman, French, and

*A *Wilayat* was an Ottoman province. Present-day Iraq comprises two such former provinces, Baghdad and Basra.

British colonial legislation. In the field of contracts the *Majalla*
remained in force. The *Majalla* and much Ottoman legislation
also remained in effect in Trans-Jordan. Between World Wars I
and II new legislation was enacted on a considerable scale in both
countries, but fundamental reforms in such fields as contracts,
real estate, and personal status law came only after World War II.
Neither in Iraq nor in Trans-Jordan were there any British courts
and on the whole the legal system of these two countries has
retained a continental European rather than a British flavor,
although a number of statutes enacted during the mandatory
period were patterned after British colonial laws.

The situation was different in Palestine which remained under
direct British rule. (In both Iraq and Trans-Jordan British control
was indirect. Iraq had become a kingdom under King Faysal I and
Trans-Jordan an Amirate under Amir Abdullah. Both rulers were
members of the Hashimite family.) The Palestine Order-in-
Council gave the courts in Palestine residuary power to apply the
rules of the English common law and equity.

Palestine Order-in-Council of 1922, Article 46.

The jurisdiction of the Civil Courts shall be exercised in conformity with the Ottoman Law in force in Palestine on 1st
November 1914, and such later Ottoman laws as have been or may
be declared to be in force by Public Notice, and such Orders-in-
Council, Ordinances and Regulations as are in force in Palestine at
the date of the commencement of this Order, or may hereafter be
applied or enacted; and subject thereto and so far as the same shall
not extend or apply, shall be exercised in conformity with the substance of the common law, and the doctrines of equity in force in
England, and with the powers vested in and according to the
procedure and practice observed by and before Courts of Justice
and Justices of the Peace in England, according to their respective
jurisdictions and authorities at that date, save insofar as the said
powers, procedure and practice may have been or may hereafter be
modified, amended, or replaced by any other provisions. Provided always that the said common law and doctrines of equity
shall be in force in Palestine so far only as the circumstances of
Palestine and its inhabitants and the limits of His Majesty's
jurisdiction permit and subject to such qualifications as local
circumstances render necessary.

Comment: Thus, during the British mandatory rule in Palestine
much Ottoman legislation was replaced by new legislation which
followed mainly British patterns. A new criminal law was enacted
which followed the broad outlines of the codes in British domin-
ions and colonies. New statutes were also enacted in such fields as
partnerships, limited liability companies, bills of exchange, checks,
and cooperative societies. In the field of procedure, English
principles replaced the Ottoman criminal procedure, and the law
of evidence was brought into fundamental agreement with rules of
British law. A number of the rules of the *Majalla* on proof and

presumptions were, however, retained, together with many of the *Majalla*'s provisions on substantive matters. Since the courts were staffed by British or British-trained judges and since an appeal lay with the Privy Council in London, the influence of common law and equity, given a subsidiary role by the Palestine Order-in-Council, made itself increasingly felt. Also, the decisions of the Palestine Supreme Court were collected in the manner of British and American decisions, and legal education followed British lines rather than European ones with a law school being established by the British in Jerusalem.

The system established in Palestine under the mandate is still to a large extent applied in Israel, although new legislation has been introduced in a number of fields. In Jordan the amalgamation in 1949 of parts of Palestine and the former Trans-Jordan, where much of the Ottoman legislation had continued in force, raised serious problems of unification of the law. Generally speaking, new legislation which was enacted for all of Jordan followed continental European rather than British legal principles.

In Syria and Lebanon the French-supported legal reforms were based, of course, on French prototypes. Among the major legislative enactments of the mandatory period still in force is the Lebanese Code of Obligations and Contracts which was promulgated in 1932. This code followed strictly continental European lines. It was drafted by a French lawyer, a M. Ropers, then judge in the French *département* of Seine, and revised by an outstanding French jurist, M. Josserand, then Dean of the Law School of Lyon and a member of the French committee which together with a similar Italian committee was at that time engaged in drafting a joint French-Italian Code of Obligations and Contracts which, incidentally, was never enacted into law in either country. Dean Josserand contributed primarily the section on a general theory of obligations to the Lebanese code. The draft of the code was then submitted to the Consultative Committee for Legislation by the Lebanese Government, which examined the draft in detail, primarily to make sure that the new code would be in harmony with other legislation in force in Lebanon. According to one of its members, Professor Choucri Cardahi, an eminent Lebanese jurist and one-time President of the Lebanese Court of Cassation, the committee looked to the French-Italian draft, mentioned above, as a model in solving various difficulties it perceived in the draft.* The committee, however, also took into account with regard to specific contracts various customary legal institutions connected with agricultural credit.† The draft was then passed to the Lebanese Chamber of Deputies and was signed into law by the President of the Lebanese Republic on 9 March 1932.

The Lebanese code, while French in inspiration, showed in its content the influence of other European codes and of the interpretive work of the French courts. No comparable code was en-

---

*Choucri Cardahi, *Code des Obligations du Liban*, première partie, *Théorie générale des Obligations,* (offprint from *Bulletin mensuel de la Société de Législation Comparée*, no. 10–12 of 1931), p. 17.
†*Ibid.*, p. 18.

acted in Syria where the *Majalla* and various statutes continued to apply until after World War II.

3. Developments in Egypt and the Fertile Crescent Countries since World War II

a. The New Civil Codes

HERBERT J. LIEBESNY, "Stability and Change in Islamic Law," pp. 30–31.

The period since World War II has been characterized in the Arab countries by intense codifying activities, both in areas regulated by Islamic law and in those already secularized. In the new codifications two main tendencies have made themselves felt: a trend toward synthesis of Islamic and Western legal ideas in fields such as contracts, and eclecticism in the selection of sources. The codes, including those which were based exclusively on Western law, no longer followed one specific European enactment but took principles and rules from a variety of European statutes. The foremost advocate in the Arab world of synthesis between the *shariʿa* and Western law has been an Eygptian jurist, Dr. ʿAbd al-Razzaq al-Sanhuri, who has been prominent in the drafting of new civil codes for a number of Arab countries. Codes or statutes based on Dr. Sanhuri's ideas and largely drafted by him have been enacted in Egypt, Iraq and Kuwait. The new civil codes of Syria and Libya have borrowed large portions of the Egyptian code. It can thus be said that a new family of civil codes has developed in the Arab world which is less closely related to French law than was the case with the previous Egyptian legislation [or is still the case with the Lebanese Code of Obligations and Contracts] and which is much farther removed from Islamic law than was the *Majalla* . . . .

Comment: Dr. Sanhuri expressed his ideas that *shariʿa* law could be used as a source for modern codifications first in a book, *Le Califat, son évolution vers une Société des Nations Orientale* (*The Caliphate, Its Evolution Towards an Oriental Society of Nations*), Paris, 1926. This study, written under the impact of the abolition of the Ottoman Caliphate by republican Turkey, envisaged an Islamic renaissance which would also, of course, encompass *shariʿa* law.

SANHURI, *Le Califat*, pp. 578–583.*

. . . The Islamic system could not be applied again . . . particularly with regard to certain of its provisions dealing with economic matters and real estate without prior adaptation to the needs of modern civilization . . . . Until this adaptation has been completed, the legal systems presently applied in the Muslim countries

*Reprinted by permission of Librairie Orientaliste Paul Geuthner.

should remain in effect since Islamic law is not equipped for immediate application. Before Islamic law could be substituted, the work of readaptation of this legal system to the needs of present-day society will have to pass through two successive stages: the research phase and the legislative phase.

. . . [The research phase] will consist of scholarly investigations aimed at a study of Islamic law in the light of [modern] comparative law. We believe that the point of departure for this research should be a separation of the religious from the temporal portion of Islamic law . . . .

[In the legislative phase] it will be essential to proceed prudently and gradually. Personal status law which is already based on the Islamic system as far as the Muslims are concerned, could furnish the first area of legislative experimentation . . . . [Sanhuri then discusses the application of Islamic law in the personal status field to non-Muslims]. The research phase will precede the legislative phase, adapting the personal status law to modern needs and divorcing it from religious considerations. Therefore, the legislator by making the changes in the Islamic system suggested by modern social science will be able to make this system more acceptable to non-Muslims.

If the experience in the field of personal status law is successful, one could go a step further and branch out into other fields of law. Here countries such as Egypt present difficulties of a different kind. Foreign legal systems have penetrated the legal thought and practice of these countries as a result of long application. An abrupt change would endanger the stability of legal relationships. The process of replacing these imported laws by national and Islamic legislation will therefore have to be gradual . . . . [Note: As a beginning, for example, a legislative declaration could state that Islamic law as set forth by the best modern authoritative doctrines (which resulted from the scholarly research envisaged above) should form the common law. That is, in the absence of a provision in the imported legislation not yet abrogated, Islamic law should be applied. The courts will thus become used to consulting Islamic law in case of silence of the foreign systems and by the same token the basic legal thought of the country will change. A second step would consist in the abrogation of those elements of the imported laws which appear to us to be inferior to Islamic law after its evolution through research. Whatever remains of the foreign systems once these two steps have been completed should be replaced by Islamic law when and if such a replacement is possible without endangering the stability of legal relationships.]

Comment: While the broad visions set forth in Dr. Sanhuri's study have not been realized, he has been able to translate some of his basic ideas into practice in the civil codes which he drafted. The first of these codes to be enacted was the Egyptian Civil Code of 1949. It was taken over in the same year by Syria, with the exception of provisions relating to real estate and proof. In Iraq the new civil code was enacted in 1951. The Libyan code was enacted in 1953. Article 1 of all these codes provides for the subsidiary application of *shari'a* law in case of silence of the code, but there are some rather significant differences in phrasing.

Egyptian Civil Code

Article 1.

(1) The law regulates all matters to which the letter and spirit of its provisions apply.

(2) In the absence of an applicable legal provision the judge shall decide according to custom and in the absence of custom in accordance with the principles of the Islamic *shari'a*. In the absence of such principles the judge will apply the principles of natural law and the rules of equity.

Syrian Civil Code

Article 1.

(1) The law regulates all matters to which the letter and spirit of its provisions apply.

(2) In the absence of an applicable legal provision the judge shall decide in accordance with the principles of the Islamic *shari'a* and in the absence of these in accordance with custom. In the absence of custom the judge will apply the principles of natural law and the rules of equity.

[The wording of the Libyan Civil Code is the same as that of the Syrian Code.]

Iraqi Civil Code

Article 1.

(1) The law regulates all matters to which the letter and spirit of its provisions apply.

(2) In the absence of an applicable legal provision the judge shall decide according to custom, and in the absence of custom in accordance with those principles of the Islamic *shari'a* which are most in keeping with the provisions of this Code without being bound by any particular school of jurisprudence. In the absence of these principles the judge will apply the rules of equity.

(3) In all this the Court shall seek guidance from decisions which are in accordance with judicial practice and from the legal principles (*fiqh*) firstly in Iraq and then in foreign countries whose laws are similar to those of Iraq.

Comment: Thus recourse to provisions of the *shari'a* is to be had according to the Egyptian code after recourse to custom, whereas in the Syrian and Libyan codes recourse should first be had to the principles of the *shari'a* and then to custom. While in actual practice the difference may not always be great, the variants in phrasing seem to indicate a somewhat different approach to *shari'a* law as a source between Egypt on the one hand and Syria and Libya on the other. The Iraqi code has the same phrasing as the Egyptian code, but is more explicit in this Article than the

other three codes. This is probably due, at least in part, to the fact
that a considerable part of Iraq's population belongs to the
heterodox Shi'i sect. This factor may account particularly for the
phrase "without being bound by any particular school of jurisprudence."

Professor Anderson has examined the general problem of the
synthesis between *shari'a* law and Western law with regard to
the Egyptian and Syrian codes.

J. N. D. ANDERSON, "The Shari'a and Civil Law (The Debt
Owed by the New Civil Codes of Egypt and Syria to the Shari'a),"
pp. 30–32.*

Considerable publicity was given at the time [of the enactment of
the new codes], particularly in Egypt, to the fact that the new
code had drawn extensively on "the decisions of Egyptian courts,
comparative legislation and the *shari'a*" as its sources of amendment and enrichment. This must not, however, be allowed to
obscure the fact that its chief architect, 'Abd al-Razzaq Ahmad
al-Sanhuri remarked in the course of its discussion before the
Committee of Civil Law set up for that purpose by the Senate:
"I put it on record now that three-quarters or five-sixths of the
provisions of this Law are based on the decisions of Egyptian
courts and on the existing legislation." All the same, the Explanatory Memorandum states unequivocally that its authors derived
from the *shari'a* "many of its general concepts and many of its
detailed provisions;" while the Report of the Committee of Civil
Law reiterated this claim and remarked that "the strengthening of
the links between this draft Code and the provisions of the *shari'a*
represents a retention of a spiritual heritage which deserves to be
preserved and used." Again, certain members of this committee
strenuously maintained that a suitable code could have been drawn
up based on the *shari'a* alone: but Sanhuri himself, while claiming
that he would yield pride of place to none in his love for the
shari'a not only admitted that little new had been borrowed exclusively therefrom (although the great majority of former borrowings had been retained), but stated categorically: "I assure
you that we did not leave a single sound provision of the *shari'a*
which we could have included in this legislation without so
doing . . . . We adopted from the *shari'a* all that we could adopt,
having regard to sound principles of modern legislation; and we
did not fall short in this respect". . . .

In Syria, on the other hand, comment on the new code naturally
took a different form. Here the introduction of a code which represented the adoption of the greater part of the Egyptian Code
almost verbatim amounted, in the abstract at least, more to a
retreat from the *shari'a* (in the form of the *Majalla*) than to an
extension of its scope. So the emphasis was placed primarily on
the inadequacy of the *Majalla*, both in form and in content, as a
civil code for a modern and progressive State; on the similarity

*Reprinted by permission of the Islamic Cultural Center, London, and the
author.

of the cultural, social, and commercial background in Syria and Egypt; and on the desire throughout the Arab world, as a long-term policy, to introduce uniform legal systems.

The debt which these codes actually owe to the *shariʿa* can, perhaps, best be summarized under four headings. There is, firstly, the inclusion of the *shariʿa* as one of the sources from which an appropriate rule or principle may be derived by the courts in default of any relevant provision; secondly, the influence which a desire for conformity with the *shariʿa* has exercised on the choice made in this code between certain concepts on which modern European codes are divided; thirdly, a few principles or provisions newly borrowed from the *shariʿa*, whether exclusively, chiefly, or in part; and, fourthly, those principles or provisions taken over by the previous legislation from the *shariʿa*, in whole or in part, and preserved, whether in their original or an amended form, in the new codes . . . .

The inclusion of the *shariʿa* as one of the sources from which a suitable rule or principle may be derived by the courts in default of any relevant provision is chiefly enshrined in Article 1. This enacts that "The provisions of this Code govern all matters to which they apply in letter or spirit. In the absence of any provision that is applicable, the judge will decide according to custom, and, in the absence of this, in accordance with the principles of the *shariʿa*. In the absence of these the judge will apply the principles of natural justice and the dictates of equity." It is noteworthy, moreover, that the Explanatory Memorandum puts considerable emphasis on the importance of this provision, and remarks: "The circumstances in which a judge may not be able to find any relevant provision will not be few in number, so the court will in many cases go back to the *shariʿa* and seek inspiration from its principles—a fact which represents an outstanding victory for the *shariʿa*." In discussion before the Senate Committee of Civil Law, moreover, the further point was made that the *shariʿa* had deeply influenced the customs of the country, particularly in rural districts. The Introduction to the Syrian Code, on the other hand, emphasizes not only that "custom and Islamic law" had been accorded a place "consonant with their importance as a fundamental and flexible source from which an important part of any deficiency which may appear in this Code may be supplied," but also that the article does not limit such derivation to the authoritative view of any one school but allows it, without limit or restriction, from the whole scope of relevant *shariʿa* principles. The value of this article seems more sentimental than practical.

It may, perhaps, also be added here that Article 32–34 expressly provides that "missing persons and absent persons are subject to provisions enacted in special legislation; in the absence of such, the *shariʿa* will be applied"; that Article 875–836 enacts that "The establishment of the heirs, the computation of their shares in the inheritance, and the devolution upon them of the property of the estate, is governed by the provisions of the *shariʿa* and by the legislative enactments concerning inheritance and estates . . ."; and that Article 915–876 provides that "Wills are governed by the provisions of the *shari'a* and by legislative enactments concerning wills." Special provisions regarding missing persons (*al-mafqud*) were introduced in Articles 7 and 8 of Law No. 25 of 1920 and regarding absent persons (*al-gha'ib*) in Articles 50–53 of the Law of the *Hasbiya* Courts of 1947; while the law of testate and intestate succession was summarized in the Law of Testamentary Dispositions and the Law of Inheritance, of 1946 and 1943 respectively. All of these are held to represent partial codifications of the *shari'a*, based on an eclectic principle of free selection of the most suitable provisions from the rules of any recognized school or the dicta of any reputable jurist. But the Explanatory Memorandum to the present law remarks that Article 875–836 has "resolved two basic points of dispute in regard to inheritance, for it decrees that it is the *shari'a* which is to be applied in regard to the inheritance of Egyptians even where they are not Muslims, and even if they have all agreed that the law of their sect is to apply; and it also makes the *shari'a* applicable in all matters of inheritance, including the devolution of the ownership of the estate upon the heirs." With regard to testate succession, again, the memorandum attached to the original draft declares that "The *shari'a*, and codifications and legislation based thereon, govern the substantive law of bequests . . . in regard to which Muslim and non-Muslim Egyptians are on a par; while in matters of form the Code of Procedure for *shari'a* courts has laid down provisions to which all bequests must conform."

Comment: An Egyptian jurist also has commented on this problem

CHAFIK CHEHATA, "Les Survivances Musulmanes dans la Codification du Droit Civil Egyptien," pp. 852–853.*

However, how can a provision of this kind [stipulating the subsidiary application of *shari'a* law] be applied in practice? Some have maintained that this is a purely theoretical statement without meaning for the legal practice. It is true that the period which has elapsed since the promulgation of the [Egyptian] code has not yet given the judges time to put the new provision to a test. Actually this provision will show its effect only in the long run . . . .

Besides, this provision will be applied only in the case of silence of the [written] law and absence of any custom. The [written] law actually covers all aspects of the civil activity of persons and custom often comes to the rescue where the law is silent.

However, no matter how inclusive legislation and how abundant custom may be, quite evidently needs develop faster in any society than legislation. Particularly in the period in which we live and of which it is often said, that history is accelerating, new situations may well arise before the legislation in force has found an adequate solution. Silence of the law is an obvious phenomenon and legislators the world over have anticipated this phenomenon and have tried to find a remedy.

In some countries the judge is asked to apply the general principles of law; in others he is asked to turn to natural law or

*Reprinted by permission of the author.

the rules of equity. This latter solution was contained in the old Egyptian civil codes and is maintained in the new code. However, in the new code it constitutes a last resort to which the judge only turns after having sought to find a solution according to the "principles of Islamic law.". . .

. . . The text stresses that the principles of Islamic law should be applied. It is thus not a question of having recourse to the works of the Muslim jurists to find a precise solution there. Besides, to what works should the judge turn? To the works of the Hanefite school to the exclusion of other works as is the case where personal status problems are concerned? The text is general and does not exclude any school, current, or tendency of thought in Islamic law. If a solution is sought for, it is likely that several, even contradictory ones, will be found in the various schools of Islamic law. Thus, the principles governing the solutions have to be sought after and not the solutions themselves.

However, the general principles of Islamic law have never been formulated by the Muslim jurists. The authors of purely theoretical works never tried to systematize Islamic law. They were content to establish logical legal rules . . . . *Fiqh* is essentially empirical in character. One looks in vain, for example, for a general theory of contracts and obligations.

If matters are looked at from this angle one might be inclined to believe that Article 1 presents the judge with an impasse.

One should not, however, be discouraged by this difficulty. The Egyptian legislator does not refer the judge to the Islamic legal system. The various theories of contracts and obligations or of real estate are elaborated and fully dealt with in the code itself. Article 1 does not wish to borrow from the technique of Islamic law. Rather it refers the judge to the basic principles of that law, that is to its spirit. This general spirit of Islamic law is presented to the judge as a last resort before turning to natural law or the rules of equity.

Natural law provides the solution dictated by sound reason. It is based upon the abstract idea of justice. Before turning to this primary natural law, . . . the judge must look to that formulation of natural law . . . established for a given society . . . the Muslim society, namely Islamic law. We should not forget that we are concerned here with the basic principles of that law, the spirit which animates it, the underlying reasons which have given rise to its specific provisions. Within these limits Islamic law constitutes merely a kind of prelude to natural law in its specific sense.

At this point the question should be asked whether applying Islamic law within these limits can be considered as establishing Islamic law as a formal source of the positive law of Egypt.

We have established that the judge is not required to search the texts of treatises on Islamic law for a specific solution for the case before him. He must, however, turn to the works on Islamic law, no matter what school they belong to, to determine the spirit which has inspired the various solutions found there. This effort will provide contact with the traditional sources of the law which was dominant in the country for many centuries.

And thus after some time has elapsed, there will be through the
court practice, helped, of course, by legal writings, a new reception of Islamic law . . . .

Comment: The Iraqi Civil Code is distinguished from the
Egyptian and Syrian codes because it has preserved a number of
provisions of the *Majalla.* As mentioned above, the *Majalla* never
applied in Egypt, and in Syria it had at least partially been replaced
by other legislation. By contrast, it still applied fully in Iraq.
Examples of general provisions taken over literally from the
Majalla are the following articles of the Iraqi Civil Code:

Iraqi Civil Code

Article 2. Where there is a text, independent interpretation
(*ijtihad*) cannot be applied. (*Majalla* Article 14.)

Article 3. What has been proven to be contrary to analogy
(*qiyas*) cannot be used by way of analogy in other cases. (*Majalla*
Article 15.)

Article 4. When prohibition and necessity conflict, preference is
given to the prohibition. When a prohibition is removed, the
thing to which such prohibition attaches reverts to its former
status of legality, but a thing that is gone is not restored.
(*Majalla* Articles 46, 24 and 51.)

Article 5. It is an accepted fact that the rules of the law change
with the change in times. (*Majalla* Article 39.)

Comment: These articles, and a number of others, express principles
not contained, in this form at least, in the Egyptian and Syrian
civil codes. They illustrate, however, the mixture between the new
and the traditional which is considerably more marked in the
Iraqi code than in the two others.

b. *New Penal, Commercial and Procedural Codes.*

Comment: In these fields new comprehensive statutes were enacted
in many of the Near Eastern Arab countries during or since
World War II. These new codes follow in general continental
European prototypes, but here too the method of the drafters has
been eclectic. In Egypt new legislation in the procedural field and
in commercial law followed the abolition of the Mixed Courts in
1949. A new Code of Civil Procedure, replacing the Procedure
Code of 1949 was enacted in 1968. A new Code of Evidence was
enacted during the same year. The latter Code brings together,
with some modifications, the rules of evidence contained in the
Civil Code, the Commercial Code, and the Code of Civil Procedure of 1949. The latter Code was not completely abolished,
some of its provisions, particularly those dealing with procedure
in personal status cases, have remained in effect.

In 1949, the disappearance of the Mixed Courts left Egypt still
with a dual procedural system, that of the courts of general
jurisdiction and that of the personal status courts. In 1955 the

Egyptian government abolished the personal status courts and thus unified its courts system. Substantively, *shari'a* law is still applied in personal status cases, but much of it has been codified. (See p. 103.)

Law No. 462 of 24 September 1955 Concerning the Abolition of the Shari'a Courts and the Courts of the Religious Minorities.

Article 1. The *shari'a* courts and the courts of the religious minorities shall be abolished effective 1 January 1956. Cases pending in these courts on 31 December 1955 shall be transferred to the National Courts for further consideration in accordance with the Code of Procedure and without additional costs.

In this connection the following principles shall be observed:

Article 2. Cases pending in the *Shari'a* High Court or in the Chamber of Appeals of the courts of the religious minorities shall be assigned to the Court of Appeal in which the [religious] court of first instance is located whose judgment is being appealed.

Suits pending in the [religious] courts of first instance shall be assigned to the appropriate National Courts of First Instance. Cases pending in the summary *shari'a* courts or summary courts of the religious minorities shall be tranferred to the appropriate National Courts of Summary Jurisdiction or of First Instance.

Article 3. Cases previously under the jurisdiction of the *shari'a* courts or the courts of the religious minorities, shall be brought before the National Courts beginning 1 January 1956.

Article 4. Within the National Courts special summary chambers, chambers of first instance and chambers of appeal shall be set up in accordance with the law on court organization. These chambers shall deal with cases concerning personal status or *waqfs* which previously were under the jurisdiction of the *shari'a* courts or the courts of the religious minorities.

In cases of this type decisions of the Court of Cassation shall be rendered by the Chamber for Personal Status Matters. The President of the *Shari'a* High Court shall be a member of this Chamber.

[The rest of this article deals with the organization of these chambers in the lower courts and the assignment of members of the former religious courts to them.]

Article 5. The provisions of the Code of Procedure shall be applied in all matters concerning personal status or *waqfs* which previously came under the jurisdiction of the *shari'a* courts or the courts of the religious minorities, except for matters for which special rules are laid down in the decree on the organization of the *shari'a* courts or legislation supplemental thereto.

Article 6. In cases concerning personal status or *waqfs* which previously came under the jurisdiction of the *shari'a* courts, decisions shall be based on the provisions of Article 280 of the decree on the organization of these courts.

[That article states that judgments should be rendered in accordance with the most authoritative opinions of the Hanefite rite, except where laws relating to *shari'a* matters provide special rules.]

In suits concerning personal status matters of non-Muslim Egyptians belonging to the same sect or denomination and for which religious courts were organized at the time of the publication of this law, decisions shall be rendered, within the framework of public order, according to their religious law.

Article 7. The application of paragraph 2 of the preceding Article shall not be affected by a change in religion with one party to the suit transferring from one religious group to another, unless he has embraced Islam. In that case paragraph 1 of Article 6 shall be applied.

[The remainder of the law deals with the transfer of the personnel of the religious courts to the National Courts, admittance to practice before the National Courts of lawyers having practiced before the religious courts and a number of other matters of detail.]

Comment: Paragraph 2 of Article 6 was interpreted by a decision of an Egyptian court as follows:

Court of First Instance, Cairo, Chamber for Personal Status Matters of Non-Muslims, Case No. 600 of 1956.

Article 6 of Law No. 462 of 1955, concerning the abolition of the *shari'a* courts and the courts of the religious communities provides: [follows text of Article 6, paragraph 2]. There is no doubt that the term "religious law" in its wider sense extends to the contents of the holy scriptures, to the opinions of the doctors of the Church and to the decisions handed down by the religious and judicial organs of the community which have acquired the character of a constant custom by virtue of their long-time application . . . .

Comment: In Lebanon a new penal code was enacted in 1943 and went into effect in 1944. It was based upon modern continental European legal thought and drew particularly from the Italian Penal Code of 1930 and the Polish Penal Code of 1932. A code of penal procedure was enacted in 1948. It has been amended at various times and was affected particularly by Decree Law No. 7855 of 16 October 1961, which revamped the judicial organization of the country. A commercial code, which replaced the old Ottoman Commercial Code, was enacted in 1943. It too is based on continental European prototypes, particularly French, but with some influence also from Italian, Portuguese, and Spanish law. The Lebanese Code of Civil Procedure, originally enacted during the mandatory period in 1933, has been subject to a number of important amendments, particularly in 1938, 1950, and 1961. It is, of course, largely based on French law. Lebanon still maintains a dual court system with religious courts having jurisdiction in personal status matters. The *shari'a* courts and the courts of the Druze community are part of the state's judicial system. The judges of these courts are appointed and paid by the state and the state can, and does, legislate on procedural and substantive matters. The situation is different with regard to the courts of the other religious communities. These communities may establish their own legislation and organize their own tribunals under the general control of the state which may restrict the prerogatives of these communities. A comprehensive law regulating the *shari'a* courts was enacted on 16 July 1962.

Syria has adopted the Lebanese Penal Code. Its Commercial Code shows strong influence of the corresponding Lebanese code. The Penal Procedure Code is based on Lebanese, French, and Egyptian models and the Civil Procedure Code follows European prototypes. There is still a dual system of secular and religious courts.

Iraq enacted a new penal code in 1969, a new law of commerce and a new civil procedure law in 1970. Iraq too still has a dual court system.

c. *New Personal Status Legislation*

Comment: In this field some codification was undertaken in Egypt in the interwar period and very intensive codifying activity has taken place in most Arab countries since World War II. These statutes are all based generally on Islamic law as found in the classical works, but they are eclectic and do not follow one individual school. Rather, they adopt those Islamic legal principles which are best suited to modern needs.

J. N. D. ANDERSON, "Law Reform in the Middle East," pp. 46–50.*

... [I]t was not until 1920 that the first reform of the substantive law of marriage and divorce ... was promulgated [in Egypt] to be followed by further reforms in 1923 and 1929 ... Yet these Egyptian reforms, though later and much more fragmentary than the Ottoman Law [of Family Rights], went considerably beyond it; for they found their basis, in some particulars, not merely in a variant Hanafi opinion or the dominant view of one of the other three Sunni schools, but in opinions attributed to certain early Muslim jurists, or to later, but somewhat unorthodox, reformers, or even occasionally in what virtually (but unoficially) amounted to a new exercise of *ijtihad*.

.   .   .   .

... [I]n 1936 a new Committee was set up which produced ... a Law of Inheritance in 1943 ... and a Law of Testamentary Dispositions ... in 1946. Each of these represents a comparatively complete codification of the relevant law, and thus largely displaces reference to the authorities previously applicable.

.   .   .   .

*Reprinted by permission of the author and the Royal Institute of International Affairs.

... In Jordan ... the Law of Family Rights, 1951, represents a recent codification based partly on the Ottoman Law of Family Rights and partly on the more drastic Egyptian reforms .... [This Law] ranges over the whole law of personal status and family relations except for testate and intestate succession ....

... In family law [of Lebanon] the *shari'a* courts still apply the Ottoman Law of Family Rights, as promulgated in Lebanon, in regard to Sunnis—and also (but only insofar as this does not contravene their own personal law) to Shi'i litigants—while the Druzes are governed by the Law of Personal Status for the Druze Community promulgated in 1948 ....

... [T]he Syrian Law of Personal Status, 1953 ... emulates the Jordanian Law of Family Rights in including a number of matters, such as legal guardianship and representation, ... while it also—unlike the Jordanian Law—comprises sections covering the law of testate and intestate succession. It is applicable, moreover, to all Syrians except, as expressly provided, for three communities, the Druzes, the Christians and the Jews; in regard to the Druzes the points specifically excepted represent the major divergencies from Islamic law covered in the Lebanese Law of Personal Status for the Druze Community, while in regard to the Christians and the Jews it may be stated that the Law is applicable only in matters of testate and intestate succession, paternity, and legal capacity and representation. Thus the Nusayri, Ithna 'Ashari, and Isma'ili communities in Syria are, it seems, made subject to this law in all particulars.

The principles of the Law, which runs to 308 articles, were derived, according to the Explanatory Memorandum, from five different sources: the Ottoman Law of Family Rights, the Egyptian reforms, the code prepared by Qadri Pasha some years ago in Egypt, certain points in regard to which the drafting committee decided to adopt some non-Hanafi opinion or some provision "not contrary to the *shari'a*," and a draft code prepared by a Syrian jurist. Of these the most significant is the fourth, which clearly opens the door extremely wide; but it is also obvious that the committee owed a considerable, if unacknowledged, debt to the Jordanian Law of 1951 ....

J. N. D. ANDERSON, "A Law of Personal Status for Iraq," pp. 542–545.*

On December 30, 1959, the *Iraqi Gazette* promulgated, as Law No. 188 of 1959, a Code of Personal Status. This code was to be brought into force on the day of its publication; it was to apply to all Iraqis except those who were specifically excepted by some special law; and any legislative enactments contradictory to its provisions were thereby repealed. It was thus that the revolutionary regime brought to an end a controversy regarding the codification of the law of personal status which had ebbed and flowed in Iraq for more than twelve years; and it is significant that

*Reprinted by permission of the International and Comparative Law Quarterly and the author.

it produced, in the event, a code which was much more radical than anything which had previously been proposed.

It was as long ago as 1947 that a draft Code of Personal Status had been approved by the Committee for Judicial Affairs of the Iraqi Chamber of Deputies. In spite, however, of the recommendation of this committee that it should be enacted by Parliament and promulgated as law, this code had been repeatedly shelved. Initially this was occasioned—in part, at least —by a change of government and· the election of a new Chamber; but the fundamental reason why it was allowed to remain in abeyance was the opposition it aroused in certain religious quarters—most of all, perhaps, among the leaders of the [Shi'ite] Ithna 'Ashari or "Ja'fari" sect, which claims approximately half of the total population of Iraq as adherents.

Iraq was, in fact, the only part of the previous Ottoman Empire —with the exception of those parts of the Arabian Peninsula over which the Porte claimed sway—which had been left virtually untouched by the series of legislative enactments in the sphere of the law of personal status which appeared in almost every other country in the Middle East. It is true that the two Imperial Edicts issued by the Sultan in 1915 . . . had been applied in Iraq; but the Ottoman Law of Family Rights had had no effect in that territory . . . because Iraq had already been occupied by the Allies at the date when it was promulgated in Istanbul.

.   .   .   .

The code which has now been promulgated differs from the draft code in three fundamental respects: it is far shorter, and therefore leaves much more to the discretion of the *qadi*; it is far more radical, and includes a number of quite daring innovations; and it eliminates all differences between Sunnis and Ja'faris, even in regard to inheritance.

The code is accompanied by a brief "Statement of Objects and Reasons" which prompted its promulgation. This emphasizes the absence, in Iraq, of any one Law "which brings together those opinions of the jurists which are generally accepted and best suited to contemporary needs," and asserts that the multiplicity of the sources on which judgments might be based, together with the differences between the law concerned, had occasioned a lack of stability in family life and a failure to guarantee the rights of individuals. One of the primary aims of the revolutionary regime from the very first, therefore, had been the "promulgation of a unified code of personal status which would provide a foundation on which the structure of the Iraqi family in its new era might be built, and which would guarantee the stability of its relationships and ensure to women their legal rights and family independence." It was with this end in view that the Ministry of Justice had set up a committee, by Order dated February 7, 1959, to "draft a Code of Personal Status the principles of which were derived from those rules in the *shari'a* which were generally agreed and those enactments of Muslim countries which were accepted, together with the settled jurisprudence of the Iraqi courts." The result of the committee's work was the present code, covering "the most important sections of Islamic law in the sphere of personal status, including matters of marriage, divorce, childbirth, paternity, custody, maintenance, bequests and succession." It is significant, moreover, that the statement then proceeds to mention, *seriatim*, "the most important provisions the committee adopted from the articles of the Civil Code and from the legislation of Muslim countries, which either had some support in the Islamic law or were not contradictory thereto."

The brevity of this code compared with the draft code of twelve years ago, on the one hand, and the Syrian Law of Personal Status, on the other (88 articles as against 177 and 308, respectively), is dismissed with the remark: "The committee has tried to bring together in this code the most important of the general principles of the law of personal status, leaving it to the *qadi* to consult the legal compendia in order to extract the detailed rules from those texts which are most suited to the provisions of this code, since the committee considers it impossible to draft a law which includes all matters, general and detailed." As a consequence it is provided in Article 1 (1) that "The legislative provisions of this code shall govern all matters covered by them, whether expressly or by implication"; in Article 1 (2) that "If there is no legislative provision which can be applied, judgment shall be given according to those principles of Islamic law which are most suited to the provisions of this code"; and in Article 1 (3) that "The courts shall be guided in all this by the law established by legal precedents and Islamic jurisprudence in Iraq and in other Muslim countries whose legislation approximates to that of Iraq." On this article the Statement of Objects and Reasons comments: "The committee took over the provisions of Article 1 from the Civil Code, after remoulding them in a form that corresponds with the principles of the *shari'a*"...

Comment: Among the most radical features of the code were the severe limitation of polygamy and the extension of certain provisions in the Civil Code applicable to land held in a form of lease from the government (so-called *miri* land) to intestate succession to property of every description. The pertinent provisions of the Civil Code had been taken from the Ottoman Land Law and were in part based on German law. They ran directly counter to a number of major principles of the Islamic law on inheritance. When Qasim was overthrown in 1963, the new regime introduced an amendment abrogating those provisions of the Code of 1959 which were "incompatible with Islamic Law." The eliminations were confined to one point regarding polygamy and the law of intestate succession as a whole.

Outside the Arab Near East, comprehensive personal status legislation was enacted in Tunisia in 1956 (amended in 1959), in Morocco in 1958, and in Pakistan in 1961.

4. *The Law of Saudi Arabia and of the Gulf Amirates*

a. *Saudi Arabia*

Comment: Saudi Arabia is one of the relatively few countries, others are Yemen and Afghanistan, where *shariʿa* law is still the basic law of the country. In various areas, however, royal decrees have been enacted which for all intents and purposes have the force of law. Since the *shariʿa*, as stated before, does not give legislative power to the ruler, legislation in Saudi Arabia has the character of administrative regulations which are permissible under *shariʿa* law. Consequently, the term *qanun* is not used in Saudi Arabia, the legislation enacted is rather termed *nizam*, regulation or ordinance. Legislation is issued by the Council of Ministers and sanctioned by the king. All such enactments are published in the official journal, *Umm al-Qura*.

King ʿAbd al-ʿAziz Ibn Saʿud unified the legal system of the country in 1926, basing this unification on the Hanbali rite. The customary tribal law also was outlawed. The courts of general jurisdiction in Saudi Arabia are the *shariʿa* courts staffed by *qadis*. The *qadis* decide on the basis of authoritative works of the Hanbali school. Six works of this school were established as fundamental by a decree issued by King Ibn Saʿud in the 1920s. The most famous of these, which is widely used, is *al-Mughni* by Ibn Qudama, a Hanbali jurist who lived in the twelfth—thirteenth century A.D. Other works have been added to this list by decision of the Judicial Board.

The substantive law administered by the *shariʿa* courts thus is gathered from works of the Hanbali scholars, but the organization of the courts and their procedure have been regulated by royal decree.

In addition to the *shariʿa* courts there exist in Saudi Arabia a number of boards and committees which have judicial functions in specific areas of the law. Thus a commercial court was established in Jidda in 1926, but gradually declined and was abolished in 1955. With the growth of modern business in Saudi Arabia, pressures grew, however, for a revival of a commercial tribunal. As a result, the Commercial Disputes Arbitration Boards were set up in 1965 and a Commercial Disputes Appeals Board was created in 1967. There are three of these Arbitration Boards, one each in Jidda, Riadh, and Dammam. Each board has three members taken from the Ministry of Commerce and Industry. The Appeals Board also has three members, the Deputy Minister of Commerce and Industry and two high-ranking officials of the same ministry. The boards are not bound to apply *shariʿa* law, but can draw upon *shariʿa* law, Western law, and international law and agreements in deciding cases before them.

Under the Saudi Labor and Workmen Regulations of 1969, Labor Disputes Arbitration Preliminary Hearing Committees and Labor Disputes Arbitration Appeal Committees were established. The police have a considerable amount of jurisdiction under the Motor Vehicle Regulations. Of considerable importance has also been the creation of a Grievance Board (*Diwan al-Mazalim*) by Royal Decree of 8 June 1955. This board has jurisdiction similar to that of an administrative tribunal as it exists in other Arab and European countries. The much needed step of setting up a Ministry of Justice was taken in 1970.

On the substantive side, important legislation also has been enacted to meet problems arising out of the modern needs which have been created through the oil industry in the eastern part of the country and the expansion of commerce which has followed in the wake of the development of the oil industry and the greatly expanded income of the country. There have been income tax regulations (applicable to non-Saudis), motor vehicle regulations, company regulations, labor regulations, to cite a few. In these regulations some modern Western principles make themselves felt. Thus the Labor and Workmen Regulations of 1969, for example, recognize liability for moral damages in some cases, whereas *shari'a* law does not recognize moral damages.

b. *The Yemen Arab Republic.**

Comment: Yemen still applies *shari'a* law in civil and criminal cases. This law is that of the Zaidi sect (a Shi'i group) in the north of the country and that of the Shafi'i rite in the southern section. Procedure has not been codified, but the courts apply a combination of customary and *shari'a* procedure. A procedural law was under consideration at the beginning of 1972. Also pending at that time was a bill to establish a hierarchical court structure. In the field of administrative, economic, commercial and other modern government activities statutes have been enacted.

c. *The Gulf Amirates.*

Comment: The small principalities on the west coast of the Gulf were under British control from the early part of the nineteenth century. Britain sought control of the Gulf as a protection of the imperial lifeline to India. With the discovery of oil, first in Iran, then in Iraq and the Gulf states, the Gulf assumed a new importance as a source of oil for Britain and other countries of Western Europe. The amirates were never integrated into the British Empire as colonies, but retained a status which was officially described by the British as being that of "independent states in special treaty relations with H.M. government." Treaties were concluded which gave the British control over foreign relations and over the award of concessions and the alienation of territory. The British establishment in the Gulf consisted of a political resident with seat on Bahrein and political agents in the various principalities.

In addition to political control the British also had judicial jurisdiction to various degrees in the Gulf principalities. This jurisdiction was regulated by Orders-in-Council and extended generally to all Westerners. One of the amirates under British

---

*I am indebted for the above information to Mr. Husayn 'Ali al-Hubaishi, Legal Advisor of the Government of the Yemen Arab Republic.

control, Kuwait, gained its independence in 1961. The others
became independent in 1971. Judicial jurisdiction was retroceded
as independence approached and by the end of 1971 British extraterritorial jurisdiction in the Gulf region had come to an end.

The end of British political control and above all the termination of British judicial jurisdiction made it necessary for the Gulf
states to establish a more elaborate system of statutes and courts.
Kuwait, anticipating the grant of independence, invited the outstanding legal draftsman of the Arab World, Dr. ʿAbd al-Razzaq
al-Sanhuri, in 1959 to help modernize the Kuwaiti legal system.
Under Dr. Sanhuri's guidance a new court system was established which consisted of courts of first instance staffed by a
single judge, a High Court of Appeal with a bench of three
judges, and a Court of Cassation with jurisdiction in personal
status and contract matters. A Code of Civil and Commercial
Procedure was enacted as Law No. 6 of 1960 and a Code of Penal
Procedure as Law No. 17 of the same year. The Civil and Commercial Procedure Code follows in form the Egyptian Code of
Civil and Commercial Procedure of 1949, but in substance is
patterned after the Egyptian Regulations for *Shariʿa* Courts of
1909, 1910, and 1931.

In matters concerning contracts and torts the *Majalla* was and
is applicable in Kuwait, but Dr. Sanhuri drafted a number of
substantive statutes which were enacted into law. Prominent
among these is the Commercial Law, No. 2 of 1961. The explanatory memorandum to this law describes briefly in its introductory
section from what sources the five books of this law were derived.
The first book dealing with commercial acts, merchants, and
commercial establishments was based upon the commercial codes
of Lebanon, Syria, Iraq, and Egypt and the draft commercial
law of the United Arab Republic. The second book deals with
obligations in general, a topic not usually treated in a commercial
code. The explanatory memorandum states, however, that the
Majalla is the civil law of Kuwait and that the Commercial Law,
based on sources derived from the West, cannot refer to the
Islamic legal provisions of the *Majalla* "as a complement to its
provisions." Therefore the second book sets forth general
Western principles of obligations. The memorandum stressses that
the provisions of this book were not taken from the Egyptian
Civil Code but from the Iraqi Civil Code because in that code
provisions of Western law are intermingled with provisions of the
Majalla. Since the *Majalla* is applicable in Kuwait, a code of the
Iraqi type was evidently considered preferable as a model by
Sanhuri. Iraqi law is followed also in other enactments, such as
the Law on Damages, No. 6 of 1961. The third book of the Law of
Commerce deals with commercial contracts and is based on the
same sources as the first book. The fourth book, dealing with
commercial papers, is drawn from the Syrian Commercial Code
and the draft law of the United Arab Republic. The fifth book
which regulates bankruptcy is based mainly on the draft law of
the United Arab Republic. Special laws deal with commercial
companies, commercial registers, and chambers of commerce. A

penal code was enacted in Kuwait as Law No. 16 of 1960. This code too is based mainly on modern principles.

Kuwait thus has modernized its legal system largely along lines followed by other Arab states, that is, Westernization was based upon continental-European, largely French, prototypes. The *shari'a* court jurisdiction has been limited to personal status cases. In Kuwaiti practice some difficulties arose initially, since the courts, staffed by lawyers from Arab countries whose system had been modernized many years ago, were not familiar with the background of the Kuwaiti system and the Kuwaiti court clerks and police officers on their part found the precipitous introduction of a largely alien system hard to cope with.

In the other amirates of the Gulf, that is Bahrein, Qatar, and the Trucial States (Abu Dhabi, Dubai, Sharjah, Ras al-Khaymah, 'Ajman, Umm al-Qaywayn, and Fujayrah) a similar process of reform started a few years ago stimulated, as in Kuwait, by the impending departure of the British. In Bahrein the process of developing the legal system was begun in the 1950s when a British judicial adviser was appointed. A number of statutes were enacted which followed the pattern of British colonial codes. Thus a code of criminal procedure was promulgated in 1966, a contract law in 1969, and a civil wrongs ordinance in 1970. The Contract Law is patterned very closely after the Indian Contract Act of 1872. However, as independence approached, Bahrein turned away from British-inspired statutes. In March 1970 a Legal Committee of the then State Council (now the Council of Ministers) was appointed which began to draft important pieces of legislation. The Legal Committee turned for prototypes to the Egyptian legal system, thus bringing Bahrein into the group of Arab states following basically continental-European patterns in their legal modernization. A new judicature law was enacted on 7 August 1971. It provided for a dual court system, civil courts, and *shari'a* courts. The civil courts are divided into summary courts, a High Court, and a High Court of Appeal. The *shari'a* court system consists of a High Court and a Court of Appeal. The *shari'a* courts have a Sunni and a Shi'i division since there is a sizeable Shi'i population on Bahrein. A law of civil and commercial procedure was enacted as Law No. 12 of July 1971, which generally follows the continental-European and Near Eastern pattern of such procedural enactments. It should be noted that there are no special personal status courts for non-Muslims. Personal status causes of non-Muslims are adjudicated by the civil courts. Like other Arab states in this area, Bahrein has appointed experienced Egyptian and Jordanian judges to serve on the Bahreini bench, since there are not enough Bahreinis available as yet to fill these positions.

The developments in the other Gulf states have been similar. In Qatar comprehensive civil, commercial, criminal, and procedural codes have been drafted, mainly along Egyptian and French lines, without, however, trying to embody the idea of synthesis of Islamic and continental-European legal ideas which Dr. Sanhuri advocated and attempted. In Sharjah the ruler asked two Jordanian lawyers in 1968 to set up and preside over a law court and assist the ruler in enacting a codified legal system. The new court has general civil, commercial, and criminal jurisdiction. On the substantive side, a criminal code and a criminal procedure code have been completed and a law of contracts has been drafted. A commercial code and a company law also have been prepared. In Abu Dhabi several statutes have been enacted and a court system has been set up. On the constitutional side, the small principalities of the Trucial Coast federated in December 1971 as the United Arab Amirates, with the ruler of Abu Dhabi as head of the Federation.

Modernization in the Gulf states thus is proceeding along several different lines. There is a sizeable legacy of statutes enacted by the British, which became applicable to all inhabitants of the various amirates as the British retroceded jurisdiction. The comprehensive codes enacted in recent years by the amirates on the other hand follow generally Egyptian or Kuwaiti, that is basically continental-European, patterns. Lastly, the extent to which *shari'a* law is reflected in the new codifications also appears to vary from country to country. *Shari'a* courts have not been abolished, but their jurisdiction has been restricted generally to personal status cases of Muslims. The overall trend in the amirates thus seems to be toward a largely Egyptian-oriented legal system, notwithstanding the long British control. This phenomenon can be explained by the fact that, in contrast to the situation in India and Pakistan and in the British mandate of Palestine, the British-staffed courts did not have general jurisdiction and the British substantive enactments were, at least until the recent retrocessions, applicable only to those categories of persons subject to British extraterritorial jurisdiction. In addition, few local lawyers were trained and there were no local British-type law schools. Therefore, there was no legacy of British practice comparable to that found in India and Pakistan or in British-mandated Palestine.

5. Developments in the Former French North African Possessions: Algeria, Tunisia, Morocco.

Comment: In the former French North African territories the influence of French law has been profound. This influence was strongest in Algeria, which was occupied by the French in 1830 and which became independent after more than a century of French rule in 1962. Under French rule Algeria was divided into two distinct parts. The three northern departments were regarded virtually as part of France and were administered in a fashion very close to that of the metropolitan area. The so-called Southern Territories, by contrast, remained under military control. All legislation of general content enacted in France before the formal annexation of Algeria in 1834 applied automatically. Later legislation had to be extended specifically to Algeria. French citizens and persons legally assimilated to French citizens were under the exclusive rule of French law except insofar as that law had been modified by special statutes for Algeria.

Indigenous noncitizens remained under the rule of Islamic law with regard to personal status matters, inheritance, and those parcels of real estate which were not regulated by French law. Most of the judicial functions were exercised in Algeria by French courts. *Qadis'* courts continued to exist, but their jurisdiction was limited to personal status cases, inheritance of non-naturalized Muslims, and, in some instances, to personal suits involving limited amounts. All other suits were justiciable by justices of the peace. There were no *shari'a* courts of appeal. Rather, appeal from the *qadis'* courts lay in the courts of first instance which also heard appeals from the justice of the peace courts. From the courts of first instance appeal lay in the Court of Appeal in Algiers. The latter was given special powers in 1892 to achieve greater uniformity in the application of Islamic legal principles and a special Chamber of Muslim Appeals (*Chambre des révisions musulmanes*) was created.

The *qadis'* courts of Algeria were thus integrated into the French judicial system, and French courts had broad jurisdiction, particularly on appeal, on questions of Islamic law. In principle the French courts in Algeria were enjoined to follow the custom of the people rather than the texts of the Muslim jurists. In practice, however, the judges looked to the *Qur'an* and to works of Muslim jurists for solutions in cases involving Islamic law. Equity and natural law were adduced to achieve the desired results where the French courts felt that otherwise their decision would be inequitable. The situation thus was somewhat similar to that in British India and French courts, too, created a large amount of case law on points of Islamic law. However, following the French habit of wide-ranging discussion of legal problems in articles and books, a very considerable literature of authoritative writings (*doctrine*) also was created. One of the most influential French jurists was Marcel Morand, for many years Dean of the law school of the University of Algiers. Among other studies, Dean Morand wrote a draft of a Code of Algerian Muslim Law, which was submitted to a Commission for the Codification of Algerian Muslim Law, but was never enacted. The code is a careful piece of work and abundantly annotated. As such it is still useful for study purposes. Because of their preoccupation with North Africa, most French writers on Islamic law, including Morand, have concentrated on the Malikite rite.

The organization outlined above applied to the three northern departments of Algeria. The Berber tribes of the mountain areas had no *qadis* and judicial powers had at one time been exercised by tribal assemblies. Under French rule justices of the peace had jurisdiction in the Berber region, the Kabylia. In the Southern Territories the *qadis'* courts remained the courts of general jurisdiction.

In contrast to Algeria, Tunisia and Morocco were not annexed by France, but remained protectorates. The French protectorate over Tunisia was established by the treaties of 1881 and 1883, while the protectorate over Morocco was established by a treaty of 1912. Not all of Morocco was under French control, however.

There was a Spanish zone in the north, and a special international status was accorded the city of Tangier. Both Tunisia and Morocco retained their indigenous governments, headed in Tunisia by the bey and in Morocco by the sultan. The French were represented in both countries by residents general and subordinate French officials. Legislation emanated in form from the Sultan of Morocco and the Bey of Tunis, but French influence was, of course, very strong. French and indigenous administrations were more closely inter-woven in Tunisia than in Morocco.

A dual court system existed in both protectorates. French courts had jurisdiction over French nationals and nationals of third countries which had given up their capitulatory rights. Nationals of Tunisia and Morocco were justiciable by local courts. In both countries personal status matters, inheritance, and certain real estate matters were adjudicated by *qadis*. Other cases were heard by administrative officials in Morocco and by secular courts in Tunisia.

The French protectorate over Morocco ended in 1956 and so did Spanish control in the northern zone. The city of Tangier was completely integrated into the Kingdom of Morocco, as the country is now styled, in 1960. Tunisia likewise obtained its independence from France in 1956. Algeria became independent in 1962. Basic reforms of the legal and judicial systems were undertaken by the three countries and some phases of these reforms were not as yet completed by 1973.

Morocco faced specific problems in regard to judicial and legal reforms. Theoretically the powers of the sultan had always extended over the whole of Morocco, but developments had differed in the French protectorate, the Spanish zone, and the city of Tangier. The legal and judicial system of Morocco thus had not only to be reformed but also had to be unified. Unification of the judicial machinery was achieved by the so-called Unification Law of 26 January 1965. This law established a unified court system; the administrative officials no longer have judicial powers. The lowest courts, the so-called *sadad* courts, correspond to justice of the peace courts, above them are the regional courts, equivalent to courts of first instance. There are also courts of appeal and at the apex of the judicial pyramid stands the Supreme Court. The latter was created by a law of 27 September 1957 and has the power of cassation with regard to judgments by the lower courts. It also has the power to annul administrative decisions where the administrative authorities have exceeded their powers.

The Unification Law abolished the *qadis'* courts and the courts of the Jewish community. The *sadad* courts have original jurisdiction in matters which used to be adjudicated by the religious tribunals, and the regional courts have appellate jurisdiction. Substantively, *shari'a* law and Hebrew law remain applicable except as far as pertinent statutes have been enacted. The law also established Arabic as the sole language of the courts and stipulated that only Moroccan nationals can be judges. This latter provision is significant, because after independence French judges continued to play some role in the Moroccan judiciary.

In Tunisia the French courts were eliminated by a French-Tunisian treaty of 9 March 1957. For a transitional period of five years beginning 1 July 1957 French judges were still to play a role in civil suits in Tunisia. The judicial hierarchy established in Tunisia is similar to that of Morocco. The lowest courts are the cantonal courts, which have limited jurisdiction, above them are the courts of first instance. There are three courts of appeal and the court of last resort is the Court of Cassation. As in Morocco religious courts have been abolished.

In Algeria too the judicial system has been unified. The present judicial organization is based on an ordinance of 16 November 1965. The Algerian system is somewhat more simplified than the systems used by Morocco and Tunisia. There are no longer any justice of the peace courts, but just one category of courts of original jurisdiction. Appeal from these courts, except in certain instances where the amounts involved are small, lies in the courts of appeal. At the apex is again a Supreme Court, established by a law of 18 June 1963 and modeled after the Moroccan Supreme Court. The religious courts have also been abolished in Algeria.

Legal reform in these three countries could not, of course, stop with the reorganization of the judicial system. The procedural and substantive codes and statutes also had to be adjusted to the new situation. In Morocco, Tunisia, and Algeria new codes of civil and penal procedure have been enacted. New penal codes were enacted in Morocco in 1962 and in Algeria in 1966. A new commercial code was promulgated in Tunisia in 1959. These new codes follow continental-European and particularly French prototypes.

In the field of contracts no new comprehensive legislation has as yet been enacted. A draft of a Tunisian civil and commercial code taking into account Islamic as well as continental-European precepts, was prepared by the famous Italian jurist and specialist in Islamic law, David Santillana. Only part of this code became law in Tunisia on 16 December 1906 under the title of Code of Obligations and Contracts. Morocco enacted a shortened version of the Tunisian code in 1913 as its Code of Obligations and Contracts. The Moroccan code did not include procedural rules, commercial law regulations, and a number of other matters that had been contained in the Tunisian code. The Tunisian-Moroccan Code of Obligations and Contracts is distinguished from the *Majalla* by the fact that it contains a good deal of Western law whereas the *Majalla* is purely Islamic. In contrast, however, to some other codes of the region, for example the Lebanese Code of Contracts and Obligations, the Tunisian-Moroccan code draws not only on French law, but also on other continental-European systems, such as German and Swiss law.

In the field of personal status and inheritance, Tunisia enacted a comprehensive law on marriage, divorce, and inheritance in 1956, amended with regard to wills in 1959. Morocco enacted comprehensive personal status and inheritance legislation in 1957 and 1958. Algeria promulgated some legislation on marriage and divorce in 1959 and a personal status code has been drafted. As elsewhere in the Arab world this personal status legislation is basically Islamic.

Thus direct French participation in the legislative and judicial processes in the states of North Africa has come to an end. In Algeria in particular endeavors have been strong, to eliminate French influence and Islamicize the legal system, both through court decisions and legislative enactments.*

C. Legal Reforms in Iran

HERBERT J. LIEBESNY, "Stability and Change in Islamic Law," p. 30.

In Iran the modernizing influence of Reza Shah brought about a thorough-going reform of the legal system. In contrast to Turkey, however, Iran did not turn away completely from Islamic law. Instead, the Iranian Civil Code attempted a synthesis of Islamic and Western legal rules. This code, issued in three parts between 1928 and 1935, regulates all fields normally found in a continental-European civil code, including family law and inheritance. In these areas the influence of Islamic law is still very strong, elsewhere modern Western rules, taken largely from French, Belgian and Swiss law, prevail. Of considerable interest in the Iranian legislation is the intermingling of *shariʿa* and Western legal patterns. For example, the code recognizes such strictly Islamic institutions as the temporary marriage (peculiar to Shiʿite law) and the repudiation of the wife by the husband, but follows Western patterns in determining the legal capacity of persons and in requiring the registration of acts affecting personal status, such as marriage and divorce. In the field of inheritance law, the code follows the *shariʿa* in restricting disposition by will to one-third of the decedent's estate, but a special statute deals with the form of the will, generally along Western lines.

[In contrast to European civil codes, the Iranian Code also contains a section on evidence.] The personal status law and law of inheritance of non-Shiʿites were not regulated by the Civil Code and the customary law of these groups continued to be applied. [The provisions of the Iranian Civil Code with regard to divorce and related matters were revised by the Family Protection Act of 1967 which introduced a number of new ideas. The provisions of this new Act are apparently applicable to Shiʿis as well as non-Shiʿis.] In other areas of the law, such as penal law, procedural law and commercial law, new codes also were enacted which generally follow modern European lines. In the application of the new codes Iran's experience appears to have been somewhat similar to those of Turkey: resistance to change in the rural areas and consequent persistence of old forms.

*See the speech of the Minister of Justice at the opening of the judicial year 1971–72, *Revue Algérienne des sciences juridiques économiques et politiques*, vol. 8 (1971), pp. 1003–1010.

D. Legal Reforms in Afghanistan

Comment: In Afghanistan legal reforms received a strong impetus with the enactment of a new constitution in 1964. As stated before, the basic law of Afghanistan has been *shari'a* law according to the Hanefite rite and at this time the *shari'a* courts still have wide jurisdiction. The constitution of 1964, however, gave *shari'a* law a subsidiary role by providing in Article 69:

> ... a law is a resolution passed by both houses and signed by the King. In the area where no such law exists, the provisions of the Hanafi jurisprudence of the *Shari'a* of Islam shall be considered as law,

and stipulating in Article 102:

> The courts in the cases under their consideration shall apply the provisions of this Constitution and the laws of the State. Whenever no provision exists in the Constitution or the laws for a case under consideration, the courts shall, by following the basic principles of the Hanafi rite of the *shari'a* of Islam and within the limits set forth in this Constitution, render a decision that in their opinion secures justice in the best possible way.

The constitution also established a court system with the Supreme Court at its apex. The Supreme Court consisted of nine justices appointed by the king, one of whom was designated by the king as chief justice. The Afghan Supreme Court had administrative as well as judicial functions. It issued administrative regulations for the courts, prepared the budget, and participated in the nomination of judges for the higher courts. For other than administrative purposes the Supreme Court was divided into chambers. There was a Chamber for Criminal and Disciplinary Actions Against Judges, a Chamber on Conflicts of Jurisdiction, and a Court of Cassation with three chambers.

The monarchy in Afghanistan was terminated by a coup on 17 July 1973. The leader of the coup, Muhammad Daud, proclaimed a republic of which he is president. A decree issued on 28 July 1973 declared Afghanistan a Republic, retroactive to 17 July, "in accordance with the true spirit of Islam." The provisions of the 1964 Constitution were abrogated unless specifically upheld by new decrees. The sections of the 1964 Constitution dealing with the king and his powers, with Parliament and with emergency powers of the king and the royal government were expressly declared void. The powers of Parliament and the emergency powers will be exercised by the president pending the proclamation of a new constitution. The government also has the power to issue new legislation. Laws which do not contravene the spirit of republican decrees remain in force.

Another decree, issued on the same day and also retroactive to 17 July, dealt with the judicial organization. Section 7 of the 1964 Constitution which dealt with the judiciary was abrogated. The administrative powers of the Supreme Court were transferred to a newly established Council of Justice which is part of the Ministry of Justice and is chaired by the Minister of Justice-Attorney General. Other members of this council are high-ranking Ministry of Justice officials, including the President of the Court of Cassation. The Prime Minister has the right to appoint one or several other "learned persons" to this council. Such members may also be proposed by the Minister of Justice. The Council of Justice also will function as the High Court of the Judiciary. The ordinary court structure remains largely unchanged. At the apex is the Court of Cassation, below it are a Central Court of Appeal, provincial courts and courts of primary jurisdiction. Special courts enumerated in the decree are juvenile courts, labor courts, and the High Court of the Judiciary mentioned before.

Among the three chambers of the Court of Cassation the most important is the Chamber of Civil and Criminal Law, which deals with cases involving *shari'a* or statutory law. This chamber at present (July 1973) consists of seven judges who must be well versed in *shari'a* law according to the Hanefite rite and in the statutory law of Afghanistan. Another chamber is concerned with commercial matters, including labor disputes, patents, insurance, and the like. A third chamber deals with public law and administrative cases and has many of the functions of a court of claims or an administrative tribunal.

All judges in Afghanistan are appointed. Under the decree of 28 July 1973 judges are appointed by the President of the Republic upon proposal by the Minister of Justice. The decree of 28 July 1973 also abrogated the Law on the Organization and Function of the Judiciary of October 1967, but left intact those provisions of that law which did not contravene anything in the decree. At this time there are 28 provincial courts in Afghanistan. Below these courts are 207 primary courts distributed over the 28 provinces of the country.

On the substantive side, Afghanistan has endeavored to modernize its legal system without, however, abandoning the Islamic basis of the law. Among the major codes so far enacted is a commercial code, which was promulgated on 15 December 1955 and which follows closely the Turkish Commercial Code of 1926. A code of criminal procedure was enacted in 1966 which is generally patterned after the corresponding Egyptian code. A penal code and a civil code are still in the drafting stage.* A marriage law was enacted originally in 1962 and replaced by a new law on 10 October, 1971. Both these laws are based on Islamic principles.†

*Much of this discussion is based upon information obtained on visits to Kabul, particularly from Justice Ghulam 'Ali Karimi, Chief Judicial Administrator, Deputy Minister of Justice Samiuddin Zhouand, other officials of the Ministry of Justice, and members of the faculties of Islamic Law and of Law and Political Science of Kabul University.

†G. M. Dari, "The Latest Change in the Marriage Law of Afghanistan," *Hokouk*, no. 4 (January 1972): 1–3. See also in the same issue, 24–31, Assadullah Raid, "Comparaison entre les codes du statut personnel Syrien, Afghan, et Marocain," continued in *Hokouk* no. 3–4 (June 1974): 15–29. An English translation of the law by Prof. Dari appeared in *Hokouk* No. 1–2 (September 1973): 1–6.

Chapter 5   Anglo-Muhammadan Law

Comment: As stated before, the influence of British common law and equity has been strongest in areas where the courts were staffed by British or British-trained judges. An outstanding example of this phenomenon has been India (that is present-day India and Pakistan). It would go too far to trace here in detail the involved history of the establishment of British courts and judicial processes in India. Under the rule of the Mogul Emperors, *qadis* appointed by them administered primarily Hanefite law with the advice of *muftis*. The standard Hanefite work utilized in the Mogul courts was the *Hidaya* of Marghinani. Around 1663 the Emperor Aurangzeb (also known as 'Alamgir) appointed a commission which compiled a collection of *fatwas* and excerpts from Hanefite works. This collection became known as the *Fatawa 'Alamgiriyya*. When British courts were established in India, the British judges were aided by so-called "law officers" who, in the case of Muslims, were akin to *muftis*. In 1772 a British Regulation laid down the rule that in suits "regarding inheritance, succession, marriage and caste and other usages or institutions, the laws of the Koran with respect to the Mahomedans . . . shall be invariably adhered to." An important characteristic of the Indian judicial system as it developed under the British was that there were no religious courts. Where required, the courts of general jurisdiction applied Muslim or Hindu law. This system has been continued in present-day India and Pakistan. For the use of the British courts the *Hidaya* was translated into English from a Persian version by Charlés Hamilton and parts of the *Fatawa 'Alamgiriyya* were translated into English by Neil B. E. Baillie in his book *A Digest of Moohumudan Law*.

The practice of the British courts in India was characterized by a reliance upon the Islamic legal texts used authoritatively in India and a rejection of any deductions made by contemporary jurists of new rules of law from the ancient texts. This tendency was due to the combined influence of *taqlid* and the common-law doctrine of *stare decisis*. The British judges apparently were inclined to equate *taqlid* more or less with *stare decisis*. Appeal from the British courts in India lay in the Judicial Committee of the Privy Council in London which expressly set forth this reliance on authoritative texts in several decisions.

In *Abul Fata v. Russomoy Dhur Chowdhury* (1894) 22 I.A. 76 at 86–87, a case dealing with the validity of a family *waqf*, the Privy Council stated:

. . . The opinion of that learned Mahomedan lawyer [Ameer Ali, with regard to the character of a family *waqf*] is founded as their Lordships understand it, upon texts of an abstract character, and upon precedents very imperfectly stated. For instance, he quotes a precept of the Prophet Mahomet himself, to the effect that "A pious offering to one's family, to provide against their getting into want, is more pious than giving alms to beggars. The most excellent of *sadaqa* [a gift made to obtain merit in the eyes of God] is that which a man bestows upon his family." . . .
. . . Clearly the Mahomedan law ought to govern a purely Mahomedan disposition of property. Their Lordships have endeavored to the best of their ability to ascertain and apply the Mahomedan law, as known and administered in *India*; but they cannot find it is in accordance with the absolute, and as it seems to them extravagant, application of abstract precepts taken from the mouth of the Prophet . . . . [Nevertheless, the Privy Council in this case did not follow strict Hanefite law, but was influenced by considerations alien to the *shari'a*.]

Comment: Reliance on *taqlid* was more clearly stated by the Council in *Baker Ali Khan v. Anjuman Ara* (1903) 30 I.A. 94 at 111–112, a case dealing with the problem whether a Shi'i *waqf* can be created by will. The Council ruled on the point of interpretation of Islamic legal texts:

In *Abul Fata v. Russomoy Dhur Chowdhury*, in the judgment of this Committee delivered by Lord Hobhouse, the danger was pointed out of relying upon ancient texts of the Mahomedan law, and even precepts of the Prophet himself, of taking them literally, and deducing from them new rules of law, especially when such proposed rules do not conduce to substantial justice. That danger is equally great whether reliance is placed upon fresh texts newly brought to light, or upon fresh logical inferences newly drawn from old and undisputed texts. Their Lordships think it would be extremely dangerous to accept as a general principle that new rules of law are to be introduced because they seem to lawyers of the present day to follow logically from ancient texts however authoritative, when the ancient doctors of the law have not themselves drawn those conclusions . . . .

Comment: Modifications in the law of India were introduced, however, primarily through legislation and through the application of the British principle of "justice, equity and good conscience." British legal thought generally as reflected in decisions of the courts in India and particularly of the Privy Council in London also played an important role.

In the early nineteenth century a liberal reform movement was strong in England, and Jeremy Bentham, one of the greatest English law reformers, advocated codification of the law. Bentham himself was interested in applying his ideas to the Indian legal system. He himself never had an opportunity to initiate law reform in India, but his ideas were influential in starting and carrying through the preparation of codes. When the Charter Act of 1833, which established one legislature for the whole of British India with authority over Indians as well as Europeans, was debated in Parliament, Thomas Babington Macauly, a British lawyer, politican, and writer, stressed the need for codification in India. In a famous speech he stated:

> What is administered [in India] is not law, but a kind of rude and capricious equity . . . . We do not mean that all the people of India should live under the same law; far from it . . . . We know how desirable that object is; but we also know that it is unattainable . . . . Our principle is simply this: uniformity where you can have it, diversity where you must have it, but in all cases certainty . . . . I believe that India stands more in need of a code than any country in the world . . . . This seems to me . . . to be precisely that point of time at which the advantage of a complete written code of laws may most easily be conferred on India . . . . It is a work which especially belongs to a government like that of India, to an enlightened and paternal despotism.*

Macauly became chairman of the first Indian Law Commission, established by the Charter Act of 1833, which drafted a penal code based on English law. This code was submitted to the government in India in 1837, but the legislature did not act on it. In 1858 the government over India was assumed by the British Crown and various codes were enacted. Among these were: the Indian Penal Code, the Indian Code of Civil Procedure, the Indian Code of Criminal Procedure, and the Indian Contracts Act. The Indian Succession Act of 1865 was also based on English law and was applicable to non-Muslims and non-Hindus. Generally, personal status matters of Muslims and Hindus remained regulated by their own laws.

Comment: An Act expressly providing for the application of *shari'a* law to Muslims in India was promulgated in 1937.

The Muslim Personal Law (Shariat) Application Act, 1937.†

An Act to make provision for the application of the Muslim Personal Law (*Shariat*) to Muslims in the Provinces of India.

Whereas it is expedient to make provision for the application of the Muslim Personal Law (*Shariat*) to Muslims in the Provinces of India.

---

*Thomas Babington Macauly, *Miscellanies*, (Boston: Houghton Mifflin & Co., 1901).
†In Pakistan this Act has been replaced by the *West Pakistan Muslim Personal Law (Shariat) Application Act* (Act V of 1962, *Gazette of West Pakistan Extraordinary* of 31 December, 1962). In addition to defining, in somewhat different terms, the matters subject to *shari'a* law, the Pakistani Act also deals with some rules of inheritance regarding limited interest of females in estates.

It is hereby enacted as follows:

1. (1) This Act may be called the Muslim Personal Law (*Shariat*) Application Act, 1937.

(2) It extends to all provinces of India.

2. Notwithstanding any custom or usage to the contrary, in all questions (save questions relating to agricultural land) regarding intestate succession, special property of females, including personal property inherited or obtained under contract or gift or any other provision of Personal Law, marriage, dissolution of marriage . . . maintenance, dower, guardianship, gifts, trusts and trust properties, and *waqfs* (other than charities and charitable institutions and charitable and religious endowments) the rule of decision in cases where the parties are Muslims shall be the Muslim Personal Law (*Shariat*).

3. (1) Any person who satisfies the prescribed authority

(a) that he is a Muslim, and

(b) that he is competent to contract within the meaning of section 11 of the Indian Contract Act, 1872, [that section provides that any person can contract who has reached majority, is of sound mind and not disqualified from contracting], and

(c) that he is a resident of a Province of India, may by declaration in the prescribed form and filed before the prescribed authority declare that he desires to obtain the benefit of the provisions of this section, and thereafter the provisions of section 2 shall apply to the declarant and all his minor children and their descendants as if in addition to the matters enumerated therein adoption, wills and legacies were also specified . . . .

Comment: With regard to the use of "justice, equity and good conscience" the following has been stated:

J. DUNCAN M. DERRETT, "Justice, Equity and Good Conscience," pp. 139–140.*

The provisions of the Regulations of 1781 for the judge to apply justice, equity and good conscience were copied from Regulation to Regulation, and from Regulation to Statute, and this residual source of law is now firmly fixed in South Asia. The area in which it can operate is progressively narrowed, but gaps in the personal laws (especially Hindu and Islamic) and gaps left in the interstices between them, where a conflict of personal laws can occur,—gaps, too, in the judge-made uncodified topics of private and public law—may still be filled by reference to this source. [After discussing the historical development of this source of law in India, the author continues.]

Ibid., pp. 143–147.

From 1880, or thereabouts to the present day the formula has meant consultation of various systems of law according to the context. The dictum in the Privy Council which is so often cited

*Reprinted by permission of George Allen and Unwin, London, copyright 1963.

[*Waghela v. Sheikh* (1887) 14 I.A. 89 at 96], and which leads to the view that English law will first be consulted wherever the formula applies, is just not true, In trusts, guardianship, tort and contract, English law is indeed looked to first. So also in conflict of laws questions (on topics like domicile), and constitutional matters, though American rules frequently compete for attention, if not as frequently as might be desirable. In those contexts where English law is consulted as a matter of course, there is no reason to suppose that English common law, as distinct from English law as a whole, ought to be regarded. The suggestion that we have to consider particularly the common law, to the exclusion of statutory amendments, is incorrect: it is to a developed system of law that we must refer, and we cannot ignore the developments which have occurred in the system we chose for first reference . . . .

In other fields of law the priority of English rules is by no means admitted. Where the systems of personal law are silent, or where they are inapplicable because the religions of the parties differ, the English law, and indeed other systems of foreign law, seem hardly the obvious choice. In practice analogies are sometimes drawn from the nearest personal law. The effects can be incongruous, but perhaps less harm is done than by the application of a system utterly unconnected with the parties' contemplation when they entered into the transaction which gave rise to the action. Where there is no possibility of reference to a personal law, reference to no specific law, to a statute, or to the English law as a last resort is found.

．　　．　　．　　．

A further use for the formula arises where the doctrines of the personal laws are obscure because of differences of opinion between the native jurists. In *Aziz Bano v. Muhammad Ibrahim* [(1925) 47 All. 823] it was held that a choice most consistent with justice, equity and good conscience could be made between the conflicting opinions in Islamic law . . . .

It remains to discuss a peculiar feature of "justice, equity and good conscience" as known in South Asia. Repeatedly advocates attempt to argue that a provision of the personal law or indeed of some statutes, is not to be applied in the circumstances because it would be contrary to equity and good conscience so to do. In no case have they succeeded. It is very curious that this argument should be raised, since in *Moonshee Buzloor Ruheem v. Shumsoonissa Begum* [(1867) 11 M.I.A. 551] the Privy Council indignantly and with great emphasis repelled the notion that a definite rule of the personal law could be nullified because it did not square with the court's notion of justice, equity and good conscience . . . .

Comment: On the basis of these principles and enactments a very large body of case law has developed with many cases decided by the Privy Council. Cases involving Islamic law were decided by British courts also in other parts of the Empire, such as East Africa or Zanzibar. These cases have contributed to the case law on this subject. These developments have given Islamic law as applied in these formerly British territories a distinctive quality. It was Islamic law as seen primarily by British judges, who not always fully grasped it in its intrinsic meaning and who interpreted it according to English principles of equitable justice. Therefore, this Anglo-Muhammadan law is a specific growth and cannot readily be used as a guide to the rules of Islamic law as applied in countries which have been outside this system, such as, for example, Egypt, Syria, or Lebanon.

The approach of the British courts in India and of the Privy Council has been criticized in Pakistan by the Commission on Marriage and Family Laws in its Report published in the *Official Gazette of Pakistan* on 20 June 1956. The Commission stated:

. . . Like the Romans the British adopted the policy of non-interference in the personal laws of the different religious communities and so the Muslims in this respect were ruled by what is called Anglo-Muhammadan Law. Muslim law, thus introduced ceased to be a growing organism responsive to progressive forces and changing needs. What was accepted as the personal law of the Muslims was conservative, rigid, and in many respects undefined . . . .*

The Pakistani courts have continued to take into account the case law created during the period of British control. However, they have struck out on their own and particularly with regard to the application of Muslim law have gone considerably further than the courts did during the British period. A good example is *Khurshid Jan v. Fazal Dad, 1965 Pakistan Law Reports (West Pakistan) 1*, 312. The case was relatively simple. Khurshid Jan, the appellant, had been given in marriage before attaining puberty and on attaining puberty exercised the option, given her by Islamic law, of repudiating the marriage. She filed a civil suit for a declaration to that effect. However, after filing suit, the girl went to the house of her husband, where cohabitation took place. The claim of the appellant that she was forced to come to the house of the respondent with the help of the police and that she did not cohabit with him was dismissed by the courts below. Nevertheless, the trial judge held that the repudiation had taken effect with the institution of the suit and that therefore the later cohabitation was not relevant. This decision was reversed on appeal by the district judge who held that according to an authoritative Hanafi text, the court cannot make a declaration on the repudiation of the marriage if the wife after exercising her option of puberty cohabits with the husband.

Khurshid Jan appealed against this decision to the High Court. In their briefs both sides raised basic questions of interpretation of Islamic law and three questions were referred to the full bench of five judges for comment. These questions were:

1. What are the sources of Muslim law?

2. What are the rules of interpretation of Muslim law and can courts differ from the views of the *imams* and other juris-consults of Muslim law on grounds of public policy, justice, equity, and good conscience?

*Pakistan, *Gazette Extraordinary*, 20 June 1956, 1197 at p. 1203.

3. In case of conflict of views found in text books on Muslim law, such as the Hidaya, the Fatawa 'Alamgiriyya, the Radd al-Mukhtar, how are the courts to determine which of the views is correct. This question was reframed so as to read: How are the courts to be guided in case of conflict of view among the founders of different schools of Muslim law and their disciples, other *imams* and *faqihs* [Islamic jurists]?

In a very lengthy opinion the court addressed itself to these three questions. The majority opinion (three of the five judges) held:

Khurshid Jan v. *Fazal Dad*, p. 360, paragraph 38.

. . . As seen above, the primary sources of Law are the Qur'an and *Hadith*, while *ijma'*, *qiyas, ijtihad* and *istidlal* are the secondary sources; *istihsan* and *istislah* being doctrines of equity and not an independent source. [In defining the sources of Islamic law, the court thus diverges somewhat from the classical theory of the four roots of Islamic jurisprudence. *Istidlal* is defined by the court in paragraph 37 as inferring one thing from another. The opinion states that the Hanefite jurists used this term in connection with the rules of interpretation, whereas the Malikites and Shafi-'ites consider it as a distinct method of juristic deduction not falling within the scope of *qiyas*.]

As to the rules of interpretation of Muslim Law: A clear injunction in the Qur'an and *Sunna* is binding and no departure is permissible provided that if the effective cause of an injunction has disappeared or an injunction was confined to the facts of a particular case its extension is not warranted . . . .

P. 374, paragraph 45. As to the competence of courts to differ from the view of earlier *imams* and *faqihs* on the grounds of public policy, justice, equity and good conscience, it may be admitted that this part of the question is not properly framed. As seen above, a *qadi* or a court of law may differ with the *qiyas* of earlier *imams* and *faqihs*, but that will be on the basis of interpretation and extension of the rule of decision contained in Qur'anic and Traditional text or *ijma'* and not on the basis of what appears to be more agreeable to the judge. A reference has been made earlier to the rules of *istihsan* and *istislah*, two distinct doctrines of Muslim jurisprudence. If there is no clear rule of decision in Qur'anic and Traditional text nor an *ijma'* or a binding juristic analogy (*qiyas*), a *qadi* or a court may resort to private reasoning (*istidlal*) and, in that he will undoubtedly be guided by the rules of justice, equity and good conscience, or in terms of the *fiqh*, by the doctrines of *istihsan* and *istislah* . . . .

P. 377, paragraph 48. The answer to the third question may be summed up thus:

There can be no disagreement in matters which are provided for in the Qur'anic and Traditional text. Similarly, *ijma'* is binding upon all until changed or modified by another *ijma'*. There is thus no room for a court to disagree with it, for according to the tradition relied upon by *Imam* Shafi'i "Whatever the community of Islam may agree upon at any time is of God." In the case of juristic analogy and *istidlal* it is open to courts to adopt any one of the conflicting views of the earlier *imams* and *faqihs*, subject, of course, to the qualification that they possess the requisite knowledge. Lastly, *ijma'* and *ijtihad* in the form of law made by the competent legislative bodies, as envisaged by the modern reformist jurists, will be binding on courts and it is not permissible for them to differ from those laws on the grounds that they conflict with the views of the earlier *imams* and *faqihs*. [The appeal was accordingly sent back for disposal in the light of the reply of the full bench. Actually, a second case, substantively unrelated had been joined for purposes of this opinion to the case of *Khurshid Jan v. Fazal Dad*. It was a petition by Zohra Begum in a guardianship case which raised similar fundamental questions. That petition also was sent back for disposal.]

Comment: Of the remaining two judges only one dissented, the other filed a concurring opinion. This concurring opinion stated the issue of the court's right to differ from the earlier Muslim jurists very succinctly:

Ibid., p. 399.

. . . the courts must be given the right to interpret for themselves the Qur'an and *Sunna*; and . . . they may also differ from the views of the earlier juris-consults of Muslim Law on grounds of *istihsan* (i.e., equity) or *istislah* (i.e., public good) in matters not governed by a Qur'anic or Traditional text or *ijma'* or a binding *qiyas*. At the same time, it must be reiterated that the views of the earlier jurists and *imams* are entitled to the utmost respect and cannot be lightly disturbed, but the right to differ from them must not be denied to the present-day courts functioning in Pakistan, as such a denial will not only be a negation of the true spirit of Islam, but also of the constitutional and legal obligation resting on all courts to interpret the law they are called upon to administer and apply in cases coming before them.

Comment: In this decision the Pakistani Full Bench thus asserted far-reaching powers for the courts which in effect amount to a denial of *taqlid* and, within limits, reestablish a right of *ijtihad*. Of interest is also the endeavour of the court to harmonize Islamic legal concepts and those derived from English common law, particularly justice, equity, and good conscience.

Part Two

Systematic Survey of Selected Principles of Classical Islamic Law and Present-day Near and Middle Eastern Law

While usul al-fiqh (*roots of the law*) *refers to the basic principles of Islamic jurisprudence,* furu' al-fiqh (*branches of the law*) *characterizes what we would call positive law. This section presents a selection of principles of the positive law of Islam as set forth in well-known texts of the orthodox schools. For each major area of the law the Islamic rules are followed by excerpts from codes and statutes now in effect as well as from legal writings and decisions to show the changes which have been made and also to provide some insight into the present-day law of the various countries discussed.*

Chapter 6   The Law of Marriage and Divorce

A. Classical Islamic Law

Comment: In Islamic law the marriage contract was patterned after the contract of sale which generally was regarded as the basic form of contract serving as a model for others. Characteristic of classical Islamic law was the ease of divorce for the husband. Divorce for the woman was not impossible, but much more difficult. Polygamy was permissible, but the Muslim was restricted to four wives and had to give equal treatment to them. The marriage is concluded between the nearest male relative of the bride (*wali*) and the bridegroom. The bridegroom must give a dowry to the bride. In the following some of the important provisions on marriage and divorce are given on the basis of the Qur'an and of authoritative works of the orthodox schools.

1. Marriage Generally

Qur'an, Sura IV.

Verse 3 . . . marry of the women, who seem good to you, two or three or four; and if ye fear that you cannot do justice (to so many) then one only or (the captives) that your right hand possesses. Thus it is more likely that ye will not do injustice.

Verse 4. And give unto the women, (whom ye marry) free gift of their marriage portions; but if they of their own accord remit unto you a part thereof, then ye are welcome to absorb it (in your wealth).

Comment: The following discussion is taken from a Hanefite work. Its author is Abu al-Husayn 'Ali bin Muhammad bin Ahmad bin Ja'far bin Hamdan al-Quduri who lived in Baghdad from A.D. 974 to 1039 and in his day was the head of the Hanefite school in Iraq. His most important work was his *Mukhtasar* (compendium).

2. The Conclusion of the Marriage

a. Formalities

AL-QUDURI, *Mukhtasar*, pp. 12–13.

The marriage is concluded by the offer [by one party] and acceptance [by the other]. [These acts] are expressed by two formulas either both of them being in the perfect or one in the perfect and the other in the imperfect. Thus, for example, the bridegroom may say: "Give me [your daughter] in marriage." And the person asked answers: "I have given her to you in marriage." The marriage of Muslims must be concluded in the presence of two witnesses who are free, of age, sound in mind and Muslims, or in the presence of one male and two female [witnesses] . . . .

Comment: The provision regarding the tenses to be used in the exchange of the formulas is needed because Arabic does not have tenses in the sense in which English has them. The Arabic verb has two basic forms, one which expresses completed action (the so-called perfect or past) and one which expresses incomplete action (the imperfect or aorist). The latter form can apply to present or future action. Thus in concluding a contract at least one party would have to use a verb form indicating completed action, otherwise the undertaking could be construed merely as a promise for the future.

b. Impediments to Marriage

Ibid., pp. 12–15.

A man is not permitted to marry his mother, his grandmothers, ancestors on the male and female side, his daughter or the daughter of his child and further in the descending line. [A man is also not permitted to marry] his sister or the daughters of his sister, the daughters of his brother, his paternal aunt, his maternal aunt, or the mother of his wife, whether or not the marriage with the daughter has been consummated. [The prohibition also applies] to the daughter of one's wife if the marriage had been consummated with the wife . . . etc. [He also may not marry] his mother or sister through milk kinship . . . .

Comment: This enumeration, not all of which was included, provides a good example of a painstaking and casuistic approach to the problem of prohibited degrees. The relationship through milk is that established between a child and his wetnurse and is still regarded as an impediment to marriage in modern Near Eastern statutes. Islamic law is not unique in attaching legal consequences to this relationship. In Roman law the slave who was linked with the master through milk kinship had certain advantages with regard to manumission.

c. *The Role of the Wali*

Ibid., pp. 16–21.

The marriage of a free woman who is of age and of sound mind is validly concluded through her consent, even if a *wali* does not intervene for her in this transaction. This is according to the opinion of Abu Hanifa, whether the woman is a virgin or not. However, according to Abu Yusuf and Muhammad a valid marriage can be concluded for a woman only through the *wali*. A *wali* must not force a virgin who is of age into marriage. If he requests her authorization and she is silent or laughs, this is regarded as constituting authorization. If she refuses he may not make her marry. If the *wali* requests authorization from a woman who is no longer a virgin, express consent is required . . . .

The *wali* may conclude a marriage in the name of persons of either sex who are minors, whether the girl is a virgin or not. The *wali* must be an agnate. Thus if the boy or girl who are minors are given in marriage by the father or grandfather, they do not have an option after reaching majority. If, however, they have been given in marriage by somebody other than the father or grandfather, they have an option upon reaching majority and may decide whether to continue or dissolve their marriage. A slave, a minor, or a psychopath may not function as *wali*. An unbeliever may not be the *wali* of a believer . . . .

d. *Equality of the Spouses*

Ibid., pp. 22–23.

In concluding a marriage, equality of the spouses must be observed. If a woman is married without the existence of equality, then it is incumbent upon the *wali* to have the spouses separated. Equality must exist with regard to lineage, piety and means, that is, the husband must be able to pay the dowry and provide for the wife's upkeep. There must also be equality of occupation between the father of the woman and the future husband.

e. *The Dowry*

Ibid., pp. 22–35.

If a woman concludes the marriage herself and agrees to a lesser dowry than is her due on the basis of the principle of equality, then the *wali* shall object to the marriage, according to Abu Hanifa, until the husband provides the remainder of the proper dowry. Otherwise he shall have the marriage dissolved. If the father has given in marriage his minor daughter on the basis of a lesser dowry, or his minor son and the latter has consented to a dowry for his wife larger than required by the principle of equality, these stipulations shall remain valid to the detriment of the minors. However, these transactions shall only be valid if concluded by the father or grandfather. A marriage is valid whether a dowry has been stipulated or not. The minimal dowry is ten *dirhem*. If one has stipulated less than ten, the woman still has a right to ten . . . . If the husband repudiates his wife before consummation of the marriage or before they are alone together, the wife has a right to half of the dowry stipulated. If the husband has married his wife without any stipulation regarding the dowry or specifying that there will not be a dowry, she has the right to an appropriate dowry after the marriage is consummated or if the husband dies leaving her a widow. If in this case the husband repudiates the wife before consummation of the marriage, she has a right to a consolation gift, namely three pieces of clothing as women of her station wear . . . .

If the husband increases the dowry after the marriage is concluded, such increase is to be paid, except in the case of repudiation before consummation. If the wife consents to a decrease in the dowry, such decrease is valid.

If the husband is left alone with his wife and there is no obstacle to the consummation of the marriage, and then he repudiates her, she has a right to the whole dowry. If, however, one of the spouses is ill or is fasting during Ramadan or is in a state of sexual abstinence because of a compulsory or voluntary pilgrimage, or a "little pilgrimage," or if the woman is menstruating, then no real seclusion is taking place . . . .

The appropriate dowry of a woman is determined by the dowries of her non-uterine sisters, of her paternal aunts, and of the daughters of her paternal uncle. It is not determined by the dowries of her mother or of her maternal aunts, unless they belong to the same tribe. In determining the dowry one should also take into account that [the women whose dowry is being compared] must be equal in age, beauty, chastity, wealth, intelligence, piety, and place of residence. They should also be contemporaries [in outlook and habits].

3. Support of the Wife and of Children (nafaqa)

Ibid., pp. 54–55.

Support has to be given by the husband to his wife, be she a Muslim or an unbeliever, provided she submits herself to him in his house. The husband should give his wife maintenance, clothes and shelter. [In evaluating the support] one should take into account the respective situation of the two spouses and whether the husband is rich or poor . . . .

Ibid., pp. 64–65.

The support of minor children is the duty of the father exclusively.

4. *Repudiation (Divorce)*

a. *Qur'anic Provisions*

Qur'an, Sura II.

Verse 226. Those who forswear their wives must wait four months; then, if they change their minds, lo! Allah is Forgiving, Merciful.

Verse 227. And if they decide upon divorce (let them remember that) Allah is Hearer, Knower.

Verse 228. Women who are divorced shall wait, keeping themselves apart, three (monthly) courses. And it is not lawful for them that they should conceal that which Allah has created in their wombs if they are believers in Allah and the Last Day. And their husbands would do better to take them back in that case if they desire a reconciliation. And they (women) have rights similar to those of (men) over them in kindness, and men are a degree above them. Allah is Mighty, Wise.

Verse 229. Divorce must be pronounced twice and then (a woman) must be retained in honor or released in kindness. And it is not lawful for you that ye take from women aught of that which ye have given them; except (in the case) when both fear that they may not be able to keep within the limits (imposed by) Allah. And if ye fear that they may not be able to keep the limits of Allah, in that case it is no sin for either of them if the woman ransom herself. These are the limits (imposed by) Allah. Transgress them not. For whoso transgresseth Allah's limits: such are wrongdoers.

Verse 230. And if he hath divorced her (the third time), then she is not lawful unto him thereafter until she hath wedded another husband. Then if he (the other husband) divorce her it is no sin for both of them that they come together again if they consider that they are able to observe the limits of Allah. These are the limits of Allah. He manifested them for people who have knowledge.

Sura XXXIII

Verse 49. O ye who believe! If ye wed believing women and divorce them before ye have touched them, then there is no period that ye should reckon. But content them and release them handsomely.

b. *Writings of Jurists*

AL-QUDURI, *Mukhtasar*, pp. 80–89.

There are three types of repudiation (*talaq*): the so-called better (*ahsan*) one, the recommended one (*sunna*), and the new (*bid'a*) one. In the *ahsan* repudiation the man repudiates his wife by a single repudiation during one inter-menstrual period during which he does not have sexual relations with her and also does not touch her until the end of her *'idda* [the legal period that must elapse before a woman can remarry after divorce or the death of her husband].

The *sunna* repudiation consists in the threefold repudiation of a wife with whom the marriage has been consummated, during three inter-menstrual periods.

The *bid'a* repudiation consists of the threefold repudiation of the wife in a single statement or during a single inter-menstrual period. If the husband does this, the repudiation is irrevocable and the husband commits a sin.

The recommended (*sunna*) method of repudiation has two aspects, the proper timing and the proper number. With regard to the proper number, it is not important whether or not the marriage has been consummated. Proper timing is only important in case the marriage has been consummated. Then the husband must repudiate his wife during an inter-menstrual period and must not have sexual relations with her. If the marriage has not been consummated, the repudiation may take place during the inter-menstrual period or during menstruation . . . . The repudiation can be pronounced validly by any husband who is of age and sound in mind. A repudiation pronounced by a minor, a person of unsound mind or a person who is asleep is invalid . . . .

Repudiation can be accomplished in two ways: through an explicit declaration or through implication. The explicit declaration states either "you are repudiated," or "you have been repudiated," or "I repudiate you." These formulas bring about a revocable repudiation. This repudiation counts only as a single one, even if the husband intended it to be multiple. Intent does not influence the effectiveness of this repudiation. If a husband without any special intention [regarding the number of repudiations] uses the formula "for your repudiation," or "you are repudiated through a repudiation," or "you are repudiated according to the repudiation," a revocable single repudiation results. If, however, he intended a triple repudiation it shall be regarded as such. The second kind is repudiation through implication. This is not effective unless the husband had the intention to repudiate his wife or the situation is evident . . . .

5. Revocation of Repudiation

Ibid., pp. 108–109.

If a husband repudiates his wife through a revocable repudiation or through two repudiations he can take her back during her *'idda* whether she consents or not . . . .

Ibid., pp. 114–115.

If it is an irrevocable repudiation of the new kind but not a triple one, the husband may again marry his wife during her *'idda* or after her *'idda* has ended. However, if it is a triple repudiation . . . he may not marry the woman until after she has married another husband in a valid marriage which has been consummated and which has been dissolved either through repudiation by the second husband or through his death which has taken him away from her . . . .

6. Divorce Through Payment by the Wife (khulʿ)

Ibid., pp. 118–121.

If there is discord between the spouses and they are loath to transgress the prescriptions of Allah, it is not wrong if the wife buys her freedom from her husband by means of something of value. He then divorces her through *khulʿ*. If he does that, the *khulʿ* has the effect of a single irrevocable repudiation and she has to pay the promised value. If the fault is on the part of the husband, it is wrong for him to receive compensation from his wife. If the fault lies with the wife, it is wrong if he accepts a compensation greater than what he has given her [as dowry] . . . . Anything that can lawfully constitute a dowry can also constitute a compensation in this type of divorce.

7. The ʿIdda

Ibid., pp. 156–159.

If a husband repudiates his wife through irrevocable or revocable repudiation or if the spouses have separated without repudiation, and the wife is free and has menstruations, then her *ʿidda* shall be three periods, the periods being the menstrual periods. [This is according to the Hanefites, the other orthodox rites take the inter-menstrual periods.] If the wife does not have menstrual periods because she is too young or too old, her *ʿidda* shall be three months. If the wife is pregnant, her *ʿidda* ends with the end of her pregnancy . . . .

If a man dies and leaves a widow who is free, the *ʿidda* lasts four months and ten days . . . . If the widow is pregnant, the *ʿidda* lasts until the end of pregnancy.

8. Maintenance of the Divorced Wife

Comment: Islamic law, like Roman law, did not know alimony as it is understood today in Western legal systems. Restitution of the dowry provided support for the repudiated wife, but in addition the husband had to provide maintenance for a limited period. The Qur'an enjoins husbands to provide reasonable maintenance for their divorced wives (Sura 11, 241). Al-Quduri gives the following details:

Ibid., pp. 56–57.

If the husband repudiates his wife, she has a right to maintenance and lodgings during her *'idda,* whether the repudiation is revocable or irrevocable. The widow does not have a right to maintenance. If the separation is due to a grievous wrong on the part of the wife, no maintenance is due her. Likewise, if the husband repudiates his wife because she has been guilty of apostasy, he does not have to provide maintenance . . . .

B. Present-day Islamic Countries

1. General

Comment: This field of law is still covered by Islamic legal principles in most Muslim countries, but the need felt for adaptation to present-day requirements has brought about significant modifications.

J. N. D. ANDERSON, "Recent Reforms in Family Law in the Arab World," pp. 3–7.*

The expedients by means of which recent reforms in family law have been effected within the Islamic system itself—nominally at least—represent a fascinating example of how an allegedly immutable law can in fact be changed in practice. They all come under the broad heading of the right of the Ruler to confine and define the jurisdiction of his courts, and include:

a. *The Procedural Device of Excluding Certain Claims, in Specified Circumstances, from all Judicial Enforcement.*

This makes it possible for the reformers to disclaim any intention of changing the substantive law as such, yet at the same time to deprive that substantive law of most of its practical relevance.

From one point of view, it is true, this may be regarded as no more than a further example of the expedient by which, from the middle of the last century, whole chapters of the law have been removed from the competence of the *shari'a* courts and entrusted to secular courts which apply codes of a wholly different origin. Yet, from another point of view, there is this essential difference; that, in this case, no alternative courts or law have been provided, and certain claims which the *shari'a* would have enforced are simply left without any means of judicial enforcement. It is precisely on this point that the critics, not unnaturally, have seized; they admit the ruler's right to transfer litigation of this sort or that from the competence of one court to that of another, but they insist that this must never involve a denial of justice.

*Reprinted by permission of Ferdinand Enke Verlag, Stuttgart, and the author.

A good example of the use of this device may be found in the measures adopted in Egypt to restrict the evils of child marriage. In deference to Muslim sentiments (and the example of the Prophet himself) child marriage was not actually forbidden; instead, the courts were precluded from entertaining any matrimonial cause in respect of a disputed marriage where the contract had not been registered, and the registrars of marriage were forbidden to register any union in which the parties had not reached the ages of eighteen and sixteen respectively. And many other problems have been somewhat similarly solved, both in Egypt and elsewhere; for the hazards of relying on that oral testimony which is fundamental to the pure *shari'a* have been repeatedly minimized, for instance, by legislation which precludes the courts from entertaining, in specified circumstances, any claim which is not based on documentary evidence.

b. *The Eclectic Device of Deriving a Code of Law from the Dicta of a Variety of Different Schools and Jurists.*

This expedient is indeed basic to the contemporary movement for the reform of the *shari'a* law as enforced by the courts, and has been applied on a number of different levels.

It has long been admitted by Muslim jurists that the individual Muslim, in his private life, is not bound in every particular to follow the dominant opinion in the school to which he happens to belong. Instead, he may elect to follow the view of some other reputable authority of the past in this matter or that. It is true that the jurists have differed greatly as to the principles on which such choice should be made; but the salient point, in this context, is that they have commonly denied any such latitude whatever to the judge and the juris-consult in their public capacity, and have insisted that these are bound to follow the dominant view of their school in every particular. Authority can, however, be found in the Shafi'i and Hanafi texts for the proposition that it is within the competence of the ruler to require his judges to adopt, instead, the opinion of some other reputable Muslim jurist, wherever the public interest may so require.

It was on this principle that the compilers of the *Majalla* relied in abandoning the dominant Hanafi doctrine, on occasions, for some other view for which some Hanafi support might be adduced. But it was not until 1915 that this expedient was applied in the sphere of family law. In the Decrees of 1915 and the Ottoman Law of Family Rights, 1917, the Turks contented themselves with the substitution of some "weaker" Hanafi opinion, or the dominant doctrine of some other Sunni school, in place of the authoritative Hanafi view; but the Egyptian reformers soon went much further, and adopted the doctrines of extinct schools such as the Zahiris, of early jurists who lived before the schools crystalised, of independent reformers such as Ibn Taymiya and Ibn al-Qayyim, and even (although without acknowledgement) of "heterodox" sects such as the Shi'is. In addition, they sometimes combined part of the doctrine of one school or jurist with part of the doctrine of another in such a way as to produce a result which, in aggregate, was wholly new—and this despite the fact that the two views so combined might rest on wholly different, and even contradictory premises.

The outstanding examples of the milder forms of such "*talfiq*" may be found in legislation—in Turkey, Egypt and elsewhere—granting ill-used wives, in a variety of circumstances, the right to a judicial divorce, for almost all such innovations had ample authority in the dominant doctrine of some of the Sunni schools. In the same way the most obvious examples of the more radical use of this principle can be seen in some of the attempts which have been made to circumscribe the enormous scope previously given to formulae of repudiation pronounced by Muslim husbands; for the legislation which reduces the effect of the "triple" divorce, when pronounced in a single formula, to that of a single and therefore revocable divorce, or which limits or precludes the validity of a conditional repudiation which takes the form of an oath or threat, rests on much more controversial juristic authority. And the same can, of course, be said about the enactments in Egypt and Iraq which provide that effect will be given to a bequest to an heir, even by a Sunni Muslim, regardless of the attitude of the other heirs—provided only that the testator has not made bequests which, in aggregate, exceed one-third of his net estate.

It should be noted in passing that the use of this eclectic expedient inevitably involved at least a partial codification of the law by legislative enactment. It is in this context that the *Majalla* may be regarded as a major break with the theories—and practice—of the previous history of Islam.

c. *The Expedient of Re-Interpreting the Original Sources of the Law in a Way for Which There has been no Precedent in the Past.*

This procedure runs directly counter to the doctrine of the "closing of the door of *ijtihad*" (i.e., the faculty of independent deduction from the original sources) which has prevailed in Sunni Islam from the end of the third century of the Muslim era until quite recent years. It also, in most cases, runs counter to the doctrine of consensus, at least in the sense that there is a tacit consensus that, however many alternative solutions may have been put forward in the past, no new interpretation is now possible. It is for these reasons that the reformers have almost always denied that their innovations are based on this expedient, even when they have supported the right of modern Muslims to indulge in independent deductions. Instead, they have preferred to represent their reforms as resting on an eclectic choice between the authorities of the past, even in an extreme and logically contradictory fashion. It is clear, however, that in a number of cases the reformers have, in fact, felt free to improvise in a way for which there is no precedent. Such, for example, is the fixing of the maximum period of gestation at one solar year; such too, are the attempts to restrict or prevent polygamy by providing judicial enforcement for conditions which were previously regarded as binding only on the individual conscience; and such, again, are the provisions which authorise the courts to assess and decree that compensation to a wife who has been repudiated without adequate cause which the Malikis and Shafiʿis regard as always incumbent on the husband, but do not enforce by temporal sanctions.

d. *The Expedient of Promulgating Regulations Which are Regarded "Not Contrary to the Shariʿa," However Much They May Break New Ground.*

Outstanding examples of this may be found in the prohibition of child-marriage or of the unilateral repudiation of a wife without reference to a court of law. Frequently, moreover, this expedient is combined with one of the other devices in order to effect the desired reform. Examples of its use in combination with (a) above may be found in legislation which requires the registration of marriage contracts, and which denies judicial recognition to unregistered unions; of its use in combination with (b) in legislation which enforces the view of three early jurists that guardians may not give minor wards in marriage; and of its use in combination with (c) in legislation which forbids or restricts polygamy. In all such cases it is argued that the *shariʿa* itself requires obedience to those in authority: provided, therefore, that the regulation concerned is not actually contrary to the divine law, it may be regarded as virtually sanctioned thereby. All the same, a number of questions necessarily arise. What, for instance, is the status of a marriage or divorce which contravenes such regulations? If the essential validity of such marriage or divorce is recognised, many jurists are perfectly prepared to admit the right of the State to impose a criminal sanction for the breach of the relevant regulation. Others would go further, and acquiesce in the denial of any judicial recognition to such marriage or divorce. But this opens the door to a dichotomy between the law which the courts impose and the law which the consciences of many regard as incumbent—even, that is, in such a basic matter as whether A and B are married, divorced, or free to marry someone else. But this is a common phenomenon today, even in the Western world.

Comment: In the following the changes made in personal status law will be illustrated by excerpts from legislation, explanatory memoranda, and decisions of local courts. As far as the Arab states are concerned, Egyptian law has been taken as example generally, except where the law of other Arab countries was more illustrative or provided innovations not found in Egyptian law.

2. *The Law of Marriage and Divorce in the Arab Countries*

a. *Changes Concerning Divorce*

(1) Judicial Divorce for Wives

Egyptian Law No. 25 of 12 July 1920.

Article 4. If the husband refuses to provide maintenance for his wife, the judgment granting such maintenance shall be executed against his assets, if such assets are evident. If he does not have such and if the husband, without raising the question of solvency or insolvency, refuses to pay for the wife's maintenance, the *qadi* shall immediately grant a divorce. If the husband claims insolvency, but cannot prove it, the *qadi* also shall immediately grant a divorce. If, however, the husband proves that he is insolvent the *qadi* shall allow him a delay of not more than one month within which he must provide for the maintenance of his wife. If he fails to do so, the *qadi* shall grant a divorce.

[Article 5 deals with nonsupport during the husband's absence.]

Article 6. The divorce for lack of maintenance is considered a revocable repudiation. The husband may take his wife back if he establishes his solvency and shows himself ready to provide maintenance for his wife during the *'idda* period. If he does not establish his solvency and does not declare that he is ready to provide maintenance for his wife, the taking back of the wife is invalid.

. . . . .

Article 9. If the husband is afflicted with a grave disease which is incurable or likely to be of long duration and which makes the marriage relationship harmful to the wife, such as madness or leprosy, the latter can demand divorce. Provided, however, that the wife was in ignorance of the disease if it preceded the marriage or did not consent to continue the marriage relationship if the disease started after the marriage had been entered into.

Divorce cannot be pronounced if the illness was known to the wife at the time of the marriage or in case the illness began after the marriage, the wife knew about it and consented to the continuation of the marriage relationship either expressly or tacitly.

Article 10. The divorce for reasons of illness is considered as an irrevocable repudiation.

Egyptian Decree-law No. 25 of 10 March 1929.

Article 6. If the wife claims that her husband has treated her in a way that makes living together intolerable for persons of their social standing, she can demand that the *qadi* grant a divorce. The *qadi* will grant an irrevocable divorce to the wife, provided the ill-treatment is established and he cannot reconcile the spouses.

If he rejects the demand and it is renewed and the ill-treatment cannot be proven, then the *qadi* shall delegate two arbitrators and shall judge the matter as prescribed in Articles 7, 8, 9, 10, and 11 of the present law.

Article 7. The arbitrators must be men of good standing, chosen from among the members of the families of the two spouses, if possible, and if not, from among persons familiar with the situation in the household and in a position to effect a reconciliation.

Article 8. The arbitrators shall investigate the causes of disagreement between the spouses and try to effect a reconciliation. If reconciliation can be effected under certain specific conditions they shall ascertain such conditions.

Article 9. If the arbitrators cannot effect a reconciliation between the spouses and the fault is on the part of the husband or on the part of both spouses, or if the arbitrators cannot determine who was at fault, they shall rule that a separation through an irrevocable divorce should be effected.

Article 10. In case of disagreement between the arbitrators the *qadi* shall order them to resume their investigation. If the disagreement continues, he shall appoint two different arbitrators.

Article 11. The arbitrators must submit their decision to the *qadi* who shall pronounce judgment in accordance with that decision.

Article 12. If the husband is absent one year or longer without legitimate reason and the wife complains about this absence, she can demand that the *qadi* grant an irrevocable divorce, even if the husband has left behind property from which the wife could satisfy her maintenance needs.

Article 13. If it is possible to communicate with the absent husband, the *qadi* shall set a time limit and summon him to return and live again with his wife or to have her come to him, within that set time limit and under pain of divorce.

If the husband does not comply within the time limit and does not furnish a legitimate excuse, the *qadi* shall pronounce an irrevocable divorce.

If it is impossible to communicate with the absent husband, the *qadi* shall pronounce the divorce without summons to the husband and without setting a time limit.

Article 14. If the husband has been subject to a final conviction to a penalty restricting freedom for a period of three years or more, the wife may, after her husband has been imprisoned for one year, petition the *qadi* for an irrevocable divorce on grounds that the situation is harmful to her, even if the husband possesses property from which she could satisfy her maintenance needs . . . .

Explanatory Memorandum to the Draft Law Concerning Certain Questions Affecting Personal Status, Decree-law No. 25 of 10 March 1929.

Comments on Articles 6 to 11:

Disagreement between the spouses is a source of great evils, the effects of which are not restricted to the spouses, but extend to their offspring and to all persons linked to them through blood or marriage. No opinion in the doctrine of Abu Hanifa gives the wife a means of freeing herself from such a situation nor does it provide any means of making the husband mend his ways. . . .

Also, it is possible that the wife may claim separate maintenance for the sole reason of creating difficulties for her husband and to extract money from him. On his part, the husband may call upon his wife to reestablish a joint household merely to divest himself of the obligation to provide separate maintenance and to make her submit, once he has her under his power, to all kinds of ill-treatment. There are furthermore various problems which can arise from the enforcement of a judgment to reestablish a joint household or a judgment providing separate maintenance by means of execution against the person, without counting the crimes and other offenses which may result if the disagreement continues.

All these problems were demonstrated clearly to the Ministry through the many complaints which it had received and it was therefore considered in the interest of general welfare to adopt the doctrine of the Imam Ibn Malik concerning disagreement between spouses, except in the case where the arbitrators find that the fault lies exclusively with the wife. This was done so as not to encourage a quarrelsome wife to break the marriage bonds without just reasons.

Comments on Articles 12 to 14:

Furthermore, it happens that a husband absents himself for a long period without a legitimate claim of travelling for business reasons or for purposes of study, without being able to claim inability to communicate, and without inviting his wife to join him or repudiating her so that she can take another husband. Generally speaking, it is against nature that the wife should thus live alone and be able to preserve intact her honor and respectability, even if the husband has left sufficient funds for her maintenance during his absence.

It also happens that the husband commits an offense for which he is sentenced to a long prison term. In that case the wife finds herself in the same situation as the spouse whose husband is absent.

The doctrine of Abu Hanifa does not provide any remedy for these cases. It is an imperative social obligation, however, to provide such a remedy. By contrast the doctrine of the Imam Malik permits the *qadi* to grant a divorce if the husband has been absent for more than a year and the wife makes a complaint about his absence, even if he has left her sufficient funds for her needs. . . .

(2) Unilateral Repudiation

Comment: Restrictions on the husband's ability to divorce his wife at will through unilateral repudiation have been enacted in the vast majority of Arab countries. It was relatively easy to find authority among the classical jurists for denying the validity of repudiations pronounced under compulsion or when intoxication or anger deprived the husband of his reason. The reformers in effect challenged the alleged consensus of the orthodox schools, however, when they denied validity to formulae of divorce uttered as an oath or threat or decreed that the "triple" divorce, pronounced in a single formula, would be regarded as a single revocable divorce.

Egyptian Decree-law No. 25 of 10 March 1929.

Article 1. A repudiation pronounced in a state of drunkenness or under compulsion is invalid.

Article 2. A conditional repudiation which has as its only purpose to induce the commission or ommission of a certain act is invalid.

Article 3. A repudiation coupled with words or gestures indicating a number is equivalent to a single repudiation.

Article 4. Formulas which have a double meaning and which can either signify repudiation or something else do not result in repudiation unless there is an intent to repudiate.

Article 5. Any repudiation is revocable except a repudiation pronounced for the third time, a repudiation pronounced before consummation of the marriage, a repudiation in exchange for compensation, and repudiations considered irrevocable by the present law and by law No. 25 of 1920. . . .

Explanatory Memorandum.

. . . In fact Islam, while permitting repudiation, has restricted its area of application to those cases only where one of the spouses or both cannot observe the limits set by God. If people observed the limits set by God and conformed to His law, no complaints against the rules of repudiation would have arisen, the ties of the Muslim family would have remained stable and peace would always have reigned. However, weakening of character and loosening of morals have brought about a certain demoralization within the Muslim family and have disturbed the peace. . . .

The Muslim wife thus has been threatened continuously by repudiation without knowing when that repudiation might come. The husband himself might not have this knowledge. If he repudiates through an oath or pronounces a repudiation dependent upon the commission or omission of an act by a third party, neither he nor his wife knows, when the repudiation will actually take effect.

Thus the welfare of the spouses, of the children and of the whole family may be dependent upon an act which is independent from the wishes of the head or the mother of the family.

In most of these cases, dissolution of the marriage is approved by the great majority of jurists. . . . [Hanefite doctrine]. The misfortunes of family life spring from these opinions. From them stem the ruses to which spouses have recourse. . . .

It is necessary to protect Islamic law and the people themselves against the temptation to infringe that law which has for its goal the happiness of humans in this world and the beyond and which, in its principles, could be applied to all nations, at all times and in all places, if it were comprehended in its true meaning and applied with understanding.

The policy with regard to Islamic law is to facilitate the practical application of the law for the people by broad interpretation and to consult the *'ulama'* every time it is necessary to find a remedy for a social ill difficult to cure, so that the people feel that the law provides a solution in any difficulty and deliverance from any adversity.

This is why the Ministry wishes to impose upon repudiation

restrictions designed to bring it into greater conformity with principles and rules of the religion and the doctrine of the Imams and the other jurists, including those who do not belong to one of the four [orthodox] rites. It has worked out the attached draft law in conformity with these principles.

Nothing in Islamic law prohibits the adoption of the opinion of jurists not belonging to one of the four rites, particularly if such adoption assures the public welfare or prevents a public evil. . . .

The draft law is based on the following principles:

1. According to an authoritative opinion of Ahmad ibn Hanbal and an opinion taught by the other three rites and many later disciples, repudiation during intoxication is invalid. It is not known whether the companions of the Prophet admitted its validity.

Also, according to Shafi'ite and Malikite doctrine and that of Ibn Hanbal, Dawud al-Zahiri and many of the companions of the Prophet, repudiation under compulsion is invalid.

2. Repudiation is divided into repudiation pure and simple, that is, repudiation which tends to produce immediate effects; delayed repudiation, such as one pronounced with the formula: "You are repudiated as of tomorrow;" repudiation by oath: such as "I shall rather repudiate my wife than do such a thing;" and conditional repudiation: such as "If you do such and so, you shall be repudiated."

Conditional repudiation is equivalent to one made by oath, because the person making it wants to intimidate or achieve the performance or nonperformance of a certain act while not actually intending to repudiate. Conditional repudiation is not equivalent to repudiation by oath if the person pronouncing it does not intend to live with his wife once the condition has been fulfilled.

Repudiation by oath or equivalent repudiations are null and void. However, other categories of repudiation are valid.

The opinions of the ancient jurists of the Hanefite rite and those of some of the later scholars of that rite have been taken into account in ruling repudiation by oath to be null and void. This principle is in accordance with the opinion of the Imam 'Ali, Shurayh, Dawud and his followers, and a certain number of Shafi'ite and Malikite jurists. The ruling that a conditional repudiation which is equivalent to a repudiation by oath is null and void is based upon the opinion of the Imam 'Ali, of Shurayh, 'Ata', al-Hakam Ibn 'Utaiba, Dawud and his followers, and Ibn Hazm.

These rules are contained in Article 2 of the draft law.

3. The multiple repudiation made verbally or through gesture is considered as a single repudiation. This is the opinion of Muhammad Ibn Ishaq, and this opinion is also attributed to 'Ali, Ibn Mas'ud, Abd al-Rahman Ibn Uf and to Zuhayr. It is likewise attributed to the sheikhs of Cordova. . . . According to Ibn al-Munzir, it is also the opinion of the disciples of Ibn 'Abbas, such as 'Ata', Tawus and 'Amr ibn Dinar. *Fatwas* in this sense have been issued by 'Ikrima and Dawud. According to Ibn Qaiyim, this is the opinion of most of the Companions of the

Prophet, of some of the disciples of Malik, of some Hanefite jurists and some disciples of Ahmad ibn Hanbal (Article 3 of the draft).

4. Formulas which are equivocal and can either signify repudiation or something else do not bring about repudiation unless there is intent to repudiate, notwithstanding the cirumstances. This is the opinion of al-Shafi'i and of Malik.

The formulas which are here understood to be equivocal are those so considered by the doctrine of Abu Hanifa (Article 4 of the draft).

5. The doctrine of Malik and al-Shafi'i has been accepted that any repudiation is revocable, except as stated in Article 5 of the draft.

It should be noted that the doctrine of Abu Hanifa shall continue to be applied to divorce by *li'an* [where the husband accuses his wife of adultery and confirms this accusation by a ritual oath], in case of impotence, or in case the husband refuses to be converted to Islam after his wife has embraced Islam.

Comment: As in several other respects, the Tunisian Code of Personal Status has gone farther in restricting the husband's right of divorce than other Arab legislation.

Tunisian Code of Personal Status, Decree of 13 August 1956.

Article 30. Divorce outside a court of law is without legal effect.

Article 31. The court shall grant a decree of divorce:

1. At the demand of the husband or the wife on the grounds specified in this code.

2. In case of mutual consent between the spouses.

3. At the demand of the husband or wife; in this case the court shall determine the indemnity due to the wife as compensation for injuries suffered or the indemnity she shall pay to the husband.

Article 32. The court shall not grant a decree of divorce until it has exhausted all means of establishing the causes of conflict between the spouses and has failed to reconcile them.

The judge may order any urgent measures concerning the residence of the spouses, maintenance and protection of the children.

Article 33. If the divorce is granted before consummation of the marriage, the wife has the right to half of the dowry agreed upon. . . .

Comment: In practice, the most important of the grounds of divorce enumerated in Article 31, has been 31. 3 which permits the husband and the wife to sue for divorce without giving any reasons. The Tunisian courts have also permitted the plaintiff who sued on the basis of Article 31. 1 to change his pleadings to Article 31. 3, if he is unable to prove his allegations as required under Article 31. 1.

Two decisions by Tunisian courts illustrate this and related points:

Decision of the Tunisian Court of Cassation, Civil Chamber of 4 July 1968, Decision 6175.

The Court:

Regarding the appeal to the Court of Cassation by Maitre Haddad to set aside a decision of the Court of Appeal of Tunis No. 27948 of 26 February 1968 granting divorce for the first time between the appellant and the appellee, Mrs. Atal Farida and sentencing the latter to the payment of one cent as compensation for damages suffered as a result of the divorce;

Taking into account the observations of the Public Prosecutor and his oral explanations at the hearing;

On the first point of the appeal charging a wrong application of Article 31 of the Personal Status Code, because the appellee, after having based her pleading on the first paragraph of that Article, then changed her pleading basing it on the third paragraph of that Article and because the court allowed this change even though there was a contradiction in the pleadings and the court should have rejected the change;

However, it appears from the statements of the judgment attacked that the pleading was based on paragraph 3 of Article 31 and that it was on that basis that the judgment attacked pronounced the divorce. This point of the appeal thus lacks any basis in fact;

On the second and third points of the appeal, taken together, which charge violation of paragraph 4 of Article 123 of the Code of Civil and Commercial Procedure because of lack of grounds for the judgment, violation of the rights of the defense, and contradiction in the grounds because the judgment attacked did not address itself to the request of the appellant that witnesses be heard to prove that relations between the spouses were good and that therefore the allegations of the appellee were without foundation. By ignoring this essential element, the judgment attacked is based on insufficient reasons, the appellant alleges, and should therefore be set aside, and also for the reason that the Court of Appeal did not make any attempt to achieve a reconciliation;

Whereas under the terms of paragraph 3 of Article 31 of the Personal Status Code cited by the judgment attacked, divorce is pronounced "at the demand of the husband or wife . . . ;"

Whereas it follows specifically from the explicit terms of the text of the statute that the demand for divorce in this case does not have to be based on a specific allegation, but is left to the free decision of one or the other of the spouses as is the case in this suit;

Whereas it follows clearly from the statements of the judgment attacked that the judges of the Court of Appeal did attempt a reconciliation between the parties, but that the wife upheld her demand, declaring that she was prepared to make any settlement demanded by her adversary in exchange for her freedom;

Whereas it follows from the above that the second and third points of the appeal, taken together, do not have any foundation in law and must therefore be rejected;

On these grounds: the appeal is rejected.

Comment: Article 123 of the Tunisian Code of Civil and Commercial Procedure of 1960 states:

Any judgment shall contain the following:

1. the name, first name, occupation, and domicile of the parties;

2. the cause of action;

3. a summary of the allegations of the parties;

4. the grounds for the decision in fact and law;

5. the terms of the judgment;

6. the date the judgment was handed down given according to the Hijra and the Gregorian calendars;

7. indication of the type of court [i.e., court of first instance, court of appeal, etc.] and location;

8. ruling on the costs if that can as yet be done.

Decision of the Court of Appeal for Tunis of 25 June 1965.

The facts:

This is an action for divorce instituted by one spouse and based upon wrong suffered, in accordance with paragraph 1, Article 31 of the Personal Status Code.

Having been unable during the course of the suit to prove the allegations made against his wife, the plaintiff changed his pleading and demanded a divorce on the basis of paragraph 3: the court of first instance granted the divorce, but assessed damages for his wife against him.

On appeal the plaintiff attacked the decision of the court of first instance on two grounds:

That there was a contradiction in grounds for the judgment attacked since on the one hand it ruled that he had a right to divorce his wife and on the other hand assessed damages against him;

That paragraph 3 of Article 31 of the Personal Status Code cannot be construed as establishing a legal presumption of abuse of right, and that moreover the court of first instance had not investigated whether the wrong alleged by the defendant was or was not well founded.

The Court:

With regard to the first count of the appeal alleging contradiction in the grounds of the judgment:

Whereas this allegation is not substantiated by examination;

Whereas the grounds of the judgment attacked show in proper and explicit fashion that divorce being a legal right of each spouse, the spouse demanding it without proving the allegations which justify his action is considered to have abused his right and opens up for the other party the claim to damages;

Whereas this is the case with regard to a demand for divorce on the basis of paragraph 3 of Article 31 of the Personal Status Code.

With regard to the construction of Article 31, paragraph 3 of the Personal Status Code:

Whereas Article 31 of the Personal Status Code enumerates three means through which divorce can be obtained: the first being based on a wrong suffered, divorce cannot be granted unless the plaintiff proves his allegations and the wrong claimed; the second being based on an express and formal agreement of the two spouses. Finally, divorce can be granted without grounds which justify it, but in this case, in contrast to the other two means of obtaining a divorce, there is a legal presumption of an abuse of right which allows the other party to collect damages.

This conclusion follows from the very terms of paragraph 3 of Article 31 which states: "in this case the court shall determine the indemnity due to the wife as compensation for injuries suffered or the indemnity she shall pay to the husband."

On these grounds: the judgment of the court below is confirmed.

Comment: These two decisions show very clearly that the Tunisian courts have construed Article 31, paragraph 3 as establishing a right of repudiation for the wife as well as for the husband. If efforts at conciliation fail, the court has to grant the divorce requested under this paragraph. The question of damages could be somewhat more controversial. The Tunisian courts, as shown by these two decisions, have construed Article 31, paragraph 3, as giving the party opposing the divorce a claim to damages. The second decision bases this claim on the well-known civil law doctrine of abuse of right, that is a right is being used to wrong another person. It has been suggested, that the wording of Article 31, paragraph 3 and the construction of this paragraph by the courts are a reaction to the *shari'a* practice under which the husband could repudiate the wife virtually at will and without being liable for any damages no matter how willful his action.*

Another point deserves mention. In both these cases the plaintiff apparently had first attempted to base his (or her) suit on Article 31, paragraph 1, which puts on him (or her) the burden of proof that he (or she) was wronged by the other party. In both cases this attempt was apparently abandoned and the plaintiff changed his pleading. (In the first case the facts are not absolutely clear, due to the custom of French-type courts of cassation to present very little of the factual basis of the case.) The note to the second decision suggests a very probable reason, the hesitancy, in the Near Eastern setting, of the parties to reveal intimate details of their personal lives in open court and, one might add, a likely equal hesitancy to do so on the part of potential witnesses.†

While other Arab countries have not gone as far as Tunisia in their regulation of divorce, several have stipulated the necessity of judicial intervention in order to make unilateral repudiation of the wife by the husband valid. Thus the Iraqi Law of Personal Status of 1959 requires the husband who wants to repudiate his wife to obtain a judgment in a *shari'a* court. However, if he cannot take the matter to court, then he must register the repudiation in court during the period of the *'idda* (Article 39. 1). The Algerian

---

*Mohktar Maaref in a note to the second decision, *Revue Tunisienne de droit* (1966–67): 206–208.
†*Ibid.*

decree No. 59–1082 of 17 September 1959 which implemented
Ordinance No. 59–274 of 4 February 1959 provided that the
judge must be asked by one or the other of the spouses to grant a
divorce in cases where the husband has repudiated his wife
(Article 11).

In a draft for a new Personal Status Law published by Egypt in
1967, the drafters did not go as far as Tunisia, Iraq, or Algeria in
demanding a court sentence for the validity of a repudiation. They
did, however, stipulate that the divorce must be pronounced
before two witnesses. The Moroccan Code of Personal Status
contains a somewhat similar provision.

(3) The *'Idda*

Comment: The length of the *'idda* period depends on whether the
husband has died or has divorced his wife. In case of his death, as
stated before, the period of the *'idda* according to the Hanefite
jurists, is four and one half months; in case of divorce three
menstrual periods. While the main purpose of the *'idda* is to
prevent *commixtio sanguinis* in case the woman remarried, the
'idda also has another important practical significance. During the
period of the *'idda* the wife is entitled to maintenance. Since
Islamic law does not know alimony in the Western sense, this
maintenance is of great importance to the woman and various
ruses were used by women to conceal the fact of menstruation
and thereby extend the period of maintenance, if possible to the
menopause. In order to prevent such abuses the personal status
laws of various Arab countries have restricted the period of the
'idda.

Egyptian Law No. 25 of 10 March 1929.

Article 16. The amount of maintenance due to the wife by the
husband is fixed in accordance with the financial circumstances of
the latter, without regard to the financial circumstances of the
wife.

Article 17. The courts may not entertain a claim for *'idda*
maintenance which exceeds one year from the date of divorce.

Explanatory Memorandum.

. . . The rules actually applicable according to Law No. 25 of 1920
allowed the divorced wife to receive *'idda* maintenance during an
unjustifiably long period. In fact, if she nursed, she could pretend
that she had not menstruated during the period of nursing, which
is two years. She could also pretend that she menstruated only
once a year and since her statement on this subject had to be
accepted on the basis of a simple declaration on her part, she could
receive *'idda* maintenance for a total of five years [two years
during which she nursed and an additional maximum of three
years]. If the wife did not nurse, she could pretend that she menstruated only once a year for three years. Such claims are contrary
to normal female physiological processes and husbands have

frequently complained against the tricks and lies to which divorced wives resorted in order to receive unjustifiably 'idda maintenance. [Under the 1920 statute the court could not entertain a suit designed to show that the divorced wife had menstruated more than once a year.]

Under these circumstances and on the basis of the principle that the ruler has the right to forbid his *qadis* to hear certain categories of claims where frauds and tricks are frequently involved, the Ministry has considered it to be in the general interest to change the provisions relating to the length of 'idda maintenance. This was done in order to bring such length in accord with the report of a specialist in forensic medicine which demonstrated that the maximal gestation period is one year. ...

Comment: A similar rule was established with regard to legitimacy by the same statute and also justified by the ruler's right to establish procedural limitations:

Egyptian Law No. 25 of 10 March 1929.

Article 15. An action to recognize the legitimacy of a child cannot be entertained if such legitimacy is contested:

1. if it has been proven that the mother did not cohabit with her husband after marriage;
2. if the child is born after the husband has been absent for a year;
3. if the child is born to a divorced or widowed woman a year after she has been divorced or widowed.

Comment: While the Egyptian legislation thus still used procedural means to achieve certain goals in the field of personal status law, other Arab countries have established rules of substantive law for the same purpose.

An example is the Syrian Personal Status Law.

Syrian Legislative Decree No. 59 of 17 September 1953

Article 121. The 'idda of the nonpregnant woman in case of divorce or annulment of the marriage is fixed as follows:

1. Three full menstrual periods for the woman of an age where these periods are regular ....
2. A full year for the woman whose menstrual periods are extended, who has never menstruated, or whose menstruations have ceased before the menopause.
3. Three months for the woman in menopause.

Article 123. The 'idda of the widow is 4 months and ten days.

Comment: Some of the recent statutes provide for an additional payment to the wife in case the husband divorces her without reasonable cause. Thus the Syrian decree provides:

Ibid.

Article 117. If the husband repudiates his wife and it becomes clear to the *qadi* that the husband was acting arbitrarily without reasonable cause and that the wife as a result would suffer poverty or financial difficulties, the *qadi* may render a judgment in her favor against the husband, having regard to the latter's financial standing and also to the degree of his arbitrariness, for an indemnity not exceeding the amount of one year's maintenance for a woman of her social standing, in addition to the maintenance due her during the *'idda*. The *qadi* may also determine whether this indemnity is to be paid in a lump sum or in monthly installments.

Comment: The Moroccan law of 1958 goes slightly further. It provides:

Moroccan Personal Status Code of 1957 and 1958.

Article 60. If the husband takes the initiative in repudiating his wife, he should give her a consolation gift (*mut'a*) in proportion to his means and her circumstances, except in cases where the dowry had been fixed, but the wife had been repudiated before the consummation of the marriage.

b. *Polygamy*

Comment: The question of polygamy has long occupied Muslim reformers, many of whom have advocated restriction or abolition of this institution. In fact, among the Arab states only Tunisia has abolished polygamy outright.

Tunisian Code of Personal Status.

Article 18. Polygamy is prohibited. Whosoever being married contracts another marriage before dissolution of the first shall be liable to imprisonment for one year or a fine of 240,000 francs or both, even if the new marriage has not been concluded in accordance with the law.

Comment: Other statutes are less categorical.

Iraqi Law of Personal Status of 30 December 1959.

Article 3 (4). Marriage with more than one wife is not permitted without permission of the *qadi*, and such permission will not be given except on the following two conditions:
    (i) that the husband is financially competent to support more than one wife;
    (ii) that there is some lawful benefit involved.
    (5) If any failure of equal treatment between co-wives is feared, then polygamy is not permitted; and the determination of this matter is left to the discretion of the *qadi*.
    (6) Anyone who concludes a contract of marriage with more than one wife in contravention of sections (4) and (5) will be punished by imprisonment for not more than one year, or by a fine of not more than 100 dinars, or by both these penalties.

Syrian Law of Personal Status of 17 September 1953.

Article 17. The *qadi* is not permitted to authorize a married man to marry another woman, if it is proven that he cannot financially support two wives.

Moroccan Personal Status Code of 1957 and 1958.

Article 30. (1) Polygamy is forbidden, if unequal treatment of the wives is to be feared.

(2) If the husband takes a second wife, the first has the right—if she has not stipulated the option [to object to a second marriage] at the time of her marriage—to initiate court action for the purpose of determining the injuries resulting to her. The marriage with the second wife cannot be concluded until she has been informed by the man who wishes to marry her that he is already married.

Article 31. The wife may stipulate in the marriage contract that her husband cannot take another wife and that she will have the right to demand the dissolution of the marriage should this undertaking be violated.

c. *The Effect of Conversion to Islam of One Spouse in Cases of Foreign Nationality*

Comment: This specific conflict of laws question has given rise to some problems in Egypt since Article 13, paragraph 2 of the Civil Code of 1949 provided:

"Repudiation of marriage is covered by the law of the country to which the husband belongs at the time of the repudiation whereas divorce and separation are governed by the law of the country to which the husband belongs at the time of the start of the legal proceedings."

Cases have not been infrequent where husbands converted to Islam and then repudiated their wives, particularly in cases of Christians where the country of their nationality did not allow divorce, but merely separation from bed and board. This applied at the time the problem arose particularly to Italians resident in Egypt who had retained their Italian nationality. Cases of this type created a dilemma for the Egyptian courts. On the one hand it was argued by a number of decisions after the introduction of the Civil Code that in case of a convert to Islam, Islamic law should apply to all personal status matters and that he therefore should be permitted to repudiate his wife.* This, it was stated, was demanded by considerations of public policy. On the other hand, these decisions obviously ran counter to the provisions of Article 13 of the Civil Code, which disregarded religious affiliation and made nationality the exclusive criterion as to the law to be applied.

As a consequence, a number of court decisions held that the provisions of Article 13 should be observed and that the change

---

*See for further details, Y. Linant de Bellefonds, "Egyptian Judicial Decisions and Conflict of Law in Matters of Personal Status," *Journal de droit international* 89 (1960): 843.

in religion should be disregarded. Among the decisions which expressed this view was one by the Court of First Instance of Alexandria of 9 April 1951.* In the case before the court an Italian wife contested the right of her husband, who had become a Muslim, to repudiate her. The court held that the law of the nationality of the husband had to be applied according to Article 13 of the Civil Code, that accordingly the *shari'a* courts (which then still existed) did not have jurisdiction and that the conversion of the husband to Islam was not relevant. Similarly, the Court of Appeal of Alexandria in a decision of 19 December, 1954 denied a plea to the jurisdiction by a British national. This man had become a Muslim and challenged the jurisdiction of the civil courts in a suit for divorce which his wife had brought. The court below had granted the divorce applying British law with regard to alimony and custody of the children.†

When the law abolishing the religious courts was enacted in 1955, Article 7 provided that if one of the parties to a suit concerning personal status matters became a Muslim even during the proceedings, Islamic law was to be applied.‡ However, this rule is applicable only to internal conflicts of laws, that is, conflicts between the personal status laws governing Egyptian citizens, not to international conflicts of laws, that is, those involving the law of foreign countries. Nevertheless, the Egyptian courts have now adopted the attitude rather generally that in a suit concerning the personal status law of foreigners, particularly divorce suits, Islamic law will be applied if one of the parties has become a Muslim.‖ Thus the Egyptian Court of Cassation actually did not apply the rules of Article 13, overruling earlier decisions to the contrary by some lower courts. The decisions of the Court of Cassation, and the holdings of many lower courts, as well as the provisions of Article 7 of the law of 1955 demonstrate that the rule is still valid that once a person has become a Muslim he is subject to Muslim law in all respects. Such a deviation from the rules of the Egyptian Civil Code as regards international conflicts of law is not surprising, however, in view of the central position which is still accorded to the *shari'a* in Egypt and most other Islamic countries. § It should be added, however, that Egypt has erected safeguards against fraudulent conversion to Islam for purposes of an easy divorce. The courts will take conversion to Islam into consideration only if it has been established by an authenticated instrument to the court's satisfaction that the conversion was *bona fide*.

As is to be expected, Egypt is not alone in this attitude toward the rights of a foreigner who converted to Islam. A Moroccan

---

Revue Egyptienne de droit international 7 (1951): 194-196.
†*Bulletin de législation et de jurisprudence Egyptiennes* 6 (1955): 62-63.
‡See p. 102.
‖Court of Cassation, Decision of 30 January 1963. *Report of the Decisions of the Court* (in Arabic) 14: 189. See for a discussion of this decision and related matters, Y. Linant Bellefonds, "Chronique de jurisprudence de la R.A.U.," *Journal de droit international* 97 (1970): 957–958.
§See also the case given p. 192.

case may serve as an example. This case came before the courts after the enactment of the Moroccan Personal Status Law, but before the law unifying the courts. Thus *shariʿa* courts still existed and had jurisdiction over all personal status matters of Muslims, including Muslim foreigners residing in Morocco (laws of 14 August 1956 and of 24 April 1959 respectively). Though the *shariʿa* courts have been abolished, substantive *shariʿa* law is still applied by the courts of general jurisdiction. Thus, it would continue to make a difference whether a person involved in a personal status matter is a Muslim or not.

The background of the case in question was as follows. A French national married a French woman in France on 30 August 1945. He embraced Islam after the conclusion of this marriage and his profession of faith was duly registered by an Islamic notary and ratified on 20 July 1960. Subsequently the husband, still a French national, married a Muslim woman who was a Moroccan citizen. Both marriages had issue. The first wife sued in the "modern court" in Morocco (which then still existed), claiming that the second marriage was void because of bigamy. The court of original jurisdiction and the court of appeal found for the plaintiff because of the husband's French citizenship and held that Article 147 of the French Civil Code, which prohibits the contracting of a second marriage before the first marriage is dissolved, was applicable. The husband then appealed to the Supreme Court of Morocco, whose decision follows:

Morocco, Supreme Court, Civil Chamber, Decision of 24 November 1964.

The Court on the single point of Appeal 15, 998:
In view of Article 5 of the law of 14 August 1956 as amended by the law of 24 April 1959:

Considering that according to that Article the *shariʿa* courts have jurisdiction in disputes concerning the personal status of Muslim foreigners resident in the Kingdom;

Considering further that the Court of Appeal having established that S. [the husband-appellant] was a Muslim foreigner residing in the Kingdom, the *qadi* has jurisdiction with regard to a cause involving the personal status of S. even though he is a French national, namely the nullity of the second marriage alleged by Mrs. J. [the first wife-respondent];

From this it follows that in taking jurisdiction of the case, the Court of Appeal was in error and has wrongly applied the applicable statutory provisions.

The judgment of the Court of Appeal is annulled for these reasons.
Decision No. 69. Civil 15,998 and 14,412.

Comment: This case was critically reviewed by a French jurist who pointed out that the Supreme Court merely had ruled on a plea to the jurisdiction and that the substantive issue still would have to be decided by the *qadi*. He argued for the application of the rules of conflict of laws on a strictly territorial basis.* However, in view of the Egyptian decisions, it is more than likely that the *qadi* would decide the case on the basis of Islamic law.

3. The Law of Marriage and Divorce in Iran, Pakistan, and Turkey

a. *Iran*

Comment: In contrast to the practice in the Arab countries, the personal status law of Iran was codified in the Civil Code and was not at the time laid down in separate statutes. In 1967, however, a new statute was enacted, the *Law on the Protection of the Family*, which changed a number of the provisions of the Civil Code dealing with such matters as polygamy and certain aspects of divorce. This law has modified some sections of the code considerably. The Civil Code generally followed Islamic law, more specifically the law of the Ithna 'Ashari branch of the Shi'a, which is the official creed of Iran.

(1) Temporary Marriage (*nikah al-mut'a*)

Comment: The Iranian code has retained one peculiar institution, namely the temporary marriage.

Iranian Civil Code

Article 1075. A marriage is temporary if it is concluded for a specified term.

Article 1076. The length of the temporary marriage shall be clearly established.

Article 1077. The provisions concerning inheritance and dowry as set forth in the title on inheritance and in the following chapter apply to the temporary marriage.

Article 1095. Failure to mention the dowry in a temporary marriage makes the marriage null and void.

Article 1097. In a temporary marriage the wife has the right to half the dowry if the husband terminates the marriage before the expiration of its term.

Comment: The temporary marriage is probably of pre-Islamic origin and has parallels in other laws. The *mut'a* marriage may at times constitute a long-term relationship somewhat inferior in status to a regular marriage or a short-term arrangement not greatly different from prostitution. However, in Islam no sect other than the *Ithna 'Ashari* permits the *mut'a* marriage. In Iraq the Personal Status Law does not allow temporary marriage to the Shi'ites of the *Ithna 'Ashari* sect, although they are numerous in Southern Iraq.

*Maurice Morère, "Statut Personnel Etranger," *Revue Marocaine du droit*, (1965): 43–44.

(2) Divorce

Comment: According to the Ithna 'Ashari doctrine, a man may repudiate his wife, but he has to use a formula containing the word *talaq* and the repudiation has to be pronounced in the presence of two male witnesses. Most importantly, Shi'i law does not recognize the triple repudiation at one sitting. It recognizes the single revocable repudiation, divorce by agreement (*khul'* divorce where the wife "buys" her freedom), and repudiation pronounced during three periods of purity. These Shi'i rules were incorporated into the Iranian Civil Code (Book 7, Title 2).

However, the Iranian Civil Code made some efforts to make divorce easier for the wife. For one thing it permitted the insertion into the marriage contract or another irrevocable agreement of certain conditions not contrary to the purposes of marriage. Thus the wife could be given the right to sue for divorce if the husband took another wife, absented himself for a specifically stated length of time, did not provide maintenance, tried to kill his wife, or mistreated her in a manner which made continuation of conjugal life intolerable. In such cases the wife had to prove her allegations in court (Article 1119). A law on marriage and divorce of 1931 provided that a judgment in such a case could be appealed up to the Court of Cassation.

The Civil Code also introduced specific grounds on which the wife could sue for divorce without the necessity of stipulating these grounds in a contract:

Iranian Civil Code.

Article 1129. If the husband refuses to provide maintenance for his wife and a judgment in the matter cannot be enforced, the wife may petition the court to grant a divorce. In that case the judge will compel the husband to divorce his wife.* The same applies if the husband is no longer able to provide the maintenance due to his wife.

Article 1130. The provisions of the preceding article also apply:

(1) if the husband does not fulfill his other obligations to his wife and he cannot be compelled to do so;

(2) if the conduct of the husband toward his wife is such that continuation of conjugal life is intolerable;

(3) if continuation of conjugal life has become dangerous for the wife because of a contagious disease of the husband which is difficult to cure.

Comment: A further important step at reform of certain aspects of the law of marriage and divorce was taken in Iran by the Law on the Protection of the Family of 1967. This law stipulated that the civil courts henceforth would have jurisdiction in all matrimonial causes and other matters involving family disputes (Article 1). Before 1967 suits brought by wives under Articles 1119, 1129, and 1130 were also heard by the civil courts. Now, however, all jurisdiction of the *qadis* in the matters enumerated in the 1967 law has

*The law of 1931 provided that in such a case the wife could apply through the civil courts to the *shari'a* courts and demand a divorce.

been eliminated. The right of the husband to repudiate his wife without any intervention by the courts also has been abolished. Now the courts must intervene in all cases. Divorce can be requested by the husband or the wife on the grounds stated in the Civil Code or on several further grounds enumerated in Article 11 of the law of 1967.

These are:

(1) conviction of either spouse to imprisonment of five years or more;

(2) if either spouse is suffering from an addiction which in the court's opinion is prejudicial to continued conjugal life;

(3) if the husband marries a second wife without the consent of the first wife;

(4) if either the husband or the wife abandons family life;

(5) if either is convicted of an offense which in the court's opinion is repugnant to family honor or prestige. In this case the court has to take into account the position and social status of the parties as well as other relevant factors.

On any of these grounds either husband or wife can ask the court for a certificate of impossibility of reconciliation. Before granting such a certificate, the court must either directly or through an arbitrator attempt to achieve a reconciliation. If such an attempt proves to be futile, the court issues a certificate of impossibility of reconciliation. No appeal lies against the court's decision either to grant or to refuse such a certificate. A certificate of impossibility of reconciliation is good for three months. During this period it may be produced before a notary who will register it and effect an irrevocable divorce. Thus, the action of the court is not final, but merely gives the parties the right to effect an irrevocable divorce within three months. Another chance is thus provided for reconsideration. The period of three months may have been chosen because of the provision in *Ithna 'Ashari* law that a divorce is only irrevocable if pronounced during three periods of purity.

Article 17 of the Family Protection Law contains an interesting provision. It states that the provisions of Article 11 must be inserted into the marriage document as a condition of the marriage contract and an irrevocable power of attorney is given to the wife to execute a divorce. Such a divorce is regarded as irrevocable. This provision may seem superfluous in view of the other provisions of the law permitting the wife to ask for divorce. However, it has to be regarded as primarily designed to overcome the opposition of the traditionalists to the new legislation, because Article 17 upheld the fiction that the wife had a right of divorce as a result of the insertion of this right into the marriage contract. Her right thus could be regarded as a delegation of the husband's right of divorce. Professor Anderson has pointed out that he was told on a visit to Iran after the enactment of the 1967 law that no distinction would be made in practice between marriage contracts entered into after promulgation of the 1967 law, which would contain a clause inserting the provisions of Article 11 of that law, and marriage contracts concluded earlier, which would lack such a clause.*

(3) Polygamy

Comment: The Iranian Civil Code did not contain any prohibition of polygamy. Under the law of 1931 on marriage and divorce, however, a man had to declare clearly at the time of the marriage to the woman whom he was marrying whether or not he was already married. If he made a false statement he was liable to criminal prosecution and imprisonment upon complaint of the wife he had defrauded. The first wife had no recourse unless the marriage contract had stipulated her right to seek a divorce if the husband took a second wife. As stated above, the law of 1967 changed this situation by giving the first wife the right to apply for a certificate of impossibility of reconciliation and thus obtain a divorce, if the husband had married a second wife without her consent.

b. *Pakistan*

(1) Background to the Pakistani Reforms

Comment: As we have seen, it was most difficult under Hanafi law, the Sunni rite prevalent in India, for a woman to obtain a divorce, whereas Maliki law was more favorable. In India an act to remedy this situation was promulgated under British rule, the *Dissolution of Muslim Marriages Act of 1939*. This act was applicable to all Muslims in India regardless of school or sect. It allowed the wife to obtain a decree dissolving her marriage for a number of specified causes similar to those allowed by legislation in Arab countries. Other important laws enacted under British rule were the *Child Marriage Restraint Act (XIX of 1929)* and the *Indian Evidence Act of 1872*. The *Child Marriage Restraint Act* provided that no marriage may be solemnized unless the groom is over eighteen and the bride over fourteen. In Pakistan the minimal age for the bride has been changed to sixteen. Section 112 of the *Indian Evidence Act* is of importance for the determination of the legitimacy of a child. This article provides that a child shall be regarded as legitimate if it is born within 280 days after the dissolution of the marriage, provided the mother remained unmarried. These acts are still applied in Pakistan, although the *Dissolution of Muslim Marriages Act* and the *Child Marriage Restraint Act* have been amended in some particulars in order to bring them in accord with later Pakistani legislation.

(2) The Pakistani Reforms in General

Comment: In Pakistan a Commission on Marriage and Family

*The Iranian law of 1967 has been discussed by J. N. D. Anderson in "Reforms in the Law of Divorce in the Muslim World," *Studia Islamica* 31 (1970): 44–45, and by Doreen Hinchcliffe, "Legal Reforms in the Shi'i World—Recent Legislation in Iran and Iraq," *Malaya Law Review* 10 (1968): 292–305. These two articles have been drawn on in the above discussion.

Laws was appointed on 4 August 1955 with the following terms of reference:

Do the existing laws governing marriage, divorce, maintenance and other ancillary matters among Muslims require modification in order to give women their proper place in society according to the fundamentals of Islam? The Commission was asked to report on the proper registration of marriages and divorces, the right to divorce exercisable by either partner through a court or by other judicial means, maintenance and the establishment of Special Courts to deal expeditiously with cases affecting women's rights.*

Comment: The Commission's report was published in the *Gazette Extraordinary* of the Government of Pakistan on 20 June 1956. The Commission dealt in considerable detail with the basic principles of Islamic law and asserted:

This Commission considers the four sources of Muslim law enunciated by the great *Imams* as comprehensive: The Holy Qur'an, *sunna*, *ijma'* (consensus) and *qiyas* (reasoning by analogy), and intends to make proposals in accordance with the one or the other. It must also be remembered that the doctrine of *istihsan* (common weal) is an integral part of Muslim law, according to *Imam* Abu Hanifa. In the past *isthsan* has helped to solve several intricate and controversial problems, and there is no reason why we should not continue to avail of it in the future. As already stated the Commission accepts the principle of *ijtihad* and does not consider the laws and injunctions of Islam to be inflexible and unchangeable like the proverbial codes of Medes and Persians.†

Comment: This advocacy by the Commission of a reopening of the *bab al-ijtihad* aroused very strong opposition from the conservative element in Pakistan, which questioned the whole approach of the Commission to the principles of Islamic law. The problem was compounded by the fact that most members of the Commission were not specialists in Islamic law and therefore, especially in the eyes of the religious leaders, had no claim to the exercise of *ijtihad*. However, soon the religious conservatives were faced with the fact that other Muslim countries had enacted legislation on divorce, polygamy, and related matters which, in one form or another, contained important changes and even innovations. Thus, the ground had been prepared to a certain extent when the Family Laws Ordinance was enacted in Pakistan in 1961. That ordinance did not accept all of the recommendations of the Commission on Marriage and Family Laws, in a number of respects it also did not go as far as, for example, the Tunisian legislation. One feature, nevertheless, was quite revolutionary, namely, the introduction of succession by stirpes (see p. 199).

*Pakistan, *Gazette Extraordinary*, 20 June 1956, pp. 1197–1198.
†*Ibid.*, p. 1204.

The Muslim Family Laws Ordinance 1961 (Act VIII of 1961 as amended.

WHEREAS it is expedient to give effect to certain recommendations of the Commission on Marriage and Family Laws;

NOW, THEREFORE, in pursuance of the proclamation of the seventh day of October, 1958, and in exercise of all powers enabling him in that behalf, the President is pleased to make and promulgate the following Ordinance:

1. Short title, extent, application and commencement.—
   (1) This Ordinance may be called the Muslim Family Laws Ordinance, 1961.
   (2) It extends to the whole of Pakistan, and applies to all Muslim citizens of Pakistan, wherever they may be.
   (3) It shall come into force on such date as the Central Government may, by notification in the Official Gazette, appoint in this behalf.
   [entered into force 15 July 1961.]

2. Definitions:—In this Ordinance, unless there is anything repugnant in the subject or context—

a. "Arbitration Council" means a body consisting of the Chairman and a representative of each of the parties to a matter dealt with in this Ordinance: Provided that where any party fails to nominate a representative within the prescribed time, the body formed without such representatives shall be the Arbitration Council;

b. "Chairman" means the Chairman of the Union Council or person appointed by the Central or a Provincial Government, or by any officer authorized in that behalf by any such Government, to discharge the functions of Chairman under this Ordinance;

Provided that where the Chairman of the Union Council is a non-Muslim, or he himself wishes to make an application to the Arbitration Council, or is, owing to illness or any other reason, unable to discharge the functions of Chairman, the Council shall elect one of its Muslim members as Chairman for the purposes of this Ordinance;

c. "Prescribed" means prescribed by rules made under section 11.

d. "Union Council" means the Union Council or the Town or Union Committee constituted under the Basic Democracies Order, 1959 (P.O. No. 18 of 1959), and having in the matter jurisdiction as prescribed.

e. "Ward" means a ward within a Union or Town as defined in the aforesaid Order.

3. Ordinance to override other laws etc.—(1) the provisions of this Ordinance shall have effect notwithstanding any law, custom or usage, and the registration of Muslim marriages shall take place in accordance with those provisions.

(2) For the removal of doubt it is hereby declared that the provisions of the Arbitration Act, 1940 (X of 1940), the Code of Civil Procedure, 1908 (Act V of 1908), and any other law regulating the procedure of courts shall not apply to any Arbitration Council.

Comment: The Basic Democracies system was abolished in
Pakistan in 1972 by statutes issued in the various provinces of the
country and new local governing bodies were established.

(3) Divorce in Pakistan

Muslim Family Laws Ordinance.

7. *Talaq*—(1) Any man who wishes to divorce his wife shall, as
soon as may be after the pronunciation of *talaq* in any form
whatsoever, give the Chairman notice in writing of his having
done so, and shall supply a copy thereof to the wife.

(2) Whosoever contravenes the provisions of subsection (1)
shall be punishable with simple imprisonment for a term which
may extend to one year or with a fine which may extend to five
thousand rupees or with both.

(3) Save as provided in subsection (5), a *talaq*, unless revoked
earlier, expressly or otherwise, shall not be effective until the
expiration of ninety days from the day on which notice under
subsection (1) is delivered to the Chairman.

(4) Within thirty days of the receipt of notice under subsection
(1), the Chairman shall constitute an Arbitration Council for the
purpose of bringing about a reconciliation between the parties,
and the Arbitration Council shall take all steps necessary to bring
about such reconciliation.

(5) If the wife be pregnant at the time the *talaq* is pronounced,
talaq shall not be effective until the period mentioned in subsection (3) or the pregnancy, whichever be later, ends.

(6) Nothing shall debar a wife whose marriage has been terminated by *talaq* effective under this section from remarrying the
same husband, without an intervening marriage with a third
person, unless such termination is for the third time so effective.

8. *Dissolution of marriage otherwise than by talaq.*—Where the right
to divorce has been duly delegated to the wife and she wishes to
exercise that right or where any of the parties to a marriage wishes
to dissolve the marriage otherwise than by *talaq*, the provisions of
section 7 shall *mutatis mutandis* and so far as applicable, apply.

Comment: The rights of the wife to obtain a judicial divorce
established by the *Dissolution of Muslim Marriages Act, 1939*
continue in force in Pakistan. Under this act a wife can demand a
decree dissolving the marriage in case the whereabouts of the
husband have been unknown for four years, the husband has not
provided maintenance for two years, has been imprisoned for
seven years or more, has not performed his marital duties for three
years, was impotent at the time of marriage and continues to be so,
has been insane for two years or suffers from leprosy or a virulent
venereal disease.

A woman can also repudiate her marriage if she had been given
in marriage by her father or guardian before she was sixteen,
provided she does so before reaching eighteen. A new ground for
dissolution was added by the Muslim Family Laws Ordinance,

namely, if the husband takes an additional wife in contravention of the provisions of the ordinance. Cruelty is grounds for dissolution, provided the marriage has not been consummated. In addition to these specific grounds the ordinance contains a general clause permitting dissolution "on any other ground which is recognized as valid for the dissolution of marriages under Muslim Law." This gives the wife the opportunity to dissolve the marriage through a *khul'* divorce. The Supreme Court of Pakistan held in *Mst. Kurshed Bibi v. Muhammad Amin* (P.L.D. 1967 S.C.97, at 111)* that the wife "is entitled to dissolution of her marriage, on restoration of what she received in consideration of marriage, if the Judge apprehends that the parties will not observe the 'limits of God.' . . . it is only in cases where a harmonious married state, as envisaged by Islam, will not be possible, that such a decree for *khul'* will be granted. . . ." On the basis of this decision the Karachi High Court held in *Mst. Hakimzadi v. Nawaz Ali* (P.L.D. 1972 Karachi 540, at 546) that the wife merely needed to show that the marriage had broken down and there was no chance of reconciliation in order for the *khul'* divorce to be validly effected.

(4) Polygamy

Muslim Family Laws Ordinance.

6. *Polygamy.*—(1) No man, during the subsistence of an existing marriage, shall, except with the previous permission in writing of the Arbitration Council, contract another marriage, nor shall any such marriage contracted without such permission be registered under this Ordinance.

(2) An application for permission under subsection (1) shall be submitted to the Chairman in the prescribed manner, together with the prescribed fee, and shall state the reasons for the proposed marriage and whether the consent of the existing wife or wives has been obtained thereto.

(3) On receipt of the application under subsection (2) the Chairman shall ask the applicant and his existing wife or wives to nominate a representative, and the Arbitration Council so constituted may, if satisfied that the proposed marriage is necessary and just, grant, subject to such conditions, if any, as may be deemed fit, the permission applied for.

(4) In deciding the application the Arbitration Council shall record its reasons for the decision, and any party may, in the prescribed manner, within the prescribed period, and on payment of the prescribed fee, prefer an application for revision . . . to the Collector . . . and his decision shall be final and shall not be called into question by any Court.

(5) Any man who shall contract another marriage without permission of the Arbitration Council shall—

(a) pay immediately the entire amount of the dower, whether prompt or deferred, due to the existing wife or wives, which

---

*Mst. is an abbreviation of *Musammat* and is used in these Pakistani decisions before the names of women much like Miss or Mrs.

amount, if not so paid, shall be recovered as arrears of land revenue; and

(b) on conviction upon complaint be punishable with simple imprisonment which may extend to one year, or with fine which may extend to five thousand rupees, or with both.

(5) Family Courts

Comment: An act establishing family courts was enacted in West Pakistan under the title *The West Pakistan Family Courts Act* (*XXXV of* 1964). The jurisdiction of these courts is defined as follows:

West Pakistan Family Courts Act.

Section 5—Jurisdiction:—Subject to the provisions of the Muslim Family Laws Ordinance, 1961, and the Conciliation Courts Ordinance, 1961, the Family Courts shall have exclusive jurisdiction to entertain, hear and adjudicate upon matters specified in the Schedule. [The Schedule specifies: dissolution of marriage, dower, maintenance, restitution of conjugal rights, custody of children and guardianship. Conciliation Courts are constituted similar to the Arbitration Councils set up under the Muslim Family Laws Ordinance. Generally, they consist of the Chairman of the Union Council and two representatives, one each nominated by the parties to the dispute. The Conciliation Courts have wide jurisdiction, some compulsory, some only if the parties agree to go to the Conciliation Court.]

Section 21. Provisions of Muslim Family Laws Ordinance to be applicable.—(1) Nothing in this Act shall be deemed to affect any of the provisions of the Muslim Family Laws Ordinance, 1961, or the rules framed thereunder; and the provisions of sections 7, 8, 9 and 10 of the said Ordinance shall be applicable to any decree for the dissolution of marriage solemnized under the Muslim Law, maintenance or dower, by a Family Court. [Section 9 and 10 of the Family Laws Ordinance deal with maintenance and dower.]

(2) Where a Family Court passes a decree for the dissolution of a marriage solemnized under the Muslim Law, the Court shall send by registered post, within seven days of passing such decree, a certified copy of the same to the appropriate Chairman referred to in Section 7 of the Family Laws Ordinance, 1961, and upon receipt of such copy, the Chairman shall proceed as if he had received an intimation of *talaq* required to be given under the said Ordinance.

(3) Notwithstanding anything to the contrary contained in any other law, a decree for dissolution of a marriage solemnized under the Muslim Law shall—(a) not be effective until the expiration of ninety days from the date on which a copy thereof has been sent under subsection (2) to the Chairman; and (b) be of no effect if within the period specified in clause (a) a reconciliation has been effected between the parties in accordance with the provisions of the Muslim Family Laws Ordinance, 1961.

Section 22—Bar on the issue of injunctions by Family Court.—

Family Court shall not have the power to issue an injunction to, or stay of any proceedings pending before a Chairman or an Arbitration Council.

. . . .

Section 4—Qualifications of Judge.—No person shall be appointed as a judge of a Family Court unless he is or has been a District Judge, an Additional District Judge or a Civil Judge.

. . . .

Section 14—Appeals.—(1) Notwithstanding anything provided in any other law for the time being in force, a decision given or a decree passed by a Family Court shall be appealable—

(a) to the High Court, where the Family Court is presided over by a District Judge, an Additional District Judge or a person notified by Government to be of the rank and status of a District Judge or an Additional District Judge; and

(b) to the District Court, in any other case.

(2) No appeal shall lie from a decree passed by a Family Court.—

(a) for dissolution of marriage, except in the case of dissolution for reasons specified in Clause (d) of item (viii) of Section 2 of the Dissolution of Muslim Marriages Act, 1939; [this clause entitles the wife to seek a divorce on the grounds that her husband "disposes of her property or prevents her exercising her legal rights over it."];

(b) for dower not exceeding rupees one thousand;

(c) for maintenance of rupees twenty-five or less per month.

Comment: As is apparent from Section 5 of the Act, the jurisdiction of the family courts is not exclusive, but is in certain cases concurrent with the jurisdiction of the arbitration councils and the conciliation courts. The arbitration councils may try to bring about reconciliation in case of *talaq* and may also issue certificates for maintenance of the wife. Since the conciliation courts have limited jurisdiction in certain money matters, the amount of dowry or maintenance legally payable can also be recovered through the conciliation courts. A main difference between the arbitration councils and conciliation courts on the one hand and the family courts on the other is that the family courts are staffed by professional judges, whereas the other two institutions are staffed by arbitrators who do not necessarily have legal training. One advantage that it was felt the arbitration councils and similar institutions would have was that the arbitrators would be local people familiar with the circumstances of the case and with the parties. In practice, however, there seems to have been some reluctance on the part of persons who knew the parties well to become involved in family disputes and possibly incur the ill will of one or both of the litigants.

c. *Turkey*

Comment: As stated in the historical section, Turkey's family law is completely secularized and the problems encountered in drafting legislation on marriage and divorce by the countries so far discussed, did not arise in Turkey. Turkey's problems lay in the practical application of the rules formulated by its codes. The provisions on divorce are contained in the Turkish Civil Code and follow those of the Swiss Civil Code. Both codes distinguish between annulment of the marriage, divorce, and legal separation. The reasons for divorce are enumerated in both codes. Among them are adultery, attempt on the life of the spouse, commission of a felony or behavior which makes living together unbearable to the other spouse, desertion, mental illness, and incompatibility. Legal separation is ordered by the court if there is a chance for reconciliation. As to its length the following is stated:

Turkish Civil Code, 1926.

Article 139. Legal separation can be ordered for a period of one to three years. It ends automatically with the expiration of the period set, but either party may ask for divorce if reconciliation has not taken place during the period stated.

Article 140. After the period set for legal separation, divorce shall be granted even at the request of one of the spouses, unless the requestor is to be blamed exclusively for the causes justifying such action.

Even in this case divorce shall be granted if the other spouse refuses to reestablish married life. . . .

Comment: The Turkish code, following the Swiss, also establishes a delay during which the guilty party in a divorce may not marry:

Ibid.

Article 142. In granting the divorce, the judge shall set a period of at least one year and at most two years during which the guilty party may not remarry.

The period of legal separation shall be comprised in this period.

Comment: It should be noted that the Turkish and Swiss codes thus establish a temporary prohibition of remarriage as a punishment for the guilty party in the divorce action. This becomes even clearer from the Swiss code, which in Article 150 adds that the period shall be one to three years in case of adultery. Article 95 of the Turkish code prohibits remarriage to the widow, the divorced wife, and the wife whose marriage has been annulled within a period of three hundred days, unless she bears a child before the end of the period. This provision which has its parallel in other European legislations, such as the French or German is, like the *'idda* of Islamic law, directed against *commixtio sanguinis*.

Polygamy is, of course, forbidden in Turkey. This is evident from the Civil Code:

Ibid.

Article 93. Any person who wants to remarry must prove that

his preceding marriage was dissolved by death, divorce, or annulment.

. . . . .

Article 112. The marriage is null and void:
(1) if one of the spouses was already married at the time of the celebration of the marriage.

. . . . .

Article 114, paragraph 3. In case of bigamy the marriage is not void if the preceding marriage had been dissolved in the meantime and the other spouse was *bona fide*.

Comment: As we have seen in earlier discussions, the Islamic marriage is a civil contract which does not necessitate religious solemnization in the sense in which this is required in a Christian marriage. In the Ottoman Empire, however, the *imam* of the local mosque became, in the course of time, the key person officiating at the marriage ceremony. He was subordinated to the *qadi* and, according to a decree issued by the sultan, needed an authorization for every single case where he officiated. When the law was secularized in Turkey, the marriage ceremony also was secularized. This is stated in the Civil Code as follows:

Ibid.

Article 97. The promise of marriage is published if the future spouses have declared it to the president of the municipality or the official in charge of marriages in urban districts, or, in the villages, to the council of elders.
The period of publication is fifteen days.

. . . . .

Article 100. Any person concerned may register an objection to the marriage during the period of publication by alleging incapacity of one of the betrothed to contract marriage or the existence of an impediment.
The objection must be submitted in writing to one of the municipalities where publication has taken place.
The president of the municipality, his deputy, or the council of elders shall dismiss directly and simply any objection not based on incapacity to contract a marriage or on a legal impediment.
Article 105. Upon the demand of the betrothed and providing there is no objection, the president of the municipality, or the official in charge of marriages, or the council of elders, who have received the promise of marriage, must proceed to the celebration or must issue a certificate of publication . . . .
The certificate of publication entitles the betrothed to be married within six months before the president of a municipality or the official in charge anywhere in Turkey.

. . . . .

Article 108. The marriage is celebrated publicly at the town hall or the meeting hall of the council of elders by the president of the municipality, or the official in charge of marriages, or the village head in the presence of two witnesses who are of age. . . .

Article 110. The official celebrating the marriage delivers to the spouses immediately after the ceremony a certificate of marriage. The religious ceremony may not take place unless such a certificate is presented. The validity of the marriage, however, does not depend upon the religious ceremony.

Comment: As mentioned above, these provisions caused considerable difficulties in Turkish villages, at least for the first two decades or so, and marriages before the *imam*, without preceding civil ceremony continued to take place. Article 237 of the Turkish Penal Code makes the performance of such a marriage a felony:

Turkish Penal Code.

A marriage officer who knowingly solemnizes the marriage of persons who are not legally entitled to marry, parties to such a marriage, and appointed or natural guardians who consent or lead the parties to such a marriage shall be imprisoned for three months to two years.

A public officer issuing marriage certificates without abiding by the legal requirements shall be punished by imprisonment for not more than three months.

Whoever performs a religious ceremony for a marriage without seeing the certificate indicating that the parties are lawfully married shall be punished by the punishment prescribed in the preceding paragraph.

Men and women who cause a religious ceremony to be performed prior to being married lawfully shall be punished by imprisonment for two to six months.

If the man is already married, he shall be punished by imprisonment for six months to three years. If the woman knowingly marries such a man, she shall be given the same punishment.

Village heads are required to inform the authority concerned of persons whom they learn to have caused a religious marriage ceremony to be performed without a legal marriage ceremony having taken place between them. Whoever acts negligently in this respect shall be punished by a heavy fine of 5 to 100 liras, and in case of repetition in addition by imprisonment for not more than one month.

Comment: The practical difficulties which inhibited the conclusion of civil marriages were summarized cogently by a Turkish jurist:

H. TIMUR, "Civil Marriage in Turkey: Difficulties, Causes and Remedies," pp. 34–36.*

It is true that the provisions of Chapter III of the Civil Code, that is, the provisions pertaining to the celebration of civil marriage, are not uniformly applied. A simple statistical investigation

*Reprinted by permission of UNESCO, copyright 1957.

substantiates this assertion. According to the latest annual of statistics, the number of civil marriages performed each year in Turkey does not exceed 70,000. It is evident that these marriages, performed as they are in accordance with the provisions of the Civil Code, do not constitute the sum total of marriages contracted in Turkey. In countries such as Rumania and Yugoslavia which have about the same population as Turkey, the annual number of marriages is between 150,000 and 180,000.

On the other hand, the census taken every five years in Turkey shows that the population increased by 9 per cent during the same period. This, however, is a percentage to be found in countries with a larger number of marriages. This fact alone proves that there are many couples living as man and wife who were never united as prescribed by the Civil Code. Naturally, children born out of these unions are illegitimate. It is unnecessary to dwell here on the well-known disadvantages of the increase of these unions, which fall outside the scope of the provisions protecting the family, and of the children born thereof.

Various reasons can be advanced for this situation, and it can be shown that many of the present defects are not rooted in differences of culture and tradition, but that they stem rather from deficiencies in the administrative organization and from the fact that the desired cultural level has as yet not been attained. The following is a summary of the reasons:

1. The first step in the celebration of marriage is to apply to the competent official and to submit a certificate of birth. Certificates are given to those persons whose parents are themselves entered in civil registers and who have their own certificates. Consequently, it may become necessary to obtain certificates for parents and even grandparents. The engaged couple, often too impatient to wait for the completion of these long and cumbersome formalities, prefer to have a religious celebration of the marriage.

2. In the villages, as a result of old habits, which by now have lost their meaning, boys are registered a long time after their birth with the purpose of postponing military service and evading the road tax. Entry in the register occurs 5 or 10 years after the birth, as if the boy were just born. Thus, according to the register, a young man of 20 is 10 or 15 years old and the doors of civil marriage are closed to him.

3. Articles 122 and 123 of the law on public health provide that men and women who want to marry, must undergo a thorough physical examination. A medical officer must examine them as to whether they suffer from syphilis, mental disease or certain other disorders. Since doctors, even private practitioners, are mostly to be found in towns, it is difficult for the villagers to have the required physical examination. On the other hand in some regions young men do not view with approval the examination of their fiancees by male doctors.

4. The Turkish legislation on old age and retirement entitles the widowed wife and the unmarried daughter to a pension on the death of her husband or father employed by the government.

Since pensions cease to be paid in the event of marriage, the wife and daughter try to avoid a civil marriage.

5. The engaged couples are always desirous of seeing the celebration of their marriage blessed by some kind of solemnity. In the principal towns, halls of a more or less spacious character are provided for marriage ceremonies, while the peasants must content themselves with listening to a few dry stereotyped words of an uneducated official, pronounced in a small and poorly furnished chamber. Thus they prefer to have an *imam* read a chapter from the Qur'an.

6. The means of communication in Turkey cannot be compared to those in Switzerland. The journey to town for a medical examination and for the completion of other formalities is often long and exhausting, and in winter sometimes impossible.

The villagers also prefer polygamy because it provides cheaper labor for agriculture and because it is easy to divorce a childless wife . . . .

The difficulties which civil celebration of marriage encountered in Turkey, owing to a number of factors, are gradually decreasing. The second world war and the Korean war largely contributed to this development. It will help in discovering the principal causes of the difficulties if it can be shown how the war indirectly influenced family life in Turkey. During the war a law was issued providing for financial aid to the families of the men in the armed forces. Women applied by the thousand. But they had first to prove that they were married. Large numbers of the women had only gone through a religious marriage ceremony. The Turkish army temporarily released its men so that they could convert their religious marriages into civil ones. It was the same during the Korean war. And finally, the provisions of the tax laws giving relief to married taxpayers and those who have children, played an important part . . . .

Comment: An important problem which arose in cases where there had only been a religious marriage, the so-called *imam-nikah*, was the status of children born from such a marriage. As Professor Timur pointed out, these children were illegitimate and therefore would not have inherited from their fathers. In order to remedy this untenable situation, the Turkish Parliament periodically enacted legislation legitimizing children born of these unions.

Over the years the problems created in Turkey by the adoption of the Swiss marriage law have diminished. A better understanding of the practical advantages of civil marriages in terms of alimony in case of divorce, benefits from the state in certain circumstances, and others have made many Turkish women, even in the villages, aware of the usefulness of a civil ceremony. In addition, better roads, better halls for the performance of the civil ceremony, and more extended health facilities have helped to remove past obstacles. Thus in many parts of Turkey a large percentage of couples are now married in a civil as well as a religious ceremony. It is likely that the religious ceremony satisfies the need for a traditional mode of marriage in the eyes of the people whereas the civil ceremony is considered necessary because of its practical effects.

While Turkish law thus has maintained the provisions of Swiss marriage law despite initial major difficulties, there have been other areas of family relationships where the Turkish courts have sought to adjust the law to Turkish concepts. A problem of this kind was discussed by another Turkish jurist.

FERIT SAYMEN, "The Personal Relations between the Children of Divorced Parents and their Grandparents." pp. 471–477.

Article 148 of the Turkish Civil Code and Article 156 of the Swiss Civil Code deal with the personal relations of children with that parent to whom they were not entrusted at the time of divorce Paragraph 1 of this Article reads:

"In the case of divorce or legal separation, the judge shall take the necessary measures concerning the exercise of parental powers and the personal relations between the parents and the children after having heard the father and the mother."

A rich literature and an abundant number of decisions concerning this question exist in Turkey as well as Switzerland. The civil codes of the two countries do not, however, contain any provision which deals with the relations between these very children and their grandparents. The letter and spirit of the law does not permit any attempt at an extensive interpretation. This is perhaps the reason why the legal literature has not discussed this question, in fact has barely touched upon it. It has, however, considerable legal interest.

Without wanting to study this question in all aspects we intend to show in this discussion the contrast which exists between the practice of the Swiss Federal Court and the Turkish Court of Cassation.

The Swiss Federal Court in a decision of 24 February 1928 in Schmid v. Lemmenmeier (1928 *Journal des Tribunaux*, 194) ruled as follows:

"The Swiss Civil Code has not adopted the principle according to which the grandparents would have a *right* to maintain personal relationships with their grandchildren or to demand that their guardianship be entrusted to them. This principle cannot be deduced either from the provisions of the law or from any interpretation of these provisions. The law gives such a right only to the father and mother . . . . It should be noted furthermore that the right to maintain personal relations between parents and children is not a necessary consequence of parental power. . . . It should rather be stated that this right derives from the close bond which exists between parents and their children as a natural consequence of having been begotten by them."

"Even though a close family relationship exists between grandparents and grandchildren, one cannot say that there is a *gap* in the law since it does not grant grandparents as well as parents the right to visit the children. . . . The Swiss Civil Code has intentionally left to *custom and usage* the task of regulating these relationships. . . . At the time of the unification of Swiss law, the question of the right of the grandparents to maintain personal relations with their grandchildren was not raised in the projects or in the discussions in the commissions or in parliament . . . . The law would certainly have talked of the rights of the grandparents, if it had wanted to grant them such rights . . . one cannot therefore speak of a gap in the law."

"Furthermore, the statutory regulation of the personal relations between grandparents and grandchildren would certainly lead to difficulties. The same rights would have to be granted to the paternal and maternal grandparents. If each of the four grandparents would claim the right to visit with the grandchildren, the latter would be shuttled back and forth between parents and grandparents. Such a state of affairs could clearly become unbearable, if one or the other of the grandparents happened to be separated from his mate."

The action of the parent to whom the child has been assigned, of forbidding the grandparents to have personal relations with the child, merely constitutes the exercise of parental power which is exclusively his. The grandparents "cannot therefore claim that the exercise of this power constituted the abuse of a right in the sense of Article 2 of the Civil Code. Actually, if the refusal of the defendant constituted an abuse of a right, such abuse would exist not only with regard to the grandparents but also with regard to the child herself and the child only could claim the protection of Article 2. . . . The defendant did not abuse his paternal power. . . . However, if the grandparents should become more reasonable, the defendant should not make it impossible for them any longer to have any relations with their granddaughter. A prolonged suspension of such personal relations would result in a mutual estrangement, the child could be hurt emotionally and suffer a serious injury. Besides, the father in thus keeping the child and the grandparents apart could damage the child's chances to inherit from her grandparents. All this would not be compatible with what is generally understood as the proper exercise of parental power and with the established usages of our people, so that it may be possible to have the authorities intervene [as they can do in the protection of the rights of the child if the parents do not exercise their powers in accordance with their duties]. . . ."

[In very similar cases the Turkish Court of Cassation reached different conclusions:]

Second Chamber of the Court of Cassation, Decision of 9 March 1944, No. 3144/4361.

[The Court confirmed the judgment of the court below and endorsed that court's reasoning:]

"Although the law does not contain any applicable provision and although the mother exercises parental power, the natural bond of blood and the legal bond of succession which bind the grandfather to his grandson make the desire irresistible for the former to maintain personal relations with the latter. On these grounds and on the basis of the powers granted to the judge by the law. . . [the right of visit was granted to the grandfather]."

Decision of the Court of Casssation of 11 December 1947, No. 6134/6501.

[The lower court had granted the right of visit to the grandparents on the following grounds:]

"The establishment of personal relations between grandparents and grandchild flows naturally from humanitarian principles and principles of justice."

"The law does not contain an applicable provision [and] the judge is authorized to decide according to Article 1 of the Civil Code." [This article allows the judge in cases where the code is silent to use customary law or, where there is none, follow the rule he would formulate were he the lawgiver.]

". . . [T]he desire of the plaintiff to visit his grandchildren is due to bonds of blood which cannot possibly be ignored. Also, the law does not prohibit at all the establishment of such relations and the judge's discretion is supreme in this matter. Judgment confirmed."

Comment: To summarize the rest of Saymen's study: the Turkish Court of Cassation, in contrast to the Swiss Federal Court, held that a gap existed in the law which permitted the judge to follow Article 1 of the Turkish Civil Code:

The law is applicable to all legal questions for which it contains either an explicit rule or one which can be derived through interpretation.

If no provision of the Code can be applied, the judge shall decide according to customary law. If no customary law rule is applicable, the judge shall follow the rule he would formulate were he the lawgiver. In that case he shall follow established doctrine and practice as set forth by judicial decisions.

The Swiss decision emphasizes legal logic and the code provisions, the Turkish decisions place greater weight on moral concepts. It should be noted that the Turkish judge cannot utilize in his construction of the code provisions the legislative history as is done so well by the Swiss court in the above-quoted decision. The Turkish code was translated from the Swiss code with certain modifications in detail and adopted *in toto* by the Turkish legislature. There was no preparatory work except that of the translation commission, no discussion of details in Parliament and no explanation of the reasons behind specific provisions. Therefore, the Turkish judge, endowed with supreme discretionary power, may well see a gap in the law where the Swiss judge aided by a long tradition, by cantonal laws and customs, and by the preparatory work for the Civil Code sees no oversight on the part of the lawgiver. Also, to the Swiss the Civil Code is traditionalist, it preserves the local laws and customs. To the Turks the code is revolutionary and breaks all ties with the Islamic law which preceded it.

Finally, the structure of the Turkish family is very different from that of the Swiss family. The family ties, and particularly those between grandparents and their descendants, are probably less close in Switzerland than they are in Turkey, where in many regions the patriarchal family has not yet disappeared.

Chapter 7   The Law of Inheritance

A. Classical Islamic Law

Comment: The Islamic law of inheritance is characterized by an emphasis on intestate succession. The prevalence of intestate succession has raised many practical problems. It makes joint property an important legal phenomenon and leads to fragmentation of agricultural holdings. Classical Islamic law divides the heirs into two major groups, those who possess a right to a definite share, the sharers, and those who take the remainder, the residuaries. In pre-Islamic Arabia the system of inheritance was purely agnatic, that is, the heir was normally the nearest agnate, thereby excluding women, cognates, and also minors. The important reform Islam brought about was to assign definite shares to certain female relatives and to ascendants. According to the Sunni jurists, the sharers are first given their share and then the remainder of the estate goes to the nearest agnate.

Other important features of the Islamic law of inheritance are: distribution of the estate *per capita*, not *per stirpes*, and restriction of the disposition by will to one-third of the estate, the so-called disposable third.

1. *Intestate Succession*

a. *Qur'anic Provisions*

Qur'an, Sura IV.

Verse 7. Unto the men (of a family) belongeth a share of that which parents and near kindred leave, and unto the women a share of that which parents and near kindred leave, whether it be little or much—a legal share.

Verse 11. Allah chargeth you concerning (the provision for) your children: to the male the equivalent of the portion of two females, and if there be women more than two, then theirs is two-thirds of the inheritance, and if there be one (only) then the half. And to his [the decedent's] parents a sixth of the inheritance, if he has a son; and if he has no son and his parents are his heirs, then to his mother appertaineth the third; and if he has brethren, then to his mother appertaineth the sixth, after any legacy he may have bequeathed, or debt (hath been paid). Your parents or your children; Ye know not which of them is nearer unto you in usefulness. It is an injunction from Allah. Lo! Allah is Knower, Wise.

Verse 12. And unto you belongeth a half of that which your wives leave, if they have no child; but if they have a child then unto you the fourth of that which they leave, after any legacy they may have bequeathed, or debt (they may have contracted, hath been paid). And unto them belongeth the fourth of that which ye leave if ye have no child, but if ye have a child then the eighth of that which ye leave, after any legacy ye may have bequeathed, or debt (ye may have contracted, hath been paid). And if a man or a woman have a distant heir (having left neither parent nor child), and he (or she) have a brother or a sister (only on the mother's side) then to each of them twain (the brother and the sister) the sixth, and if they be more than two, then they shall be sharers in the third, after any legacy that may have been bequeathed or debt (contracted) not injuring (the heirs by willing away more than a third of the heritage) hath been paid. A commandment from Allah. Allah is Knower, Indulgent.

b. *Writings of Jurists*

The following passages are taken from a brief Malekite work the *Risala* (Treatise) of Ibn Abi Zayd al-Qayrawani. The author was born in Nefza (Spain) in A.D. 922/23. He spent most of his life in Kairuan in present-day Tunisia where he died in A.D. 996. He was one of the famous scholars of the Malekite school. The *Risala* was most recently edited and translated into French by Leon Bercher. Parts were edited and translated into English by Alexander David Russell and Abdullah al-Ma'mun Suhrawardy under the title *First Steps in Muslim Jurisprudence*. Both works contain the Arabic text as well as the translation.

IBN ABI ZAYD AL-QAYRAWANI, *Risala*, pp.274–279.

There are only ten categories of male heirs; the son and son's son and further down [in the direct line]; the father; the paternal grandfather and up [in the direct line]; the brother; the son of the brother and further male descendants; the paternal uncle; the son of the uncle and further male descendants; the husband; and the patron [of a freedman].

There are only seven categories of female heirs; the daughter; the daughter of the son; the mother; the grandmother; the sister; the wife; and the patroness [of a freedman].

The husband's share in his wife's estate is one-half if she does not leave a child or a child of a son. If she leaves a child or a child of a son, be it the husband's offspring or that of another, the husband's share is a fourth.

The wife's share in her husband's estate is a quarter if he does not leave a child or a child of a son. If he leaves a child or a child of a son, be it the wife's offspring or that of another, the widow's share shall be one-eighth.

The share of the mother in the estate of her son is one-third if there are no children or children of a son nor two or more brothers or sisters. There are two special cases of distribution. If the decedent leaves a wife and both his parents, the wife receives a quarter of the estate, the mother a third of what is left, and the father the rest. If the heirs are the husband and the parents of the wife, the husband receives half, the mother a third of what is left, and the father the rest. In all other instances the mother receives one-third of the estate. . . . However, if there are children or children of a son, or two brothers or sisters, the mother's share is one-sixth.

If the father is the sole heir of his child, he takes the whole estate. If the decedent has left a male child or children of a son, the share of the father is one-sixth. If the decedent has left neither a male child nor children of a son, the share of the father is still a sixth, then other heirs who are entitled to a share receive their share and the father takes the remainder.

If a male child is the sole heir he takes the whole estate. If not, he takes the remainder after those entitled to a fixed share who compete with him have received their share. These are the wife of the decedent, his parents and grandparents.

. . . If there are a son and a daughter, the share of the son is equal to that of two daughters. This rule applies no matter what the number of sons and daughters. . . .

The share of an only daughter is one-half, that of two daughters two-thirds. If there are more than two daughters their total share is still two-thirds . . . .

Brothers and sisters do not inherit if the father, son or male children of the son of the decedent are living . . . .

Comment: The above passages give some idea of the detailed and complex rules which Islamic law established for the shares to be received by the various relatives of the decedent. In order to clarify these rules further, a more schematic presentation will be given.*

As set forth in the Qur'an there are two categories of heirs, the sharers, also called Qur'anic heirs, and the residuaries.

   (a) *the Sharers* are:
      (1) the husband or
      (2) the wife
      (3) the daughter
      (4) the daughter of a son however far removed in descendance
      (5) the father
      (6) the mother
      (7) the true grandfather, however far removed
      (8) the true grandmother, however far removed

*This brief presentation follows the majority Sunni opinion in all instances and omits details particularly with regard to collateral relatives. A thorough discussion of the Islamic inheritance law is available in N. J. Coulson, *Succession in the Muslim Family*, (Cambridge: Cambridge University Press, 1971).

(9) the full sister
(10) the consanguine sister
(11) the uterine brother
(12) the uterine sister

Definition of terms:

A *true grandfather* is an ascendant between whom and the decedent no female is interposed in the line of descent.

A *true grandmother* is a female ascendant between whom and the decedent no male ancestor is interposed who is separated from the decedent by a female. Thus the father's mother and the mother's mother are true grandmothers; the mother's father's mother is not.

A *consanguine sister* is a half-sister related to the decedent through the father.

A *uterine brother or sister* is a half-brother or half-sister related to the decedent through the mother.

A *daughter of a son, however far removed* includes a son's daughter, a son's son's daughter etc.

The shares of the various sharers are as follows:

(1) *husband*	$\frac{1}{4}$ if there is a child or a son's child no matter how far removed; $\frac{1}{2}$ if there is no such child.
(2) *wife*	$\frac{1}{8}$; if there are several wives they take $\frac{1}{8}$ collectively, to be divided equally among them. $\frac{1}{8}$ is received if there is a child or son's child no matter how far removed; if there is no such child, the share is $\frac{1}{4}$.
(3) *daughter*	$\frac{1}{2}$; several daughters take $\frac{2}{3}$ collectively. These shares apply if there is no son. If there is a son, daughters take as residuaries (see p. 180).
(4) *the daughter of a son, no matter how far removed*	$\frac{1}{2}$; $\frac{2}{3}$ if there are several daughters in this category taking collectively. These shares apply if there is no son or daughter, no higher son's son, no higher son's daughter, or no equal son's son. If there is a son, a higher son's son, or if there are several daughters or higher son's daughters, the daughter of a son does not take anything, she is excluded from the inheritance. If, however, there is only one daughter or higher son's daughter, the daughter or higher son's daughter will take $\frac{1}{2}$, the daughter of a son dealt with here will take $\frac{1}{6}$. If the daughter of a son competes with an equal son's son she becomes a residuary.

(5) *the father* — $\frac{1}{6}$ if there is a child or a son's child however far removed; if there are no descendants he takes as a residuary. In the presence of daughters he is a sharer as well as a residuary (see p. 180).

(6) *the mother* — $\frac{1}{6}$ if there is a child or a child of a son however far removed, or two or more brothers or sisters of the decedent, whether such brothers or sisters are full, consanguine or uterine. If there is no child or son's child however far removed or not more than one brother or sister, the mother takes $\frac{1}{3}$. However, although collaterals may restrict the mother to $\frac{1}{6}$, they will not inherit if the decedent's father survives. If a wife or husband of the decedent survives together with the decedent's father, the mother takes $\frac{1}{3}$ of what remains after the share of the wife or husband has been deducted.

(7) *grandfather however far removed* — $\frac{1}{6}$. He is entirely excluded by the father of the decedent or a nearer true grandfather. Otherwise his position is the same as the father's would be were he living.

(8) *grandmother however far removed* — $\frac{1}{6}$ whether there is one or several. The maternal grandmother is entirely excluded by the mother or a nearer maternal or paternal grandmother. The paternal grandmother is entirely excluded by the mother, the father, a true grandfather, a nearer true maternal or paternal grandmother.

(9) *full sister* — $\frac{1}{2}$ if there is one, $\frac{2}{3}$ collectively if there are several. A full sister is entirely excluded by a son, a son's son however far removed, the father or the true grandfather. If there is a full brother, the full sister becomes a residuary.

(10) *consanguine sister* — $\frac{1}{2}$ if there is one, $\frac{2}{3}$ collectively if there are several. A consanguine sister is entirely excluded by a son, a son's son however far removed, the father, or a true grandfather, as well as a full brother or more than one full sister. If there is only one full sister the consanguine sister or sisters will take $\frac{1}{6}$. The consanguine sister becomes a residuary with a consanguine brother.

(11) *uterine brother* — $\frac{1}{6}$ if there is one, $\frac{1}{3}$ collectively if there are several. The uterine brother is entirely excluded by a child, a son's child however far removed, the father or a true grandfather.

(12) *uterine sister* — same as uterine brother.

Illustrative Diagrams to (4) Above

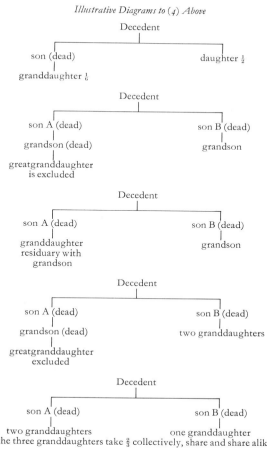

Decedent
son (dead) — daughter ½
granddaughter ⅙

Decedent
son A (dead) — son B (dead)
grandson (dead) — grandson
greatgranddaughter
is excluded

Decedent
son A (dead) — son B (dead)
granddaughter
residuary with
grandson — grandson

Decedent
son A (dead) — son B (dead)
grandson (dead) — two granddaughters
greatgranddaughter
excluded

Decedent
son A (dead) — son B (dead)
two granddaughters — one granddaughter
the three granddaughters take ⅔ collectively, share and share alike.

Illustrative Diagrams to (6) Above

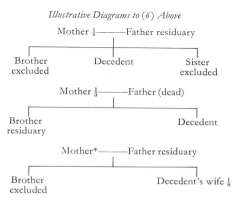

Mother ⅙———Father residuary
Brother excluded — Decedent — Sister excluded

Mother ⅓———Father (dead)
Brother residuary — Decedent

Mother*———Father residuary
Brother excluded — Decedent's wife ⅛

*Mother takes ⅓ of estate after deduction of ⅛.

(b) *the Residuaries or Agnatic Heirs.*

An agnate is a person who is related to the decedent through male links only. This would include such persons as the son, the son's son, but also the son's daughter, the father, the father's father and so forth. The residuaries can be divided into descendants, ascendants, and collateral relatives, among the latter are included not only brothers and sisters of the decedent, but also the paternal uncle, both full and consanguine, and his son and remoter descendants. Among the male agnates, the son takes only as a residuary, that is, assuming there is only one son, he will take what is left after the shares of the Qur'anic heirs have been satisfied. Let us say the decedent left a wife and one son, then the wife will get $\frac{1}{8}$ of the estate and the son will get the rest. As we have seen in the discussion of the Qur'anic heirs, there are some who may take as residuaries. Thus, if there is a son, the daughter of the decedent does not take as a sharer, but as a residuary with the son. She does not, however, share equally with him. There is a general rule that when a male residuary competes with a female residuary, the male residuary takes double the female portion. Therefore, if a man has left a son and two daughters, the son will take $\frac{2}{4}$ of the estate and each daughter will take $\frac{1}{8}$.

The following are the classes of the residuaries in order of succession:

(1) *Descendants*

   (i) *Son.* Several sons inherit equal shares.

   (ii) *Son's son however far removed.* The nearer in degree excludes the more remote one. Two or more son's sons in the same degree inherit equal shares.

(2) *Ascendants*

   (i) *Father.* The father has a special position, he inherits as both a Qur'anic heir and an agnatic heir if he competes with a daughter of the decedent. Let us assume the decedent has left a daughter and his father. In this case the daughter receives $\frac{1}{2}$ of the estate and the father, since there is a surviving child, receives $\frac{1}{6}$. This leaves $\frac{1}{3}$ of the estate still unassigned. Sunni law allots this share to the father as a residuary, so that in effect the decedent's father and the decedent's daughter each inherit $\frac{1}{2}$ of the estate.

   (ii) *True Grandfather, however far removed.* The nearer in degree excludes the more remote one.

(3) *Collateral Relatives of the Decedent*

   (i) *full brothers*

   (ii) *full sisters*

   (iii) *consanguine brothers*

   (iv) *consanguine sisters*

   (v) *full brother's son*

   (vi) *consanguine brother's son*

   (vii) *full brother's son's son*

   (viii) *consanguine brother's son's son*

then follow more remote male descendants of the last two categories.

(4) *Collateral Relatives of the Decedent's Father*
    (i) *full paternal uncle*
    (ii) *consanguine paternal uncle*
    (iii) *full paternal uncle's son*
    (iv) *consanguine paternal uncle's son*
    (v) *full paternal uncle's son's son*
    (vi) *consanguine paternal uncle's son's son*

then follow the more remote male descendants of the last two categories. Male descendants of more remote true grandfathers are treated in the like order and manner as the persons in category (4).

In the distribution of the estate among the heirs, two anomalous situations can arise. One is that the sum of the shares of the sharers exceeds the total. To take a simple example, a female decedent leaves a husband and two full sisters. Under the law the husband is entitled to $\frac{1}{2}$ of the estate and the two sisters collectively take $\frac{2}{3}$. Using a common denominator, this means $\frac{3}{6} + \frac{4}{6} = \frac{7}{6}$. In such a case the shares have to be reduced. This is done by making the denominator the sum of the numerators and leaving the numerators as they are. The sum of the numerators in this case is 7. Thus we have $\frac{3}{7}$ for the father and $\frac{4}{7}$ collectively for the two sisters of the decedent. The sum is $\frac{7}{7}$.

This case is, of course, rare. Somewhat more frequent would be the case where there are no residuaries and the shares of the sharers do not add up to the total (so-called return or *radd*). In this case the residue is distributed among the sharers in proportion to their share. Again the shares are reduced to a common denominator and the denominator then is made the sum of the numerators with the numerators remaining unchanged. Thus, for example, the decedent leaves a mother and one daughter. The share of the mother is $\frac{1}{6}$, that of the daughter is $\frac{1}{2}$. Together these shares are $\frac{2}{3}$, leaving a residue of $\frac{1}{3}$. According to the above formula the estate is then distributed as follows: the mother receives $\frac{1}{4}$ and the daughter $\frac{3}{4}$. Husband and wife are not entitled to an increase under *radd*.

2. *Wills*

Comment: As stated above, a Muslim is permitted to dispose only of one-third of his estate by will. The Qur'an sanctions bequests.

Quar'an, Sura II

Verse 180. It is prescribed for you, when one of you approacheth death, if he leave wealth, that he bequeath unto parents and near relatives in kindness. (This is) a duty for all those who ward off (evil).

Comment: A *hadith*, however, gives more detailed rules:

AL-BUKHARI, *Sahih*, Book 23, Chapter 37.

Sa'd bin Waqqas said: The Messenger of Allah used to visit me at Mecca, in the year of the farewell pilgrimage because of my illness which had become very severe. I said: "My illness has become very severe and I have much property and there is no one to inherit from me except a daughter, shall I bequeath two-thirds of my property to a charity?" He said: "No." I said: "Half?" He said: "No." Then he said: "Bequeath one-third and one-third is a great deal, because if you leave your heirs free from want it is better than if you leave them in want, begging of other people ...."

Comment: Al-Qayrawani states on this matter:

AL-QAYRAWANI, *Risala*, pp. 220–221.

Whoever has assets which could be the object of disposition by will, should make his will. However, there cannot be bequests in favor of a legal heir. All bequests must come out of the bequeathable third. Any excess beyond this third shall be restored [to the legal heirs], unless the latter agree to the bequest ....

3. *Shi'i Law of Inheritance*

Comment: The law of inheritance is one field where Shi'i law differs significantly from Sunni law. According to the law of the Ithna 'Ashari sect, which for our purposes is the most important one, heirs are divided into three classes. Qur'anic heirs in the first class are husband and wife, father and mother, sons and daughters as well as further linear descendants. One peculiar feature of Shi'i law is that grandchildren take *per stirpes*, that is, they divide the portion of their parent. The second class of heirs, comprises maternal and paternal grandparents how-soever high, as well as brothers and sisters and their descendants. The third class consists of paternal and maternal uncles and aunts of the decedent, then their descendents, uncles and aunts of the father and mother of the deceased how high so ever and their descendants. These groups take in order of priority. In Shi'i law the higher class excludes the lower.*

B. Present-day Islamic Countries

1. *The Arab Countries*

Comment: This field of law too is still covered by Islamic legal principles in most Muslim countries—Turkey, of course, is again an exception—but here also adaptations to modern needs have been made.

In terms of time, some of the reforms in the field of marriage and divorce preceded those in the field of inheritance law, primarily because reforms in the area of divorce particularly were considered more urgent. In Egypt a comprehensive law of intestate

*The shares are generally the same as in Sunni law.

succession was enacted in 1943, and a Law on Wills in 1946. A number of the more recent statutes have included rules on inheritance as well as rules on marriage and divorce. Such comprehensive statutes were enacted in Syria (1953), Tunisia (1956, as amended in 1959), and Morocco (1958).

Generally, the modern statutes have introduced only comparatively minor changes in the law of intestate succession. The basic edifice has remained intact (a significant exception is Pakistan). In the following some general provisions of the Egyptian Law on Intestate Succession are given.

Egyptian Law No. 77 of 1943.

Article 1. The succession opens with the death of the decedent or as a result of a judicial decree declaring him presumed dead.

Article 2. The right of succession comes into being with the establishment of the actual existence of the heir at the moment of death of the decedent or at the date of the decree of his presumptive death. . . .

Article 3. If two persons die without its being known who died first, neither shall succeed to the other, whether or not death has been caused by the same event.

Article 4. The charges against the estate are satisfied in the following order:

(1) The expenses necessary to cover the funeral of the decedent and that of any person for whose support the decedent was responsible, from the time of death to interment;

(2) the debts of the decedent;

(3) any bequest within the limits of the bequeathable portion.

The remainder is distributed among the legal heirs. If there is no heir, distribution of the remaining estate takes place as follows:

(1) The portion to which a person is entitled who was acknowledged as a kinsman by the decedent;

(2) the bequests made by the decedent in excess of the bequeathable third;

(3) in default of such persons, the estate or the residue thereof shall be paid into the Public Treasury.

[The "acknowledged kinsman" is defined in Article 41:

If the deceased acknowledged anyone's relationship to him as a child of someone else, the one so acknowledged will be entitled to his estate provided he be of unknown parentage, provided further that the lack of any relationship to the decedent cannot be proven and that the decedent has never retracted this acknowledgment . . . .]

Article 5. One of the bars to inheritance is that the heir should have deliberately caused the death of the decedent, whether as principal, accessory or false witness whose testimony led to the sentence of death and its execution, provided the act was carried out without justification or excuse and the perpetrator was sane and no less than 15 years of age.

Abuse of the right of self-defense is considered as an excuse.

Article 6. There is no right of inheritance between Muslims

and non-Muslims, but non-Muslims may inherit from each other. Difference in domicile is no bar to inheritance between Muslims. It is also no bar to inheritance between non-Muslims unless the law of the foreign state bars foreigners from inheritance.

Article 7. The claims to the estate are based on marriage, blood relationship or agnation by law.

Those who inherit by reason of marriage are entitled to a prescribed share.

Those who inherit because of blood relationship are entitled to a prescribed share or inherit as residuaries or inherit under both these rights, or they inherit as uterine relatives in accordance with the rules of exclusion and the return respectively.

.   .   .   .

Article 30. If the prescribed shares do not exhaust the estate and there are no agnates by blood, the residue will be given to those entitled to prescribed shares, other than the surviving spouse, in proportion to their respective shares, while the remainder will be returned to the surviving spouse if there are no agnates by blood, no relatives entitled to a prescribed share and no uterine relatives. [This article thus deals with the so-called "right of return" (*radd*), that is, the distribution of the remaining estate, if the claims of the sharers have been satisfied and there is no residuary heir.]

Comment: The law of wills was regulated in Egypt by Law No. 71 of 1946. This law has some important features, particularly with regard to so-called "obligatory bequests."

Egyptian Law No. 71 of 24 June 1946.

Article 1. The will is an act through which the testator disposes of his estate for the time after his death.

Article 2. The will can be oral or in writing. If the testator is incapable of expressing himself in either of these manners, the will may be established through intelligible signs . . . .

Article 3. In order to be valid, the will must not contain provisions contrary to religious precepts or have a motive which runs counter to the intentions of the legislator.

The will of a non-Muslim is valid unless it is forbidden by his own religious law or by Islamic law.

.   .   .   .

Article 13. A will which has as its objective the distribution of the estate among the [legal] heirs of the testator and designation of the portion of each one of the heirs or of some among them, is valid and becomes irrevocable upon the death of the testator. If the value of the portion given to one of the heirs exceeds his [legal] share of the estate, the excess is regarded as a bequest.

.   .   .   .

Article 37. The will drawn in favor of a legal heir or a non-heir is valid up to a third of the estate and does not require ratification by the legal heirs. Beyond this third the will is valid, provided the excess is ratified by the heirs expressly after the death of the testator . . . .

. . . . . .

Article 76. If the decedent does not make a bequest for the descendants of a child who has predeceased him, has died at the same time, or has been presumed dead, equal to the portion of the estate of the decedent that would have been due him had he survived, the descendants shall by right be entitled to a bequest equal to that portion up to one-third of the estate, provided that they are not legal heirs and that they have not received from the decedent under whatever title as a gift a portion equal to that which is due them. If the descendants have received a share smaller than that to which their forebear was entitled, they shall have a right to the remainder under the title of an obligatory bequest.

These bequests are due the children of a daughter and the descendants of a son no matter what degree they belong to, provided they are linked to the decedent exclusively through the male line. In the latter case any ascendant excludes his own descendants, but not those of others. The portion of each ascendant shall be distributed among his descendants of whatever degree they may be in accordance to the rules concerning intestate succession in the same manner as if he or his ascendants who link him with the decedent had died after the death of the latter and as if the death of these ascendants had taken place in order of their lineage.

Article 77. If the bequest made by the decedent to a person having a right to an obligatory bequest exceeds the portion due him then the excess will be regarded as an ordinary bequest; if it is smaller, the beneficiary has a right to a complementary portion.

If the decedent makes bequests to some of those entitled to obligatory bequests and not to others, the latter have a right to their share. . . .

Article 78. The obligatory bequests take precedence over other bequests.

If the decedent has not made any bequests to those who have a right to an obligatory bequest, but has made bequests to other beneficiaries, each of those having a right to an obligatory bequest takes his share out of the remainder of the estate if that remainder suffices. If not he takes his share from the remainder as well as from the goods bequeathed to other beneficiaries.

Comment: As was the case with the legislation on marriage and divorce, the Egyptian legislator emphasized that it had been necessary to go beyond Hanefite law in the drafting of the statute on wills.

Explanatory Memorandum to the Law on Wills.

At the beginning of the reign of Muhammad ʿAli the Sublime Porte issued an Imperial Firman and an *irade* which provided that the court decisions and the *fatwas* had to conform to the rite of Abu Hanifa. . . . However, studies which were undertaken revealed that it was extremely difficult to adhere to this rule in the administration of justice and to follow the most authoritative opinion of the Hanefite rite. The reasons were the following:

(1) A number of problems are the subject of controversies within the Hanefite rite, and it is impossible to determine which one of the various opinions is the most authoritative one. Hence there have been serious divergencies in court decisions.

(2) Certain changes which have occurred in the course of time make it necessary to apply rules taken from the Hanefite rite or some other rite, so that the legislator can provide the best possible means of resolving disputes between litigants.

(3) The rules of the Hanefite rite are scattered among various works and it is not easy for the public to ascertain these rules. It is only right that the public should know exactly the rules on the basis of which justice is dispensed. . . .

Comment: In the debate in the Egyptian Senate, the rapporteur of the bill made the same point:

Annals of the Senate, Session of 25 March 1946.

In the bill on wills the government has not confined itself to the use of rules of the Hanefite rite. Rather it has searched among other rites for sources of inspiration so as to draft a bill which is well adapted to present-day circumstances and which is well in line with the practical needs. . . .

However, if there is no provision laid down in the statute, one has to turn to Hanefite opinion in conformity with the Regulation for the Organisation of the *Shari'a* Courts, Article 280.

Comment: Provisions similar to those of the Egyptian statute are contained in the Syrian, Moroccan, and Tunisian legislation. However, all these statutes are more restrictive than the Egyptian one. The Syrian Law of Personal Status of 1953 restricts the beneficiaries of obligatory bequests to children of a son, the Moroccan Law of Personal Status of 1958 includes among those entitled to obligatory bequests descendants of a son how low so ever, but, like the Syrian law, excludes descendants of a daughter. The Tunisian law of 1959 finally gives the right to an obligatory bequest to the sons and daughters of a son or daughter who has predeceased the decedent, but not to any lower descendant. All these statutes, like the Egyptian one, stipulate that the obligatory bequests may not be larger than the bequeathable third.

A Tunisian decision makes it clear that in the establishment of the right to an obligatory bequest the date of the death of the person under whose will the obligatory bequest is taken is decisive. The date of the death of the predeceased son or daughter is immaterial.

*Tribunal of First Instance of Tunis, Judgment No. 25,685, 13 June
1967.*

[The plaintiffs in this suit were the children of a son and two
daughters all of whom had predeceased their mother. A certificate
had been drawn up by two notaries stating that the sole heirs
were two surviving daughters of the decedent. The grandchildren
of the decedent now prayed the court to declare void that certificate and recognize the rights of the grandchildren according to the
law of 1959.]

The Court:
Considering that the plaintiffs' request that the certificate drawn
up by the notaries Ibrahim bin Shadly Klibi and Muhammad bin
Hadi bin Yusuf Ismail dated 4 February 1966, be declared void;
Considering that they requested in addition to be recognized as
heirs in the succession of their grandmother Mrs. Ghazala bint
'Ali according to the provisions on obligatory bequests and in
accordance with Article 191 of the Personal Status Code;
Considering that counsel for the plaintiffs has produced:
1. An excerpt from the civil status register of deaths delivered
by the municipality of Tunis under number 1,546 and dating from
1964;
the certificate, the annulment of which is requested, and which
indicates that Mrs. Ghazala died on 20 March 1964 at the Rabta
hospital and that the sole heirs are her two daughters Khadduja
and Tumiya, born to her and her husband Muhammad bin
Firjani al-'Awini.
2. A certificate executed by the Sheikh of Manouba attesting that
Mrs. Ghazala died on the date indicated without having remarried.
3. A certificate also executed by the Sheikh of Manouba on
21 April 1967, attesting that 'A'isha and Manubia, daughters of
Ghazala and her husband Muhammad bin Firjani al-'Awini died
in Manouba, the first around 1934, the second around 1943.
4. A certificate executed by the Sheikh of Manouba attesting that
Ghazala died at the time and place indicated and that her heirs are
her daughters Khadduja and Tumiya on the one part and the
grandson Muhammad, son of her son al-Hattab, as well as the
following grandchildren all of whom are of age: Muhammad,
'Ali, Aziza and Zahra, children of her daughter 'A'isha and of
Hamadi bin Amara, and Kamar daughter of her daughter Manubia
and of Belkacem Yazidi on the other part.
5. A death certificate executed by [two notaries] dated 10 March
1965 and a list of heirs established on 30 January 1967 by two
notaries of Tunis . . . showing that the sole heirs of Ghazala are
[follow the same names as given above under 4];
Considering that counsel for the defendants conceded that the
plaintiffs were the grandchildren of Ghazala, but claimed that they
could not be recognized as heirs because their progenitors had
died before the promulgation of the Personal Status Law [al-Hatta,
'A'isha and Manubia, parents of all the plaintiffs involved had
died during the 1930's or 1940's] and that the law is not
retroactive;

Considering that it is evident from the documents submitted and from the admission of the parties that the decedent is the grandmother of the plaintiffs;

Considering that Article 191 of the Code of Personal Status provides that "the children ... whether male or female, of a person who dies before or at the same time as the children's grandparent, are beneficiaries of an obligatory bequest equal to the share which would have gone to their father or mother;"

Considering that the claim that the law is not retroactive is not relevant because the critical date is that of Mrs. Ghazala's death who is the parent of all the branches involved and who died on 20 March, 1964, that is after the promulgation of the Personal Status Code;

Considering that also the Public Prosecutor requested annulment of the notarial certificate of 4 February 1967 and recognition of the plaintiffs as heirs after their grandmother Ghazala;

On these grounds:

the tribunal decides in first instance [i.e., the judgment can be appealed] that the notarial certificate executed by the two notaries of Tunis, Messrs. Ibrahim bin Shadli Klibi and Muhammad bin Yusuf Ismail dated 4 February 1967 is annulled, that this annulment shall be noted on the death certificate of Mrs. Ghazala and in the register of the two notaries, that the plaintiffs shall be recognized as being entitled to the succession after their grandmother Ghazala according to the provisions on obligatory bequests as contained in Article 191 of the Personal Status Code. Defendants will bear the costs.

Comment: Obligatory bequests and some other aspects of the statutes here discussed were examined by Anderson.

J. N. D. ANDERSON, "Recent Reforms in the Islamic Law of Inheritance," pp. 354–365.*

What then ... of the excessive rigidity which ... characterises the Islamic law of inheritance in its Sunni form? This point has been tackled in the Sudan, Egypt and Iraq, in each of which countries it has now been decreed that a testator has complete freedom to make what legacies he likes, whether to heirs or non-heirs, within the bequeathable third, and that any such bequests which he may make to an heir are no longer subject to the other heirs' consent. This reform was effected in the Sudan by Judicial Circular No. 53 of 1945, which prefaces its provisions by the statement that "Experience has shown that people are in need of a relaxation in the provisions of the law of bequests as currently applied and that the adoption of the following provisions will be to their manifest advantage ...." As for Egypt the Explanatory Memorandum issued with the Law of Testamentory Dispositions 1946, maintains that the essential validity of a bequest to an heir, provided it is within the bequeathable third, is supported by the majority of jurists, while its implementation rests on the "Verse

*Reprinted by permission of *The International and Comparative Law Quarterly*.

of Bequest" in the Qur'an. This is the view of "a number of expositors, including Abu Muslim al-Asfahani, and also of a number of jurists from outside the four (Sunni) schools"; and this view was adopted in Article 37 "because people stood in need of it."

This may, no doubt, seem at first sight a very minor and natural reform. But it must be emphasized that it runs directly counter to what has continually been claimed as the "consensus" of the four Sunni schools and represents in fact if not in explicit acknowledgment, an adoption of the "heterodox" doctrine of the Ithna 'Ashari Shi'is in this respect. . . .

It is noteworthy that this reform not only allows a parent to make special provision for a particularly needy child, or other relatives, to make similar distinctions between one heir and another, but that it also expressly permits a testator to distribute his whole estate, item by item, between his heirs, provided only that this distribution does not favor some heirs at the expense of others to more than the extent of the "bequeathable third." In addition, this reform clearly goes a certain way towards remedying the unenviable position of the widow, for it at least allows her husband to augment her paltry entitlement on intestacy by a bequest of up to one-third of his net estate. A further concession in her favor (and indeed, that of the widower too) was made in the Sudan by Judicial Circular No. 28 of 1925, which provided that the spouse relict might take the residual estate of the deceased, by the doctrine of the "return," in the absence of any agnate, quotasharer or other relative. Similar (although not quite identical) provisions are included in the Egyptian Law of Intestate Succession, 1943, and the Syrian Law of Personal Status, 1953 . . . .

When we turn to the problem of the exclusion of grandchildren from any share in their grandparents' estate by the survival of an uncle (i.e., the son of such grandparent)—a problem which must have been present throughout the history of Islam but which has assumed much more serious proportions today with the progressive decay of family solidarity—the obvious remedy would seem to be to give them the right of representation, i.e., the right to step into the shoes of their deceased parent and inherit what he or she would have inherited had he or she survived the grandparent concerned . . . .

It was, obviously, in order to avoid . . . difficulties and to make provision for orphaned grandchildren while still keeping intact the general structure of the Islamic law of inheritance that the Egyptian reformers in 1946 tackled this problem by means of the device known as "Obligatory Bequests." But it seems advisable to consider this device, in the first place in the considerably simplified form in which it was subsequently adopted in the Syrian Law of 1953 and the Moroccan Law of 1958—for in both these countries (by contrast with the situation in Egypt and Tunisia) these bequests were confined to grandchildren through a predeceased son or son's son. Otherwise, the general provisions were much the same as in Egypt. . . . This ingenious device does not in any way affect the structure of the Islamic law of intestate succession, which it leaves completely untouched, while it yet makes provision for orphaned grandchildren. In most cases, moreover, it will give them precisely what their deceased father would have taken. Where, however, the deceased grandparent had only two sons, one of whom predeceased him, then his orphaned grandchildren would be confined to the bequeathable third; but where, on the other hand, the grandparent had made other bequests then it might well be that his orphaned grandchildren would receive more under the system of obligatory bequests than their deceased father would have received had he survived....

... The juristic justification for this exceedingly ingenious and beneficial expedient ... finds its primary support in the Qur'anic "Verse of Bequests" which commands a Muslim to make bequests in favor of "parents and relatives," and in view of a number of early authorities that this verse, however much it may have been abrogated in regard to those relatives who were subsequently accorded a fixed share in the "Verses of Inheritance," still makes it incumbent on a Muslim to make provision by will for any close relative who is not otherwise provided for. Next, it rests on the view of Ibn Hazm, some dicta attributed to very early jurists, and one report in the school of Ahmad Ibn Hanbal, that where a testator fails to make such an "obligatory" bequest it should nonetheless be executed out of his estate. Finally, it claims that the selection of orphaned grandchildren, as the only relatives in whose favor such action is to be taken, and the details as to what they are to be given, represents a legitimate exercise of the ruler's discretion in accordance with the public interests.

.   .   .   .

... [I]t is clear that this provision of obligatory bequests, in the form in which it is found in Egypt, has the further effect of favoring, in part, the immediate family of the deceased as against the claims of the tribal heirs. For example, if a man is survived by a daughter, the son or daughter of a predeceased daughter and a distant agnatic cousin, the daughter will take one-half, the grandchild one-third, and the cousin one sixth—instead of the one-half he would otherwise have taken. And where the only relatives are a deceased daughter's children and a distant agnate, the former will at least take one-third.

But this problem of the immediate family when in competition with the extended family of tribal life has been tackled in a much more direct and comprehensive way in Tunisia and Iraq. In Tunisia this took the form of an addendum added in 1959 to Article 143 of the Law of Personal Status, 1956. The first paragraph of this addendum ... provided that the doctrine of the "return" to quota-sharers, as accepted by almost all Sunnis today, except the Malikis, should be introduced in Tunisia. But the second paragraph was much more radical, and it reads "As for the daughter, whether one or many, or the son's daughter how low soever, she shall take the residue of the estate by the 'return' even in the presence of an agnate in his own right, like a brother or an uncle, or the Public Treasury." It is noteworthy, moreover, that this section has been added to the chapter on "Exclusion"; and it has been pertinently remarked that the effect of this provision is virtually to put the daughter or son's daughter in the position of an agnate in her own right, who will totally exclude even a brother of the full or consanguine blood (and equally, of course, a full or consanguine sister) . . . .

When we turn to Iraq it is well to remember that the law of Personal Status, 1959, took the unparalleled step of completely abandoning the Islamic law of inheritance, for both Sunnis and Shi'is, in favor of the law of succession—itself of German origin —which had previously been applicable only to holdings in government land. This audacious innovation, which aroused fierce opposition, was justified by 'Abd al-Karim Qasim on three distinct grounds: first, that Iraq must have a unified law of succession, and that the Sunni and Shi'i systems of inheritance were so different as to be irreconcilable; secondly, that men and women must be put on an equal footing, with no preference (for example) to sons over daughters, and this was contrary to both systems; and, thirdly, that there was nothing impious in this innovation, since the Qur'an, in allotting a double share to the male in such circumstances, used an Arabic word which implied advice rather than command. (Note: There is, however, no real substance in this argument.)

In the circumstances it is not surprising that when the regime of 'Abd al-Karim Qasim was overthrown by another *coup d'etat* in February, 1963, the new government issued an amendment to the Law of Personal Status, 1959, to cover those provisions which were "incompatible with the Islamic law," and that this phrase was intended principally to refer to intestate succession. But the interesting point is that the new provisions regarding intestate succession follow the main structure of the Shi'i law, and divide all relatives into three classes—first, children and children's children, together with the father and mother; next, brothers and sisters and their children, together with grandparents; and, finally, uncles and aunts and their children—and make this applicable to all Iraqis.

This seems eminently reasonable. One of the chief purposes of the Law of Personal Status, 1959, had been to unify the law; and its consistent method was to choose, in each particular, the rule which was most suitable to modern life, whether it was of Sunni or Shi'i origin. There can be little doubt, moreover, that the Shi'i system, with its wholehearted championship of the immediate family as against the tribal heirs, is much closer to the ethos of contemporary society, at least in its urban form. It seems, indeed, that a number of Iraqis who had daughters but no sons had, in recent years, professed conversion to the Shi'i faith just because they did not want a considerable part of their estate to go to a distant agnate.

As so often happens in the case of such legislative enactments, this new law is, however, open to differences of interpretation when it comes to detailed application. This is, indeed, particularly characteristic of the Iraqi law of 1959 (as amended), since this law represents, in parts, little more than a skeleton and leaves a vast amount to the discretion of the courts. But the major problem in regard to the law of inheritance comes from a combination of Article 1 (2) of the original law, which reads: "If there is no legislative provision which can be applied, judgment shall be given according to those principles of the Islamic law which are most suited to the provisions of this code," with Article 90 (as included in the amendment of 1963), which reads: "With due regard to the foregoing, the distribution to the heirs by relationship of their entitlement and their shares shall be according to the rules of the *shari'a* which were followed before the enactment of the Law of Personal Status No. 188 of 1959, as shall also be the case in regard to the rest of the provisions regarding inheritance . . . ." [This provision did not lead to a filling of lacunae in the statute from Shi'i law.] . . . [T]he courts in Iraq while all accepting the main structure of the Shi'i law as enunciated in the code, have each applied "the rules of the *shari'a* which were followed before the enactment of the Law of Personal Status No. 188 of 1959" in their own system, insofar as these could be combined therewith. And this means that while the Shi'is have, no doubt, applied their law in its integrity, the Sunnis have interpreted the statutory provisions, insofar as this was possible, in terms of Sunni law. The result is that whereas a daughter, for example, will totally exclude a germane brother, whether the case is decided in a Shi'i or Sunni court, she will exclude the son of a predeceased son only in a Shi'i court. . . .

At first sight this seems most unsatisfactory, since it runs directly counter to the desire for unification of the law which was one of the major motives behind the legislation of 1959. But . . . it is possible to argue that the amendment of 1963, as interpreted by the courts, still succeeds in promoting the interests of the immediate family against the tribal heirs, as desired by many modern Sunnis, while yet allowing scope for those differences of application in detail—particularly in regard to the relative position of agnates and "uterine" heirs—the summary eradication of which would have so deeply upset the long traditions of Sunni orthodoxy. Much the same principle also applies to other sections of the Law of Personal Status, and it seems probable that the skeleton nature of many of its provisions may be explained, in part at least, by a deliberate desire to allow for a measure of diversity within a basic uniformity.

Comment: One of the problems which has achieved added importance through the enactment of various statutes, is that of their application to foreigners and the conflict of laws questions which arise when a foreigner dies in one of these countries and leaves an estate there. A pertinent case was decided by the Egyptian courts as follows:

Court of Appeal of Alexandria, Decision of 17 May 1956.

The Court of Appeal of Alexandria: Considering that the Italian Consul General acting as representative of the Italian Government in the matter of the succession of the late Mrs. Concetta Olivo, widow of the late Gatio, of unknown parents and deceased the 6th February 1955, has presented to the President of the Court of First Instance in Alexandria a request for a ruling confirming the death of Mrs. Olivo of Italian nationality and resident in Alexandria, and stating that the succession should devolve upon the Italian Government since the deceased had left neither heirs nor a will; that this demand was transmitted to the Personal Status Court where the Consul General of Italy pleaded that the Italian Government represented by its Consul General in Alexandria, should be recognized as the sole legitimate heir of Mrs. Olivo of Italian nationality and deceased intestate at Alexandria on the 6th of February 1955; that in effect the deceased had left neither a will nor relatives within the sixth degree and that the Italian Government is heir according to Article 586 of the Italian Civil Code which is applicable on the basis of Article 17 of the Egyptian Civil Code and Article 954 of the Code of Civil Procedure;

[Article 586 of the Italian Civil Code provides:

If there are no other heirs . . . the succession devolves upon the State . . . . Acquisition is by right without need for acceptance . . . and cannot be subject of repudiation . . . .

The State is not responsible for the debts of the estate or for bequests which exceed the value of the estate acquired.]

[Article 572 of the same code provides:

If a person dies without leaving offspring, parents, or other ascendants, or brothers or sisters or their descendants, the succession is opened for the closest relative or relatives without regard to lineage. Succession does not take place among relatives beyond the sixth degree.]

[Article 17, paragraph 1 of the Egyptian Civil Code reads:

Inheritances, wills and other dispositions taking effect after death are governed by the law of the decedent, the testator or the person disposing of the property at death.]

[Article 954 of the Egyptian Code of Civil Procedure then in effect, provides in part:

Aside from other cases provided by law, affixing of the seals can be requested: . . . .

(5) by the consul of the country whose national the deceased was, provided the consular conventions give him this right . . . .];

that after hearing the advice of the Public Prosecutor, the Court of First Instance found against the plaintiff; that the Consul General of Italy filed an appeal; that the appeal is in order and is declared formally acceptable;

Considering further that the decision of the Court of First Instance was based on the following reasons:

1. that Article 10 of the Egyptian Civil Code according to which "Egyptian law alone will rule to determine the nature of a legal relationship in order to ascertain the law applicable in the event of a conflict between various laws in any particular suit," necessitates the conclusion that an estate if there are no heirs passes to the State where the estate is situated at the moment of death; also that according to the *lex fori* the succession in case there are no heirs

devolves upon the State not by right of inheritance, *jure hereditatis*, according to which the succession is governed by the law of the decedent, but according to the law of sovereignty, *jure imperii*;

that in other words the succession is governed by the law of the place where the estate is located and that the State appropriates that estate as if it were abandoned property;

that one has to refer to the *shari'a* as the common law applying to personal status matters in Egypt for the determination of the character of such devolution;

2. that under these conditions the appropriate rule to be applied in this case is that contained in Article 18 of the Civil Code according to which "possession, ownership and other real rights are regulated, as regards immovables, by the law of the place in which the immovable is situate, and, as regards movables, by the law of the place where the movable was situate at the time when the event occurred which resulted in the acquisition or loss of possession, ownership or other real rights." Since the basis of acquisition has been established in this case, the last paragraph of Article 4 of Law No. 77 of 1943 has to be applied according to which succession devolves upon the Treasury if there is no heir;

3. that even if one were to admit, purely hypothetically, the applicability of the rule of Article 17, paragraph 1 of the Civil Code, it still remains true that the cause for acquisition of the property is directly related to the economic status of the country, which depends on public policy and which in turn confers upon the State by virtue of its sovereign right, *jure imperii*, the ownership of abandoned property;

and that therefore the Italian Civil Code cannot be applied to the succession in dispute, since the law is incompatible with Egyptian public policy;

Considering further that in first instance as well as on appeal the appellant has maintained that Article 17, paragraph 1 should be applied . . .; that consequently Article 586 of the Italian Civil Code according to which estates without an heir devolve upon the government shall also be applied; that according to that text, the Italian Government acquires the estates as heir and not in exercise of a right of sovereignty, *jure imperii*, and that it administers the property *ex jure gestionis* in accordance with the rules of private law; that the exercise by the Italian Government of such a right regarding the estates of its nationals excludes all interference with the public policy of Egypt, since the rules regarding monetary relationships for contracts as well as wills are left to the free determination by the interested parties;

that an Italian who dies without leaving an heir is considered as having known that his estate will devolve upon the Italian Government; that this is, tacitly, the expression of the last will of the decedent, as is the case with a will made for the benefit of a third person residing abroad which the Egyptian law does not prohibit; that Articles 17 and 23 of the Preliminary Provisions of the Italian Civil Code provide that with regard to succession the national law of the foreigner at the time of his death shall be applied irrespective of the place where his estate is situate, consequently the estate of an Egyptian who dies in Italy would devolve upon his own government.

Considering further that on appeal the appellant added that Article 18 concerning possession, ownership and other real rights is not applicable and that the suit is governed by Article 17 . . .;

that in this regard and concerning the succession after Mrs. Olivo, of Italian nationality, the national law is that which gives the Italian Government the right to collect the estates of its nationals as legitimate heir coming after the relatives up to the sixth degree (Articles 565 and 572 of the Italian Civil Code); also that the succession was not vacant and that therefore Article 4 of Law No. 77 of 1943 could not be applied which subjects the succession to the law of the location of immovables; that therefore the decision of the first instance is in error regarding its interpretation of the Italian Civil Code, since the Italian Government inherits from its nationals as a relative in the seventh degree; and that it follows therefrom that the legal nature of its right is a right of succession *jure hereditatis* and not a sovereign right, *jure imperii*;

that the Italian law did not want to divorce this right of succession authorizing the State to appropriate the estate of the decedent from the classical rule which assimilates the position of the State to that of a legitimate heir; that consequently Article 586 of the Italian Civil Code applies to Italian nationals whether they die in Italy or abroad;

Considering further that the Public Prosecutor concluded that the establishment of the nature of a legal relationship for the purpose of determining the law applicable in Egypt to succession is governed by the *shari'a* to which the Egyptian law refers and to which one must turn in this case;

that a devolution of this kind is not governed by the rules of succession but is assimilated to the appropriation of abandoned property, that this excludes the application of Article 17, paragraph 1 of the Civil Code and that the rule applicable is that established by article 18 of the same code; that Article 4 of Law No. 77 of 1943 concerning inheritance applies to all vacant successions in Egypt whether the decedent be an Egyptian or a foreigner; that even if it were admitted that the rule applicable were that provided in Article 17 paragraph 1 of the Egyptian Civil Code and that Italian law ought to be applied, it still remains that the provisions of that law are incompatible with Egyptian public policy;

that finally it follows from Article 938 of Title III of the Code of Civil Procedure concerning the formalities in the case of the inheritance from foreigners, that the Egyptian legislator considered the devolution of all vacant successions to the State as a territorial rule, applicable also to estates left by foreigners; that therefore a foreign law cannot be applied whose provisions are contrary to this rule [Article 938 reads: In case the heirs are not present or not known or if present or known have renounced the estate, the appropriate judge may upon demand of an interested party or the Public Prosecutor appoint a curator for the estate. The curator must draw up an inventory of the assets and liabilities of the estate. In case the curator named is not the Administration of Public Property, he must notify that Administration of his appointment within ten days. The Administration must undertake in the country of origin of the deceased the searches necessary to discover possible heirs. If within a year of the date of the above notification, no heir has presented himself, the curator must turn over the estate to the Administration of Public Property. An official report has to be drawn up.];

Considering further that Mrs. Olivo, whose death was established at Cairo on 6th February, 1955, was before her death of Italian nationality and that she did not leave descendants or other relatives entitled to inherit and that all her assets, real and personal, are in Egypt;

Considering further that in order to establish which Egyptian or Italian laws are applicable to the present suit, the nature of the legal relationship has first of all to be determined; that the Egyptian law is solely qualified to do so as the law of the court *lex fori* in accordance with Article 10 of the Egyptian Civil Code;

Considering further that the determination of the legal relationship according to Egyptian law leads to the inevitable conclusion that a vacant estate devolves upon the State where the assets are located, that therefore the State has the right to appropriate by virtue of public authority the estate of the decedent who has died without heirs; that in effect for immovables generally and for movables found in a certain place at the moment when the event occurred which led to their acquisition, the law of the place applies in one case and the other;

that it follows from the foregoing that the rule deriving from the legal relationship in the present case leads to the conclusion that this relationship is governed by the law of the forum, that it is the Egyptian law which should be applied on the basis of an extensive interpretation;

that since an estate left by a decedent who died without heirs, is involved, succession legitimately and legally devolves upon the Treasury not by virtue of inheritance, but as an attribute of public authority to which all estates stemming from a vacant succession shall pass in accordance with Article 4, last paragraph of Law No. 77 of 1943 concerning inheritance whose provisions are founded upon the rules of the *shari'a*;

Considering further that the appropriation by the State of an estate on the basis of these provisions and in conformity with Article 938 of the Code of Civil Procedure as to the formalities to be fulfilled in the matter, is based upon the territorial power of the State which applies to the possession, ownership and other real rights concerning property to the exclusion of any other system of personal law;

that in contrast to what has been stated, the application of the law of the decedent, as maintained by the appellant rests upon different considerations;

that, in effect, the arguments submitted by the apellant concerning the structure of the family, its protection and the method of transfer of the estate of the decedent to his heirs, are completley foreign to the suit since Article 10 of the Egyptian Civil Code has determined the legal relationship stemming from the existence of immovables and movables left by the decedent whose possession and ownership are governed by Egyptian law to the exclusion of any other system;

that even admitting that the law applicable, according to legal rules, could be the national law of the decedent, it still remains that its application is incompatible with Egyptian law concerning public policy which excludes the application of a personal law to succession; that in effect the estate of a person who died without heirs falls to the Treasury, since the determination of the legal relationship by the *lex fori* establishes this devolution on the basis of sovereign right; that under these conditions a vacant succession remains submitted to the law of the place where the estate is located and that possession or ownership of the estate is regarded as acquired by the State where it is found and that such possession and ownership are established by appropriation, since abandoned property is involved;

that these principles derive from the *shari'a* and from the law on inheritance whose provisions touch upon public policy as deriving from the law concerning the position of immovables and justified furthermore by the exercise of the right of sovereignty *jure imperii*; this being in accordance with the authority deriving from the law of the place, in order to insure the protection of contracts concerning movables and immovables;

Considering further that these considerations exclude the application of the personal law to successions even where the decedent is of foreign nationality;

that therefore the estate of Mrs. Olivo who died without leaving heirs must be submitted to the law of the place where it is situate, this applying to immovables as well as movables, in accordance with Article 18 of the Civil Code;

that as a result the arguments of the appellant are contrary to the principles and rules set forth above;

that since Italian law is not applicable, no importance can be attached to the legal character of the right of the State being regarded as a legitimate heir in the seventh degree in order to recognize the devolution upon the State of estates left by its nationals in accordance with Italian inheritance law, justifying the appropriation of the estate by the Italian State;

that it is also necessary to discuss the question of reciprocal treatment resulting from the adoption of the rule established by that law, in the sense that the estate of an Egyptian who died in Italy would devolve upon his government, such a hypothesis does not permit the setting aside of the rule discussed and established by the Egyptian Civil Code, since there exists neither a special law nor an international convention applicable to Egypt in accordance with Article 23 of the Civil Code [that Article provides that the general rules of conflict established by the Civil Code are not applicable if provisions contrary to them "are included in a special law or in an international convention in force in Egypt."];

that from the foregoing it follows that the trial court's decision is well-founded and must be confirmed (Court of Alexandria, case 40–11°, Presiding Judge Yahiya Muhammad Massud, 17 May 1956).

Comment: This case illustrates well the attitude taken by the Egyptian courts with regard to the rules governing succession. It should be noted that continental European law applies the notion of "public policy" (*ordre public*) more widely than American courts; in general on the use of the concept of public policy in conflict of law situations by the French courts, see René David and Henry P. de Vries, *The French Legal System, An Introduction to Civil Law Systems*, New York, Oceana Publications, 1958, p. 134. In the present case the argument that a ruling for the appellant would be against public policy is reinforced by reference to the fact that the law of inheritance is based on the *shari'a*.*

In a decision of 2 July 1957 the Civil Chamber of the Court of Cassation of Egypt ruled on the legal character of the agreement of the legal heirs to a bequest.

Court of Cassation, Civil Chamber, Decision of 2 July 1957.

Syllabus by the Court.

In accordance with Law No. 18 of 1923, wills do not have to be registered. The same is true of their ratification. Actually, according to the opinion of the jurists of the Hanefite School, ratification is a clearance on the part of the heir. The transfer of the property is accomplished not by the heir, but by the testator. This doctrine follows from the principle which these jurists admit, according to which the will made in favor of an heir in any event, and the will made in favor of a non-heir if it exceeds one-third (of the estate) is valid and not void, but will have effect only if ratified by the heirs. Consequently, ratification does not establish a right and the view cannot be supported that the transfer of the property originates with the heir. In the present instance, the declaration contained in a contract among the heirs constitutes merely a ratification by the son of the decedent of the will executed by the latter in favor of his wife and his daughter within the limits of one-third of the estate. The said son thus set a declarative act and the contract confirming such declaration does not have to be registered. Consequently, this contract is also not subject to dues at the time of the registration of the instrument of partition of the realty of the estate drawn up on the basis of this declaration, the instrument of partition being subject to registration in accordance with Law No. 18 of 1923 and the ministerial order of 26 May 1926. [Law No. 18 of 1923 regulates the registration of various transactions concerning real property.]

*Compare with this case and the ruling that the State's right is that of the sovereign and not of an heir, the modern doctrine of escheat in the U.S. See *in re Lindquist's Estate*, 25 Cal. 2d 697, 154 P. 2d 879, 1944, 19 Am. Jur. 380 at 381. See also Thomas E. Atkinson, *Handbook on the Law of Wills*, 2d ed., 97.

2. *Pakistan*

Comment: In Pakistan only one aspect of the law of inheritance was regulated by the Family Laws Ordinance, namely succession by *stirpes*.

The Muslim Family Laws Ordinance, *1961*

Article 4. In the event of the death of any son or daughter of the propositus before the opening of succession, the children of such son or daughter, if any, living at the time the succession opens, shall *per stirpes* receive a share equivalent to the share which such son or daughter, as the case may be, would have received if alive.

Comment: The Marriage Commission Report stated on this matter:

Report of the Commission on Marriage and Family Laws, pp. *1222–1223*

Is there any sanction in the Holy Qur'an or any authoritative *hadith* whereby the children of a predeceased son or daughter are excluded from inheriting property?

It was admitted by all members of the Commission that there is no sanction in the Holy Qur'an or any authoritative *hadith* whereby the children of a predeceased son or daughter could be excluded from inheriting property from their grandfather. It appears that during the period of ignorance* this custom prevailed amongst the Arabs, and the same custom has been made the basis of the exclusion of deceased children's children from inheriting property of their grandfather. It may be mentioned that if a person leaves a great deal of property and his father has predeceased him, the grandfather gets the share that the father of the deceased would have gotten. This means that the right of representation is recognized by Muslim law amongst the ascendants. It does not, therefore, seem to be logical or just that the right of representation should not be recognized among the lineal descendants. If a person has five sons and four of his sons predeceased him, leaving several grandchildren alive, is there any reason in logic or equity whereby the entire property of the grandfather should be inherited by one son only and a large number of orphans left by the other sons should be deprived of inheritance altogether? The Islamic law of inheritance cannot be irrational and inequitable. Moreover, as the right of representation entitles a grandfather to inherit the property of his grandsons even though the father of the testator has predeceased him, why can the same principle be not applied to the lineal descendants, permitting the children of a predeceased son or daughter to inherit property from their grandfather? There are numerous injunctions in the Holy Qur'an expressing great solicitude for the protection and welfare of the orphans and their property. Any law depriving children of a predeceased son from inheriting the property of their grandfather would go entirely against the spirit of the Holy Qur'an.

*I.e., the pre-Islamic period.

It was stated by Maulana Ehtishamul Huq that all the four *Imams* are agreed that the son of a predeceased son or daughter shall be excluded from inheritance. The Maulana Sahib was not prepared to reopen this question in view of the unamimous opinion of all the *Imams*. . . .

It has been suggested in some of the replies that the grandfather can by will, leave one-third of his property to his grandchildren. This provision does not do full justice to the orphans as is evident from the example given above. We, therefore, recommend that legislation should be undertaken to do justice to the orphans in respect of the property of their grandfathers.

Comment: The Pakistani law has been critically discussed by Anderson.

J. N. D. ANDERSON, "Recent Reforms in the Islamic Law of Inheritance," pp. 356–358.

. . . [The principle of representation] was actually adopted in Pakistan in 1961. Clearly, it has much to commend it, for it is eminently straightforward and practical. It may be thought, moreover, that it represents a reproduction of what would have happened had the deceased parent survived till one minute after the demise of the grandparent concerned, instead of dying, perhaps, two minutes before. In reality, however, things do not always work out quite like that—as a simple example will show. Let us suppose that P has two children, a son A and a daughter B, and that B, who herself has a daughter C, predeceases P. If there are no other claimants the Pakistani law would result in C inheriting the whole of her mother B's share, namely one-third of the net estate; but whereas B, had she survived, would indeed have taken one-third of her parent's estate, her daughter C would have been entitled to no more than half of this, and the other half would have gone to her uncle as the nearest agnate.

But there is a far more common—and important—objection to this solution: namely, that it radically upsets the whole structure of the Islamic law of inheritance. Of this three examples must suffice. First, let us suppose that P has two children, a daughter A and a son B, and that B predeceases his parent leaving a daughter C. If no other relatives are involved the Pakistani law will result in the son's daughter C taking two-thirds of the estate, as the share which her deceased father would have taken, and the daughter A taking one-third; whereas the usual rule in all the Sunni schools would have initially allotted one-half to the daughter and one-sixth to the son's daughter, and would then have given them (after application of the principle of the return) three-quarters and one-quarter respectively. Secondly, let us suppose that P dies survived by the daughter of a predeceased son and a brother of full blood. In this case the Pakistani law would enable the granddaughter completely to exclude the brother, in the same way as her deceased father would have done; whereas the law ordinarily applied in all the Sunni schools would have given her one-half of the estate and left the other half to the brother, as would, indeed, have been the case had the deceased been survived by a brother together with one of his own daughters. Thirdly, let us suppose that P has a son A and a daughter B, and that both of them die in his lifetime, the son leaving a daughter C and the daughter leaving a son D. In this case the Pakistani law would allot two-thirds of the estate to the granddaughter C and one-third to the grandson D, as representing in each case their deceased parents, whereas the law applicable in all the Sunni schools would have given the whole estate to the son's daughter, as a quota-sharer, to the total exclusion of the daughter's son, as neither a quota-sharer nor an agnate.

It is clear, then, that this solution introduces the most radical changes in the Islamic law of inheritance; but the question remains as to whether these changes are to be welcomed or deprecated. In this context it must be noted in passing that the Pakistani law has a considerable bearing on the further problem . . . of the priority which many Muslims today would prefer to give to their immediate family as against the old tribal heirs or agnates; for the Muslim Family Laws Ordinance would clearly have the effect that the child of a predeceased daughter would take half the grandparent's estate as against even his or her full brother, while the daughter of a predeceased son would totally exclude such a brother, instead of sharing the estate with him. This may, indeed, be regarded as a gain, but as a gain achieved at the cost of a considerable number of anomalies; for the brother who would be excluded from such an estate by the granddaughter of the deceased through a predeceased son would not be excluded by the deceased person's own daughter. . . .

Comment: Since there is no statute regulating other aspects of the law of inheritance, Pakistani courts must still rely upon the general rules of Sunni or Shi'i law in deciding cases dealing with intestate succession. Since Sunni and Shi'i laws of inheritance differ considerably from each other, as we have seen above, it is important to determine whether the decedent was a Sunni or a Shi'a, if there is litigation concerning the estate. A Pakistani case deals with this problem.

Pathana—Apellant versus *Mst. Wasai and Another—Respondents, in the Supreme Court of Pakistan.*

Civil Appeal No. 9 of 1964, decided on 9th December 1964. (On appeal from the judgment and order of the High Court of West Pakistan, Peshawar Bench, Peshawar, dated the 7th May 1962, in Civil Appeal No. 54/30 of 1957.)

JUDGMENT

S. A. Pahman, J.—This appeal by special leave, arises out of a suit brought by Pathana appellant for possession of ⅔ share of the property left by one Salara, who died on the 18th of June 1951. The suit was resisted by Mst. Wasai, widow of the deceased, and Mst. Mehrajan, his daughter. The plaintiff's case was based on the allegation that Salara professed the Sunni (Hanafi) faith. The defence to the suit was founded on the counter plea that he died a Shi'a. The trial judge found the issue in favour of the respondents and dismissed the suit with costs. On appeal, the District Judge reversed the finding and held that Salara was governed by the Hanafi Law. He therefore decreed the suit with costs. In second appeal, the respondents succeeded before the High Court of West Pakistan. The judgment of the District Judge was reversed and that of the trial judge restored. Special leave to appeal was granted in this case to consider the question whether the High Court were right in interfering in second appeal, with what was essentially a finding of fact, in the circumstances of this case.

The crucial question in the case was whether the deceased Salara died professing the Hanafi creed or he belonged to the Shi'a sect. If the former was the case, then the appellant was entitled, as a residuary, to $\frac{2}{3}$ths of the property left by the deceased, he being his cousin. The remaining property would then have gone to the two heirs, namely, the widow and the daughter. If, however, Salara was a Shi'a by faith, then the appellant was not entitled to any share in his property.

Second appeals from appellate decrees are dealt with in section 100 of the Code of Civil Procedure, 1908. This section is expressed in these terms:—

"(1). Save where otherwise expressly provided in the body of the Code or by any other law for the time being in force, an appeal shall lie to the High Court from every decree passed in appeal by any Court subordinate to a High Court, on any of the following grounds, namely:—

"(a) the decision being contrary to law or to some usage having the force of law;

"(b) the decision having failed to determine some material issue of law or usage having the force of law;

"(c) a substantial error or defect in the procedure provided by the Code or by any other law for the time being in force, which may possibly have produced error or defect in the decision of the case upon the merits."

Subsection (2) of this section clarifies that an appeal may lie under this section from an appellate decree passed ex parte. This section has to be read with section 101 of the Code which declares that no second appeal shall lie except on the grounds mentioned in section 100.

It is common ground between the parties that the instant case did not attract clauses (a) and (b) of subsection (1) of section 100 of the Code. Justification for interference in second appeal could therefore have been found only in clause (c) of that subsection.

The learned Single Judge who disposed of the appeal in the High Court, held that the judgment of the District Judge in appeal, was vitiated for two reasons. In his opinion, firstly, the learned District Judge had completely missed the statement given by Mst. Allah Wasai, defendant, as her own witness, and secondly, "he had failed to take into consideration important circumstances arising out of the evidence produced in the case."

He therefore felt that it was open to him to re-assess the evidence in the case, afresh. He then discussed the evidence and recorded the finding that the deceased had died a Shi'a and consequently the plaintiff's suit merited dismissal.

In support of the first ground that prevailed with the learned Single Judge, he relied on an observation occurring in the judgment of the District Judge in the following passage:—

> Nizam has gone to the length of saying that all the relations of the deceased, professed Shi'a faith, including the plaintiff. Plaintiff repudiates this allegation and the two defendants have not come into the witness-box to assert themeslves as Shi'as.

Apparently, the last sentence in this extract from the judgment, was construed to mean that the learned District Judge was under the impression that Mst. Allah Wasai had not been examined as a witness in the case at all. It is explained, however, that what the learned District Judge meant was merely that she had not stated from the witness-box that she herself was a Shi'a. This contention appears to be well-founded. In the paragraph preceding the one which contains the above extract, the learned District Judge has indicated how the case was presented to him.
He states:

> He has come up in appeal and the learned counsel who represented him, vehemently contended that the learned trial court did not properly appreciate the evidence produced before it. He, therefore took me through the evidence which the parties had produced on the record.

This obviously means that the learned District Judge went through the whole evidence on record, which was not voluminous in nature, consisting as it did, of seven witnesses on behalf of the plaintiff and six examined by the defendants, including Mst. Wasai as D.W.1. It is not conceivable therefore that he was unaware of Mst. Wasai having been examined as a witness in this case. The interpretation of the sentence in question advanced by learned counsel for the appellant, appears consequently to be correct. Mst. Wasai did not, in so many words, assert that she herself was a Shi'a and this is apparently what the learned District Judge was commenting on. The second defendant had not offered herself as a witness in the case at all. The learned Single Judge in the High Court appears to have misconceived the position in this respect.

Mr. Abdur Rashid who appeared for the respondents before us, attempted to argue that the learned District Judge was guilty of misreading of evidence in the case and therefore the High Court had jurisdiction to reopen the finding of fact arrived at by him. In support of this position, he invited our attention to the observation of the learned District Judge, to the effect that *Maulvi* Zaboor Ahmad, P.W.3, had asserted that he was the ancestral *Maulvi* of the plaintiff's family. Learned counsel suggested that this witness had merely averred that he was himself an ancestral

Maulvi, i.e., his own forefathers were also *Maulvis*. We have perused the statement of this witness, and the context in which this sentence occurs, lends itself to the construction which was adopted by the learned District Judge. The witness started by saying that the deceased was known to him to belong to the Sunni sect of Islam, that he was ancestral *Maulvi* and that he had officiated as *Imam* at the funeral prayers on the death of a sister of Gulsher, P.W.2, who is a cousin of the deceased. It is apparent that Zahoor Ahmad was trying to make out that he was the *Maulvi* who performed various religious services for the family of the plaintiff. At best, the sentence was capable of either interpretation and the District Judge could not be said to have misdirected himself by adopting one of them.

Another instance of the alleged misreading of evidence that learned counsel for the respondents pressed into service, was said to consist in the District Judge's remark, while discussing the testimony of *Imam* Bakhsh, D.W.4, and Singar Khan, D.W.6, that they had not disclosed their own faith. It is pointed out that D.W.4, *Imam* Bakhsh, had stated in his cross-examination that he was himself a Shi'a though such an assertion is absent from the testimony of Singar Khan, D.W.6. In this respect, apparently, the learned District Judge had committed a slight error. Even if the correct position had, however, been present to his mind on this point, we do not consider that the main line of his reasoning would have been affected materially. This would be borne out by the following observations in his judgment:—

> Some other evidence was also led by the defendants to show that the deceased was in his lifetime a Shi'a by faith because he used to hold *majlis* in the Shi'a fashion and used to say his prayers without folding his hands, and in this respect, reference may be made to the testimony of *Imam* Bakhsh (D.W.4) and Singar Khan (D.W.6). If he was really holding Shi'a *majlisses* as is alleged by these witnesses, he must have been inviting some *zakirs* because without them the *majlis* could not be held. Not a single *zakir* had come forward to support this allegation. The evidence of these witnesses that they had occasions to say their prayers with the deceased, cannot be properly checked. They have not disclosed their own faith. If they themselves were not Shi'as, it is very doubtful that they had many occasions to say their prayers along with the deceased because the Shi'as do not say their prayers after a Sunni *Imam*; and if these witnesses are Shi'as they must be knowing the Shi'a *Maulvis* after whom they said prayers jointly with the deceased. No such *Maulvi* has been mentioned and I am not prepared to believe these bald statements without the relevant details to make them convincing.

The omission to note therefore that D.W.4, *Imam* Bakhsh, had claimed to be a Shi'a, made no difference to this reasoning. It is to be observed that only a substantial error or defect in the procedure, which may possibly have produced error or defect in the decision of the case upon the merits, would fall within the purview of clause (c) of subsection (1) of section 100 of the Code of Civil Procedure. The mistake pointed out here was certainly not of that character.

As regards the "important circumstances," which, according to the learned Single Judge, the District Judge had ignored, it was mentioned before him that the mutation in favour of the respondents was sanctioned by the Revenue Authorities on the 8th of June 1952, and that the plaintiff-appellant had raised no objection to its sanction at that time. He had waited till the 21st of February 1956, to bring his suit. It was suggested that he did so only because his relations with Mst. Allah Wasai had become strained, as she had married off her daughter with one Farid, instead of to a son of a nephew of the plaintiff, despite the latter's protests. The point was also given prominence in the High Court judgment that the funeral prayers of the deceased were performed by Sakhi Muhammad or Sakha Muhammad, D.W.1, a Shi'a *Maulvi*, with the permission of the deceased's widow and that Pathana was present on that occasion and does not appear to have objected. Moreover, "the positive statements" of the D.Ws. to the effect that they had been participating in *majalis* organized by the deceased and had offered prayers in his company in the Shi'a mode, were said to be preferable to the evidence "of negative character" given by the plaintiff's witnesses. The phrase "of negative character" in this context appears to be inept to describe the positive allegation of the P.Ws., that Salara was a Sunni. All these circumstances were matters of inference from the evidence, which was duly considered by the District Judge and furnished no ground for interference in second appeal.

In a similar case reported as *Mst. Durga Choudhrani v. Jawahir Singh Choudhri* (17 IA 122), the Judicial Committee of the Privy Council held that an erroneous finding of fact is a different thing from an error or defect in the procedure and that there is no jurisdiction to entertain a second appeal on the ground of such an erroneous finding, however gross or inexcusable the error may seem to be. Their Lordships observed that where there is no error or defect in the procedure, the finding of the first Apellate Court, upon a question of fact, is final, if that Court had before it evidence proper for its consideration in support of the finding. This principle was also affirmed by the Federal Court of Pakistan in a case reported as *Abdul Majid v. Khalil Ahmad* (PLD 1955 FC 38). It was pointed out in that case that a fallacy in appraising the evidence as to a fact, unless it amounts to a material mistaken assumption, is merely an error in coming to a finding as to that fact, and such error has never been held to be an error of law justifying interference in second appeal. With respect, we find ourselves in agreement with these dicta.

It was, in our opinion, therefore, not open to the learned Single Judge to set aside the finding as to the faith of the deceased, Salara, recorded by the District Judge, on the grounds mentioned by him.

It may be added that the finding of the District Judge was reasonably supported by the evidence on record. In the Indo-Pak.

Sub-continent there is the initial presumption that a Muslim is governed by Hanafi Law, unless the contrary is established by good evidence (vide Mulla's *Muhammadan Law*, Section 28). Even Sakhi Muhammad, D.W., who was the star witness of the respondents and had officiated at the funeral prayers of the deceased Salara, at the instance of his widow, was careful enough to say that he did not know what faith the deceased professed. He led the funeral prayers for him merely because his widow had asked him to do so. The widow might have been anxious to make out that Salara was a Shi'a, to serve her own property interests. In fact, it appears from the evidence that the services of Sakhi Muhammad were requisitioned as the Sunni *Maulvi* was not available on this occasion. Sakhi Muhammad admitted that Zahoor-ud-Din or Zahoor Ahmad (who was examined as P.W.3, in this case) was a Sunni *Maulvi* who used to officiate at *nikah* ceremonies of the family of the plaintiff and the defendants and also used to lead funeral prayers for members of that family. Sakhi Muhammad himself being a Shi'a *Maulvi* should have been aware of the true position if Salara belonged to his sect and could not have hesitated to claim him as a member of his fold. After going through the whole evidence on record, we have reached the conclusion that the inference drawn by the learned District Judge fairly arose on that evidence and was indeed, in all probability, in accord with the facts. No fault could therefore be found with the appreciation of the evidence by the District Judge, in second appeal.

The appeal succeeds and is hereby allowed. The order of the High Court will be set aside and that of the learned District Judge restored. In the circumstances of the case, we leave the parties to bear their own costs.

Appeal allowed.

3. *Iran*

Comment: The provisions on testate and intestate succession in the Iranian Civil Code are based essentially on Shi'i law.

On bequests the Code states:

Iranian Civil Code.

Article 843. Bequests in excess of the disposable third are void, unless ratified by the heirs. If only some of the heirs ratify, the ratification is valid and prorated according to the share of those who have given it.

Article 849. If the testator has indicated an order of preference in bequeathing more than the disposable third to several different legatees and the heirs refuse to ratify the excess over the disposable third, the bequests shall be distributed in the order indicated by the testator, until the disposable third is reached and those bequests which cannot be implemented because the disposable third is exhausted are declared void.

In the case where the various bequests are made without an order of preference, they are all subject to reduction to the disposable third and are then prorated.

Comment: This provision is not in strict accordance with Shiʿi law which in case the bequests exceed the disposable third and the heirs do not ratify, provides that the bequest first in time shall be satisfied, then the second, and so forth until the disposable third is exhausted. The Hanefite school, by contrast, rules that the bequests shall be prorated in case they exceed the disposable third and the heirs do not ratify.

Intestate succession is regulated in the Code in great detail according to the rules established by the Shiʿi Ithna ʿAshari sect. The Code also preserves succession by *stirpes* for the grandchildren, as provided by the Ithna ʿAshari law.

Iranian Civil Code.

Article 910. If the decedent leaves children or even one child, his grandchildren will not be called to take any share in the estate.

Article 911. If the decedent has not left any living children, his grandchildren replace them by right of representation. Since they are then considered as heirs within the first group, they compete with the surviving mother or father of the decedent.

The distribution among grandchildren is *per stirpes*, that is each branch takes the share of the person through whom it is related to the decedent. Thus children of the son take double the share of children of the daughter.

In the distribution among members of the same branch the males take double.

Article 912. The descendants of the decedent of whatever degree they may be on the descendant scale, shall inherit according to the preceding article, provided however, that the closer relative excludes the more distant one.

Comment: The rules for representation are thus narrower than in the Pakistani statute. The grandchildren's right of representation does not exist if there is a surviving son or daughter. Thus the aim that the Egyptian statute pursued by providing for compulsory bequests, and that the Pakistani statute sought to meet by introducing the principle of representation without restriction, namely, to provide for grandchildren whether or not there are any living children, is not met by the Iranian legislation.

The form of the will is regulated in a separate statute of 13 January 1939, which is Western-inspired to a large extent.

A law of 22 July 1933 deals with the

Personal Status Law of Non-Shiʿi Iranians.

In suits concerning the personal status, the testamentary rights and the succession of non-Shiʿi Iranian nationals, the usages and religious customs of the parties shall be taken into account as follows, provided they are not contrary to public policy:

1. In suits concerning marriage, divorce, and the rights of the spouses toward each other, the rules and customs of the husband's religion shall be applied.

2. In suits concerning succession and wills, the rules of the religion of the decedent are applicable.

3. In suits concerning adopted children and the inheritance rights of the adopted child and of the father or mother by adoption, the rules and customs of the religion of the parents is applied.

4. *Turkey*

Comment: In Turkey the Islamic system of inheritance was completely abandoned and the Swiss system was introduced, which provided for the distribution of the estate *per stirpes*.

Turkish Civil Code of 1926.

Article 439. The nearest heirs are the descendants of the decedent.

Children inherit in equal parts.

Predeceased children are represented by their descendants who succeed *per stirpes* in all degrees.

Article 440. If the decedent has not left any descendants, his father and mother are his heirs. They take in equal parts.

If the father and mother have predeceased the decedent, they are represented by their descendants, who succeed *per stirpes* in all degrees. If there are no heirs on one side, the whole estate devolves upon the heirs of the other side.

Article 441. The heirs of a decedent who has left neither descendants nor father or mother, nor any of their descendants, are the grandfather and the grandmother. They take in equal parts.

The predeceased grandparent is represented by his descendants who succeed *per stirpes* regardless of degree.

In case one grandparent on the father's side or on the mother's side has predeceased the decedent and there are no descendants of that grandparent, his share devolves upon the heirs of the same side.

If the grandparents of one side are dead and have not left descendants, the whole estate shall devolve upon the heirs of the other side.

Article 442. The grandparents and their descendants are the final heirs through blood relationship . . . .

Article 444. The surviving wife or husband has a choice between the usufruct of half of the estate or ownership of a quarter, provided the decedent leaves descendants.

In competition with the father or mother of the decedent or their descendants, the surviving wife or husband has a right to ownership of one-quarter of the estate, together with usufruct of one-half; in competition with the grandparents or their descendants, he has a right to ownership of half of the estate and to usufruct of one-quarter; if there are no grandparents or their descendants, he takes the whole estate.

Comment: There are no restrictions on a person to dispose by will. However, a certain portion of the estate must go to certain intestate heirs. This portion is expressed in fractions of the share in the estate the respective survivor would have received had the decedent died intestate. For example, a descendant receives three-quarters of his share, a parent half and so forth. The surviving spouse receives half of his statutory share, if he is the sole legal heir, and his full share, if there are other heirs besides him.

This practice of reserving a portion of the estate for the legal heirs is a result of European legal development; the provisions are taken straight from Swiss law and have no relation to Islamic law. The reform of Turkish law in the field of succession has not given rise to as many difficulties as were encountered in the law of marriage and divorce. Some problems have arisen, however, with regard to the grandparents. While the Swiss system is straightforward and simple, simpler indeed than the Islamic system, it was devised with the Swiss family structure in mind. We have seen earlier that the Turkish courts have had a different attitude toward the position of the grandparents with regard to grandchildren whose parents are divorced. With regard to inheritance too it has been felt that the grandparents were not given their proper position. They are excluded from the inheritance in present-day Turkish law by brothers or even nephews of the decedent, whereas in Sunni law they would be excluded only by closer grandparents or the parents. While the grandparents, if they are in straightened circumstances, can apply to the courts for support, this is, of course, not the same as having a definite legal share. The remedy here is not as simple as in the case of the visiting rights discussed above. In the case of the visiting rights a lacuna existed which the courts could easily fill. In the present instance, however, there are definite provisions of the code which bind the courts.

Chapter 8 Contracts and Torts in Classical Islamic Law and Modern Near Eastern Law

A. Contracts

Comment: Islamic law did not develop a theory of obligations. Sale, however, was the typical contract on which other contracts were patterned. A brief definition of sale and a description of the conclusion of the contract of sale is provided by a Hanefite author, Ibrahim al-Halabi (died A.D. 1549), in his *Multaqa al-Abhur*. This author lived in the sixteenth century and his work was highly regarded in the Ottoman Empire. Parts of the *Multaqa* were translated into French by H. Sauvaire.

HALABI, *Multaqa al-Abhur* (p. 458, translation Sauvaire pp. 5–6).

Sale, in the legal sense, is the exchange of property against property. Sale is concluded by offer and acceptance expressed by two verbs in the past tense, such as "I have sold" and "I have bought." . . . If the seller says: "Take the thing for such and such" and the buyer answers: "I have taken," or "I have consented" the sale is valid.

AL-QAYRAWANI, *Risala*, pp. 200–201.

Allah permits sale and forbids usury (*Qur'an*, Sura II, 275). In the period before Islam usury was permissible in transactions . . . . It is usury if one . . . exchanges silver against silver from hand to hand and one amount exceeds the other. The same is true when gold is exchanged for gold. Thus it is not permitted to exchange silver for silver and gold for gold except in equal value and from hand to hand. To exchange silver for gold is usury, unless it is from hand to hand.

Majalla

Article 167. Sale is concluded through offer and acceptance.
   Article 168. Offer and acceptance are made by employing the terms customarily used in the particular locality in concluding the contract of sale. . . .
   Article 169. The past tense is usually employed for offer and acceptance. . . .
   Article 170. A contract of sale may be concluded by employing the imperfect tense, provided it is meant to imply the present. If, however, the future is meant, no sale is concluded.

Article 171. If terms are used meaning the future, such as "I will buy," or "I will sell," no sale is concluded, since the parties are merely making promises.

. . . .

Article 173. Offer and acceptance may be made in writing or by word of mouth.

. . . .

Article 175. The principal objective of offer and acceptance is to demonstrate the agreement of the parties. Therefore a contract of sale is concluded also if this agreement is demonstrated through any suitable conduct. Such a sale is called a sale through conduct of the parties . . . .

. . . .

Article 181. The place where the sale is concluded is the place where the parties meet together with the intention of concluding the sale.

Article 182. Both parties have an option during their meeting from the time the offer has been made to the end of the meeting. . . .*

Article 183. If after the offer has been made, but before there has been acceptance, one of the parties, by word or by deed signifies the intention to dissent, the offer is null and void and there can be no reason for acceptance. . . .

Article 184. If one of the two parties makes an offer, but withdraws it before the other party has accepted it, the offer is void and the sale cannot be concluded by a later acceptance.

Article 185. If a second offer replaces the first before acceptance, the first offer is void and its place is taken by the second. . . .

Article 186. If a contract of sale is concluded with a condition attached which results from the very nature of the contract, both the sale and the condition are valid.

. . . .

Article 369. The effect of a concluded sale is transfer of ownership, that is to say, by virtue of the sale the purchaser becomes the owner of the thing sold and the vendor becomes the owner of the price.

Comment: The modern Near Eastern codes contain general provisions on contracts which are generally based on continental European prototypes. The pertinent provisions of the Egyptian Civil Code and of the codes derived from it are largely taken from French law.

A contract is defined in the Egyptian Civil Code as follows:

---

*This option is not permitted by all schools. The Malikites, for example, regard the sale as concluded when the offer is accepted.

Egyptian Civil Code.

Article 89. A contract is created, subject to any special formalities that may be required by law for its conclusion, from the moment that two persons have exchanged two concordant intentions.

Comment: Of particular interest is the treatment of the cause of the contract. There is a basic difference between cause as continental European law and Near Eastern law understand it and consideration as understood in American law. Classical Islamic law did not develop a theory on cause, but from classical writings certain rules can be deduced which show that the Islamic concept was close to the continental European one. Santillana has summarized the position of classical Islamic law:

DAVID SANTILLANA, *Istituzioni di Diritto Musulmano Malichita,* vol. 2, pp. 22–23.

In a contract the cause, even if not expressly stated, is always presumed, because it is not assumed that a person of sound mind mind would decide to contract without a motive. The cause expressed is considered valid until the contrary is proven. If absence of a cause is proven, the obligation is void.

Comment: The Egyptian Civil Code generally follows continental European law with regard to cause.

Egyptian Civil Code.

Article 136. A contract is void if the obligation is assumed without cause or for a cause contrary to public policy or morals.

Article 137. An obligation is considered to have a lawful cause, even if such cause is not expressed in the contract, unless the contrary is proven.

The cause expressed in the contract is considered to be the true cause until evidence to the contrary is produced. Upon evidence produced that the cause is feigned, the burden of proving that the obligation had another lawful cause falls upon the person who maintains that such is the case.*

Comment: Although the Turkish Civil Code, following the Swiss Code of Obligations, does not stipulate the need for a cause in a contract, Turkish law does require that every contract have a cause.

According to Article 217 of the Iranian Civil Code the cause of a contract need not be expressly stated.

*The difference between cause and consideration has been discussed by E. G. Lorenzen, "Causa and Consideration in the Law of Contracts," *Yale Law Journal* 28 (1919): pp. 621–646. On the concept of cause in French law see Amos and Walton, *Introduction to French Law* (2d ed., Oxford: Clarendon Press 1963), pp. 166–172.

B. Joint Ownership and Preemption

Comment: In a legal system where intestate succession was, and still is, prevalent, joint ownership plays a particularly important role. The rights of the individual joint owner with regard to disposing of his share are extensive.* However, the co-owners have an option to purchase the share at the same price as the outsider. This right of preemption (Arabic: *shuf'a*) has been preserved in the law of most countries of the region.

Majalla.

Article 1045. Joint ownership consists of a thing itself belonging absolutely to more than one person, so that such persons enjoy a special position in relation to such thing. . . .

Article 1060. Joint ownership of property held in absolute ownership is brought about when more than one person join in the ownership of a particular thing, that is to say, where such thing belongs to them, as where ownership therein is acquired by any of the causes of acquiring ownership such as purchase, or taking by way of gift, or by acceptance of a bequest, or inheritance, or by mixing or causing to mix one property with another, that is to say, by uniting them in such a way that they cannot be distinguished or separated from one another.

·   ·   ·   ·

Article 1069. The joint owners of property held in absolute ownership may by agreement deal with their property in any way they wish, in the same way as a single owner of such property.

·   ·   ·   ·

Article 1071. One of the joint owners of property held in absolute ownership may deal with such property alone, without the permission of the other. He may not, however, deal with it in such way as to cause injury to the other joint owner.

Article 1072. Neither of the joint owners may force the other to sell or purchase his share. If the property held in absolute ownership jointly by them is capable of division, and the other joint owner is not absent, such property may be divided. If it is not capable of division they may share the usufruct thereof. . . .

·   ·   ·   ·

Article 1075. The joint owners of property held in absolute ownership are strangers to one another as regards their shares. Neither is the agent of the other. Consequently, neither joint owner may deal with the share of the other without the latter's permission. But in the case of dwelling in a house which is jointly owned and as regards matters pertaining thereto, such as coming in and going out, each of the joint owners is considered to be an absolute owner of such property. . . .

·   ·   ·   ·

*See also p.225.

Article 950. Preemption consists of acquiring possession of a piece of property held in absolute ownership which has been purchased, by paying the purchaser the amount he gave for it.

Article 951. The preemptor is the person having the right of preemption.

Article 952. The subject of preemption is real property to which the right of preemption is attached.

.   .   .   .

Article 1008. There are three causes of preemption:

(1) Where a person is the joint owner of the property itself which is sold. Such as is the case where two persons jointly own a parcel of real estate.

(2) Where a person is joint owner of an easement in the property sold. As where a person shares in a private right of taking water or in a private road . . . .

But if a house taking water from a public river which is open to the use of the public or the doors of which give on to a public road is sold, the owners of the other houses taking water from such a river, or which give on to the public road, do not possess any right of preemption.

(3) Where a person is adjoining neighbor of the property sold.*

Article 1009. The right of preemption belongs:

First, to the person who is a joint owner of the property sold.

Second, to the person who is a joint owner of an easement over the property sold.

Third, to the adjoining neighbor.

If the first person claims his right of preemption, the others lose theirs. If the second person claims his right of preemption, the third person loses his.

.   .   .   .

Article 1013. Should there be several persons enjoying a right of preemption, they are dealt with according to their numbers and not according to the number of parts, that is shares, which they hold. . . .

.   .   .   .

Article 1017. The property to which the right of preemption attaches must be real property held in absolute ownership. Therefore no right of preemption can attach to a ship or other movable property, nor to real property which has been made a *waqf*, nor to *miri* land.

.   .   .   .

Article 1021. Preemption can only be affirmed on the basis of a contract of sale [between a joint owner and another person].

.   .   .   .

Article 1028. The claim made in cases of preemption must have three elements:

*This right of the neighbor exists only in Hanefite law.

(1) it must be made immediately upon hearing of the sale;
(2) it must be made formally and in the presence of witnesses;
(3) the person alleging the right of preemption must claim that he is entitled to bring action and to be granted absolute ownership of the property.

Comment: The present Egyptian Civil Code has preserved this right of preemption.

Egyptian Civil Code.

Article 935. Preemption is the option that a person has to substitute himself in a sale of immovable property in the place of the purchaser, in the cases and subject to the conditions laid down in the following articles.

Article 936. The right of preemption belongs:
(a) to the bare-owner, in the case of a sale of all or part of the usufruct attached to a bare property;
(b) to the joint owner, in case of a sale to a third party of part of the property held jointly;
(c) to the usufructuary, in case of a sale of all or part of the bare property which produces his usufruct;
(d) in case of *hikr*, to the bare-owner if the sale relates to the right of *hikr*; and to the beneficiary of the *hikr* if the sale relates to the bare property;*
(e) to the neighboring owner in the following cases:
 (i) in the case of buildings or building land whether situated in a town or village;
(ii) if the land enjoys a right of servitude over the land of the neighbor, or if a right of servitude exists in favor of the land of a neighbor over the land sold;
(iii) if the land of a neighbor adjoins the land sold on two sides and the value is at least half of the value of the land sold.

Article 937. When several persons preempt, the right of preemption will be exercised in the order set forth in the preceding article.

If several persons of the same degree exercise the rights of preemption, the right of preemption will belong to each one of them in proportion to his share.

If a purchaser is, in accordance with the provisions laid down in the preceding article, entitled to exercise the right of preemption, he will be preferred to other preemptors of the same degree or of a lower degree, but those of a higher degree will have priority over him.

.　　.　　.　　.

Article 939. Preemption cannot be exercised:
(a) if the sale is made by public auction in accordance with the procedure prescribed by law;

---

*Hikr is a long-term lease of land, not to exceed sixty years under Egyptian law, and giving the lessee the right to construct buildings or cultivate the land. It is a contract similar to the Roman *emphyteusis.*

(b) if the sale is made between ascendants and descendants, between spouses, or between relatives to the fourth degree, or between relatives by marriage to the second degree;

(c) if the property sold is destined for religious purposes or to be annexed to property already used for such purposes. . . .

Article 940. Whoever desires to exercise the right of preemption must, on pain of forfeiture of his right, notify both the vendor and the purchaser of his intention within a period of fifteen days from the day of a formal summons served on him either by the vendor or by the purchaser. This period is increased, if necessary, by the time allowed for distance.

Article 941. The formal summons provided for in the preceding article must, on pain of nullity, contain the following particulars:

(a) an adequate description of the property subject to preemption;

(b) the amount of the price, the official dues, the conditions of sale, and the first names, surnames, professions, and domiciles of the vendor and the purchaser.

Article 942. Notification of intention to exercise the right of preemption must, on pain of nullity, be made through official channels. It is not valid as against third parties unless it is registered.

The actual sale price must within thirty days at the most from the date of notification, be deposited in full at the pay office of the court of the district in which the property is situated, and in any event before the introduction of the action in preemption. If this deposit is not made within the prescribed time and manner, the right of preemption shall be forfeited.

Article 943. An action in preemption must, under pain of forfeiture, be introduced against the vendor and the purchaser before the court of the district where the property is situated, and entered on the court docket within thirty days from the date of notification provided for in the preceding article. The case will be disposed of as a matter of urgency.

Article 944. Without prejudice to the rules regarding registration, the judgment which finally establishes the right to preemption will constitute the title of ownership of the preemptor.

Article 945. The preemptor is vis-à-vis the vendor substituted for the purchaser in all his rights and obligations. . . .

.   .   .   .

Article 948. The right of preemption is forfeited in the following cases:

(a) if the preemptor renounces his right, even before the sale;

(b) if four months have elapsed since the date of the registration of the deed of sale;

(c) in all other cases prescribed by law.

Comment: Article 942, paragraph 2 which requires deposition of the sale price in full within thirty days of notification has been interpreted strictly by the Egyptian Court of Cassation.

Court of Cassation, Civil Chamber, No. 3–4/100 of 10 February 1955.

Syllabus by the Court.

... Article 942 of the Civil Code provides in paragraph 2 that the preemptor must within at most thirty days from the date of notification of preemption deposit in full at the pay office of the court of the district in which the property is situated the actual sale price. If the deposit is not made within the period and in the manner prescribed by the law the right of preemption will be forfeited. It follows from the foregoing that the deposition of the full sale price within the prescribed time period has become an essential condition for the admissibility of an action in preemption and one of the necessary formalities. Thus the action legally cannot be entertained until it has been established that the deposit has been made. In the case before this court it is established that the preemptor was so anxious to commence action that he did so on the basis of his personal information without awaiting the summons by the vendor or purchaser which antecedes the declaration of intention to exercise the right of preemption. He therefore deposited what he thought was the full sale price, but which was in fact an amount smaller than the actual price. Under these circumstances the preemptor alone must bear the risk of his action and he has exposed his right to forfeiture because of the deposit of only a portion of the sale price.

Comment: The basic rules of preemption are similar in other countries, for example in Lebanon where this right is based on a law of 5 February 1948. In Iran the right of preemption is regulated by Articles 808 through 824 of the Civil Code. In the Turkish Civil Code Article 659 gives co-owners a right of preemption in case a share of the individual property is acquired by a person who is not a co-owner. This provision is, however, taken from Article 682 of the Swiss Civil Code and is, of course, much narrower than the right of preemption under Islamic law as reflected in other legal systems in the region.

C. Torts

Comment: The Islamic law of torts differs in several important respects from modern European and American law. These differences are not merely of academic interest, but can be of practical importance especially because the Islamic law of torts is still applied in Saudi Arabia. Tort actions may arise in this country involving Saudi law, because action may be brought, and in a number of cases has been brought in this country on the basis of the fact that the contract of employment between an American employee and an American company doing business in Saudi Arabia was concluded in this country. If an employee in such a case is injured in Saudi Arabia he is likely to sue in this country and Saudi law of torts may be applied to the case.* Islamic law gives a much narrower scope than American law does at present to the doctrine of respondeat superior, restricting this doctrine generally to cases where a direct order has been given to the employee. Also, in Islamic law moral damages (compensation for pain and suffering) are unknown. Absolute liability has a broader application than in modern American law. The treatment of tort law by Islamic jurists is generally very casuistic, actually rather similar to the treatment given the subject in Roman law.†

Abu Yusuf provides an example on the problem of respondeat superior.

ABU YUSUF, *Kitab al-Kharaj*, p. 96 (French translation, p. 248).

If one of the merchants one finds in the bazaar, the outskirts of town, or the streets orders one of his employees to water down the outside of neighboring houses and this action causes someone's death, the one who has given the order [i.e., the merchant] is responsible. If, however, he has ordered his employee to make his ablutions and this employee goes out into the street [and causes an accident there], the employee is liable, the reason being that the ablution is for the benefit of the one who performs it, whereas the watering down benefits the one who ordered it. . . .

Comment: In the case of contractual obligations, too, the master is responsible only if he gave direct orders. The following example is from a Malekite compendium:

SAHNUN, *Al-Mudawwana*, vol. 11, p. 31.

A launderer who has much clothing to launder, hires a helper whom he orders to go to the river to wash some of the garments. He is responsible if the helper loses any of the clothes.

Comment: The *Majalla* does not deal with the problem of respondeat superior. In its treatment of torts generally it distinguishes between direct and indirect destruction.

Majalla.

Article 887. Direct destruction consists of the destruction of a thing by a person himself. The person destroying the thing is called the direct perpetrator [of the destruction].

Article 888. Indirect destruction consists of the indirect causation of the destruction of a thing. This means the commission of an act which will inevitably lead to the loss or deterioration of an object. . . .

Thus, if a person cuts the cord by which a lamp is suspended, the lamp will inevitably fall on the floor and break. The one who

*See Walton v. Arabian American Oil Company 233 F.2d 541, cert. denied 352 U.S. 872, 77 S.Ct. 97, 1 L.Ed.2d 77 (1956). In similar more recent cases the U.S. District Court for the Southern District of New York has required proof of Saudi law.

†See the examples from Roman and Islamic law, above pp. 32 and 33.

cut the cord is the direct author of the damage to the cord and the indirect cause of the lamp's destruction. . . .

. . . .

Article 912. If a person destroys the property of another, intentionally or unintentionally, and whether it be in the owner's custody or that of a person to whom it has been entrusted, the person who has committed the destruction is liable for the loss . . . .

Article 913. If a person slips and falls upon a thing owned by another and destroys it, he is liable for the loss he caused.

Article 914. If a person destroys someone else's property believing that it is his own, he is liable to make good the loss.

Article 915. If someone pulls at the clothes of another person and tears them, he is liable for the full value of the clothes. However, if he takes hold of the clothes and the owner in pulling them tears them, he is liable only for half of the value of the clothes.

Similarly, if someone sits on the seam of another's clothes and that person gets up from his seat not knowing that someone is sitting on his clothes' seam and tears them, then the one who sat on the seam is liable only for half of the value of the clothes.

. . . .

Article 922. If a person causes the destruction of the property of another or a diminution of its value, in other words, if he commits an act which has as a necessary consequence the destruction of the property or a diminution of its value, he must make good the damage caused. . . .

Article 923. If an animal frightened when seeing a person runs away and is lost, the person involved is not responsible for the loss, unless he has deliberately frightened the animal.

Similarly, if an animal is frightened by the noise of a gun fired by a huntsman, takes flight and perishes or breaks its leg, the huntsman is not liable to make good the loss. However, if he has fired the gun with the intention of frightening the animal, he is liable.

Article 924. The liability established by the preceding articles concerning a person who is the indirect cause of damage depends upon whether or not his act is wrongful. In other words, in order to be liable the person who has committed the act the inevitable consequence of which was damage to be caused to another person, must have acted without justification. . . .

Comment: The basic principles underlying the above provisions are spelled out in the introductory title of the *Majalla* which deals in its second section with the basic principles of the *shari'a.*

Majalla.

Article 92. Anyone is responsible for the damage he has caused another directly, even though unintentionally.

Article 93. Whoever is the indirect cause of damage is liable only if he has acted intentionally.

Comment: Liability without fault, which is stipulated in Islamic law in those cases where damage is caused through direct action, is known in other legal systems too, including the common law. In the old Germanic laws, for example, absolute liability was the rule and this principle continued to be applied until the reception of the Roman law, which introduced the idea of liability for negligence. The same has been true in English law. A modern American authority on torts has dealt with the development of the idea of negligence in English law and the reemergence of the doctrine of absolute liability in more recent times.

WILLIAM L. PROSSER, *Handbook of the Law of Torts* (4th ed., 1971) p. 17.*

Certainly at one time the law was not concerned very much with the moral responsibility of the defendant. "The thought of man shall not be tried," said Chief Justice Brian, "for the devil himself knoweth not the thought of man." (Y.B.7 Edw. IV, f. 2, pl. 2.) The courts were interested primarily in keeping peace between individuals by providing a substitute for private vengeance, and the party injured was quite as likely to take the law into his own hands when the injury was an innocent one. The man who hurt another by pure accident or in self-defense was required to make good the damage inflicted. [Page 17, footnote 27: "Although the defendant's intent was good, still the intent is not material, though in felony it is; as where one is shooting at butts [targets] and kills a man, it is not felony . . . But when one shooting at butts wounds a man unintentionally, he shall be called a trespasser against his will." 1506, Y.B. 21 Hen. VII, 27.5 . . . .]

Ibid., p. 492.

. . . Until about the close of the nineteenth century, the history of the law of torts was that of a slow, and somewhat unsteady progress toward the recognition of "fault" or moral responsibility as the basis of the remedy. With a growing moral consciousness in the community, there was a general movement in the direction of identifying legal liability with conduct which would not be expected of a good citizen. This tendency was so marked that efforts were made by noted writers to construct a consistent theory of tort law upon the basic principle that there should be no liability without fault.

Ibid., p. 494.

. . . [T]he last hundred years have witnessed the overthrow of the doctrine of "never any liability without fault," even in the legal sense of a departure from reasonable standards of conduct. It has seen a general acceptance of the principle that in some cases the defendant may be held liable, although he is not only charged with no moral wrongdoing, but has not even departed in any way from a reasonable standard of intent or care. . . .

*Reprinted by permission of the West Publishing Company.

Comment: In present-day Egyptian law, and in most other Near Eastern legal systems, the basic principle is that of liability for fault.

Egyptian Civil Code.

Article 163. Every fault which causes injury to another imposes an obligation to make reparation upon the person by whom it was committed.

Article 164. Every person in possession of discretion is responsible for his unlawful acts. . . .

Article 165. In the absence of a provision of the law or an agreement to the contrary, a person is not liable to make reparation, if he proves that the injury resulted from a cause beyond his control, such as unforeseen circumstances, *force majeure*, the fault of the victim, or of a third party.

[However, Article 178 provides:]

Whoever is in charge of a thing whose supervision requires special care, or of a machine, is liable for the damage caused by it, unless he shows that the damage was due to a cause beyond his control, subject always to any special provisions of the law in this respect.*

Comment: As stated above, Islamic law does not know compensation for moral damages. The injury or loss must be concrete, a specific injury or a specific amount of damage to a thing. Specific amounts were due for certain injuries, but only if these injuries left a permanent damage. Compensation for injuries which healed completely were admitted only by some Hanefite jurists, but even here the judge had to follow specific rules of evaluation. However, under the influence of French law, the concept of moral damages has been introduced into Near Eastern statutes. Moral damages are generally allowed by the Egyptian Civil Code.

Egyptian Civil Code.

Article 222. Damages also include compensation for moral prejudice [pain and suffering]. The right to compensation for moral prejudice cannot, however, be transmitted to a third party unless it has been fixed by agreement or unless it has been subject of legal proceedings. . . .

Comment: Identical provisions are contained in Article 223 of the Syrian Civil Code and Article 225 of the Libyan Civil Code. The Iraqi Civil Code is somewhat more explicit. Article 205, paragraph 1, enumerates various forms of moral prejudice, such as injury to honor, dignity, freedom of a person. This paragraph was reproduced verbatim in Article 23, paragraph 1 of Kuwaiti law no. 6 of 1961. The similarity among these various statutes is due, of

*The materials to the Egyptian Civil Code refer in connection with this article to several provisions of the *Majalla*, among them Articles 92 and 93 (see p.219).

course, primarily to the fact that they were all drafted, or taken from statutes drafted by Dr. Sanhuri.

In Saudi Arabia damages for pain and suffering (moral damages) generally are not recognized. However, some inroads are beginning. One such instance is contained in the Saudi *Labor and Workmen Regulations*.

Labor and Workmen Regulations of 15 November 1969.

Article 74. If the [labor] contract is cancelled for no valid reason, the party who is prejudiced by such cancellation shall be entitled to an indemnity to be assessed by the competent Commission, provided that such an assessment shall take into account actual and contingent material and moral prejudice suffered by such party . . . .

Comment: It should be noted, however, that damages for moral prejudice are to be awarded by a special commission established by the law to decide labor disputes. The *qadi*, still the judge of general jurisdiction in Saudi Arabia, would apply *shari'a* law and would not recognize moral damages.

Chapter 9   Property and Waqf

Comment: As was the case with regard to contracts, the Muslim jurists did not develop a cohesive theory of property rights. They did, however, establish certain basic principles. According to the classical jurists, a thing in order to be owned must have the following attributes: it must have some value; must be capable of ownership; and its use must be permitted. Thus something that has no value, such as a free person or a drop of blood, cannot be owned. Things common to all also cannot be subject to property rights, as the air or the sea. The same is true, at least as far as Muslims are concerned, of things forbidden to Muslims, e.g., wine and pork. The classical jurists differed on the question as to whether non-Muslims could own wine or pork.

The classification of property in the Egyptian Civil Code of 1949 is not divergent in essentials from that of the Muslim jurists, but it does not allude to the religious prohibition of certain things to Muslims.

Egyptian Civil Code.

Article 81. Anything that is not outside the bounds of commerce by its nature or by virtue of the law may be the object of property rights.

Things outside the bounds of commerce by their nature cannot be owned exclusively by anybody. Things which are outside the bounds of commerce by virtue of the law are things which cannot be subject of property rights according to law.

Comment: Within these limits then the right of ownership is basically absolute. This is expressed by the *Majalla*.

Majalla.

Article 125. Anything that can be so owned can be the object of absolute ownership [the Arabic term is *mulk*], whether it be a specific object or its use.

Comment: The *Majalla*, following classical Islamic law, thus includes in ownership both the right to a thing itself and the right to certain uses of the thing, such as usufruct or an easement. This is somewhat different from Roman law which regarded a usufruct not as a form of ownership but as an interest *sui generis*.

The Egyptian Civil Code generally follows the French Civil Code in defining the right of ownership.

Egyptian Civil Code.

Article 802. The owner of a thing has, within the limits of the law, the sole right to use it, enjoy it, and dispose of it.

Article 803. The owner of a thing also owns everything that constitutes an essential element of the thing owned, of the kind which cannot be separated from the thing without the latter perishing, deteriorating, or being changed.

The ownership of land includes what is above and below, as far as it can be usefully enjoyed in height and depth. . . .

.   .   .   .

Article 806. An owner must, in the exercise of his rights, comply with the laws, decrees, and regulations having for their object the interests of the public and of individuals. . . .

Comment: These provisions of the Egyptian Code are also in accord with Islamic law which likewise limited the right of ownership by the right of others and by the public interest.

Islamic law and the modern codes also distinguish between personal and real property. Ottoman law, as stated on p. 164, divided real property into five categories: *mulk* land, that is, land held in freehold ownership; *miri* land, that is, state land leased to individuals; *matruka* land, that is, land reserved for public purposes; *waqf* land, that is, land established as a pious foundation; and *mawat* or dead land. *Mawat* land was desert or unused land which if brought into cultivation became *miri* land, that is, the cultivator acquired a right of usufructuary ownership as in other *miri* land.

In Egypt the regulation of land tenure had been similar to that in the rest of the Ottoman Empire. However, although ownership by the state had been widespread, this ownership was very much weakened during the seventeenth and eighteenth centuries by the use of the so-called *iltizam* system under which land was assigned to individuals by public tender in exchange for a sum of money. In the course of time these *iltizam* lands came to be held for life and could even be sold and inherited. When Muhammad 'Ali became pasha of Egypt in the early nineteenth century, he abolished the *iltizam* system. He also confiscated much of the agricultural land which had become *waqf* land. Much of the land thus reverted again to the state.*

Following Muhammad 'Ali's reforms there was no longer an intermediary between the state and the fellah. The latter, of course, did not have ownership but only usufruct in the land. The status of this land was changed significantly by a law the Khedive Sa'id enacted on 5 August 1858. This law went far in establishing private ownership for the cultivator in the land he held from the state. Among other things this land could now be inherited,

*For further details see Gabriel Baer, *A History of Landownership in Modern Egypt,* 1800–1950, (London: Oxford University Press, 1962), pp. 1–7.

pledged as security for a mortgage, and alienated. Further reforms followed and by the end of the nineteenth century most of the land in Egypt was held in full ownership.

In those Arab countries which had been part of the Ottoman Empire until its dissolution at the end of World War I, the Ottoman Land Law continued in effect for some time and the differentiation between *mulk* and *miri* land is still made, at least in theory. Both the Lebanese Land Law of 12 November 1930 and the Syrian Civil Code of 1949 retain this distinction. However, in practice it has become largely meaningless, even though with regard to *miri* land the state retains bare ownership. One rule, that *miri* land reverts to the state if it is not cultivated within five years or if cultivation is interrupted for five years (Article 19 of the Lebanese Land Law and Article 775 of the Syrian Civil Code), is apparently not enforced in practice. Another, that *miri* land cannot be constituted into a *waqf* has lost most of its importance due to the disappearance of family *waqfs* in most countries and restrictions on the establishment of new *waqfs*.*

Intimately connected with rights in real property and also with taxation of real estate has been the problem of registration of property rights, which the Ottoman Land Law had already tried to regulate. Great progress has been made in various countries in the establishment of land registers, but various difficulties still remain.

The problem of joint ownership has already been mentioned in connection with preemption (p. 213). It is mainly an outgrowth of the Islamic law of inheritance and is akin to tenancy-in-common.

The Egyptian Civil Code contains the following provisions:

Egyptian Civil Code.

Article 825. When two or more persons are owners of the same thing, but their respective shares are undivided, they are co-owners and, in the absence of proof to the contrary, their shares are considered to be equal.

Article 826. Every co-owner in common is the absolute owner of his share. He may alienate it, collect the fruits thereof and make use of it, provided he does not injure the rights of the other co-owners. . . .

Comment: A decision by the Egyptian Court of Cassation provides some insight into some of the problems which can arise.

Court of Cassation, Civil Chamber, No. 3–4/98 of 10 February 1955.

Syllabus by the Court.
In order for personal property to become real property as a fixture, it is necessary for both the personal and real properties to belong to the same person. Therefore, if one co-owner of undivided real

---

*Land reform has brought about many changes in land ownership in countries of the Near and Middle East, but a discussion of these developments is outside this study.

property is the sole owner of irrigation machinery which he installed on the said undivided property and which he used for himself only and his own account, then this machinery does not become a fixture and part of the real property.

Comment: A peculiar institution of Islamic law and one which has played an important role in the past is the *waqf* (Arabic plural *awqaf*). In North Africa the *waqf* is known as *hubs* or, in a French spelling, *habous*. A *waqf* is the allocation of some piece of property to charitable or pious purposes. The person establishing the *waqf* (*waqif*) loses his ownership in the *waqf* property. The property cannot be alienated either by the former owner or by the administrator of the *waqf*. Every *waqf* must have an ultimate charitable or pious objective, such as support of the poor or of a mosque. However, this objective may be in the future and the *waqf* may be used to establish a fund for the maintenance of the descendants of the *waqif*, who would be designated as beneficiaries, if the *waqif* so desires, until the line dies out. Under Hanefite law the *waqif* can designate himself as the first beneficiary of the *waqf*. The other orthodox schools do not permit this. The *waqf* is administered by a trustee.

Generally speaking, anything that is tangible can be the object of a *waqf*, but it must have permanency. However, objects permanently attached to real property can be made into individual *waqf* property. For example, one or more trees in an olive grove can become *waqf*. Animals, such as horses or camels, also can be objects of a *waqf*. Books and furniture also can be made into *waqf*, while money or stocks and bonds cannot. In practice most *waqfs* consist of real estate.

In contrast to the trust, a *waqf* is established in perpetuity. It also is irrevocable. Although the *waqf* property cannot be alienated, it can be leased, but usually only for limited periods so as to avoid a circumvention of the principle of inalienability through excessively long leases. Since a *waqf* can be designated for specific beneficiaries, it can be used to avoid the limitations of the Islamic law of inheritance, such as the restriction of disposition by will to one-third of the estate. A *waqf* can also help to avoid the excessive fragmentation of property which the Islamic law of inheritance so often brings about. However, because of the rules of perpetuity and inalienability, *waqf* property is forever withdrawn from commerce and therefore can be a hindrance in economic development, particularly land reform. A *waqf* which is devoted to the endowment of a permanent charitable or pious institution, such as a hospital or a mosque, is called a *waqf khayri* (charitable waqf), a *waqf* that is designated to provide support for certain descendants of the *waqif* before being assigned to a charitable purpose is called a *waqf dhurri* (descendants' or family *waqf*). This distinction is frequently of practical importance in the treatment of *waqf* property in modern legislation.

In most countries of the Near and Middle East *waqf* property, once widespread, has now been greatly restricted. Family *waqfs* particularly, have been abolished in a number of countries, such as

Egypt, Syria, Pakistan, Iran. In Lebanon, the courts, based on certain opinions of classical jurists, have ruled *waqfs* to be revocable and capable of becoming extinct. Charitable *waqfs* have generally been less affected by reform legislation than the family *waqf*, but these *waqfs* are as a rule administered by state organs, such as a ministry of *waqf* administration. Thus, the *waqf* as a legal institution has now lost a great deal of its former importance.

Chapter 10   Penal Law

Comment: Penal law is that area of the law which was least developed by the Muslim jurists and where administrative regulations by Muslim rulers found broad application. Very important in Islamic penal law is the distinction between offenses for which the punishment is determined in the Qur'an and offenses for which the punishment may be established by the judge in his discretion. A famous treatise by Abu al-Hasan 'Ali al-Mawardi, *Kitab al-Ahkam al-Sultaniyya* (Book of the Rules of Government) is one of the works which deals with this matter in considerable detail. Al-Mawardi was born in Basra in A.D. 972 and died in Baghdad in A.D. 1058. He became a very learned teacher of law and was appointed *qadi*. He exercised this office in various towns before becoming *qadi* in Baghdad, the capital of the empire at that time. Mawardi's *Ahkam al-Sultaniyya* might be termed a treatise of constitutional and administrative theory which deals with the bases of the power of the caliph, various administrative and judicial organs, and other subjects of administrative law. This work was translated into French by E. Fagnan under the title *Les statuts gouvernmentaux ou règles de droit public et administratif*, Algiers, 1915.

A. Offenses in General

AL-MAWARDI, *Al-Ahkam al-Sultaniyya*, p. 219 (Fagnan p. 469).

Offenses are forbidden acts which God punishes by a legal penalty [*hadd*] or discretionary punishment [*ta'zir*].

B. Offenses to which <u>Hadd</u> Punishment Applies

Comment: These offenses are: fornication, false accusation of fornication, drinking of wine, theft and brigandage. The punishment for fornication is set at one hundred lashes, for adultery it is stoning. The proof of fornication or adultery was difficult. The Qur'an (Sura IV, 15) demanded proof by four

reliable male witnesses. The jurists have interpreted this requirement as meaning that these witnesses must have been present at
the sexual act itself. False accusation of fornication or adultery is
punishable according to the Qur'an by eighty lashes (Sura XXIV,
4).

Drinking of any intoxicating beverage is forbidden by the
Qur'an and according to the classical jurists. The punishment for
the offender was forty strokes or lashes. Punishment for theft is
cutting off of the hand, according to the Qur'an (Sura V, 41).
According to a *hadith* of the Prophet, this harsh punishment does
not apply to petty larceny. However, the classical jurists differ as
to the definition of petty larceny in terms of the value of the
thing stolen.

Brigandage or endangering the peace of the land are punished
by death, possibly through crucifixion, or through amputation of
alternate hand and foot (Qur'an, Sura V, 36).

Qur'anic punishments are still meted out in some countries,
such as Saudi Arabia, for larceny, fornication, and adultery.

C. Discretionary Punishment (Ta'zir)

AL-MAWARDI, *Al-Ahkam al-Sultaniyya*, pp. 237–239 (Fagnan
pp. 504–509).

Discretionary punishment is inflicted in cases of offenses for which
the *shari'a* has not established written [*hadd*] punishment. . . . It has
this in common with *hadd* penalties: it, too, is a means of punishment which differs with the type of offense. However, discretionary punishment differs from *hadd* punishment in three respects:

The punishment for respectable persons belonging to the upper
classes is less than for low class persons who lead a bad life. . . .
Discretionary punishment thus varies according to the status of a
person, whereas all men are treated the same way in the application of *hadd* punishments. Thus in the case of a man of high
standing, it may be enough to turn away from him; with a man of
lesser rank it may suffice to speak to him sternly; another may
have to be reprimanded sharply in humiliating terms, but
without slanderous or injurious implications. Finally, those in the
lowest group shall be imprisoned for such a term as may be
necessitated by their rank in society and their offense. Some will
be held for a day, some for a longer time and some even for an
indefinite period. . . . Others will be exiled, if their offenses would
tempt other believers to do wrong. . . . Some finally will be
flogged, the number of lashes being dependent on the gravity of
the offense and the behavior of the offender.

· · · ·

The second difference [between *hadd* punishment and discretionary punishment] is that there cannot be pardon or intercession [for

the offender] in the case of *hadd* punishment, whereas in discretionary punishment the offender can be pardoned and intercession is permissible.

.   .   .   .

The third difference is that injuries caused by the application of a *hadd* punishment do not establish any responsibility [for damages], whereas discretionary punishment does. As a result of the punishment ʿUmar al-Khattab inflicted on a woman, she miscarried and her child was stillborn. ʿUmar consulted ʿAli on this matter who made him pay blood money for the foetus.

Comment: Imprisonment was used widely in Islamic law, both before and after trial. Abu Yusuf in his *Kitab al-Kharaj* (p. 89) admonishes governors to have those released who are imprisoned without cause.

D. Talion (Retaliation) and Blood Money (Compensation, Weregild; Arabic: diya)

Comment: Retaliation for a slaying is a very old form of punishment which is also extended to other injuries. It is a replacement for the blood feud. A further step away from the blood feud is the payment of the blood money, that is, instead of retaliating against the person of the transgressor, a certain amount of money is paid to the family of the slain person or to the person who has been injured. The amount of these payments is generally fixed. In Islamic law the family of the transgressor is liable for the payment of blood money in some cases. The fundamental rules for retaliation and blood money are laid down in the *Qurʾan*.

Qurʾan, Sura II.

Verse 178. Oh ye who believe! Retaliation is prescribed for you in the matter of the murdered; the freeman for the freeman, and the slave for the slave, and the female for the female. And for him who is forgiven somewhat by his (injured) brother, prosecution according to usage and payment unto him in kindness. This is an alleviation and a mercy from your Lord. He who transgresseth after this will have a painful doom.

AL-MAWARDI, *Al-Ahkam al-Sultaniyya*, pp. 231–233 (Fagnan pp. 493–498).

. . . Assaults on persons can be intentional or accidental, or intentional but resembling the accidental. The offense is intentional if the offender aims to kill someone with an instrument which pierces with the point or cuts with the edge. . . . According to Abu Hanifa, intention which gives rise to talion exists when a thing made of iron or other material is used which causes death by piercing or cutting the flesh. Such intention does not exist if stones or pieces of wood are used which kill through their weight or through the pain which they cause. The rule to be applied if intention exists, is, according to Shafi'i, to give the claimant for the victim . . . the choice between talion and blood money. According to Abu Hanifa, however, the claimant may only apply talion, and blood money can be asked for only with the agreement of the murderer.

The claimant for the victim or the one having the right of talion is the person, man or woman, who is the heir of the victim either as sharer or as residuary. Malik gives this right only to the male heirs of the victim but not to the females . . . .

Purely accidental homicide, where a person causes the death of another unintentionally, does not call for the death of the offender by virtue of talion. . . . Such cases . . . of purely accidental killing give rise to a claim to blood money, but not to talion. The *diya* must be paid by the relatives of the offender liable for such payment . . . . Those liable ['*aqila*] include all the agnatic relatives with the exception of the father and sons. Thus the father and all ascendants and the son and all descendants are excluded. Abu Hanifa and Malik, however, include them. . . .

The *diya* payable for the [accidental] killing of a free Muslim is one thousand gold dinars. . . . Expressed in camels it is one hundred camels. . . . The *diya* payable for a woman, whether her life was taken or one of her limbs severed is half that due for a man. . . .

Involuntary manslaughter exists if the offender had the intention of [inflicting bodily harm] but not to kill. For example he hits another person with a piece of wood or throws stones at him . . . or a prince inflicts a discretionary punishment upon an offender and causes his death. In such cases there is no talion, but an aggravated *diya* payable by those liable. Aggravation means that the *diya* payable in gold or silver is increased by one-third. . . .

The *diya* for intentional homicide, if there is no talion, is also aggravated and levied first against the property of the offender.

Comment: Accidental homicide is dealt with in the Qu'ran.

Qur'an, Sura IV.

Verse 92. It is not for a believer to kill a believer unless (it be) by mistake. He who hath killed a believer by mistake must set free a believing slave, and pay the blood money to the family of the slain, unless they remit it as a charity. If he (the victim) be of a people hostile to you, and he is a believer, then (the penance is) to set free a believing slave. And if he cometh of a folk between whom and you there is a covenant, then the blood money must be paid unto his folk and (also) a believing slave must be set free. And whoso has not the wherewithal must fast two consecutive months. A penance from Allah. Allah is Knower, Wise.

Comment: The Islamic jurists basically distinguish three types of homicide which are based on certain general criteria, such as the weapon used, rather than the real intention of the person committing the offense. The three categories are:

a. intentional homicide;
b. homicide caused by negligence (quasi-intentional);
c. accidental or mistaken homicide.

The negligent homicide is defined as an intentional act against another person which does not generally cause death, but which could do so sometimes. The homicide by mistake includes cases where there was no intent to act against the person killed, but the action itself was intended. For example, someone shoots at a deer and kills a man.

The Hanefite jurists distinguish a fourth category, namely, indirect homicide. This is the case, for example, if a man digs a well and another man falls in and is killed.

It should be noted that the killer himself is not responsible for the blood money in case of negligent or accidental homicide, only his agnates, the so-called *'aqila* are. The Hanefite school differs and makes the killer responsible together with his agnates.

Blood money for homicide and bodily injuries is still imposed by the *qadi*'s courts in Saudi Arabia and other countries in the Arabian Peninsula. The amount of the blood money is fixed. According to a legal opinion of the Mufti of Saudi Arabia of 1955, the blood money for the intentional or quasi-intentional killing of a male Muslim is one hundred camels, for accidental killing the number is the same, but the camels are of less value. The Mufti in his opinion translated the value of the camels into Saudi riyals. Accordingly, the blood money for intentional or quasi-intentional killing is 18,000 riyals, for accidental homicide 16,000 riyals.* The blood money for a female Muslim is half that of a male one. The *diya* for the loss of limbs, fingers, toes, etc. was and is figured in fractions of the *diya* payable for homicide.

Retaliation and blood money are both widespread in the laws of many peoples. The code of Hammurabi and other Mesopotamian laws as well as the Old Testament (particularly in Exodus and Deuteronomy) contain provisions comparable to those in Islamic law. Blood money was well known also in Germanic law where the agnatic relatives were liable for the blood money. In Anglo-Saxon law, blood money played an important role. A detailed list of payments for various injuries is contained in the laws of Ethelbert (about A.D. 600) published in Roscoe Pound, *Readings on the History and System of the Common Law*, 2d edition, (Boston, 1913), pp. 28–30. Payment for the slaying of a man was stipulated in Alfred's and Guthrum's peace (A.D. 879): "Then this is this: If a man be slain, we estimate all equally dear, English and Danish, at eight half marks of pure gold. . . ." (*Ibid.*, p. 31).

---

*This would correspond to about $3,900 and $3,500 respectively.

E. Present-day Penal Law

Comment: In most Near and Middle Eastern countries modern penal codes have been enacted which follow generally the continental European system. Offenses are divided into three categories: crimes (felonies), delicts (major misdemeanors) and contraventions (petty offenses). In some instances, particularly where family honor is involved, local customs have, however, been taken into account, either by statutes or by the courts. Syria and Lebanon are examples of countries with statutory provisions, which in this case are identical.

Lebanese Penal Code of 1949.

Article 562. Whoever having surprised his wife, his female ascendant or descendant or his sister in the act of committing adultery or having illicit sexual relations with a third person and having committed non-premeditated homicide or injury on one or the other of the persons involved shall benefit from a defense which wholly excuses him.

Whoever commits such homicide or injury where he surprises his wife or his female ascendant or descendant or his sister in compromising circumstances shall benefit from extenuating circumstances. [The Syrian Penal Code of 1949 contains the same provision in Article 548.]

Comment: In Iraq where the Baghdad Penal Code, in force until 1969, did not contain a comparable provision, executive clemency was used for a long time to shorten sentences imposed by the courts in cases where homicide was committed in the protection of family honor.

In Pakistan the courts have utilized Section 300 of the Penal Code to achieve a similar result.

Penal Code of 1860.

Section 300. Except in the cases hereinafter excepted, culpable homicide is murder, if the act by which death is caused is done with the intention of causing death. . . .

[Exception 1 states:]

Culpable homicide is not murder if the offender whilst deprived of the power of self-control by grave and sudden provocation, causes the death of the person who gave the provocation or causes the death of any other person by mistake or accident.

Comment: This exception has provided a basis for Pakistani courts to mitigate punishment when faced with crimes committed to preserve the family honor. A fairly recent case illustrates the problems faced by the courts.

Appeal against the order of the Sessions Judge, Kalat, dated 10 December 1963.*

The judgment of the Court was delivered by:

Muhammad Gul, J.—The appellant Behram, aged 25 years and his paternal aunt's son Mahmud, aged 20 years, were jointly tried by the learned Sessions Judge, Kalat, under sections 302/34 Pakistan Penal Code (P.P.C.) [Section 302 establishes the penalty for murder. Section 34 establishes equal responsibility for all persons participating in a criminal act "in furtherance of the criminal intention of all"], for the murders of Dad Karim and Musammat Rahim Bibi. Mahmud was acquitted of the charge under sections 302/34 P.P.C., but was convicted under section 304 Part I P.P.C. and sentenced to imprisonment till the rising of the Court† [section 304 part I sets forth the penalty for culpable homicide]. However, the appellant was convicted on the same facts under section 302 P.P.C. [that is, for murder] and sentenced to transportation for life.‡ He appeals against this conviction and sentence as aforesaid.

The appellant and Mahmud along with the latter's parents lived in the same *Haveli* [house or compound] in village Ghulam Paraiz. Mst. Rahim Bibi, deceased, aged about 25 years, was the real sister of Mahmud. She and her husband Jangi Khan (Prosecution Witness 6), also used to live in the same *Haveli* till a few days prior to the occurrence when they shifted to their own house in a nearby village at a distance of about two furlongs from village Ghulam Paraiz. Dad Karim, deceased, belonged to village Kacha Khad, but had settled in village Ghulam Paraiz where he ran a shop.

The case for the prosecution is that on 7 April 1963, about midday, Mahmud, accused, came out of his house and went toward *Baghecha* [garden] of Badal Khan. As he jumped over the wall of *Baghecha*, he was shocked to see his sister Mst. Rahim Bibi and Dad Karim in a compromising position. He challenged the miscreants to get up and rushed towards them. Being thus surprised by Mahmud, they got up. Dad Karim made a bid to escape but Mahmud, accused, succeeded in getting hold of him. Even then Dad tried to free himself by pushing as under his captor. This led to a scuffle between the two. Mahmud shouted to the appellant for help asking him to bring weapons because he had caught a "*Siahkar.*" [The word means wicked. It is here used for the alleged adulterers. *Siahkari* is used for the act of adultery.] The appellant immediately responded to the call and taking a sword and a pick-axe ran to the spot and saw Dad Karim and Mahmud still grappling with each other. Mahmud told the appellant that his sister Mst. Rahim Bibi and Dad Karim had been guilty of "*Siahkari.*" Thereupon the appellant threw the sword towards Mahmud

*Quetta is the capital of the province of Baluchistan, which is in the southwest part of Pakistan bordering on Iran. Kalat is the capital of a district of the same name in Baluchistan.

†This means until the end of the day's court session.

‡This is today rigorous imprisonment, usually twenty years.

and himself attacked Dad Karim with the pick-axe. Mahmud also gave him blows with the sword and when Dad Karim was incapacitated and fell down, Mahmud slaughtered him with the sword. Dildar (Prosecution Witness 2) saw the appellant and Mahmud inflicting injuries upon Dad Karim with their respective weapons. Having finished with Dad Karim, the appellant and Mahmud followed Mst. Rahim Bibi, who had in the meantime disappeared from the scene. They found her going towards the village and having overtaken her also killed her with the weapons they were carrying. She was also slaughtered by Mahmud after she had fallen on the ground. Ghulam Nabi (Prosecution Witness 3) saw the appellant and Mahmud in pursuit of her and Ata Muhammad (Prosecution Witness 4), and Mira Khan (Prosecution Witness 5) saw her being actually killed. Having killed her, the appellant and Mahmud dragged her body to the place where Dad Karim lay dead and stayed with the dead bodies till Takri Nawab (Prosecution Witness 1), on hearing the commotion came to the scene of occurrence. On inquiry by the witness, the appellant and the accused told him that they had killed Dad Karim and Mst. Rahim Bibi because they were guilty of "*Siahkari*." Takri Nawab went to report the matter to the *Tehsildar* [Officer-in-Charge of the Sub-Division], who in turn informed the Station House Officer [the police officer commanding the police station] over the telephone. The latter immediately proceeded to the scene of occurrence. The appellant and Mahmud remained at the spot till the arrival of the police and handed over the pick-axe (Prosecution Exhibit 1) and sword (Prosecution Exhibit 2) to the police.

On 11 April 1963, the appellant was produced before the *Tehsildar-cum-Magistrate* [this officer having some judicial functions], for recording his confession. After the Magistrate had satisfied himself that the appellant was going to make confession of his own free will and not under any pressure from the police, he recorded his statement (Prosecution Exhibit U). In his statement he gave a graphic description of the entire transaction and made a down-right confession as being a partner in crime with Mahmud and having killed both Dad Karim and Mst. Rahim Bibi with pick-axe and sword respectively. On the following day, i.e., on 12 April 1963, Mahmud, accused, was also produced before the *Tehsildar* and he made a similar confessional statement (Prosecution Exhibit V).

In the course of trial both before the Committing Magistrate and in the Sessions Court, Mahmud modified his statement in so far as it implicated Behram appellant. In both statements, he entirely exculpated the appellant from being concerned in the killing and himself assumed the sole responsibility for having killed both Dad Karim and Mst. Rahim Bibi in the circumstances mentioned above. When confronted with his earlier confession (Prosecution Exhibit V), he admitted having made the statement but repudiated it so far as it implicated the appellant and said he was innocent. The appellant too completely went back upon his confessional statement (Prosecution Exhibit U) and denied all knowledge or participation in the commission of the crime.

However, the learned Sessions Judge relied and rightly so, upon the two confessional statements (Prosecution Exhibits U and V). That apart, the ocular evidence (which is of the un-impeachable character) and the medical report (which shows that two different weapons, namely sword and pick-axe, were used), clearly point to two persons taking part in the crime. The appellant's participation in the crime is established beyond doubt.

Faced with this overwhelming evidence both ocular and circumstantial, appellant's learned counsel frankly conceded that the appellant was co-partner in crime with Mahmud, accused, and argued in support of the appeal on that basis. He contended that on the evidence produced in the case, which the learned Sessions Judge had accepted in the case of Mahmud, he ought to have allowed the benefit of grave and sudden provocation to the apellant as well and should have also similarly convicted him under section 304 part I P.P.C. instead of section 302 P.P.C. We feel that there is force in the learned counsel's contention. The learned Sessions Judge distinguished the case of the appellant from that of Mahmud, in paragraph 14 of his judgment, in the following words:

"The only point to be determined in his case, therefore, is as to whether he (the appellant) too acted under grave and sudden provocation or not. From the circumstances of the case, I am, however, of the opinion that he did not act under any grave and sudden provocation. He admittedly did not see the two deceased in a compromising position and it is in evidence that Rahim Bibi was not present at all when he arrived for the help of Mahmud. In the circumstances there was therefore, nothing to give grave provocation. The mere telling of Mahmud that Dad Karim had committed adultery with Rahim Bibi could not in my opinion give him any sudden provocation."

The learned Sessions Judge reached this conclusion against the unanimous opinion of the Assessors who assisted him in the trial. [The Assessors participate in the trial, much like a jury would, and the judge must ascertain their opinions before pronouncing judgment. However, he is not bound by the opinion of the Assessors.] They were of the opinion that the plea of grave and sudden provocation was equally available to the appellant as in the case of Mahmud. Whether plea of grave and sudden provocation will avail in a case will depend upon its circumstances and it is nowhere laid down as an inflexible rule, that an outraged relation should also be an eyewitness to the sexual indecency before he can take advantage of the mitigating circumstances. The view taken by the trial court appears to us to be an unwarranted limitation on the operation of the first exception of section 300 P.P.C. The learned Sessions Judge perhaps overlooked the very important fact in this case, that the appellant besides being a close relation of Mst. Rahim Bibi also lived with Mahmud and his parents as member of the family in the same *Haveli* and, therefore, he was so much honor-bound as Mahmud himself to assert his right to redeem the infamy that has been brought upon the family by Mst. Rahim Bibi by her sexual relation with Dad Karim.

The learned Sessions Judge further overlooked the fact that the appellant responded to the call for help by Mahmud, accused, who actually had seen the two miscreants in the act of sexual intimacy. Not only that: Dad Karim gave him further provocation by offering resistance to make good his escape and indeed during the initial stage had better of Mahmud, who was comparatively younger in age and, therefore, not strong enough to overpower him single-handed. All these factors are, in our opinion, very material and go a long way to bring the appellant's case at par with that of Mahmud. Indeed, the learned Assistant Advocate General could not support the proposition enunciated by the learned Sessions Judge in respect of the appellant's case. Therefore, we hold that the appellant's conviction under section 302 P.P.C. cannot be maintained.

On the point of sentence, learned counsel for the appellant next urged that prior to integration of Kalat Division with the rest of the province, for the purposes of the administration of justice, the tribal custom recognized the right of male members to kill with impunity a "*Siahkar*" female member of the family and her paramour and that it was precisely for this reason that the learned Sessions Judge let off Mahmud with a token sentence of imprisonment till the rising of the court. Therefore he pleaded for a similar token sentence in the case of the appellant also. To this aspect of the case we have given our anxious consideration and, if we may say so, the learned Sessions Judge misdirected himself when he allowed extraneous considerations to weigh with him in awarding trifling sentence to Mahmud. Having found him guilty under section 304 part I P.P.C. he was bound to impose a sentence as warranted by law and if in his opinion any extra-judicial consideration had any bearing on the case, then he ought to have brought the case to the notice of the Provincial Government who have ample powers under section 401 of the Criminal Procedure Code of 1898 to deal with the case and to mitigate the rigor of the law as the justice of the case may require. [The section cited gives the Provincial Government the power to suspend the execution of a sentence or to remit it in whole or in part, conditionally or unconditionally.] It is not permissible to courts to encroach upon the prerogative power of the Executive reserved under section 401 Cr.P.C. or Article 18 of the Constitution. [This article gave the president the right of pardon and of commutation and remission of sentences.] The offense under section 304 part I P.P.C. is punishable with transportation for life or imprisonment which may extend to ten years and also a fine. As a rule, sentence actually awarded must bear some proportion to the punishment prescribed by the statute. This is not to say that in assessing the actual sentence the Court should disregard the circumstances of the case before calling for what may be a severe or, as the case may be, lenient sentence. But to award the sentence of imprisonment till the rising of the Court in case where the maximum prescribed is transportation for life and in which two human lives were lost is to reduce criminal justice to a mockery. Learned counsel for the appellant strongly relied upon *State vs. Akbar (Pakistan Law*

Decisions 1961 Lahore 24), in which the accused who pleaded grave and sudden provocation in his defense was convicted under section 304 part II P.P.C. and sentenced to imprisonment till the rising of the Court and a revision by the State for enhancement of sentence failed. That case proceeded on its own facts. For one thing, the conviction in that case was under part II of section 304, which is a lesser offense. [Whereas part I of this section deals with culpable homicide, part II deals with cases where "the act is done with the knowledge that it is likely to cause death, but without any intention to cause death or to cause such bodily injury as is likely to cause death." In that event punishment is imprisonment up to ten years and fine.] Secondly, the learned Single Judge did not quite approve of the trifling sentence imposed by the Sessions Judge in that case. It is true that the learned Single Judge made some observations underlining the desirability of preserving the moral values and notions of honor and chastity as well as social customs, which prevail in the society, and to deal with such cases with leniency. But it is wrong to read that judgment as laying down that in cases of grave and sudden provocation caused by sexual delinquency of female relatives, a trifling sentence will do. While on the one hand law gives the benefit of shock to the accused in the circumstances furnishing grave and sudden provocation within the meaning of Exception I of section 300 P.P.C. in prescribing a sentence of transportation for life or imprisonment extending up to ten years, it also inculcates a peculiar sanctity for human life. Therefore, a balance is to be maintained between the two different concepts underlying the provisions of the P.P.C. relevant to this case.

For the foregoing reasons, we set aside the conviction and sentence of the appellant under section 302 P.P.C. and convict him for an offense under section 304 part I, P.P.C. and sentence him to three years rigorous imprisonment. With the above modification, the appeal is dismissed.

Comment: This case clearly shows the difficulties the courts have to face in dealing with this type of case. As stated by the court, the tribal assemblies, called *jirgas*, which consist of representatives of the tribes in a certain area and which have some judicial functions, have generally acquitted persons charged with murder, when they had acted to preserve the family honor. The *Report of the Law Reform Commission, 1958–1959* recommended that cases involving such murders where fraud might be suspected should be tried by the ordinary courts and not by *jirgas*.

Report of the Law Reform Commission, 1958–1959, p. 112.

In the Baluchistan area, another type of reprehensible crime came to our notice. Murders are camouflaged as *Siahkari* cases, that is, cases of murder committed under grave and sudden provocation due to infidelity of the wife or a female relative. We are told that a person who wants to kill an enemy, purchases a woman, marries her and then kills her as well as the enemy, giving the whole case the guise of a *Siahkari* case. In this way he wins the sympathy of his tribesmen, and the *jirgas* before which such cases are brought, in view of the prevailing tribal sentiment, are reluctant to recommend any punishment. It also happens that a man who is fed up with his wife and wants to get rid of her, murders her and links her up with an enemy whom he also wants to dispose of. This is another class of cases in which the colour of *Siahkari* is pressed into service to escape the clutches of the law. In order to stop this kind of fraud on the law we recommend that such cases not be sent to *jirgas* at all but to ordinary courts for trial. . . .

Comment: In the case of Behram given above, adultery was apparently clearly established. Tribal *jirgas* no longer had jurisdiction in the place where the murder had been committed and the case came before the ordinary court. The sentence of the court below in the case of Mahmud, the brother of the murdered woman, reflects quite clearly the prevailing local opinion and the quandary of the judge. He had to apply a statute which was drafted by the British and essentially reflects Western views and standards of behavior, in a very different tribal setting. Thus, he imposed a token sentence. In the case of the cousin, a split developed between the judge and the assessors, laymen who no doubt were local people. The judge, against the advice of the Assessors, meted out to the cousin a very stiff sentence, giving a strict interpretation to the words "grave and sudden provocation" in the Pakistani Penal Code. On appeal the court censured the court below for merely imposing a token sentence on the murdered woman's brother, but at the same time allowed that the cousin had also acted under a "grave and sudden provocation." Both the appeals court and the court below thus attempted to adjust the penal law which did not directly deal with this type of offense (in contrast to the Lebanese and Syrian Penal Codes), without, as the appeals court put it, making a "mockery of the law." It is also interesting that the appeals court pointed to executive clemency as offering an extraordinary remedy in such cases.

The abuses cited by the Law Reform Commission were, no doubt, of grave concern to the courts and law enforcement agencies. It is likely, however, that even here at times tribal customs came into play. A tribesman may have felt justified in revenging himself upon an enemy and may have believed that he should be allowed to do so without incurring punishment. In order to have a good chance to accomplish this he would then make the case appear as a murder involving family honor. This is said, not to excuse such actions, of course, but rather to show that in penal law, as in other areas of the law, as we have seen, conflicts can arise between local attitudes and customs and a law largely based on non-indigenous models. It is essentially up to the courts then to adjust the codified law to the needs of the society to which the law has to be applied.

Chapter 11   Procedure Before the Westernization of the Law

Comment: One of the foremost characteristics which Islamic law shares with other laws of antiquity and the Middle Ages was a lack of separation of judicial and executive powers. The Islamic judge, the *qadi*, originally was the delegate of the governor of the province or of the caliph. He served at the pleasure of the person who appointed him. The *qadi*'s court was the court of general jurisdiction and, in contrast to the courts of the Mesopotamian countries, it was a single judge court. There were no regular appeal procedures and the idea of *res iudicata* was not strongly developed.

A. The Qadi and his Office

IBN KHALDUN, *The Muqaddimah*, vol. 1, pp. 452–454.

The office of the judge is one of the positions that come under the caliphate. It is the institution that serves the purpose of settling suits and breaking off disputes and dissensions. It proceeds , however, along the lines of the religious laws laid down by the Qur'an and the *sunna*. Therefore, it is one of the positions that belongs to the caliphate and falls under it generally.

At the beginning of Islam, the caliphs exercised the office of judge personally. They did not permit anyone else to function as judge in any matter. The first caliph to charge someone else with the exercise of (the office of judge) was 'Umar. He appointed Abu al-Darda to be judge with him in Medina, he appointed Shurayh as judge in al-Basra, and Abu Musa al-Ash'ari as judge in al-Kufah. On appointing (Abu Musa) he wrote him the famous letter that contains all the laws that govern the office of judge, and is the basis of them. He says in it:

Now, the office of judge is a definite religious duty and a generally followed practice.

Understand the depositions that are made before you, for it is useless to consider a plea that is not valid.

Consider all the people equal before you and in your court and in your attention, so that the noble will not expect you to be partial and the humble will not despair of justice from you.

The claimant must produce evidence; from the defendant, an oath may be exacted.

Compromise is permissible among Muslims, but not any agreement through which something forbidden would be permitted, or something permitted forbidden.

If you gave judgment yesterday, and today upon reconsideration come to the correct opinion, you should not feel prevented by your first judgment from retracting; for justice is primeval, and it is better to retract than to persist in worthlessness.

Use your brain about matters that perplex you and to which neither Qur'an nor *sunna* seem to apply. Study similar cases and evaluate the situation through analogy with those similar cases.

If a person brings a claim, which he may or may not be able to prove, set a time limit for him. If he brings proof within the time limit, you should allow his claim, otherwise you are permitted to give judgment against him. This is the better way to forestall or clear up any possible doubt.

All Muslims are acceptable as witnesses against each other, except such as have received a punishment provided for by the religious law, such as are proved to have given false witness, and such as are suspected (of partiality) on (the ground of) client status or relationship, for God, praised be He, forgives because of oath (?) and postpones (punishment) in the face of evidence.

Avoid fatigue and weariness and annoyance at the litigants.

For establishing justice in the courts of justice, God will grant you a rich reward and give you a good reputation.

Farewell

Although the personal exercise of the office of judge was to have been the task of (the caliphs), they entrusted others with it because they were too busy with general politics and too occupied with the Holy War, conquests, defense of the border regions, and protection of the center. . . .

Comment: The letter quoted by Ibn Khaldun is generally not regarded as authentic today. It gives, however, a good idea of the principles which the early Muslim lawyers and administrators regarded as guiding in the exercise of justice. It might be noted that Abu Musa, the addressee of the letter, was not only a judge but also governor of Basra. The alleged author of the letter was the Caliph 'Umar ibn 'Abd al-'Aziz (Umar II, A.D. 717–720).

AL-MAWARDI. *Al-Ahkam al-Sultaniyya*, pp. 69–71 (Fagnan, pp. 140–146).

Investiture with the judicial office results from a contract and is accomplished in the same way as that of other offices, orally if the individual is present, through a messenger or in writing if the individual is absent. . . . Its validity depends upon the acceptance of the person invested.

.   .   .   .   .

The delegation of powers to the *qadi* is necessarily either general or special. If it is general and he can act independently within the limits of his powers, the matters with which he is concerned can be divided into ten categories:

(1) He resolves differences and puts an end to difficulties and law suits either through a compromise between the two parties, taking into account what is feasible, or through coercion by pronouncing a final judgment taking into account what is due.

(2) He proceeds for the benefit of the claimants with the enforcement of their claims against those who deny them, after these claims have been proven well founded through either confession, an oath, or witnesses. There is no agreement, however, whether the *qadi* may in this case render judgment on the basis of personal knowledge of the matter in dispute. Malik and Shafi'i . . . say yes. Abu Hanifa permits reliance upon personal knowledge, if such is acquired during the exercise of his official functions, but not if it has been acquired prior thereto.

(3) He makes provision for the guardianship of those who because of insanity or youth are unable to administer their property. He does the same where such measures are necessary because of prodigality or bankruptcy in order to protect the property of such persons against claimants and to maintain the validity of contracts to which they are parties.

(4) He supervises pious foundations (*waqf*) with regard to the safeguarding of their substance and their income, the collection of the latter and its proper use. If someone is charged with the administration (of the pious foundation), he respects the rights of that administrator; if there is none, he assumes these duties himself. . . .

(5) He sees to it that testamentary provisions are executed as desired by the testator, provided the conditions set are lawful and not prohibited. . . .

(6) He marries single women who are widows or divorcees to proper husbands, provided they have no *wali* and have been asked in marriage. Abu Hanifa does not make this a right of the judge because he permits the widow or divorcee to marry herself [without *wali*].

(7) He applies the *hadd* penalties to those who are liable to them; this is a matter of public order. He proceeds by himself and without a complaint, provided the offense is proven through the confession of the accused or through witnesses. If it is an offense to which *ta'zir* punishment applies, the *qadi* intervenes only in case of a complaint. Abu Hanifa says that he may not apply a penalty in either case unless there is a complainant.

(8) He exercises police powers in his district. He stops all infringements in streets and public places and causes the removal of all projections [of buildings] and of all buildings which are too tall. He may proceed on his own initiative regarding these duties without anybody having to lodge a complaint. According to Abu Hanifa, he may do so only if a complaint has been lodged with him. However, these are questions of public order and it is hardly important whether or not there is a request for intervention. Consequently, the official's freedom of action is more marked.

(9) He undertakes the necessary investigations with regard to his reliable witnesses (*shuhud*) and his assistants, and selects those among his lieutenants who can substitute for him.

(10) He judges on a basis of equality between the powerful and the weak and equitably between the noble and the humble. He should not follow his desire to find insufficient an established right or to show partiality for the wrong. Allah has said: "Oh David! Lo! We have set thee as a viceroy in the earth, therefore judge aright between mankind, and follow not desire that it beguile thee from the way of Allah. Lo! those who wander from the way of Allah have an awful doom, forasmuch as they forgot the Day of Reckoning" (*Qur'an*, Sura XXXVIII, 27). . . .

B. Plaintiff and Defendant

Comment: The question of who is to be regarded as plaintiff and who is to be regarded as defendant was considered important by the Muslim jurists. On the resolution of this question depended the allocation of the burden of proof.

A Malikite jurist, Ibn 'Asim al-Maliki, gives a definition of plaintiff and defendant in a famous work, *al-Tuhfa al-hukkam fi nukat al-'uqud wa'l-ahkam* [*The Present to the Judges on the Fine Points of Contracts and Judgments*]. Ibn 'Asim (A.D. 1359–1426) lived all his life in Granada where he was Chief *Qadi* for many years. The *Tuhfa* is written in verses. It was edited and translated into French by Leon Bercher, Algiers, 1958.

IBN 'ASIM, *Al-Tuhfa*, vs. 21–23.

The plaintiff is he whose statement is not corroborated by a principle or by usage.

The defendant is he whose statement is supported by a principle or by usage.

According to another opinion, the one who affirms the existence of a fact is the plaintiff, the one who denies its existence is the defendant.

Comment: Another Malikite jurist, Khalil bin Ishaq (born about A.D. 1365) also discussed this problem.

KHALIL BIN ISHAQ, *Al-Mukhtasar*, p.208.

[The judge] will order the plaintiff, that is, the one whose statement is as yet unproven, to make a statement. If this criterion cannot be used, he will be regarded as plaintiff who has brought the other to court. If this criterion also cannot be used, the roles of plaintiff and defendant are determined by lot. . . .

Then [after the plaintiff has made his statement] the judge will order the defendant to reply, that is the one whose statement had more weight [before the plaintiff submitted his evidence] because of usages or of a principle.

Comment: The statement that the one whose allegation is not in accord with generally accepted principles and usages is the plaintiff and the one whose allegation is in accord with such principles and usages is the defendant, may sound strange. What is meant is that the plaintiff alleges something out of the ordinary. For example, A claims that B owes him a certain sum of money, B denies this. The normal state of affairs is for a person not to owe anything, therefore, if A claims that B owes him a certain amount he has to prove it. Similarly if A alleges that B has damaged his fence negligently, he alleges something out of the ordinary and has to prove it.

A general rule of Roman law is reminiscent of Ibn 'Asim's statement that the one who asserts the existence of a fact is the plaintiff and the one who denies it is the defendant:

Digest of Justinian 22. 3. 2.

The burden of proof is upon him who affirms, not upon him who denies.

C. Evidence

Comment: Once the roles of plaintiff and defendant have been established and the burden of proof has been allocated, the plaintiff must prove his case. According to the Muslim jurists the principle means of proof was through witnesses. In legal theory, though not in practice, documents played a very subsidiary role.

1. Documentary Evidence

Comment: A modern Lebanese jurist has dealt with this subject.

EMILE TYAN, *Le Notariat et le régime de preuve par écrit dans la pratique du droit musulman*, pp. 5–12.*

The general and fundamental principle, which unanimous and uninterrupted opinion of the jurists teaches during the course of all the history of Islamic law, is "that the document in itself is without value; that a written document does not make proof." Certain justifications for this principle became very popular and were presented as clichés by all writers. These justifications are: one document can easily be confused with another document; a document may merely represent an intention to try a formulation, may merely be a draft; the document may have mistakes in it; or the seal may be counterfeit. If a written document was produced, it had itself to be proven through admissible means of evidence. The written document was therefore excluded from the

*Reprinted by permission of the author and the Faculty of Law and Economics of Beirut.

means of proof. "Legal means of proof are restricted to three: testimony of witnesses, confession, and oath." The last two means of proof had a relatively restricted application in practice. The testimony of witnesses, however, became the most important means of proof. . . .

Nevertheless, the use of written documentation in the performance of legal acts—private as well as public—is very old in the Muslim Arab world. It actually goes back to its origins. According to the Muslim chroniclers themselves, court clerks had been employed in the courts to keep a record of the proceedings since the first half of the first century of the Hijra (seventh–eighth century A.D.). Orders and decisions of the administrative authorities from the same period also were reduced to writing. Contracts among private individuals also were written. . . .

It could not have been different. Actually, in the provinces which the Arab invaders conquered from the Byzantine Empire and where Islamic law and judicial practice developed, the written document had been in use for a long time. . . . These populations remained the same, having simply changed religion and language. They obviously could not renounce in their daily practice the old established usages which, besides, presented such great advantages regarding the security and convenience of legal relationships. Furthermore, in applying these usages they did not come in conflict with any precept taught by the new religion. In fact, the Qur'an formally recommends to the believers to put their contracts in writing (Sura II, 282). . . .

In their disdain for the written document, the jurists came in conflict with this verse of the Qur'an. They did not, however, change their attitude. Rather they strove . . . to downgrade the importance of the Qur'anic provision. In fact, the jurists refused to regard this provision as a binding rule, but saw it merely as a recommended act.

For purposes of the present study it is not necessary to investigate the historical origins of the rule propounded by the jurists. We simply should ask ourselves . . . how, in view of the widespread use of the written document, the rule established by the jurists which definitely denies any value to the written document could be reconciled with the general practice and under what conditions a written document could be validly employed in legal transactions.

The answer to this question appears simple. The legal technique applied by the practice and approved by the jurists actually derived from the proof through witnesses. A written legal document is not regarded to make proof in and by itself. Just as any legal act can be proven through witnesses, so can a legal act which has been reduced to writing be proven through at least two persons . . . who testify that they have witnessed the act in question.

Strictly speaking, proof of the legal act thus is not established by the written document, but by the testimony of witnesses. Therefore there is no basic difference, from an evidentiary point of view, between a legal act which has been reduced to writing and one which has not been put in writing. In both cases the testimony of witnesses makes proof. The written document, however, has the advantage of assuring the preservation of the exact terms of the transaction.

This procedure was not original or new. It was employed in all systems which could have provided precedents for the Islamic system. In the law and practice of the Roman and Byzantine Empires, even at times of the greatest diffusion of the system of notaries, legal acts registered by notaries (*tabelliones*) required the participation of at least two persons acting as witnesses. . . .

Pre-Islamic practice in Arabia followed, and the Qur'an consecrated, an analogous procedure. In the verse cited above, the Qur'an, after having recommended the use of written documents, urges the contracting parties to have two honorable persons witness the contract thus drawn up.

This procedure is applied to all written documents, private or public. Proof of judicial actions, especially judgments, is made as a matter of principle not through a written document issued by the judge or the court registry, but through the testimony of witnesses whom the judge has asked to be present during the court proceedings.*

Comment: The pertinent parts of the Qur'anic verse cited by Tyan read as follows:

Qur'an, Sura II.

Verse 282. Oh ye who believe! When ye contract a debt for a fixed term, record it in writing. Let a scribe record it in writing between you in (terms of) equity. No scribe should refuse to write as Allah has taught him, so let him write, and let him who incurreth the debt dictate, and let him observe his duty to Allah his Lord, and diminish naught thereof. But if he who owes the debt is of low understanding, or weak or unable himself to dictate, then let the guardian of his interests dictate in (terms of) equity. And call to witness, from among your men, two witnesses. And if two men be not (at hand) then a man and two women, of such as ye approve as witnesses, so that if the one erreth (through forgetfullness) the other will remember. And the witnesses must not refuse when they are summoned. Be not averse to writing down (the contract) whether it be small or great, with record of the term thereof. That is more equitable in the sight of Allah and more sure for testimony, and the best way of avoiding doubt between you. . . .

2. *Testimony of Witnesses*

Comment: The use of witnesses and of the oath in procedure is described by al-Qayrawani.

*The use of documents in transactions and the nature of formularies prepared by Muslim jurists have been discussed by Jeanette A. Wakin, *The Function of Documents in Islamic Law* (Albany: State University of New York Press, 1972).

AL-QAYRAWANI, *Risala*, pp. 260–265.

The plaintiff must prove [his claim through witnesses], he who denies the claim [i.e., the defendant] must take the oath. No oath is required if the connection between the parties is uncertain or if there is doubt concerning the validity of the claim. This is the rule of the Medinese authorities. . . .

If the defendant declines to take the oath, judgment will be given for the plaintiff provided he confirms by oath his precise claim. The oath is sworn "by Allah besides Whom there is no deity." It is sworn in a standing position and by the pulpit of the Prophet (the Lord bless him and give him salvation!) if the value is at least a quarter dinar. In places other than Medina it shall be taken in the mosque and in that part of it which is most venerated. The nonbeliever shall swear by God wherever he worships.

If, after the defendant has taken the oath, the plaintiff discovers proof [through witnesses] of which he had been unaware, the judgment will be in his favor. If, however, he knew about this evidence before the defendant took the oath, it will not be admitted. According to another opinion the new evidence will be admitted in any case.

Judgment will be given on the basis of the testimony of one witness and an oath [taken by the plaintiff] in cases concerning property. This is not the case, however, when the suit concerns marriage, divorce, *hadd* punishment, intentional physical injuries or homicide. . . .

The testimony of women is not admitted except in property cases. A hundred of them count for as many as two of them. Two women equal one man. The judge can thus decide on the basis of the testimony of one man and two women or of two women and the oath of the plaintiff in cases where this method of proof is admitted. . . .

The testimony of an adversary or of an unreliable person is not admitted. Only the testimony of wholly reliable [*'adl*] Muslims will be accepted. . . .

In attesting the reliability of witnesses only the formula is accepted: "He is very reliable and one can be satisfied." A single witness will not be accepted either for the attestation of reliability or the lack of same. . . .

Comment: This system of reliable witnesses developed into a very important institution in the Islamic law of procedure. Emile Tyan has dealt with this institution extensively in his basic work on Islamic legal procedure.

TYAN, *Histoire de l'Organisation Judiciaire en Pays d'Islam*, pp. 236–239.

Testimony of witnesses [*shahada*, the term for witness is *shahid*, plural *shuhud*] is one of the most important institutions not only in the system of evidence, but also in judicial organization as such in Islamic law. . . .

In Islamic law the testimony of witnesses is the foremost means of proof. . . . Documentary evidence had always been regarded with disfavor in legal writings. It had never been regarded in principle as a means of establishing proof by itself. The jurists treated it only as subsidiary evidence . . . . The reason for this low regard lies in the fact that as the jurists have stated "the written statement can be subjected to mistakes," and "the seal as well as the writing can be falsified." Although documents were widely used in legal transactions and sytematic registries were established in the courts with all that this implies concerning documentation and archival organization, proof of the content of private and public documents was not established by the content as such, but by the witnesses who appeared in the document. This is why all documents, be they under private seal or certified, are always signed by at least two witnesses. . . . One can say . . . that written proof developed only under the cover of proof established through witnesses . . . .

In the first centuries of the Hijra, . . . the judge apparently enjoyed great freedom concerning the acceptance or rejection of the testimony of witnesses.

. . . .

Such a system of evidence obviously had great disadvantages. According to Kindi [a Muslim scholar of the ninth century], an Egyptian *qadi*, Jawt ibn Sulayman, in the middle of the second century of the Hijra instituted a procedure designed to provide the judge with information about the moral standing of witnesses called upon to testify in court. This system was known as *tazkiya* [testifying to the integrity of the witness]. The judge accepted or rejected the testimony according to the favorable or unfavorable result of this inquiry which he had undertaken. The *tazkiya*, however . . . could not in itself avoid all the disadvantages of the earlier system. It, in fact, pointed up the dangers of that system. . . . The fate of legal acts remained therefore precarious. The whole transaction might become void, if a dispute arose between the contracting parties and if the judge, rightly or wrongly, rejected the testimony of the witnesses who had been called. It was thus necessary to provide a means of avoiding in advance the danger that the testimony of witnesses, which constituted the basic element in proving legal acts, be contested. This need gave rise to the institution of the *shahada* in the technical sense of the term.

This institution is based on a procedural rule according to which the judge, after verifying the moral standing of an individual, recognizes him from then on as a reliable witness whose testimony cannot in principle be rejected. The persons so recognized become permanent witnesses and are called "*shuhud 'udul*" reliable witnesses. . . . The establishment of these permanent witnesses, does not, of course, prevent the parties from introducing the testimony of other persons. The testimony of these persons remains exposed, however, to the risk of rejection according to the general principles of the law.

Ibid., pp. 242–248.

The appointment of a person as a permanent witness is dependent first of all upon fulfillment of the conditions required for admission as a witness. These are according to the jurists: being of age, of sound mind, a free man, and a Muslim. He must also not have been convicted of having accused another of a dishonorable offense, and he must be wholly reliable [*'adl*, plural *'udul*]. The testimony of women is not admitted, unless it is reinforced by that of a man. . . .

Aside from these conditions, the judge is free in his choice of permanent witnesses and has in this regard nearly fully discretionary powers. . . .

The *qadi* has the same powers in the dismissal of the witnesses. . . . Often the advent of a new *qadi* was the occasion for a complete change in the personnel of the *shuhud*. . . .

The judges did not, however, exercise in these respects a wholly uncontrolled power. There was always the possibility of referring the matter to higher authority or even to the caliph.

. . . . .

We have seen already that the system of permanent witnesses was instituted originally to protect legal acts against the risk of a challenge to their means of proof. In this system, however, can be found the origins of the institution of notary in Islamic law. . . . The essential function of the *shuhud* was to serve as witnesses of the proceedings in court and of the judgment.

. . . . .

In the eighth and ninth centuries of the Hijra, the diplomas of investiture of the judges contain passages directing the new judge not to give judgment without the permanent witnesses being present. The judgments themselves stated . . . that they were certified by the testimony of the *shuhud* who had assisted the judge during the law suit.

In the description given by *Maqrizi* of the formalities of a trial before the chief *qadi* it is specifically stated that the *shuhud* sit by the side of the judge. . . .

As to the number of the *shuhud* of a judge, no precise rules can be deduced from the texts. This was apparently a practical problem and much depended on the *qadi*'s own estimate.

. . . . .

Since the institution of the *shuhud* had for its purpose to assure the proof of the trial proceedings and of the judgment, should one then conclude that there were no court clerks who could keep a record? This was not the case. The two institutions existed and functioned side by side. . . . The court clerk always had been a necessary assistant of the judge, even though the judge also had to be assisted by the *shuhud*. It can probably be said that the institution of the *shahada* is later than that of the court clerk. The historical texts show the presence of court clerks at the beginning of the second century of the Hijra, whereas the *shahada* of the *qadi* apparently does not start until about the end of the same century. How can this be explained? Why was it felt necessary to introduce officials whose sole function was to remember details of the proceedings, if this function was also, and better, fulfilled by the reduction of these details to writing? We believe that there is only one answer, namely, lack of understanding of the written word as a means of proof. . . .

Comment: In the course of time the functions of the *shuhud* were extended and they even assumed judicial duties by delegation from the *qadi.*

The great importance assigned to witnesses in Islamic law is by no means a rare phenomenon in legal development. Obviously, oral testimony would be more important than documentary proof in times where there was little documentation and where writing was not widespread. The importance of the testimony of witnesses continued, however, even in cultures where the document played an important role. Thus, in ancient Mespotamia where documents were widely used as proof, witnesses maintained at least parity with documents. Special types of witnesses also were known. For example, in the settlement of Nuzi (at the site of the modern Kirkuk in northern Iraq) around 1500 B.C. there existed special official witnesses to sales. Persons who had special knowledge of the condition of real estate in the community and also knew the law appear as witnesses in suits concerning real estate (see H. J. Liebesny, "Evidence in Nuzi Legal Procedure," *Journal of the American Oriental Society*, 61, p. 132).

In Rome witnesses were practically the only means of proof in early times. Even in the time of Constantine the Great (fourth century A.D.) witnesses and documentary evidence had equal value. A decree of that emperor of A.D. 317 states:

Codex Justinianus, 4. 21. 15.

In the trial of lawsuits the same weight is given to the reliability of documents as to the deposition of witnesses.

Comment: This approach changed in favor of documentary evidence by the time of Justinian (sixth century A.D.) who stated in:

Codex Justinianus, 4. 20. 1.

Against written evidence unwritten evidence cannot be adduced.

3. *Oath*

Comment: The oath plays a specific role in Islamic legal procedure and in modern procedure in the countries of the Near and Middle East as well as in a number of civil law countries in Europe. It is one of the oldest institutions in legal procedure. It can be utilized to solemnize a statement and affirm its truth as in modern American law, with the court evaluating the statement freely and giving it proper weight in the context of the total evidence. The oath, however, also has been and is being employed as a means to decide a dispute. The sworn statement by one of the parties, usually the defendant, ends the suit and the judge must decide in conformity with the sworn statement.

This decisive oath was, originally at least, close to an ordeal and can be found in early Mesopotamian law in the second millenium B.C., in the Old Testament, Talmudic law, Roman law, and Islamic law. It is still used in many modern legal systems, those of France, Italy, and many countries of the Near and Middle East among them.

In Islamic law the decisive oath played an important role. A *hadith* stipulates that the plaintiff has to prove his case through two witnesses or that the defendant must swear an oath. This legal maxim was embodied in a *hadith* at a relatively late period. It appears as a formal tradition for the first time in Shafi'i (see Joseph Schacht, *The Origins of Muhammadan Jurisprudence* [Oxford: The Clarendon Press, 1950], pp. 187–188). Among the earlier jurists there seems to have been considerable disagreement as to the use of the oath in the system of evidence. Some early jurists apparently demanded an oath as well as witnesses from the plaintiff. From this practice the doctrine developed that one witness and the oath of the plaintiff constituted proof. Divergencies in the judicial practice in the first half of the second century of the Hijra (eighth century A.D.) indicate that the utilization of the oath to decide a lawsuit was not yet fully developed. Its development was probably due to the desire to diminish exclusive reliance on witnesses.

In Arabic the term *yamin* is commonly used for oath, promissory as well as affirmative, and it occurs in several passages of the Qur'an. However, in pre-Islamic times there was a special type of oath which was used as a means of proof, called *qasama*. This was an oath sworn with oath helpers or compurgators, usually fifty. The oath helpers were not witnesses, but supported the oath of the principal. Also, the *qasama* was sworn by the plaintiff rather than by the defendant. In the Islamic period the oath called *qasama* was restricted to the oath by relatives of a man who had been murdered. Fifty oaths had to be sworn, but they could be sworn by fifty people or less. If the plaintiff refused to swear this oath, then the defendant had the duty of swearing fifty oaths with oath helpers.

This type of oath survives today among Bedouin tribes.

AUSTIN KENNETT, *Bedouin Justice, Laws and Customs among the Egyptian Bedouin*, pp. 40–42.*

The oath is only used where evidence is either non-existent or insufficient to adopt any other means of ascertaining the truth. In this connection, the ordinary oath taken by a witness before giving evidence is not referred to; but the oath in the technical sense means the Oath of Purgation, i.e., the act of clearing oneself

*Reprinted by permission of the Cambridge University Press.

from the suspicion of guilt by swearing that one is innocent, or alternately, of swearing to the guilt of the other party. The procedure in Bedouin law is apt to be confusing, as on some occasions plaintiff swears that his plaint is true, and other occasions defendant swears that the plaintiff's case is not true, and that he (the defendant) is innocent. . . .

It may be accepted as a general rule that it is the defendant who swears, either by himself or supported by others according to circumstances. . . . Among the Aulad 'Ali in the Western Desert (of Egypt), the oath of the defendant alone is considered sufficient to clear himself in small, unimportant or trivial cases. If, however, A accuses B of stealing a camel, or other goods to the value of twenty pounds or so, B's oath is not considered sufficiently weighty, and the court will demand that four other men of his family or tribe swear with him. . . .

In all cases of the oath . . . A invariably has the right, not only to dictate the form of the oath, but also to choose the men of B's family or tribe to back him in his oath, and still further to choose the particular sheikh's tomb at which the oath should be taken. . . .

In blood money cases the number of men chosen to back the defendant's oath is naturally increased, in corresponding ratio to the importance of the case. This number is usually fifty men chosen by the plaintiff from the defendant's tribe to back his oath, but in some tribes custom demands that this number shall be fifty-five. In all the above cases, however, the names of the men chosen must be submitted to, and approved by, the court.

In blood money cases another example of apparent casuistry is observed. It may happen that in B's family there are only thirty-seven men, whereas custom demands that fifty should swear in addition to the defendant himself. In a case like this B himself and the remaining thirty-six adult men of his family will take the oath first, and subsequently thirteen of them will swear a second oath. . . .

It is important to remember that if the defendant himself or one single man of those chosen by the plaintiff to back the defendant in his oath fail or refuse to swear as directed, the whole case for the defense crumples up, and judgment is awarded automatically to the plaintiff.

Comment: The oath with oath helpers is found also in other legal systems, such as the Germanic laws and the early common law.

POLLOCK AND MAITLAND, *The History of English Law*, vol. 2, p. 600.*

. . . In some rare cases a defendant was allowed to swear away a charge by his own oath; usually what was required of him was an oath supported by the oath of oath helpers. There are good reasons for believing that in the earliest period he had to find kinsmen as oath helpers. When he was denying an accusation

*Reprinted by permission of the Cambridge University Press, copyright 1968.

which, if not disproved, would have been cause for a blood-feud his kinsmen had a lively interest in the suit, and naturally they were called upon to assist him in freeing himself from the consequences of the imputed crime. The plaintiff, if he thought that there had been perjury, would have the satisfaction of knowing that some twelve of his enemies were devoted to divine vengeance. In the course of time the law no longer required kinsmen, and we see a rationalistic tendency which would convert the oath helpers into impartial "witnesses of character." Sometimes the chief swearer must choose from among a number of men designated by the court or by his opponent; sometimes they must be his neighbors. . . .

Comment: The oath with oath helpers, the *qasama* of Islamic law, thus appears to be a completely different institution in origin and application, from the decisive oath for which the term *yamin* is used. The decisive oath was very highly developed in Roman law and also known in Hebrew law, and it would therefore be tempting to conclude that this type of oath was taken over by Islamic law from another legal system. However, the wide distribution of the decisive oath in the Near Eastern legal systems, literally since the dawn of history, dictates extreme caution in assuming any direct takeover.

The classical jurists of Islam accepted in principle the rule that the plaintiff had to prove his case through witnesses and that the defendant could clear himself through an oath (see p. 240). Many refinements and detailed provisions were worked out, however, and the various schools differ on some specifics. Generally, the Hanefite rules are stricter than those of the Malikites and Shafi'ites. As a rule, the defendant must take the oath if the plaintiff cannot prove his case. The oath has to be requested by the other party, but the defendant is ordered to swear by the *qadi*. The request by one party that the other take the oath is called tendering the oath. If the party to whom the oath is tendered does not want to take the oath, he can frequently retender it. In Islamic law, the Malekite and Shafi'ite schools permit retendering the oath, the Hanefite school does not. There are certain cases where the plaintiff rather than the defendant takes the oath. Thus the Shafi'ite and Malekite schools permit the plaintiff to take an oath in suits concerning property if he can produce only one witness.

It is a general characteristic of the decisive oath in practically all systems that, with few exceptions, it terminates the case and that even proven perjury does not constitute valid grounds for reopening it. This latter rule is due to the belief that a false oath will be punished by God, as expressly stated in Roman law as well as Islamic law.

Codex Justinianus, 4. 1. 1 and 2.

If a case is decided through an oath, be it agreed upon between the parties or tendered by one party or retendered, it cannot be reopened because perjury is charged, except where an exception is made by this law.

It is sufficient to leave vengeance for the violation of the sanctity of the oath to God.

AL-BUKHARI, *Sahih*, Book 52, Chapter 20.

... Later al-Ashaz bin Qais having met us told us: ... I had a lawsuit with someone concerning a certain matter. We laid our dispute before the Prophet who told me: "Produce your two witnesses or he shall take the oath." "In this case," I replied, "he will swear for he is without scruples." The Prophet answered: "He who takes an oath in bad faith in order to appropriate some goods will find God angry at him when he meets Him . . . ."

Comment: In the discussion of present-day procedure we shall see that basically the same idea still applies today.

D. The Settlement of Grievances

Comment: As many other legal systems, Islamic law provided an extraordinary means of redress in the form of the *mazalim* courts. The word *zalama* means "to treat unjustly" and the *mazalim* courts were established to redress injustice. They had wider powers and were bound by fewer rules than the ordinary courts. The *mazalim* courts derived their authority from the sovereign and his fundamental right to deal with all litigation and to adjudge all grievances. Mawardi deals with the *mazalim* jurisdiction in considerable detail.

AL-MAWARDI, *Al-Ahkam al-Sultaniyya*, pp. 77–83 (Fagnan, pp. 157–174).

The *mazalim* jurisdiction aims at inducing through fear those who have committed unjust acts to behave equitably toward others and at inducing, through a feeling of respect, the parties to a lawsuit from being too obstinate in their mutual denials. Therefore, whoever fulfills this function has to be a man of importance who is firm, highly respected, of high moral standards, with few desires, and very scrupulous. In this office a man must have the fierceness of guards and the firmness of judges.

. . . . .

The person charged with *mazalim* jurisdiction fixes a day when the victim of injustice can appeal to him and when the litigants can appear, so that he can devote the other days to administrative and executive duties which are entrusted to him. However, if he is one of those whose sole responsibility is to deal with *mazalim* cases, then he shall deal every day with these matters. Access to him shall be easy. . . . The personnel in his audience hall shall comprise five categories. . . : (1) guards and bailiffs. . . ; (2) the *qadis* and other authorities from whom he can inquire about the rights established before them and from whom he can get information concerning the proceedings between the parties in their court; (3) jurists whom he can consult in difficult, doubtful and puzzling cases; (4) scribes who record what transpires between the parties and the rights and obligations which are claimed; (5) witnesses who certify the right he has recognized and the decision he has declared enforceable.

When these five groups of people are present in the audience hall the official charged with *mazalim* jurisdiction can begin to exercise his functions which concern particularly six categories of cases:

(1) Investigation of the abuse of power by the governors with regard to their subjects. He proceeds against them because of unjust conduct. This is an inherent right of the position and its exercise does not depend upon a complaint by the victim. . . .

(2) Extortions committed by the tax collectors in collecting the revenue. . . .

(3) Management of the clerks in the public offices, since these are men to whom the Muslims have entrusted the task of keeping the balance between receipts and expenditures. . . .

(4) Claims by those entitled to salaries concerning reductions or delays in payment. . . .

(5) Restitution of property taken by force. . . .

(6) Supervision of pious foundations [*waq fs*]. . . .

(7) Enforcements of judgments of *qadis* which have not been executed, because the *qadis* were too weak and without power to proceed against the convicted party in view of the latter's power, high position, or great importance. The *mazalim* judge has greater power and superior authority. Thus he can enforce the judgment against the loser in the suit either by taking from him whatever he is withholding or by forcing him to surrender whatever he has been judged to owe.

(8) Maintenance of public order to the extent to which the *muhtasib* [an official exercising certain police powers] is powerless to maintain it. . . .

(9) Supervision of religious practices, such as observance of rest on Friday and of feast days, performance of the pilgrimage and of the Holy War, so that there is no negligence and the rules are followed, for the right of Allah must be wholly enforced and His injunctions carried out.

(10) Intervention as arbitrator between persons who have a dispute. He decides between the parties. However, in the exercise of this arbitral power he must not deviate from what the law imposes and demands. In handing down a decision [in such a case] he must follow the rules which bind other officials and the *qadis*. . . .

The differences between the *mazalim* judge and the *qadi* can be set forth in ten points:

(1) The *mazalim* judge, because of the greater fear he inspires and the more powerful means of action at his disposal, can, in contrast to the *qadi*, inhibit reciprocal denials by the parties and prevent acts of violence and excesses of evildoers.

(2) The *qadis* in their decisions have to keep within the limits set by the *shari'a*, whereas the *mazalim* judge is not bound by these rules. His freedom is limited only by those legal precepts which establish definite prohibitions.

(3). . . .

(4) He imposes a discretionary punishment on those whose unjust actions are manifest and restrains through reprimand and criticism persons whose hostile intentions cannot be doubted.

(5). . . The *mazalim* judge may in the higher interest of justice postpone the judgment on the basis of his free appraisal, whereas the *qadi* cannot postpone his judgment if one of the parties demands that he hand it down. . . .

(6) The *mazalim* judge may, even against the will of the parties, transfer the case to arbitrators . . ., while the *qadi* may not make such a transfer except with the consent of the parties.

[The rest of these points deals with the greater freedom of the *mazalim* judge with regard to the collection and evaluation of evidence.]

Comment: The *mazalim* jurisdiction thus introduced into Islamic procedure an element of equity, a freedom from the strict forms of the law, thereby permitting the redress of injustices. The concept of the ruler protecting his people against injustice is very old. In the prologue to his code, the Babylonian King Hammurabi says:

JAMES B. PRITCHARD, ed., *Ancient Near Eastern Texts*, p. 164.

. . . Anum [the Babylonian sky god] and Enlil [the Babylonian storm god] named me to promote the welfare of the people, me Hammurabi, the devout god-fearing prince, to cause justice to prevail in the land, to destroy the wicked and the evil, that the strong might not oppress the weak. . . . [and in the Epilogue he repeats the same theme:]

Ibid., p. 178.

. . . I became the beneficient shepherd whose scepter is righteous; my benign shadow is spread over my city. In my bosom I carried the peoples of the land of Sumer and Akkad; they prospered under my protection; I have governed them in peace; I have sheltered them in my strength. In order that the strong might not oppress the weak, that justice might be dealt the orphan (and) the widow . . . I wrote my precious words on my stela, . . . to give justice to the oppressed.

Comment: In Roman law the principle of *aequitas*, which is close to but not wholly identical with equity in Anglo-American law, gave relief from the requirements of the *ius strictum* and provided for the further development of the law through the activities of the *praetor*.

In English law, of course, the application of the principle of equity gave rise to a separate system of law administered by the

Chancery. The early Chancery records give many examples of cases which were similar to those brought before the *mazalim* judge. The chancellor's jurisdiction was sought in cases where the parties did not have a common law remedy, where proper evidence could not be had or where it was claimed that the ordinary course of justice was impeded through fraud. It should be noted, however, that Roman *aequitas* and English equity gave rise to legal principles which coexisted with the strict law and eventually developed into a system of their own. This is not the case with the *mazalim* jurisdiction. It was not systematized in a manner comparable to the equity jurisdiction of the Chancery. The development of the *mazalim* jurisdiction in the Seljuk and Ottoman periods has been described as follows:

H. A. R. GIBB AND HAROLD BOWEN, *Islamic Society and the West*, vol. 1, part 2, p. 116.*

... Under the Selcuqids, the *mazalim*, delegated to royal officers, became still further assimilated to administrative courts, and (although evidence on this point is still lacking) presumably still more subject to administrative regulation. With the development of the system of military *iqta's* or fiefs, some of the regular functions of the *mazalim* were transferred to the court of the *qadi 'l-'asker* (military judge) before whom alone the members of the standing military forces were justiciable, and to whose courts ,in consequence, suits relating to property were generally referred. The *qanuns* of the Ottoman sultans and the extensive jurisdiction of the *qadi 'l-'asker* were the logical end of this process.

Ibid., pp. 129–130.

... [In the eighteenth century] the generality of European observers were struck by the arbitrary conduct and indifference to human life shown by the military and the police [in the Ottoman Empire]. Conditions in this respect no doubt varied as between provinces, but the impotence of the provincial authorities to protect the population from their tyranny is evidenced by the practice of sending memorials to the Sublime Porte itself, and in Egypt by the action of the *Sheykh el-Beled* 'Othman Bey Dhu'l Fiqar in reviving, about 1743, the custom of *mazalim* courts, two of which he set up in his house, one for men and one for women.

*Reprinted by permission of the Oxford University Press, copyright 1957.

Chapter 12   Procedure in Present-day Near Eastern Countries

A. Introductory

Comment: With the exception of a few countries, such as Saudi Arabia and Yemen, the *qadi*'s court is no longer the court of general jurisdiction. The court system and procedure of most Near Eastern countries have been westernized and a modern appeal procedure has been established. Except in countries where British influence has been strong, procedure follows continental European lines. Consequently, the judge, or the presiding judge, plays an important role and the procedure has inquisitory features.

B. The Organization of the Courts

Comment: Taking Egypt as an example, the following picture of the court organization of a country following continental European patterns can be given:

1. Courts of summary jurisdiction; these courts have a restricted jurisdiction in civil cases and jurisdiction over misdemeanors.

2. Courts of first instance (twenty-one in number). These are the courts of general jurisdiction in civil matters and courts of appeal regarding civil and criminal judgments of the courts of summary jurisdiction.

3. Courts of appeal (six in number) which have appellate jurisdiction in cases where the courts of first instance have original jurisdiction. They also have original jurisdiction as courts of assizes in cases of felonies.

4. The Court of Cassation in Cairo.

The Court of Cassation is divided into civil and criminal chambers. In civil cases appeal lies in the Court of Cassation against decisions of the courts of appeal if the decision of the court of appeal was based on a violation, wrong application, or faulty interpretation of the law, or if the decision was affected by a nullifying procedural error. The parties can also appeal to the Court of Cassation if a final judgment had been handed down by any court which was contrary to another judgment between the same parties with the latter judgment having already achieved the force of *res judicata*. The General Procurator can appeal a case to the Court of Cassation if the decision of the court below was based on a violation, wrong application, or faulty interpretation of the law and if the parties either had no recourse against the decision, failed to appeal within the time limit set for appeal, or had undertaken not to appeal.

As a rule the Court of Cassation in granting an appeal will set aside the decision and remand the case to the court which had made the decision. That court is bound to decide in conformity with the decision of the Court of Cassation.

Egyptian Code of Civil Procedure of 1968.

Article 269. If the judgment attacked is set aside for lack of jurisdiction, the Court of Cassation has to rule on the question of jurisdiction. . . . If the judgment is set aside for other reasons, the Court shall remand the case to the court which had made the judgment for retrial. . . . In this case the court to which the case has been remanded must conform with the decision of the Court of Cassation concerning the point of law adjudicated by the Court of Cassation. No judges are allowed to sit in the remanded case who took part in the judgment set aside. If, however, the judgment is set aside and the case can be decided on its merits or an appeal has been lodged for the second time, then the Court can decide on the merits of the case.

Comment: The powers of the Court of Cassation are similar in criminal cases.

The right of the Court of Cassation to rule on the merits of a case was stated in a decision.

Court of Cassation, Decision of 30 October 1956.

[The question on which the Court was asked to rule was that of the proper limits of legitimate defense against an attack.]

Syllabus by the Court.

To estimate the force necessary to repel an attack and to determine whether the recourse to force was within the limits of legitimate defense or exceeded them is within the purvue of the court of original jurisdiction. However, if the facts as stated in the decision, reveal beyond any doubt that the defendant was exercising legitimate defense, and the court nevertheless reached a conclusion incompatible with these facts, then it is the duty of the Court of Cassation to intervene in order to rectify this conclusion on the basis of logic and law.

Comment: In its decisions the Court of Cassation very frequently refers to articles of the codes or of statutes, but quite often also to the "line of decisions" (*jurisprudence*) of the Court itself.

In other countries of the Near East where procedure follows

continental European patterns, the court organization is essentially similar. However, in a number of these countries there are still religious courts, both for Muslims and non-Muslims. Where this is the case, the nonreligious courts are the courts of general jurisdiction, whereas the religious courts have jurisdiction over specific subject matters. This jurisdiction is exclusive.

In Pakistan procedure generally follows British lines. There are codes of civil and criminal procedure which were enacted under British rule, but have, of course, been amended in various respects. There were no religious courts in British India and there are none now in Pakistan or India. The courts of general jurisdiction will consider *shari'a* law in certain cases where the parties are Muslims.*

C. Penal Procedure

Comment: The penal procedure in most Near and Middle Eastern countries is patterned after that of continental Europe, especially France, and shows significant differences from that of the U.S. Again to take Egypt as an example, there is a hierarchy of public officials who constitute the so-called *ministère public* [to use the French term, since the institution was derived from the French prototype; Arabic: *niyaba umumiya*]. These officials fulfill the functions of public prosecutors in penal cases. They may represent the public interest in civil cases. At the head of this hierarchy is the *Procureur Général*. Members of the *ministère public* are essentially civil servants. They are all appointed and can be transferred freely. In the exercise of their functions they are under the direction of the *Procureur Général*.

If an offense allegedly has been committed, it is up to the public prosecutor (as representative of the *ministère public*) to decide whether there is a case. In cases of misdemeanors the public prosecutor may bring the case directly to the court, provided the police report contains enough information. If the case involves a major misdemeanor, the public prosecutor may at his discretion pass the case for preliminary investigation to an investigating magistrate (French: *juge d'instruction*). In felony cases a preliminary investigation by the *juge d'instruction* is mandatory, provided the public prosecutor believes that there is cause for further investigation of the allegations made. Investigating magistrates are attached to every summary tribunal and to every court of first instance. The investigating magistrate is in full control of and has sole responsibility for the investigation. The investigation is nonpublic, but the parties may demand copies of various documents and are informed of such acts of investigation as took place during their absence. In Egyptian law, as in the law of most Near and Middle Eastern and European countries, a party

* *West Pakistan Muslim Personal Law (Shariat Application) Act of 1962*, section 2.

injured by the alleged offense, whether physically or financially, may join in the penal action as a so-called civil claimant. During the investigation, the accused, the victim, and, if there is such, the civil claimant may be represented by counsel. Counsel for the defendant may, however, speak only with the permission of the judge during the interrogation of the accused.

At the end of the preliminary investigation the investigating magistrate transmits the file to the public prosecutor. In case of a petty offense the accused is brought to trial in the summary court, and the same is the case, with a few exceptions for specific misdemeanors which are tried in the court of assizes, for misdemeanors (*délits*). If the investigating magistrate has come to the conclusion that the offense constitutes a felony, the accused is brought before the so-called *chambre des mises en accusation*. This body is part of every court of first instance and consists of three judges. The term may be translated as chamber for indictment, the body is somewhat comparable in function to a grand jury. The chamber makes its determination on the basis of the file which one of its members reports on and statements by the parties. The procedure is not public. The chamber can remand the case to the investigating magistrate, if it feels that further investigation is needed, can undertake such investigation itself, or, if it is satisfied that a felony has been committed, it sends the case for trial to the court of assizes. If the chamber believes that a misdemeanor only has been committed, it sends the case to the summary court. The chamber may also conclude that there is no punishable offense, in which case it can so find and the accused, if he was under arrest, is set free.

At the trial the indictment is read and then the prosecution and the civil party, if there is one, make their statements. The defendant is thereafter asked whether he pleads guilty or not guilty. If he pleads guilty, the court may pronounce judgment without hearing further evidence, if it is satisfied with the confession. In a decision of 25 March, 1957 (*Bulletin Officiel des Tribunaux* 56 [1958], No. 161) the Court of Cassation stated that the evaluation of a confession is left to the discretion of the court of original jurisdiction.

D. Evidence

1. Witnesses

Comment: In civil matters the law of Egypt permits both parties to introduce witnesses. The court rules whether the facts which the party proposes to prove through his witnesses are pertinent and admissible. The witness is sworn and then questioned. The parties may not question the witness directly but ask their questions through the court. The party who has introduced the witness poses his questions first and then the opposing party poses his questions. The judge or judges also may ask questions independently. The procedure is similar in penal cases. In the latter case prosecution witnesses are heard first and then the defense witnesses. This system of interrogation does not allow for cross-examination as it is known in the American system. In actual practice the presiding judge, if there is a bench of several judges, asks most of the questions. This is very clearly expressed in:

Syrian Code of Civil Procedure of 1953.

Article 139, (1) The presiding judge of the court directs the discussions during the trial and is charged with interrogating the parties and witnesses, the other judges must obtain the permission of the presiding judge before asking the questions they consider necessary. . . .

Comment: The result is frequently that judges have much more experience in formulating questions properly than many lawyers and the role of the judge or the presiding judge is much more active than it is in an American trial. It might also be mentioned that instruction in most European and Near Eastern law schools with continued emphasis on lectures and relatively little discussion of cases (although the latter is increasing), and with an absence of moot court or clinical experience, would not prepare the law student well for the type of adversary procedure common in the U.S.

2. *The Decisive Oath*

Comment: The decisive oath, which was discussed as a feature of Islamic law, has maintained considerable importance in modern Near Eastern law and survives also in a number of European legal systems.

The following provisions are from the Egyptian Law of Evidence of 1968 which follows here nearly verbatim provisions of the Egyptian Civil Code of 1949. The numbers of articles of that code are also given.

Egyptian Law of Evidence of 1968.

Article 114. Each party may tender the decisive oath to the other party; the judge may, however, refuse to allow the oath to be tendered if the party who tenders the oath does so vexatiously.

The party to whom the oath has been tendered may tender back the oath to the other party. The oath cannot, however, be tendered back when it has for its object a fact in which the two parties did not both participate, but which is purely a personal matter affecting the person to whom the oath has been tendered (Civil Code 410).

Article 115. The decisive oath cannot be tendered regarding a fact contrary to public policy. The fact which is the object of the oath must be personal to the party to whom the oath is tendered;

if the fact is not personal to that party, the oath will be taken only on the mere knowledge that the party has of the fact. . . . The decisive oath may be tendered at any stage of the proceedings (Civil Code 411).

Article 116. A party who has tendered or who has retendered the oath cannot retract once the other party has agreed to take the oath (Civil Code 412).

Article 117. When the oath tendered or retendered has been taken, the other party is not entitled to prove that the oath is false. When, however, such an oath is established to be false by the decision of a penal court, the party damaged as a result of the false oath may claim compensation without prejudice to his possible right of recourse against the judgment rendered against him (Civil Code 413).

Article 118. The party to whom the oath has been tendered and who has refused to take it without tendering it back to the other party, or the other party to whom the oath has been tendered back and who has refused to take it, will lose the case (Civil Code 414).

Article 119. The judge may on his own initiative, tender the suppletory oath to either party with a view of deciding on the merits of the claim or on the amount of the award.

The judge may tender this oath only when the claim is neither completely proven, nor wholly without proof (Civil Code 415).

Article 120. The party to whom the judge has tendered the suppletory oath cannot tender the oath back to the other party (Civil Code 416).

Article 121. The judge may only tender the suppletory oath to the plaintiff as regards the amount of the claim, when it is impossible to fix this amount in any other way.

The judge, even in this case, will determine the amount up to which the plaintiff should be believed on his oath (Civil Code 417).

Comment: In contrast to the provisions of Article 413 of the Egyptian Civil Code of 1949 (Article 117 of the Law on Evidence), the French Civil Code does not permit the collection of damages if perjury is established by a penal court. This prohibition is due to the French theory that tendering the oath constitutes an agreement between the two parties which cannot be affected even by proven perjury. The old Egyptian Mixed and National Civil Codes followed the French doctrine. The Egyptian Civil Code took the provision for damages from the Portuguese Civil Code of 1867, according to the materials to the Egyptian Code. The materials stressed that the Egyptian Code had abandoned the French concept of a contract and, as did Islamic law, regarded the decisive oath as a distinct legal institution. A decision rendered by an Egyptian court soon after the enactment of the new civil code well illustrates the difference between the old and the new law concerning the decisive oath.

Court of Appeal, Alexandria, Decision of 8 January 1952.

[The case concerned a claim by the sons of a deceased man that the father had been co-owner of a cafe on the basis of a partnership contract. They sued the alleged partners in the Court of First Instance of Alexandria demanding an accounting. The defendants claimed that there had been no partnership. The court of first instance denied the claim of the plaintiffs as not having been proven. On appeal the plaintiffs tendered the decisive oath to the defendants, only one of whom took it. The court of appeal thereupon confirmed the judgment of the court below with regard to the defendant who had taken the oath, but continued the case with regard to the defendants who had failed to do so. At a later hearing one of the remaining defendants produced a partnership contract which clearly established that the father of the plaintiffs had been a partner in the enterprise. The defendant who had taken the oath that there had been no partnership and that he had been sole owner of the cafe was shown to have been one of the signatories of the partnership contract.

On the basis of this evidence the plaintiffs entered a plea to set aside the judgment because the defendant had fraudulently influenced the judgment by producing documents in the court below purporting to show him as sole owner of the cafe and that furthermore the introduction in evidence of the partnership contract had demonstrated that the decisive oath taken by the defendant had been false. The defendant tried to counter these charges among other things by stating that the decisive oath constitutes an agreement between the parties and that there is no further recourse. The court held:]

While it is true that under the old Civil Code (Article 225) and the old Code of Civil and Commercial Procedure (Article 166) it was a basic principle of legal writings and court decisions that the decisive oath is equivalent to a contract and that its tender implied renunciation of all other types of evidence and relinquishment of all further rights, so that the taking of the oath put a definite end to the suit and that, therefore, the party who had tendered the oath could not claim damages if the oath of the party who had sworn had been declared to be false, or attack the decision on the basis of perjury, this is no longer true under the rule of the new Civil Code which does not consider the decisive oath to be an agreement or contract. [The decision then reproduced Article 413 of the Civil Code.]

Through the provisions of the new Code the legislator permits the party who has tendered the oath in case of a false oath to appeal the judgment or to enter a plea that the judgment against him be set aside, and to claim damages from the party who had sworn the false oath, on condition, however, that the perjury has been established first by judgment of a penal court.

Until such a judgment has been handed down, therefore, the party injured by a false judgment cannot sue for damages or attack the decision rendered against it.

For these reasons, the plea that the judgment be set aside is rejected.

Comment: This decision clearly shows that the party injured by a false decisive oath has remedies. However, these remedies are effective only if perjury has been established by a judgment of a penal court. Such a judgment thus is a precondition for an action by the injured party.

The suppletory oath differs from the decisive oath in that it does not in and by itself end the suit. This was ruled in a decision by the Egyptian Court of Cassation.

Egypt, Court of Cassation, Civil Chamber, Decision of 13 January 1955.

Syllabus by the Court.
The suppletory oath is a measure taken by the judge on his own motion in order to arrive at the truth, and the result of this measure is left to the sole appreciation of the judge. Thus this oath does not constitute incontrovertible proof as far as the judge is concerned: rather it is left to him whether or not to take it into account after it has been sworn. The appellate court is therefore not bound by the conclusion which the court of first instance drew, since the suppletory oath does not end the law suit and does not prevent an appeal against the decision which is based upon this oath. It follows that the decision of the appellate court here attacked is not voided by the fact that the defense was not refuted according to which the appeal should not have been received because the suppletory oath ended the suit. Such a defense is not conclusive and the failure to deal with it in the decision does not influence the conclusions of the appellate court.

3. Documents

Comment: As in French law, and in contrast to Islamic law, documents play a very prominent role as means of proof in Egyptian law. The Law of Evidence distinguishes between official documents and private agreements. An official document is one in which an official or a person charged with the performance of public duties states in the proper legal form and within the limits of his powers that certain facts have taken place or that certain declarations have been made to him by the parties (Article 10 of the Law of Evidence). The official document makes proof against anybody unless and until it is declared to be false (Article 11). A private agreement is assumed to have originated with the person whose writing, signature, seal, or thumb print appears on it unless he formally disavows it (Article 14). Signed letters have the same probatory force as private agreements provided they are signed (Article 16). The testimony of witnesses is definitely subordinated to proof through documentation as stated in the Law of Evidence:

Egyptian Law of Evidence of 1968.

Article 60. Except where there is an agreement or arrangement to the contrary, and outside commercial matters, proof of a legal transaction or of the extinction of an obligation cannot be accomplished through witnesses if the value involved is more than E £20, or is indeterminate. . . . (Civil Code 400 (1)).
Comment: The Law of Evidence allows only a few exceptions to this general rule, and the situation is similar in other countries which follow the French system. In Pakistan, by contrast, the Evidence Act of 1872 (Act I of 1872) states that "all facts, except the contents of documents, may be proved by oral evidence." In Turkey documentary proof is required with regard to most transactions involving a value of more than T£50. Thus, in most countries of the area the emphasis on witnesses which was found in classical Islamic law has been replaced by a primary stress on the written document.

4. Measures to Simplify and Expedite Procedure

Comment: In many of the countries of the Near and Middle East the system of procedure is rather complex and formal, particularly when seen from the viewpoint of the population in the rural areas. Also, travel to towns is often difficult and lawyers are not always easily available and, at least from the farmer's vantage point, expensive. Various steps have, therefore, been taken, especially in cases which would normally come before summary courts or their equivalents, to simplify and expedite procedure.

Thus the Egyptian Code of Civil Procedure of 1968 established conciliation committees at the seat of the courts of summary jurisdiction (Article 64). These committees will attempt to settle certain cases, where the value involved is small, before these cases are brought before the court for adjudication. The use of the conciliation committees is compulsory in all applicable cases. The conciliation committees are chaired by an assistant prosecutor. They must accomplish their mission within thirty days, although an extension for another thirty days is permissible with the agreement of the parties. If a settlement has not been reached within this period, the case goes to trial in the regular court.

In Iran the Shah as part of his "White Revolution" reform program established informal courts in the rural areas, called Houses of Justice, and in towns and cities, called Arbitration Councils. The judges of these courts are elected by the people of the town or village and are local laymen. The courts are composed of five elected judges, but not all have to be present at an individual trial. The arbitration councils have jurisdiction over minor civil disputes and petty offenses. Attached to each council is a legal advisor appointed by the Ministry of Justice who can reject the decision of the council if it is not in accordance with Iranian law.

The houses of justice in rural areas also deal with minor

disputes. Prominent among these are quarrels over grazing rights and rights to water. Disputes involving land also are frequent. Family quarrels likewise may be brought before the judges of the houses of justice, but not divorce cases. The houses of justice do not have legal advisers. Procedure in these rural courts is usually even less formal than in the arbitration councils, but the judges, elected by the people of the village and known to them, have authority. Particularly in the rural areas these informal courts have been very successful. They make it unnecessary for the farmer to go to town and deal with a complex and, to him, bewildering system of justice and in addition save the expense of a lawyer and the often lengthy waiting period before a case comes to trial.

In Pakistan the Conciliation Courts Ordinance of 1961 (Ordinance XLIV of 1961) established courts composed of the Chairman of the Union Council and two representatives nominated by the parties. [Union councils were local elected bodies and part of the system of "Basic Democracies" under the Constitution of 1962.]* The conciliation courts have jurisdiction in certain civil and criminal cases. In criminal cases they cannot as a rule impose a prison sentence or a fine, but they can award compensation to the injured party.

In Afghanistan conciliation commissions staffed by laymen were established in 1974.

These various institutions thus attempt, within the general framework of the judicial system, to simplify and expedite court procedure. Appeals are usually possible, but are limited in scope and, apparently, are not often utilized. Aside from being easier to grasp than the formal court system, these institutions also revive the idea of arbitration which is so deeply imbedded in the tradition of the region.

*Since these councils have now been abolished, a different local official will be the chairman.

Appendix 1   Suggestions for Further Reading

Chapter 1.

Joseph Schacht, *An Introduction to Islamic Law* (Oxford: Clarendon Press, 1964), chapters 1 and 2, (will be cited henceforth as Schacht, *Introduction*). This book by an outstanding authority on Islamic law provides a very good survey of the development of Islamic law and of its main institutions. The non-Arabist, however, will not find it easy reading. The critical bibliography provided for each chapter in an appendix is exhaustive and excellent.

A standard work on the position of the king in the ancient oriental monarchies and on his relationship to the deities is Henri Frankfort, *Kingship and the Gods, A Study of Ancient Near Eastern Religion as the Integration of Society and Nature* (Chicago: The University of Chicago Press, 1948). Another good treatment of this general subject is C. J. Gadd, *Ideas of Divine Rule in the Ancient East* (London: Oxford University Press, 1948).

On the law of the ancient Hebrews see further Ze'ev W. Falk, *Hebrew Law in Biblical Times* (Jerusalem: Wahrmann Books, 1964).

The problem of the personality of the law is discussed with references to further literature in Herbert J. Liebesny, "The Development of Western Judicial Privileges," in Majid Khadduri and Herbert J. Liebesny, eds., *Law in the Middle East*, vol. 1 (Washington, D.C.: The Middle East Institute, 1955): 308–312.

Chapter 2.

Joseph Schacht, *Introduction*, chapters 3 through 11. Chapters 2 and 3 in Majid Khadduri and Herbert J. Liebesny, *Law in the Middle East*, vol. 1, were written by Joseph Schacht and may be substituted for chapters 3 through 9 of the *Introduction*. These chapters are more condensed than those in the *Introduction* and make easier reading.

Noel J. Coulson, *A History of Islamic Law*, Islamic Surveys no. 2 (Edinburgh: University Press, 1964), chapters 1 through 7, 9 and 10.

Subhi Mahmassani, *Falsafat al-Tashrī fi al-Islām* [*The Philosophy of Jurisprudence in Islam*], translated by Farhat J. Ziadeh (Leiden:

E. J. Brill, 1961) presents the development of Islamic law from the viewpoint of a modern Muslim scholar in a clear and concise fashion. The book has a very good bibliography of Arabic works and a brief bibliography of non-Arabic titles.

Students who wish to gain a deeper understanding of the development of Islamic jurisprudence and particularly of the role of al-Shāfiʿī should read Joseph Schacht, *The Origins of Islamic Jurisprudence* (Oxford: Clarendon Press, 1950) and Majid Khadduri *Islamic Jurisprudence, Shāfiʿīs Risāla* (Baltimore: The Johns Hopkins Press, 1961). This study contains a translation of the *Risāla* with a very valuable introduction.

Important parts of the writings of two scholars who laid much of the foundation for the study of Islamic law in the present-day West are now available in English: G. H. Bousquet and Joseph Schacht, eds., *Selected Works of C. Snouk Hurgronje* [translations partly in English, partly in French] (Leiden: E. J. Brill, 1957) and Ignaz Goldziher, *Muslim Studies* [a translation of the author's work *Muhammedanische Studien*, by S. M. Stern] (Albany: State University of New York Press, vol. 1, 1967, vol. 2, 1972).

Valuable as an introduction to Islam and Islamic history generally are: H. A. R. Gibb, *Mohammedanism* (London: Oxford University Press, 1949) and Philip K. Hitti, *Islam, A Way of Life* (Minneapolis: University of Minneapolis Press, 1970).

There are several comprehensive works on Islamic and Arab history: P. M. Holt, Ann K. S. Lambton, and Bernard Lewis, eds., *The Cambridge History of Islam* (Cambridge: Cambridge University Press, 1970); Carl Brockelmann, *History of the Islamic Peoples* (New York: C. P. Putman's Sons, 1960) and Philip K. Hitti, *History of the Arabs,* 10th edition (New York: St. Martin's Press, Inc., 1970). A basic work on the history of the Arabs from prehistoric times to the present in its political and cultural aspects.

Shorter treatises of Arab history are: George E. Kirk, *A Short History of the Middle East*, 7th edition (New York: Praeger, 1964) and Bernard Lewis, *The Arabs in History* (Phoenix, Arizona: J. M. Hutchinson, 1966).

Various aspects of medieval Islam were examined by C. E. von Grunebaum, *Medieval Islam*, 2nd edition (Chicago: University of Chicago Press, 1953) and C. E. von Grunebaum, *Islam, Essays in the Nature and Growth of a Cultural Tradition* (London: Rutledge & Kegan Paul Ltd., 1955).

The heterodox sects are dealt with by Asaf A. A. Fyzee, "Shiʿī Legal Theories," in Majid Khadduri and Herbert J. Liebesny, *Law in the Middle East*, vol. 1: 113–131 and Noel J. Coulson, *A History of Islamic Law*, chapter 8.

Chapter 3.

Joseph Schacht, *Introduction*, chapter 13.
Majid Khadduri and Herbert J. Liebesny, *Law in the Middle*

East, vol. 1, chapter 11: Ebül'uā Mardin, "Development of the *Sharī'a* under the Ottoman Empire"; chapter 12: S. S. Onar, "The Majalla"; chapter 13: Herbert J. Liebesny, "The Development of Western Judicial Privileges."

Readers who wish to gain a deeper understanding of the Ottoman legal reforms in their historical, political, and cultural setting should consult the following two works, both of which are excellent: Bernard Lewis, *The Emergence of Modern Turkey*, 2d edition (London: Oxford University Press, Oxford Paperbacks, 1968) and Roderick H. Davison, *Reform in the Ottoman Empire, 1856–1876* (Princeton: Princeton University Press, 1963).

The standard work on the development and functioning of the mixed courts in Egypt is Jasper Y. Brinton, *The Mixed Courts of Egypt*, revised edition (New Haven: Yale University Press, 1968).

Ferhat J. Ziadeh, *Lawyers, the Rule of Law and Liberalism in Modern Egypt*, Hoover Institution on War, Revolution and Peace (Stanford: Stanford University Press, 1968) traces the rise of the legal profession in Egypt and the role which it has played.

On the nature of the civil law the following may be consulted: F. H. Lawson, *A Common Lawyer Looks at the Civil Law* (Ann Arbor: University of Michigan Law School, 1953). A very good introduction to the civil law and its characteristics.

John Henry Merriman, *The Civil Law Tradition* (Stanford: Stanford University Press, 1969) is a good basic introduction to various important features of the legal systems of Western Europe and Latin America.

Athanassios N. Yiannopoulos, ed., *Civil Law in the Modern World* (Baton Rouge: Louisiana State University Press, 1965) is a collection of interesting and useful papers presented at the first annual meeting of the Civil Law Section of the Louisiana State Law Institute held in New Orleans on 17–18 May, 1963. Chapter 2, "The Law of Family and Succession," touches upon the family law of the Islamic countries and the reforms introduced there.

John P. Dawson, *The Oracles of the Law* (Ann Arbor: The University of Michigan Law School, 1968). This study deals with the contribution made by case law to the legal systems of Rome, England, France, and Germany. A very thorough examination of this topic by an author thoroughly familiar with the historical development of the institutions concerned. Very useful for those who wish to gain a more thorough insight into this very important set of problems.

Chapter 4.

A. Treatises and Articles

Joseph Schacht, *Introduction*, chapter 12, chapter 14, pp. 97–99, chapter 15, and N. J. Coulson, *A History of Islamic Law*, chapters 11, 12, 13, and 14.

N. J. Coulson, *Conflicts and Tensions in Islamic Jurisprudence* (Chicago: University of Chicago Press, 1969) discusses some of the basic principles of Islamic law and the impact of modern thought on them.

The role of Islamic law in modern Islamic countries has been dealt with by J. N. D. Anderson, *Islamic Law in the Modern World* (New York: New York University Press, 1959) and Joseph Schacht, "Islamic Law in Contemporary States," *American Journal of Comparative Law* 8 (1959): 133–147. A recent comprehensive article on this subject is J. N. D. Anderson, "Modern Trends in Islam: Legal Reform and Modernisation in the Middle East," *The International and Comparative Law Quarterly* 20 (1971): 1–21.

A number of recent studies have dealt with the legal system of one particular country of the region. The following are some important studies in this field in English, French, and German: Turğul Ansay and Don Wallace, Jr., *Introduction to Turkish Law* (Ankara: Society of Comparative Law, Turkey, and Middle East Technical University, Faculty of Administrative Sciences, 1966); Ernst Hirsch, "Vier Phasen im Ablauf eines zeitgenössischen Rezeptionsprozesses," *Zeitschrift für vergleichende Rechtwissenschaft* 69 (1970): 183–223 (a discussion of the reception of Swiss law in Turkey); Don Wallace, Jr., "Turkey: Summary and Bibliography," *The International Lawyer* 4 (1970): 556–559 (a brief summary of the Turkish legal system, followed by a short bibliography of studies in English); Pierre Catala and André Gervais, eds., *Le droit Libanais*, 2 vols., (Paris: Librairie générale de droit et de jurisprudence, R. Pichon et R. Durand-Auzias, 1963) is a thorough discussion of the present-day Lebanese legal system by a number of authors. Samir Shamma, "Law and Lawyers in Saudi Arabia," *International and Comparative Law Quarterly* 14 (1965): 1034–39. Ahmad Hijazi, "Kuwait, Development from a Semitribal, Semicolonial Society to Democracy and Sovereignty," *The American Journal of Comparative Law* 13 (1964): 428–438. Parker T. Hart, "Application of Hanbalite and Decree Law to Foreigners in Saudi Arabia," *The George Washington Law Review* 22 (1953): 165–175.

There is little comprehensive literature in English on legal developments in former French North Africa. The situation under French rule is discussed in Herbert J. Liebesny, *The Government of French North Africa* (Philadelphia: University of Pennsylvania Press, 1943). A good survey of Tunisian law up to the late 1950s is presented in R. Jambu-Merlin, *Le droit privé en Tunisie* (Paris: Librairie générale de droit et de jurisprudence, R. Pichon et R. Durand-Auzias, 1960). Moroccan institutions are discussed in Michel Bourely, *Droit public marocain* (Paris: Librairie de Medicis, 1965). Judicial developments in Algeria are traced in Etienne-Jean Lapassat, *La Justice en Algérie, 1962–1968* (Paris: Armand Colin, 1968). The treatment of developments after 1964 is somewhat sketchy. An interesting sociological-legal study is Jean-Paul Charnay, *La vie Musulmane en Algérie d'après la jurisprudence de la première moitié du XXᵉ siècle* (Paris: Presses Universitaires de France, 1965). Recent trends in Algeria were examined in Gamal Moursi Badr, "La relance du droit Islamique dans la jurisprudence Algérienne depuis 1962," *Revue Internationale de droit comparé* 22 (1970): 43–54 and John N. Hazard, "Socializing Islamic Law in Africa," *Mélanges offerts à Pierre Andrieu-Gultran-court. Année Canonique* 17 (1973): 543–554.

The following works present a discussion of the broad philosophical and ideological framework which has provided the background and basis for specific reforms of Islamic law and of the problems faced by Muslims in the modern world: H. A. R. Gibb, *Modern Trends in Islam*, 2d edition (New York: Octagon Books, 1972); H. A. R. Gibb, *Studies on the Civilization of Islam* (Boston: Beacon Press, 1962). This is a collection of articles by Professor Gibb, edited by Stanford J. Shaw and William R. Polk and covering a wide variety of topics. Some of them deal with the impact of the West on Islamic culture. Wilfred Cantwell Smith, *Islam in Modern History* (Princeton: Princeton University Press, 1957). This book deals with the development of Islamic thought in various modern Muslim states. G. E. von Grunebaum, *Modern Islam, The Search for Cultural Identity* (Berkeley: University of California Press, 1962). A collection of essays dealing with the problems Muslims face in the modern world. E. I. J. Rosenthal, *Islam in the Modern Nation State* (Cambridge: Cambridge University Press, 1965). A discussion of classical political thought in Islam and of the impact of the idea of the modern nation state. Albert Hourani, *Arabic Thought in the Liberal Age, 1798–1939* (London: Oxford University Press, 1962). This study discusses the teachings of important Arab scholars of this period. Malcolm H. Kerr, *Islamic Reform* (Berkeley: University of California Press, 1966) deals with the political and legal theories of two outstanding Islamic modernists.

B. Codes and Official Gazettes

A number of the modern codes of the Arab countries, of Turkey, Iran, and Afghanistan are available in English or French translations. While these translations are useful, it must be remembered that any translation is in effect a construction of the statute translated. Thus the translations convey a useful general impression of the subjects treated and of the organization of the statute in question. However, if the construction of a specific provision is needed, it is imperative to go back to the code or statute in the original language.

The Egyptian Civil Code is available in an English translation. Perrott, Fanner, and Sims Marshall, *The Egyptian Civil Code* (Alexandria: Le Journal du Commerce et de la Marine, 1952). All Egyptian codes, including the new Code of Civil Procedure and the new Law on Evidence are available in French translations.

The Lebanese and Syrian codes are available in French translations. The Syrian codes have appeared in a series entitled *Recueil des lois Syriennes et de la législation financière*, edited by Jean Anhouri and Victor Syriani, Damascus.

The codes of Algeria, Tunisia, and Morocco are available in

French. The Libyan Civil Code is available in an English translation by Meredith O. Ansell and Ibrahim Massaud al-Arif (New York: The Oleander Press, n.d.).

The Turkish codes were translated into French soon after they were issued by Editions Rizzo, *La législation turque*. The Turkish Penal and Criminal Procedure Codes have been published in English as Nos. 9 and 5 respectively in the American Series of Foreign Penal Codes, Fred B. Rothman and Co., South Hackensack, N.J. The Turkish Code of Civil Procedure is available in English in Delmar Karlen and Ilhan Arsel, *Civil Litigation in Turkey* (Ankara, 1957). The new Turkish Commercial Code was translated into English by Rasim Cenani, *The Turkish Commercial Code, English Version* (Istanbul, no date).

The Iranian Civil Code has been translated into French: R. Aghababian, *Législation Iranienne*, vol. 2 (Paris, 1951). The commercial and penal codes also are available in French translations. Excerpts from the Iranian codes have been published in English: *Iranian Law and the Iranian Legal System. An Introduction to the Iranian Legal System and an English Language Collection of Portions of Iranian Law*, published by the Judge Advocate Branch, United States Military Assistance Advisory Group to Iran and the Judicial Department, Imperial Iranian Forces, no place or date. Treatise One of the Commercial Code as amended in 1969 was translated into English by Musa Sabi, *The Commercial Code, Treatise 1, Joint Stock Companies, as Ratified by Both Houses of Parliament on 15th March 1969* (Tehran, 1969). The same author also published a translation of the Iranian Civil Procedure Code as amended in 1970: Musa Sabi, *Civil Procedure Code of Iran* (Tehran, 1972).

A compilation in English of various statutes relating to the transacting of business in Kuwait, including the Commercial Code, has been published by Gabriel Anton Sfeir and Omar Abu Zlam, *Business Laws of Kuwait, A Practical Digest Comprising Decrees, Orders and Regulations* (no publisher, 1971).

The Law of Commerce of Afghanistan has been translated into English by the staff of the Public Administration Service, US/AID Kabul, Afghanistan, mimeographed, no date. An unofficial translation into English of the Afghan *Criminal Procedure Law* appeared serially in the *Kabul Times* in 1966. The Marriage Law of 1971 was translated into English by G. M. Dari in *Hokouk* No. 1–2 (September 1973): 1–6.

There are relatively few translations of pertinent works on Hanbali law as applicable in Saudi Arabia. The important recent translations follow: Henri Laoust, *Le précis de droit d'Ibn Qudāma* (Beirut: 1950). This is a French translation of the 'Umda, a brief résumé of the much larger *Mughnī* of Ibn Qudāma. The translator has given ample references to the *Mughnī*. The book also has a very good introduction. George M. Baroody, *Crime and Punishment under Ḥanbalī Law* (no place, no date). This book is a translation of part of Shaykh Ibrāhīm ibn Muḥammad ibn Salīm ibn Dūyān, *Manār al-Sabīl*, a work required to be used by Saudi *qāḍīs*.

Practically all of the countries discussed in this section publish official gazettes. These gazettes are generally published in Arabic,

Turkish, or Persian, depending on the country concerned. The Afghan Official Gazette is published in Farsi (in its Kabuli form called Dari) and Pushtu. The Pakistani gazette is still published in English. In some countries important legislation is also published by the government in English or French, at times as part of the official gazette. Thus Iraq publishes in English *The Weekly Gazette of the Republic of Iraq*. In other instances yearly volumes have been or are still being issued in French or English. However, these collections cannot be relied upon, valuable as they are to the non-Arabic speaking Western lawyer, to contain all the legislation enacted during the period the publication covers. In cases where a specific statutory or code provision is involved, it is indispensable to consult the official gazettes for possible amendments, particularly if the provision concerned is to be used in a legal argument or is relevant to the drafting of a legal document.

In the Gulf the British *Persian Gulf Gazette* was published periodically until the end of British control. It contained various enactments applicable to persons under British jurisdiction and, in recent years, ordinances retroceding jurisdiction over various matters to local rulers. Statutes enacted for the Gulf states by the British or under British aegis are often available in English, otherwise publication is in Arabic.

The gazettes of Algeria, Tunisia, and Morocco still have French versions.

Chapter 5.

Joseph Schacht, *Introduction*, chapter 14, pp. 94–97

N. J. Coulson, *A History of Islamic Law*, chapter 12, pp. 163–171. Islamic law, with ample reference to case law, has been studied by a number of authors dealing with Islamic law in India. Two such works that are well known are Asaf A. A. Fyzee, *Outlines of Muhammadan Law*, 3d edition (London: Oxford University Press, 1964) and D. F. Mulla, *Principles of Mahomedan Law*, 15th edition by Sir Syed Sultan Ahmed (Calcutta: Eastern Law House Private Ltd., 1967). Asaf A. A. Fyzee, *Cases in the Muhammadan Law of India and Pakistan* (Oxford: Clarendon Press, 1965) is a companion volume to his *Outlines*. The work contains the full text of many important cases and is indispensable for a study of Anglo-Muhammadan law. Shaukat Mahmood, *Principles and Digest of Muslim Law*, revised edition (Lahore: Pakistan Law Times Publications, 1967) takes into account Pakistani case law and statutes up to June 1967.

Seymour Vesey-Fitzgerald, *Muhammadan Law, An Abridgement According to Its Various Schools* (Oxford, 1931) takes some East African cases and ordinances into account.

J. N. D. Anderson, *Islamic Law in Africa* (London: Her Majesty's Stationery Office, 1954) is a very valuable survey of

Islamic law and its application in the former Aden Colony and Protectorate and the former British territories in Africa.

M. B. Ahmad, *The Administration of Justice in Medieval India* (Karachi: The Manager of Publications, 1951) discusses the court system of the Mughal period. Sir George Claus Rankin, *Background to Indian Law* (Cambridge: Cambridge University Press, 1946) deals with the development of the law under British rule in India. J. Duncan M. Derrett, *Religion, Law and the State in India* (New York: The Free Press, 1968) deals in chapter 15 with "The Future of Muhammadan Law in India." M. C. Setavald, *The Common Law in India*, 2d edition (Bombay: N. M. Tripathi Pvt. Ltd. and South Hackensack, N.J.: Fred B. Rothman and Co., 1970) is a reprint, with a Table of Cases, Index, and Bibliography, of a series of lectures the author gave at Lincoln's Inn, London in 1960 under the auspices of the Hamlyn Trust. During British rule, Indian cases were published very much like English cases. Those decided by the Privy Council were published in a special series as *Indian Appeals*. The publication of cases in the same general manner was continued after independence by India and Pakistan. Case law still plays a very important role in both countries and in searching for a solution to a specific legal problem very considerable attention must be paid to court decisions.

Chapters 6 and 7.

Joseph Schacht, *Introduction*, chapters 22 and 23.

J. N. D. Anderson, *Islamic Law in the Modern World*, chapters 3, 4, and 5. These chapters deal specifically with the Islamic law of marriage, divorce, and inheritance and with some of the modern reforms in this field. The extensive bibliography is particularly valuable with regard to the questions dealt with in these chapters.

J. N. D. Anderson, "Modern Trends in Islam, Legal Reform and Modernization in the Middle East," *International and Comparative Law Quarterly* 20 (1971): 1–21, is one of the latest studies of this author on reforms in the personal status law in the Near and Middle East. Professor Anderson is one of the foremost authorities among Western scholars in this field.

Muhammad Abu Zahra, "Family Law," in Majid Khadduri and Herbert J. Liebesny, *Law in the Middle East*, vol. 1, chapter 6. This is a detailed survey of the Sunni Islamic law of marriage, divorce, and inheritance by an outstanding Egyptian jurist.

Y. Linant de Bellefonds, *Traité de droit Musulman comparé*, volume 2. (Paris and the Hague: Mouton and Company, 1965). This is the second volume of the work the first volume of which was excerpted in this book (see Appendix 4). It is a very detailed study of Islamic law of marriage and divorce according to the four Sunni rites. There is some treatment of modern reforms.

A third volume deals with support of wife and children, guardianship and various types of *inter vivos* gifts (Mouton and Company, 1973).

Asaf A. A. Fyzee, *Outlines of Muhammadan Law*, 3d ed., chapters 2 through 7 deal with varous aspects of domestic relations law, chapters 11 through 14 deal with various aspects of the law of inheritance. Chapter 14 is particularly important, since it discusses the Shīʿī law of inheritance in considerable detail. The emphasis, as stated before, is on Anglo-Muhammadan law.

N. J. Coulson, *Succession in the Muslim Family* (Cambridge: Cambridge University Press, 1971) is a thorough study of the Islamic law of inheritance and of the modern reforms.

Chapter 8.

Joseph Schacht, *Introduction,* chapters 20 and 21.

Subhi Mahmassani, "Transactions in the *Sharīʾa*," in Majid Khadduri and Herbert J. Liebesny, *Law in the Middle East*, chapter 7. This is a very good survey of the subject based mainly on Ḥanefite law. Mahmassani includes a brief discussion of property and torts.

Chafik Chehata, *Droit musulman, applications au Proche-Orient* (Paris: Précis Dalloz, 1970). This book, published in a series of brief legal outlines, covers various subjects among them, in part 2, personal status, but more importantly, since the literature on personal status law is extensive in Western languages, also contracts and torts in Islamic law and the present-day systems of the Arab countries.

The same author has discussed the contract in Ḥanefite law and the differences between the Ḥanefite rite and the other schools in *Études de droit musulman* (Paris: Presses universitaires de France, 1971), part 2, chapter 3. A second volume (Presses universitaires de France, 1973) deals in part I with contractual liability.

Abraham L. Udovitch, *Partnership and Profit in Medieval Islam* (Princeton: Princeton University Press, 1970). The author investigates various forms of economic partnerships in Ḥanefite, Malikite, and Shafiʿite law.

The same author has published an interesting article on "The Law Merchant of the Medieval Islamic World," in G. E. von Grunebaum, ed., *Logic in Classical Islamic Culture* (Wiesbaden: Otto Harrassowitz, 1970): 113–130.

Chapter 9.

Chafik Chehata, *Études de droit musulman*, vol. 2, part II deals with rights in real property in Islamic law.

Doreen Warriner, *Land Reform and Development in the Middle East, A Study of Egypt, Syria and Iraq,* 2d edition (London: Oxford University Press, 1962).

Doreen Warriner, *Land and Poverty in the Middle East* (London: Royal Institute of International Affairs, 1948). An earlier study by the same author, but still valuable.

Gabriel Baer, *A History of Landownership in Modern Egypt, 1800–1950* (London: Oxford University Press, 1962). A valuable historical survey. However it does not, of course, cover the important land reform measures enacted since the Egyptian revolution of 1952.

Ann K. S. Lambton, *Landlord and Peasant in Persia* (London: Oxford University Press, 1953). A very useful survey.

The important problem of water laws and water use has been dealt with by: Dante A. Caponera, *Water Laws in Moslem Countries* (Rome: Food and Agriculture Organization of the United Nations, 1954). The book gives some background on Islamic law of water usage and on the customary and codified law of various Moslem countries. Though still useful it is somewhat out of date and also is rather compressed and marred by some inaccuracies. A. M. Maktari, *Water Rights and Irrigation Practices in Lahej. A Study of the Application of Customary and Sharī'ah Law in South-West Arabia* (Cambridge: Cambridge University Press, 1971), although restricted to a small area, is a very thorough and valuable study with an extensive bibliography.

Henri Cattan, "The Law of Waqf," in Majid Khadduri and Herbert J. Liebesny, *Law in the Middle East,* vol. 1, chapter 8. A concise discussion of the subject, including a comparison with the trust of Anglo-American law.

It should be emphasized that the books by Warriner, Baer, and Lambton are primarily focused on land use and land reform and that land law is discussed only as it relates to the broader subject matter of the study concerned.

Chapter 10.

Joseph Schacht, *Introduction,* chapter 24.

M. J. L. Hardy, *Blood Feuds and the Payment of Blood Money in the Middle East* (Beirut: no publisher, 1963). A good discussion of the various aspects of *diya.* The study was prepared while the author was Legal Officer of the United Nations Relief and Works Agency for Palestine Refugees in the Near East. It primarily reflects Hanefite law.

R. Brunschvig, "'*Āķila,*" *Encyclopaedia of Islam,* new edition, volume 1 (Leiden: E. J. Brill, no date): 337–340, thoroughly discusses the problem of the responsibility of the *'āqila* in a homicide case, pointing up the differences between the orthodox rites as to the composition of the group responsible and giving further literature.

J. N. D. Anderson, "Homicide in Islamic Law," *Bulletin of the School of Oriental and African Studies* 13 (1951): 811–828.

Franz Rosenthal, *The Muslim Concept of Freedom Prior to the Nineteenth Century* (Leiden: E. J. Brill, 1960). Chapter IV, b. of this book has a very good discussion of imprisonment and forced labor in Islam.

Uriel Heyd, *Studies in Old Ottoman Criminal Law*, edited by V. L. Ménage (Oxford: Clarendon Press, 1973) discusses developments before the Tanẓīmāt.

Chapters 11 and 12.

Joseph Schacht, *Introduction*, chapter 25.

Emile Tyan, "Judicial Organization," in Majid Khadduri and Herbert J. Liebesny, *Law in the Middle East*, vol. 1, chapter 10. A concise presentation of the subject matter dealt with in greater detail by the same author in his work excerpted in this book (see Appendix 4).

Theodore E. Mogannam, "The Practical Application of the Law in Certain Arab States," *George Washington Law Review* 22 (1953): 142–155. This article discusses the court organization and related subject matters for Syria and Jordan. Now outdated in some details, but still very useful.

G. Baroody, "Sharī'ah, Law of Islam: An American Lawyer in the Courts of Saudi Arabia," *Aramco World* 17 (1966): 26–35.

David E. Long, "The Board of Grievances in Saudi Arabia," *The Middle East Journal* 27 (1973): 71–75. A discussion of the revival of the *maẓalim* courts in Saudi Arabia and their functions.

Jeanette A. Wakin, *The Function of Documents in Islamic Law* (Albany: State University of New York Press, 1972). This book contains an edition of Ṭahawi's chapter on sales from the *Kitāb al-Shurūt al-Kabir* with extensive notes and a very valuable introduction dealing with this type of literature, namely, formularies for various transactions in Islamic law. The relationship between witnesses and documents as means of proof also is discussed.

Appendix 2 Glossary

ʿabd:	slave.
Abū Ḥanīfa (80/699–150/767):	Muslim jurist-theologian.
ʿadl (pl. *ʿudūl*):	wholly reliable, of good character.
ahl al-kitāb:	people of the Book, see *dhimmīs*.
aḥsan al-ṭalāq:	single repudiation during one intramenstrual period.
amān:	pledge of security, safe conduct, given to an individual nonbeliever to protect him in Muslim territory.
al-Azhar:	famous religious university in Cairo.
ʿāqila:	agnatic relatives liable for blood money.
al-Bukhārī, Muḥammad bin Ismāʿīl (194/810–256/870):	a leading *ḥadīth* scholar, author of a *Musnād al-Saḥīḥ*, a collection of traditions from the Prophet.
bab al-ijtihād:	gate of independent reasoning.
caliph:	successor, title of the successors of the Prophet.
Codex of Justinian:	Roman law, part of the *Corpus Juris*, compiled in the sixth century upon orders of the Byzantine Emperor Justinian. It contains excerpts from the decrees of Roman Emperors.
consensus prudentium:	in Roman law agreement among the jurists on a specific point of law.
Copts:	Christians of Egypt. The name is a corruption of the Greek word for Egyptian (*Aigyptos*). The Orthodox Coptic Church is the official Church of Ethiopia.
Corpus Juris Civilis:	Roman law, the name given in

the Middle Ages to the codifications compiled under Justinian in the sixth century A.D. They consist of the *Institutiones*, *Digest* (or *Pandectae*), *Codex Justinianus*, and *Novellae*. The latter are decrees enacted by Justinian after the other books of the *Corpus Juris* had been compiled.

dār al-ḥarb: territory of war, the region of the enemy, the unbeliever.

dār al-Islām: territory of Islam, territory of peace.

de cujus: the decedent.

dhimmīs: people of the Book or scriptuaries (Christians, Jews, Sabians, Zoroastrians). They were permitted to live in Muslim territory according to their own laws, but suffered certain disabilities.

Digest: (*Pandectae*): Roman law, the most important part of the *Corpus Juris*. The Digest contains excerpts from the writings of outstanding Roman jurists of the classical era.

diya: blood money, weregilt, compensation for wounds or loss of life.

doctrine: in French law (and Near Eastern legal systems), the opinion established by the writings of legal scholars in monographs, books or articles.

dūnum: a square measure, about 1,000 square yards.

farḍ: obligatory (a binding obligation upon the believer, such as prayer).

fatwā: a legal opinion given by a *muftī*.

fetvā: Turkish spelling of *fatwā*.

fetvāhane: the Ottoman *fetvā* office.

Fatāwā ʿĀlamgīriyya: a collection of *fatwās* and other legal rules made under the Mogul Emperor Aurangzēb or ʿĀlamgīr in India in the seventeenth century.

fiqh:	Islamic jurisprudence.
furūʿ al-fiqh:	the "branches of the law," the positive law in Islam.
Gaius:	famous Roman jurist of the second century A.D. His *Institutiones* is a textbook of Roman law and served as a model for the *Institutiones* of Justinian.
ḥadd (pl. ḥudūd):	a fixed punishment established by God in the Qurʾān for certain offenses.
ḥadīth:	an oral communication traced back to the Prophet, a specific tradition.
ḥajj:	the pilgramage to Mecca, an obligation for every Muslim.
Hammurabi:	King of Babylon, author of the famous Code of Hammurabi (eighteenth or seventeenth century B.C.).
Ḥanbal:	see *Ibn Ḥanbal.*
Ḥanbalite School:	one of the four orthodox Sunni schools or rites.
Ḥanefite School:	one of the four orthodox Sunni schools or rites, founded in Iraq.
Ḥanīfa:	see *Abū Ḥanīfa.*
ḥarām:	forbidden.
ḥasbīya courts:	guardianship courts (Egypt).
Hatt-i Humāyūn:	Imperial decree of the Ottoman Sultan.
Hatt-i Sherīf of Gülhāne:	Imperial Edict of the Rose Chamber, the Ottoman reform decree of 3 November 1839.
al-Hidāya:	a Ḥanefite work by Marghīnānī written in the twelfth century A.D. It has high standing in India.
hijra:	migration of the Prophet from Mecca to Medina in A.D. 622. It marks the beginning of the Muslim era of dating. The Muslim year is a lunar year.
ḥiyal (pl. of ḥīla):	legal devices, evasions, observing the letter, but not the spirit of the law.
ḥusn:	seemliness.

ʿibādāt:	religious performances.
Ibn Ḥanbal, Aḥmad bin Muḥammad (164/780–241/855):	Muslim jurist-theologian, founder of the Ḥanbalite school, worked mostly in Iraq.
Ibn Khaldūn (732/1332–808/1406):	Famous Muslim historian. His outstanding work is the *Muqaddimah*, the *Introduction* to his *History*.
Ibn Mālik:	see *Mālik*.
ʿidda:	period specified for the termination of the legal effects of marriage; the period of time a divorced or widowed woman has to wait before remarriage.
ijmāʿ:	consensus of the Muslim community or the jurists.
ijtihād:	lit. effort; the use of personal, independent reasoning in the solution of a legal problem.
iltizām:	to farm a branch of the revenue, tax farming.
imām:	leader; can be leader in prayer or religious-political leader, e.g., the former *imām*, king of Yemen.
imām nikāḥ:	in Turkey, a marriage entered into before an *imām*, a religious marriage.
Institutiones:	Roman law, a. an introductory textbook by the jurist Gaius; b. an introductory text compiled on orders of the Emperor Justinian in the sixth century A.D. and forming part of the *Corpus Juris Civilis* (q.v.).
iqtā:	military fief in the Ottoman Empire.
irāde:	Ottoman decree.
Ismāʿīlī:	a Shīʿī sect.
isnād:	the chain of transmitters of a *ḥadīth*.
istidlāl:	inductive reasoning.
istiḥsān:	juristic preference, exercised in breach of strict analogy.
istiṣlāḥ:	legal opinion which takes the public interest into account.

Ithnā 'Asharī:	twelvers, a Shīʿī sect.
ius respondendi:	Roman law, the right granted a jurist by the emperor to give, upon request, legal opinions which were binding on the judge (this right was awarded since the time of the Emperor Hadrian).
jihād:	holy war, just war.
jirga:	a tribal assembly.
jizya:	poll tax paid by the *dhimmis*.
jurisprudence:	French law. (also Near Eastern legal systems), the line of decisions established by the courts on a specific legal problem (German: *Rechtsprechung*).
Justinian (ruled 527–565):	Byzantine emperor who ordered the compilation of the legal works now known collectively as *Corpus Juris Civilis* (q.v.).
khalīfa:	successor, caliph.
kanun:	see *qānūn*.
khulʿ:	a divorce which the wife achieves by giving a consideration to her husband (frequently the dowry).
madhhab:	school of Muslim religious law, orthodox rite of Islam.
mahr:	dowry.
Majalla:	lit. collection, the Ottoman Civil Code of 1877.
majlis:	meeting, gathering.
makrūh:	disapproved.
Mālik bin Anas:	Muslim jurist-theologian (90/708(?)–179/795), lived in Medina; founder of the Malikite school.
Malikite School:	one of the four Sunni orthodox schools or rites, founded in Medina.
mandūb:	recommended.
maṣlaḥa:	public interest, welfare.
matn:	the substance of a *ḥadīth*.
matrūka land:	land reserved for public purposes.

maulvi:	see *mawlawī.*
mawāt land:	dead, unused land.
mawlawī:	term used in Pakistan and India for a Muslim scholar of religious law.
mazālim courts:	special courts of complaints.
millet:	religious community.
mīrī land:	state-owned land leased to individuals.
mubāḥ:	permitted, an act indifferent from the standpoint of Islamic law and religion.
muftī:	a jurisconsult, legal counsellor.
Muḥarram:	first month of the Muslim year.
muḥtasib:	inspector of the market, an official with certain police powers (including limited civil and criminal jurisdiction). Probably has his origin in the hellenistic *agoranomos*, who had the same duties. He was generally charged with "encouraging good and discouraging evil."
mujtahid:	a person who is entitled to exercise the right of *ijtihād.*
mulk land:	land held in freehold ownership.
Muslim bin al-Ḥajjāj (202/817–261/875):	a prominent *ḥadīth* scholar, author of a *Musnād al-Ṣaḥīḥ*, a collection of traditions from the Prophet.
mut ʿa:	compensation paid to a divorced woman in certain cases.
nafaqa:	support of the wife.
nikāḥ:	marriage.
nikāḥ al-mut ʿa:	temporary marriage.
niẓām:	ordinance, used of secular regulations, e.g., in Saudi Arabia
niẓāmīya courts:	the secular courts established in the Ottoman Empire during the *Tanẓīmāt* (q.v.).
qāḍī:	the Muslim religious judge.
qāḍī ' l- ʿasker:	military judge in the Ottoman Empire.
qānūn:	a legal enactment or regulation. The term is derived from the

Greek *kanon*, rule or decree. It was used for the decrees of the Ottoman sultans. Now used for law or code, e.g., *qānūn al-madanī* civil code.

qasāma: oath with oath helpers.

qibla: direction toward Mecca in prayer.

qiyās: analogy.

qubḥ: unseemliness, disgrace.

al-Qudūrī: Hanefite jurist of the tenth–eleventh century A.D. He wrote *al-Mukhtaṣar* (compendium), a work widely used in the Ottoman Empire and its successor states.

Qurʾān: the Holy Book of Islam.

Ramaḍān: Muslim month of fasting.

raʾy: opinion, individual reasoning. *Raʾy* is applied in the process of *ijtihād*.

residuaries: those heirs in Islamic law (mostly agnates) who take after the claims of the sharers (q.v.) have been satisfied.

ṣaḥīḥ: sound, authentic, used to characterize traditions from the Prophet considered genuine by the scholars.

ṣalāt: prayer.

Shaʿbān: eighth month of the Muslim year.

al-Shāfiʿī (150/767–204/820):   Muslim jurist-theologian, founder of the Shafiʿite school. Worked mainly in Iraq and Egypt.

Shafiʿite School: one of the four orthodox Sunni schools or rites.

shahāda: Muslim profession of faith; also testimony of witnesses.

shāhid (pl. *shuhūd*):   witness.

sharers: intestate heirs who are assigned a definite share of the decedent's estate in the Islamic law of inheritance.

sharīʿa: the sacred law of Islam.

al-Shaybānī, Muḥammad (132/749–189/805):	one of the leading jurists of the Hanefite school.
Shaykh al-Islām:	Chief *Muftī* of the Ottoman Empire.
Shīʿa, Shīʿī:	the partisans of the fourth caliph, ʿAlī, son-in-law of the Prophet. This is the main heterodox sect in Islam. It has several subsects.
shufʿa:	preemption.
shuhūd ʿudūl:	reliable witnesses.
sunna, (pl.) sunan:	originally any normative legal custom, later applied to the practice of the Prophet.
sūra:	a chapter of the Qurʾān.
ṭalāq:	repudiation, the divorce of the wife by the husband.
ṭalāq al-bidʿa:	triple divorce in a single statement.
ṭalāq al-sunna:	repudiation with proper timing and proper numbers.
Tanẓīmāt:	period of reform in the Ottoman Empire during the nineteenth century.
taqlīd:	conformism; to follow the the opinion of an authoritative jurist or school.
taṣarruf:	usufruct.
taʿzīr:	discretionary punishment; imposed by the *qāḍī* in cases where no *ḥadd* punishment is prescribed.
ʿulamāʾ (sing. ʿalīm):	the jurist-theologians of Islam.
umma:	the community of believers.
uṣūl al-fiqh:	the "roots" or basic principles of Islamic law.
walī:	legal guardian.
waqf:	a pious endowment.
waqf dhurrī:	family *waqf*.
waqf khayrī:	charitable *waqf*.
yamīn:	oath.
zakāt:	alms tax; to give alms is one of the duties of the pious Muslim.
zākir:	a person who recites verses from the Qurʾan and prayers from memory at religious ceremonies.

Appendix 3 Chronology

All dates A.D.

2nd century	The Roman jurist Gaius.
527–565	The Byzantine Emperor Justinian. Under him the *Corpus Juris Civilis* was compiled. It consists of the *Institutes* of Justinian, the *Digest*, and the *Code of Justinian*.
about 570 or somewhat later	Birth of the Prophet Muḥammad.
622	Migration of the Prophet to Medina. The Islamic era begins (Year of the *Hijra*).
630	Muḥammad conquers Mecca.
8 June 632	Death of Muḥammad.
632–634	The caliph Abū-Bakr.
633	Conquest of southern Mesopotamia by the Arabs.
634–644	The caliph ʿUmar.
635	Damascus conquered by the Arabs.
639	The Arabs conquer Egypt.
640	The Arabs conquer Persia.
644–656	The caliph ʿUthmān.
647	Tripolitania conquered.
653	Qurʾān recension by ʿUthmān.
656–661	The caliph ʿAlī.
661–750	Umayyad dynasty.
750	The Umayyad dynasty is overthrown and the ʿAbbāsid dynasty begins.
767	Abū Ḥanīfa, founder of the Ḥanefite School dies.
786–809	Reign of the ʿAbbāsid caliph Hārūn al-Rashīd.
795	Mālik, founder of the Malikite School dies.
795	Abū Yūsuf, important disciple of Abū Ḥanīfa and a chief *qāḍī*, dies.

805	Shaybānī, another important disciple of Abū Ḥanīfa, dies.
820	Shāfiʿī, founder of the Shāfiʿite School, dies.
855	Ibn Ḥanbal, founder of the Ḥanbalī School, dies.
tenth century	Closing of the Gate of Independent Reasoning (gradual).
1099	The Crusaders capture Jerusalem.
1187	Sultan Saladin (Ṣalāḥ al-Dīn) defeats the Franks and captures Jerusalem.
1258	The Mongol ruler Hūlāgu captures Baghdad. End of the ʿAbbāsid dynasty.
1263–1328	Ibn Taimīya, famous Ḥanbalī jurist.
1332–1406	Ibn Khaldūn.
1453	Conquest of Constantinople by the Ottoman Sultan Mehmed II (1451–1481).
1520–1566	Sultan Sulaymān the Magnificent (Qānūnī).
1490–1574	Ebüssuūd, Shaykh al-Islām under Sultan Sulaymān.
1526	Beginning of the Mogul Empire in India.
1555–1605	ʿAkbar the Great, outstanding Mogul emperor.
1658–1707	Aurangzēb ʿAlamgīr, Mogul emperor. Under him the *Fatāwā ʿĀlamgīriyya* was compiled.
1789–1807	Selīm III, sultan of the Ottoman Empire. First attempts at reform.
1804	French *Code Civil* enacted.
1805	Muḥammad ʿAlī becomes governor of Egypt.
1839–1861	ʿAbd al-Mājid, sultan of the Ottoman Empire.
1839	*Hatt-i Sherīf of Gülhāne,* reform legislation in the Ottoman Empire inaugurated (*Tanẓīmāt*).
1850	Ottoman Commercial Code enacted.
1856	*Hatt-i Humāyūn.*
1858	Ottoman Penal Code enacted.
1858	Ottoman Land Law enacted.
1875	Establishment of Mixed Courts in Egypt.
1877	*Majalla* enacted.
1914	Great Britain establishes protectorate over Egypt.
1917	Ottoman Law of Family Rights.
30 October 1918	Armistice of Mudros. Dissolution of the Ottoman Empire.

23 July 1919	First Turkish National Congress meets under Kemal Atatürk's leadership in Erzerum.
1920	Mandates for Palestine, Iraq and Transjordan given to Great Britain, for Syria and Lebanon to France at San Remo Conference.
1922	British protectorate over Egypt ended.
1923	Peace Treaty of Lausanne concluded between Allies and Turkey.
29 October 1923	Turkey becomes a republic; Kemal Atatürk its first president. Former Sultan ʿAbd al-Mājīd remains caliph.
3 March 1924	Atatürk abolishes the caliphate.
1925	Reza Khan Pahlevi becomes Shah of Iran. End of Qājār dynasty, beginning of Pahlevi dynasty.
1926	New civil code enacted in Turkey.
1932	Iraq admitted to League of Nations.
1928–1935	Iranian Civil Code enacted.
1936	Treaty of Alliance between Great Britain and Egypt.
1937	Montreux Convention on the abolition of the Mixed Courts in Egypt concluded.
1937	Muslim Personal Law (Shariat) Application Act enacted in India.
1939	Dissolution of Muslim Marriages Act enacted in India.
1943	Lebanon and Syria assume independence.
1948	British leave Palestine. State of Israel proclaimed.
1948	Transjordan becomes independent. Treaty of alliance between Great Britain and Transjordan.
1949	Armistice agreements concluded between Israel on the one hand and Egypt, Syria, Lebanon and Jordan on the other.
1949	Mixed Courts are abolished in Egypt. New Egyptian civil code and other codes come into effect.
1949	New civil code enacted in Syria.
1950	Jordan annexes the West Bank and the Old City of Jerusalem.
1951	New civil code enacted in Iraq.
1951	Jordanian Law of Family Rights enacted.
1952	Military coup in Egypt.
1953	Egypt becomes a republic.

1953	New civil code in Libya.
1953	Syrian Law of Personal Status enacted.
1954	President Nagīb removed from office in Egypt. Premier Nasser assumes the presidential duties.
1955	Religious courts abolished in Egypt.
1956	Tunisian Code of Personal Status enacted.
1956	Egypt nationalizes the Suez Canal Company.
1956	War between Israel and Egypt. British and French forces land in Suez Canal area.
1957–1958	Personal status legislation enacted in Morocco.
1958	Egypt and Syria form United Arab Republic.
1958	Monarchy is overthrown in Iraq.
1959	Iraqi Law of Personal Status enacted.
1961	Kuwait becomes independent.
1961	Military coup in Syria. Union with Egypt is dissolved.
1961	Muslim Family Laws Ordinance is enacted in Pakistan.
1962	A military coup overthrows the monarchy in Yemen.
1967	War between Israel and the Arab states.
1967	Iranian Family Protection Law enacted.
1971	The Gulf amirates gain their independence from the United Kingdom.
1971	Afghan Marriage Law enacted.
1973	Afghanistan becomes a republic.
1973	War between Israel and the Arab states.

The Muslim calendar starts counting years with the *Hijra* (Hegira), that is, the migration of the Prophet from Mecca to Medina. The Muslim year is a lunar year and there is, therefore, no direct correspondence between Muslim dates and Christian dates. A useful formula for conversion is $C = \frac{32}{33}H + 622$, where C is the year of the Christian era and H is the Muslim year. To establish exact dates, one of the available conversion tables should be used. The best is Berthold Spuler and Joachim Mayr, *Wüstenfeld-Mahler'sche Vergleichungstabellen*, new edition (Wiesbaden: Franz Steiner Verlag, 1961).

Appendix 4 List of Authors and Documents Quoted*

Abū Yūsuf. *Kitāb al-Kharāj*. Būlāq: Egyptian State Printing Office, 1885. French translation by E. Fagnan in *Livre de l'impot foncier*, Paris: Paul Geuthner, 1921.

      pp. 96–97 (Fagnan   p. 32
      pp. 248–249)
      p. 96 (Fagnan, p. 248) p. 218

Al-Ahrām, 11 September 1951 (Italian translation in *Oriente Moderno* 31 (1951): 213–214).

                  p. 42

Anderson, J. N. D. "Codification in the Muslim World," *Rabel's Zeitschrift für ausländisches und internationales Privatrecht* 30 (1966): 241–253.

      p. 245   p. 66
      pp. 245–246   p. 69

Anderson, J. N. D., "Law as a Social Force in Islamic Culture and History," *Bulletin of the School of Oriental and African Studies* 20 (1957): 13–40.

      pp. 13–14   p. 3
      p. 15   p. 12
      p. 16   p. 27
      pp. 18–21   p. 24

Anderson, J. N. D., " A Law of Personal Status for Iraq." *The International and Comparative Law Quarterly* 9 (1960): 542–563.

      pp. 542–545   p. 104

Anderson, J. N. D. "Law Reform in the Middle East," *International Affairs* 32 (1956): 43–51.

      pp. 46–50   p.103

Anderson, J. N. D. "Recent Reforms in Family Law in the Arab World," *Zeitschrift für vergleichende Rechtswissenschaft* 65 (1963): offprint, 17 pp.

      pp. 3–7   p. 136

Anderson, J. N. D. "Recent Reforms in the Islamic Law of Inheritance." *International and Comparative Law Quarterly* 14 (1965): 349–365.

      pp. 354–365   p. 188
      pp. 356–358   p. 200

---

* The page numbers on the left refer to the source of the excerpt, those on the right to this book. Because of the great variety of the source material, the uniform system of legal citation has been used only with regard to decisions where standard forms have been developed.

Anderson, J. N. D. "The Sharī'a and Civil Law." *The Islamic Quarterly* 30 (1954): 29–46.

    pp. 30–32   p. 196

Bayitch, S. A. "Codification in Modern Times." In *Civil Law in the Modern World*, edited by Athanassios N. Yiannopoulos, pp. 161–191. Baton Rouge: Louisiana State University Press, 1965.

    pp. 164–166   p. 56

Bonham-Carter, Sir Edgar, see Iraq Civil Commissioner, *Review of the Civil Administration of Mesopotamia.*

Brinton, J. Y. *The Mixed Courts of Egypt.* 2d. ed. New Haven: Yale University Press, 1968.

    pp. 64–66   p. 173

British India. *Muslim Personal Law (Shariat) Application Act 1937*, Act no. XXVI of 1937.

    Preamble, Articles 1–3 p. 120

British India, *Decisions: Abul Fata v. Russomoy Dur Chowdhury* (1894) 22 I.A. 76.

    pp. 86–87   p. 118

Baker Ali Khan v. Anjuman Ara (1903) 30 I.A. 94.

    pp. 111–112   p. 119

al-Bukhārī. *Ṣaḥīḥ.* vols. 1–3 edited by L. Krehl, Leiden: E. J. Brill, 1862–1868 and vol. 4 edited by Th. W. Juynboll, Leiden: E. J. Brill, 1907–1908.

    Book 23, chapter 37   p. 181

    Book 52, chapter 20   p. 254

Chehata, Chafik. "Les Survivances Musulmanes dans la codification du droit civil égyptien." *Revue internationale de droit comparé* 17 (1965): 840–853.

    pp. 852–853   p. 198

Codex Justinianus.

    4.1.1 and 2   p. 253

    4.20.1   p. 250

    4.21.15   p. 250

Corpus Juris Canonici, Decretum Gratiani.

    1.1,1   p. 7

David, René. *French Law, Its Structure, Sources and Methodology.* Baton Rouge: Louisiana State University Press, 1972.

    pp. 77–82   p. 59

    pp. 180–186   p. 61

Derrett, J. Duncan M. "Justice, Equity and Good Conscience." In *Changing Law in Developing Countries*, edited by J. N. D. Anderson, pp. 114–153. London: George Allen and Unwin, Ltd., 1963.

    pp. 139–140   p. 121

    pp. 143–147   p. 121

Digest of Justinian

    9.2.7.2–8; 9.2.9.4   p. 32

    22.3.2   p. 244

    50.17.1   p. 31

Egypt. *Abolition of the Mixed Courts and the Consular Courts.* Law 115 of 1948.

> Articles 1, 2, 3 and 7   p. 87

Egypt. *Abolition of the Sharī'a Courts and the Courts of the Religious Minorities.* Law 462 of 24 September 1955.

> Articles 1–7   p. 101

Egypt. *Annals of the Senate.* Session of 25 March 1946

> p. 186

Egypt. *Civil Code of 1949.*

> Article 1   p. 95
> Article 81   p. 223
> Articles 89, 136–137   p. 212
> Articles 163–165, 178   p. 221
> Article 222   p. 221
> Articles 802, 803, 806   p. 224
> Articles 825–826   p. 225
> Articles 935–937,
> 939–945, 948   p. 215

Egypt. *Code of Civil Procedure of 1968.*

> Article 269   p. 259

Egypt. *Decisions:*

Court of Appeal, Alexandria, *Decision of 8 January 1952, Courrier des Tribunaux* 1954, 118.

> p. 264

Court of Appeal, Alexandria, *Decision of 17 May 1956, Bulletin de législation et de jurisprudence Egyptiennes*, nouvelle série, 7 (1956), 156.

> p. 192

Court of Cassation, Civil Chamber, *Decision of 13 January 1955, Syllabus by the Court.* Egypt, Ministry of Justice, *Bulletin officiel des tribunaux, Répertoire alphabétique* 55 (1955) in French and Arabic. No. 333 (French Section), No. 5 (Arabic Section).

> p. 265

Court of Cassation Civil Chamber, *Decision no. 3–4/98 of 10 February 1955, Syllabus by the Court. Bull. off., Rép. alpha.*, No. 60 (French Section), No. 130 (Arabic Section).

> p. 225

Court of Cassation Civil Chamber, *Decision no. 3–4/100 of 10 February 1955. Bull. off., Rép. alpha.*, No. 314 (French Section), No. 287 (Arabic Section).

> p. 217

Court of Cassation, Civil Chamber, *Decision of 30 October 1956, Syllabus by the Court.* Egypt, Ministry of Justice, *Bulletin officiel des tribunaux*, 56, Nos. 7 and 8 (1958) in French and Arabic, No. 126.

> p. 259

Court of Cassation, Civil Chamber, *Decision of 2 July 1957, Syllabus by the Court. Bull. off.*, No. 168.

> p. 198

Court of First Instance, Cairo, *case No. 600 of 1956. Syllabus by the Court. Bull. off.*, no. 147.

> p. 102

Gaius. *Institutiones.*
    1.1   p. 6
Gibb, H. A. R. and Bowen, Harold. *Islamic Society and the West.*
vol. 1, part 2. London: Oxford University Press, 1957. Under the
auspices of the Royal Institute of International Affairs.
    p. 116   p. 257
    pp. 129–130   p. 257
Goldziher, Ignaz. *Muhammedanische Studien.* 2 vols. 1888.
Reprint (2 vols. in 1). Hildesheim: Georg Holms 1961. Vol. 2.
    p. 6   p. 14
    p. 11   p. 14
    p. 13   p. 13
    pp. 19–21   p. 13
Goldziher, Ignaz. *Vorlesungen über den Islam.* 2d. ed.
Heidelberg: Carl Winter, 1925.
    pp. 52–53   p. 17
al-Ḥalabī, Ibrāhīm, *Multaqa al-Abḥur.* Partial French translation
by H. Sauvaire in *Droit Musulman (Rite Ḥanefite), Le Moultaqa el
Abheur,* Marseille: Barlatier-Feissat Père et Fils, 1882.
    pp. 5–6   p. 210
Hatt-i Humāyūn of 18 February, 1856. French translation by
Aristarchi Bey in *Législation Ottomane.* Constantinople: Bureau du
Journal Thraki, 1874, vol. 2.
    pp. 14–22   p. 49
Hatt-i Sherif of Gülhāne of 3 November, 1839 French translation by
Aristarchi Bey in *Législation Ottomane,* vol. 2.
    pp. 7–14   p. 46
Heidborn, A. *Droit public et administratif de l'Empire Ottoman.*
Vienna and Leipzig: C. W. Stern, 1909. Vol. 2.
    pp. 267–269   p. 40
Hurgronje, C. Snouk. "Le droit Musulman." In *Selected Works of
C. Snouk Hurgronje,* edited by G. H. Bousquet and J. Schacht,
pp. 214–255. Leiden: E. J. Brill, 1957.
    pp. 225–227   p. 16
Ibn ʿĀṣim al-Mālikī. *Tuḥfat al-ḥukkām fī nukat al-ʿuqūd waʾl-aḥkam.*
Edited, translated, and annotated by Léon Bercher. Algiers:
Institut d'Etudes Orientales, Faculté des Lettres, Université
d'Alger, 1958.
    verses 21–23   p. 243
Ibn Khaldūn. *The Muqaddimah, An Introduction to History.* 2d ed.
English translation by Franz Rosenthal. Princeton: Princeton
University Press, 1967.
    vol. 1 pp. 452–454   p. 241
    vol. 2 pp. 448–460   p. 15
    vol. 3 pp. 4, 6–9   p. 19
    pp. 8–9, 13   p. 27
    pp. 3, 30–32   p. 21
Iran, *Civil Code, promulgated 1928–1935.*
    Articles 843 and
    849   p. 206
    Articles 910–912   p. 207
    Articles 1075–1077   p. 155

Articles 1095–1097   p. 155
Articles 1129 and
   1130   p. 156
Iran. *Personal Status of Non-Shīʿī Iranians, Law of 22 July 1933.*
            p. 207
Iraq. *Civil Code of 1951.*
      Article 1   p. 95
      Articles 2–5   p. 100
Iraq. Civil Commissioner. *Review of the Civil Administration of Mesopotamia.* (Cmd. 1061). London: H.M. Stationery Office, 1920.
      pp. 93–95   p. 89
Iraq, *Personal Status Law of 30 December 1959.*
      Article 3 (4)   p. 151
Kennett, Austin, *Bedouin Justice, Laws and Customs Among the Egyptian Bedouin.* Cambridge: Cambridge University Press, 1925.
      pp. 40–42   p. 251
Khadduri, Majid. *War and Peace in the Law of Islam.* Baltimore: The Johns Hopkins University Press, 1955.
      pp. 52–53   p. 10
      pp. 175–177   p. 9
Khalīl bin Isḥaq. *Al-Mukhtaṣar.* Paris: Republican Government Printing Office, 1900.
      p. 208   p. 243
Koschaker, Paul. *Europa und das römische Recht.* 4th ed. Munich: C. H. Becksche Verlagsbuchhandlung, 1966.
      pp. 161–162   p. 55
      pp. 183–187   p. 58
Lawson, F. H. *A Common Lawyer Looks at the Civil Law* (1953). Ann Arbor: University of Michigan Law School, 1953.
      pp. 76–77   p. 58
Lebanon, *Penal Code of 1949.*
      Article 562   p. 233
Lex Ribuaria.
      31. 3 and 4   p. 8
Liebesny, Herbert J. "Stability and Change in Islamic Law." *The Middle East Journal* 21 (1967): 16–34.
      p. 19   p. 29
      pp. 21–22   p. 65
      pp. 22–23   p. 64
      pp. 24–25   p. 71
      pp. 25–26   p. 78
      p. 30   p. 115
      pp. 30–31   p. 93
Linant de Bellefonds. *Traité de droit Musulman comparé.* Vol. 1. The Hague; Mouton and Cie, 1956.
      pp. 20–22   p. 28
      pp. 54–55   p. 30
Majalla. French translation by Aristarchi Bey in *Législation Ottomane*, vols. 6 and 7. English translation Hooper, C. A. *The Law of Palestine and Trans-Jordan.* Vol. 1. Jerusalem, 1933.
      Articles 92–93   p. 219

Article 125	p. 223
Articles 167–170	p. 210
Articles 171, 173 175, 181–186, 369	p. 211
Articles 887, 888	p. 218
Articles 912–915, 922–924	p. 219
Articles 950–952, 1008, 1009	p. 214
Articles 1013, 1017, 1021, 1028	p. 214
Articles 1045, 1060, 1069, 1071, 1072, 1075	p. 213

Majalla, Report of the Drafting Commission. French translation in Aristarchi Bey, *Législation Ottomane*, vol. 6.

pp. 3–18   p. 66

al-Māwardī, Abū al-Hasan ʿAlī. *Kitāb al Aḥkām al-Sulṭāniyya.* 2d ed. Cairo: Mustafa al-Bāni al-Halbī, no date. French translation by E. Fagnan in *Les Statuts governementaux*. Algiers: Aldolphe Jourdan, 1915.

Māwardī pp. 69–71 Fagnan pp. 140–146	p. 241
Māwardī pp. 77–83 Fagnan pp. 157–174	p. 254
Māwardī p. 219 Fagnan p. 469	p. 228
Māwardī pp. 231–233 Fagnan pp. 493–498	p. 230
Māwardī pp. 237–239 Fagnan pp. 504–509	p. 229

Montreux Convention of 1937 (Abolition of Egyptian Mixed Courts) US *Treaty Series* No. 939.

p. 86

Morocco, *Decision:* Supreme Court, Civil Chamber, *Decision of 24 November 1964,* No. 69. Civil 15, 998 and 14,412. *Revue Marocaine de droit* 1965.

p. 157   p. 154

Morocco, *Personal Status Code*, promulgated between 22 November 1957 and 3 April 1958. (Arabic text and French translation— which differs from official French translation—with a discussion of various provisions in André Colomer. *Droit Musulman, Manuels de droit et d'économie du Maroc*. Rabat: Editions La Porte, vol. 1, 1963, vol. 2, 1968.)

Articles 30–31	p. 152
Article 60	p. 151

New Testament, *Gospel of Matthew*. Revised Standard Version.

22:21   p. 6

New Testament. *1 Peter*. Revised Standard Version.

2:13–14   p. 6

Opet, Otto. "Die Neuregelung des türkischen Eherechts." *Niemeyers Zeitschrift für internationales Recht* 28 (1920): 338–354.

pp. 341–343   p. 70

Ottoman Penal Code of 1858. French translation by Aristarchi Bey in *Législation Ottomane*, vol. 2: 212–273.

Article 1   p. 64

Pakistan. *Decisions:*
Behram—Convict/Apellant vs. The State—Respondent, Quetta Circuit, Criminal Appeal 21 of 1963. 1966 (*Part I*) *Pakistan Law Reports, West Pakistan* 150.

p. 234

Mst. Khurshid Jan—Apellant v. Fazal Dad—Respondent. Regular Second Appeal No. 485 of 1961, Appellate Civil, Full Bench. 1965 (*Part 1*) *Pakistan Law Reports, West Pakistan* 312.

p. 123

Pathana—Appellant v. Mst. Wasai and Another—Respondents. Civil Appeal No. 9 of 1964, decided 9 December 1964. 17 (*Part I*) *Supreme Court, All Pakistan Legal Decisions* (1965) 134.

p. 201

Pakistan. *Muslim Family Laws Ordinance of 1961* (Act VIII of 1961 as amended).

Preamble	p. 160
Articles 1–3	p. 160
Article 4	p. 199
Article 6	p. 162
Articles 7–8	p. 161

Pakistan. *Penal Code of 1860* as amended.

Section 300	p. 233

Pakistan. *Report of the Commission on Marriage and Family Laws.* Gazette Extraordinary, 20 June 1956. 1197–1232.

pp. 1197–1198, 1204	p. 159
p. 1203	p. 123
pp. 1222–1223	p. 199

Pakistan. *Report of the Law Reform Commission, 1958–1959.* Karachi: Government of Pakistan Press, 1959.

p. 112	p. 238

Pakistan. *West Pakistan Family Courts Act* (Act XXXV of 1964).

Section 4	p. 164
Section 5	p. 163
Section 14	p. 164
Section 21	p. 163
Section 22	p. 163

Palestine Order in Council of 1922, Great Britain, *Parliamentary Papers.* Cmd. 1785, London, H.M. Stationery Office, 1922.

Article 46   p. 91

Pirenne, Henri. *Mohammed and Charlemagne.* New York: Harper and Rowe, 1939. Meridian Books (paperback) World Publishing Co., 6th Printing, 1961.

pp. 150–152   p. 35

Pollock, Sir Frederick and Maitland, F. W. *The History of English Law*, 2d ed., vol. 2, 1898. Reprint: Cambridge University Press, 1968.

p. 600   p. 252

Pritchard, James B. ed. *Ancient Near Eastern Texts Relating to the Old Testament.* 3d. edition. Princeton: Princeton University Press, 1969.

| pp. 164, 178 | p. 256 |
| p. 165 | p. 5 |

Prosser, William L. *Handbook of the Law of Torts.* 4th edition. St. Paul, Minnesota: West Publishing Co., 1971.

p. 17	p. 220
p. 492	p. 220
p. 494	p. 220

al-Qayrawānī, Ibn Abī Zayd. *Risāla.* Edited and translated into French by Léon Bercher, 3d edition. Algiers: Editions Jules Carbonel, 1949.

Table of Contents	p. 23
p. 200	p. 210
p. 220	p. 182
pp. 260–265	p. 247
pp. 274–279	p. 175

al-Qazwīnī, Abu Hatim Mahmūd Ibn al Hasan. *Kitāb al-Ḥiyal fil Fiqh.* Translated by Joseph Schacht. Leipzig: J. C. Hinrichs, 1924.

| p. 10 | p. 43 |
| p. 26 | p. 43 |

al-Qudūrī, ʿAlī bin Muhammad bin Ahmad bin Jaʿfar bin Hamdān. *al-Mukhtaṣar.* Edited and partially translated into French by G. H. Bousquet and L. Bercher in *Le statut personnel en droit Musulman Hanefite.* Tunis: Institut des Hautes Etudes de Tunis, no date.

p. 12	p. 130
pp. 12–15	p. 130
pp. 16–21	p. 131
p. 22	p. 131
pp. 22–35	p. 131
pp. 54, 64	p. 132
p. 56	p. 136
pp. 80–89	p. 133
pp. 108, 114	p. 134
pp. 118–121	p. 135
pp. 156–159	p. 135

Qurʾān. English translation by Mohammed Marmeduke Pickthall. *The Meaning of the Glorious Koran.* London: George Allen and Unwin, 1930; Mentor paperback edition.

Sūra II 178	p. 230
Sūra II 180	p. 181
Sūra II 226–230	p. 133
Sūra II 282	p. 246
Sūra IV 3, 4	p. 129
Sūra IV 7, 11, 12	p. 174
Sūra IV 92	p. 231
Sūra VI 146	p. 42
Sūra XXXIII 49	p. 133

Review of the Civil Administration of Mesopotamia, see Iraq, Civil Commissioner.

Saḥnūn, ʿAbd al-Salām bin Saʿīd. *al-Mudawanna*. Cairo: 1905–1906.
>   vol. 11, p. 31   p. 218
al-Sanhūrī, ʿAbd al-Razzāq. *Le Califat son évolution vers une Société des Nations Orientale*. Paris: Librairie Orientaliste Paul Geuthner, 1926.
>   pp. 578–583   p. 93
Santillana, David. *Istituzioni di diritto Musulmano Malechita con riguardo anche al sistema Sciafiita*. 2 vols. Rome: Istituto per l'Oriente, 1938.
>   vol. 1, pp. 32–33   p. 12
>   p. 46   p. 18
>   pp. 70–71   p. 18
>   vol. 2, pp. 22–23   p. 212
Saudi Arabia. *Labor and Workmen Regulations of 15 November 1969*
>   Article 74   p. 222
Saymen, Ferit. "The Personal Relations Between the Children of Divorced Parents and their Grandparents." *Annales de la Faculté de droit d'Istanbul* 1, No. 2 (1952): 471–477.
>   pp. 471–77   p. 170
Schacht, Joseph, *Droit Byzantin et droit Musulman*. Rome: Academia Nazionale de Lincei, 1956.
>   pp. 6–10   p. 33
Schiller, A. Arthur. "Jurists' Law." *Columbia Law Review* 58 (1958): 1226–1238.
>   pp. 1226–1232   p. 36
Schnitzer, Adolf F. *Vergleichende Rechtslehre*. 2d. edition. Vol. 1. Basel: Verlag für Recht und Gesellschaft, A.G. 1961.
>   pp. 59–64   p. 52
Schulz, Fritz. *Principles of Roman Law*. Oxford: The Clarendon Press, 1936. Reprint by the same publisher 1956.
>   pp. 41–52   p. 31
Selle, Friedrich. *Prozessrecht des 16. Jahrhunderts im Osmanischen Reich*. Wiesbaden: Otto Harrassowitz, 1962.
>   p. 82   p. 41
>   pp. 99–101   p. 41
al-Shāfiʿī. *Risāla*. English translation by Majid Khadduri. Baltimore: Johns Hopkins University Press, 1961.
>   p. 119   p. 14
Speiser, E. A. "Authority and Law in Mesopotamia," In *Authority and Law in the Ancient Orient*, Supplement to the *Journal of the American Oriental Society*, No. 17 (1954): 8–14.
>   p. 14   p. 6
Syria. *Civil Code of 1949*.
>   Article 1   p. 95
Syria. *Code of Civil Procedure 1953*.
>   Article 139 (1)   p. 262
Syria. *Personal Status Law, Legislative Decree No. 59 of 17 September 1953*.
>   Article 17   p. 152
>   Article 117, 121, 123 p. 150

Timur, Hifzi. "Civil Marriage in Turkey; Difficulties, Causes and Remedies." in *The Reception of Foreign Law in Turkey.*
International Social Science Bulletin 9 (1957): 34–36.

   pp. 34–36   p. 167

Tunisia, *Decisions:*
Court of Appeal for Tunis, Decision of 25 June 1965. *Revue Tunisienne de droit,* 1966–1967: 205–206.

        p. 147

Court of Cassation, Civil Chamber, Decision No. 6175 of 4 July 1968: *Revue Tunisienne de droit,* 1969–1970: 222–224.

        p. 146

Tribunal of First Instance,, Tunis, Judgment No. 25,685 of 13 June 1967. *Revue Tunisienne de droit* 1968: 120–123.

        p. 187

Tunisia, *Personal Status Code,* Decree of 13 August 1956, amended by Law No. 59–77 of 19 June 1959. (Arabic text and French translation in M. T. Es-Senoussi, *Code du statut personnel annoté,* 2d. edition, Tunis: 1958. The French text of the Amendment can be found in *Journal Officiel de la République Tunisienne,* 23–26 June 1959, pp. 657–659).

   Article 18   p. 151
   Articles 30–33 p. 145

Turkey. *Civil Code of 1926.*

   Explanatory Note p. 79
   Articles 93   p. 165
   Articles 97, 100, 105,
   108,   p. 166
   Article 110   p. 167
   Articles 112, 114,
   paragraph 3   p. 166
   Articles 139, 140, 142 p. 165
   Articles 439–444 p. 208

Turkey. *Penal Code of 1926.*

   Article 237   p. 167

Tyan, Emile. *Histoire de l'organisation judiciaire en pays d'Islam.* 2d ed. Leiden: E. J. Brill, 1960.

   pp. 219–220   p. 38
   p. 229   p. 39
   pp. 236–248   p. 247

Tyan, Emile. "Le Notariat et le régime de la preuve par écrit dans la pratique du droit Musulman." *Annales de l'École Française de droit de Beyrouth.* 1945, No. 2.

   pp. 5–12   p. 244

United Arab Republic, see Egypt.
Velidedeoğlu, H. V. "The Reception of the Swiss Civil Code in Turkey." In *The Reception of Foreign Law in Turkey. International Social Science Bulletin,* 9 (1957): 60–69

   pp. 61–63   p. 81

Vinogradoff, Paul. *Roman Law in Medieval Europe.* 1909. Reprint. Cambridge: Speculum Historiale, 1968.

   pp. 25–26   p. 8

Von Grunebaum, Gustave. *Medieval Islam*. Chicago: University of Chicago Press. Phoenix Books, 1961.

      pp. 149–151   p. 17

Wilson, John A. "Authority and Law in Ancient Egypt." In *Authority and Law in the Ancient Orient,* Supplement to the *Journal of The American Oriental Society* No. 17 (1954): 1–7.

      pp. 5–7   p. 5

Index